CONSCIENCE AND THE COMMON GOOD

Our society's longstanding commitment to the liberty of conscience has become strained by our increasingly muddled understanding of what conscience is and why we value it. Too often we equate conscience with individual autonomy, and so we reflexively favor the individual in any contest against group authority, losing sight of the fact that a vibrant liberty of conscience requires a vibrant marketplace of morally distinct groups. Defending individual autonomy is not the same as defending the liberty of conscience because, although conscience is inescapably personal, it is also inescapably relational. Conscience is formed, articulated, and lived out through relationships, and its viability depends on the law's willingness to protect the associations and venues through which individual consciences can flourish: these are the myriad institutions that make up the space between the person and the state. *Conscience and the Common Good* reframes the debate about conscience by bringing its relational dimension into focus.

Robert K. Vischer is associate professor at the University of St. Thomas School of Law in Minneapolis. Professor Vischer's scholarship explores the intersection of law, religion, and public policy, with a particular focus on the religious and moral dimensions of professional identity.

D1616851

Conscience and the Common Good

RECLAIMING THE SPACE BETWEEN PERSON AND STATE

ROBERT K. VISCHER

University of St. Thomas School of Law, Minneapolis

CAMBRIDGE
UNIVERSITY PRESS

DOMINICAN UNIVERSITY LIBRARY
SAN RAFAEL, CALIFORNIA 94901

CAMBRIDGE UNIVERSITY PRESS
Cambridge, New York, Melbourne, Madrid, Cape Town, Singapore,
São Paulo, Delhi, Dubai, Tokyo

Cambridge University Press
32 Avenue of the Americas, New York, NY 10013-2473, USA

www.cambridge.org
Information on this title: www.cambridge.org/9780521130707

© Robert K. Vischer 2010

This publication is in copyright. Subject to statutory exception
and to the provisions of relevant collective licensing agreements,
no reproduction of any part may take place without the written
permission of Cambridge University Press.

First published 2010

Printed in the United States of America

A catalog record for this publication is available from the British Library.

Library of Congress Cataloging in Publication data

Vischer, Robert K.
Conscience and the common good : reclaiming the space between person and state / Robert K.
Vischer.
    p.   cm.
Includes bibliographical references and index.
ISBN 978-0-521-11377-9 (hardback)
1. Liberty of conscience – United States.   I. Title.
BV741.V57   2009
323.44′20973 – dc22   2009038308

ISBN 978-0-521-11377-9 Hardback
ISBN 978-0-521-13070-7 Paperback

Cambridge University Press has no responsibility for the persistence or
accuracy of URLs for external or third-party Internet Web sites referred
to in this publication and does not guarantee that any content on such
Web sites is, or will remain, accurate or appropriate.

for Maureen

Contents

Acknowledgments

I am thankful for the insightful comments on various portions of this book from friends and colleagues, including Tom Berg, Matt Bodie, Rick Garnett, John Inazu, Lyman Johnson, Andy Koppelman, Joel Nichols, Eduardo Penalver, Michael Perry, Lisa Schiltz, Steve Shiffrin, Steven Smith, Susan Stabile, Julian Velasco, and John Witte Jr. I owe particularly large debts of gratitude to Brian Tamanaha and Amy Uelmen, both of whom went far beyond the call of duty in encouraging and offering constructive feedback on this project. My students, Eric van Schyndle and Paul Haverstock, provided stellar research assistance, and I appreciate the institutional support offered by Dean Thomas Mengler and the University of St. Thomas Law School. I benefited enormously from presenting earlier versions of these chapters at Vanderbilt, Marquette, Notre Dame, St. John's, Villanova, Fordham University, University of Maryland, Oklahoma University, University of Colorado, St. Louis University, Humboldt University (Berlin), Pontificia Universita San Tomasso (Rome), and the University of Exeter (U.K.). I am especially grateful to my wife, Maureen, and my daughters – Sophia, Lila, and Ava – for cheering me on in my efforts, and I apologize to Ava that the book has less to say about princesses or fairies than she might have hoped.

PERMISSIONS

I am grateful for permission to include portions of my earlier work in this volume. Portions of chapter 5 were published as *The Good, the Bad and the Ugly: Rethinking the Value of Associations*, 79 NOTRE DAME L. REV. 949 (2004). The bulk of chapter 6 was published as *Conscience in Context: Pharmacist Rights and the Eroding Moral Marketplace*, 17 STAN. LAW & POL'Y REV. 83 (2006) and chapter 7 as *Corporate Identity and Moral Pluralism: Reclaiming the Relational Dimension of Conscience*, 5 J. OF CATHOLIC SOCIAL THOUGHT 323 (2008). Part of chapter 8 was published as *The Sanctity of Conscience in an Age of School Choice: Grounds for Skepticism*,

6 MARYLAND L.J. OF RACE, RELIGION, GENDER AND CLASS 81 (2006), and portions of chapter 10 as *Legal Advice as Moral Perspective*, 19 GEO. J. LEGAL ETHICS 225 (2006); *Professional Identity and the Contours of Prudence*, 4 UNIV. OF ST. THOMAS L.J. 46 (2006); and *Heretics in the Temple of Law: The Promise and Peril of the Religious Lawyering Movement*, 19 J. L. & RELIG. 427 (2004).

Introduction

Americans justifiably cherish the liberty of conscience as a foundational limitation on state power. Few today would challenge the assessment offered in 1919 by future Supreme Court Chief Justice Harlan Fiske Stone that the liberty of conscience is so vital that "it may well be questioned whether the state which preserves its life by a settled policy of violation of the conscience of the individual will not in fact ultimately lose it by the process."[1] Stone was affirming, in the wake of World War I, the ongoing need to recognize and respect conscientious objector status. The nation's commitment to conscience has helped provide legal protection for individuals faced with direct state encroachment on their core moral convictions, not only in the draft context, but also, for example, for students facing state-required participation in the pledge of allegiance. "If there is any fixed star in our constitutional constellation," Justice Jackson wrote for the court in *Barnette*, the landmark case striking down a state's pledge requirement, "it is that no official, high or petty, can prescribe what shall be orthodox in politics, nationalism, religion, or other matters of opinion or force citizens to confess by word or act their faith therein."[2] At stake was nothing less than the court's duty to preserve "freedom of conscience to the full."[3]

When the state moves against the individual, either foreclosing dissent or coercing assent to the majority's ideals, it makes sense to view liberty of conscience as a legal protection that arises at the point of conflict between an individual's deeply held moral or religious beliefs and state power.[4] In many of today's public-square battles implicating conscience, the individual-versus-state paradigm is inapposite.

---

[1] Harlan Fiske Stone, *The Conscientious Objector*, 21 Col. Univ. Q. 253, 269 (1919) (quoted in *Seeger v. United States*, 380 U.S 163, 170 (1965)).

[2] *West Virginia Bd. of Ed. v. Barnette*, 319 U.S. 624, 642 (1943).

[3] *Id.* at 646 (Murphy, J., concurring).

[4] See, e.g., *Girouard v. United States*, 328 U.S. 61, 68 (1946) ("The struggle for religious liberty has through the centuries been an effort to accommodate the demands of the State to the conscience of the individual.")

Increasingly, the individual claiming conscience is opposed not by state power, but by the similarly conscience-driven claims of nonstate entities. Few of us would dispute the notion that liberty of conscience is an essential feature of the political order, but that broad consensus has proved to be of little help in resolving an expanding range of disputes involving conscience.

LAW'S CONSCIENCE CONUNDRUM

Consider the case of Elane Photography. Nearly ninety years after future Chief Justice Stone cautioned against using state power to force a person to participate in military combat against the dictates of his conscience, another widely publicized legal skirmish over conscience erupted from a simple email exchange. Vanessa Willock contacted Elane Photography, a husband-and-wife photo agency in Albuquerque, New Mexico, through its web site to inquire about photographing her same-sex commitment ceremony. Co-owner Elaine Huguenin emailed back: "We do not photograph same-sex weddings. But thanks for checking out our site." Willock filed a complaint with the state human rights commission, alleging a violation of the state's public accommodations law, which covers sexual orientation. At the hearing, Willock testified that the email "was a shock" and caused her "anger and fear." Jonathan Huguenin explained at the hearing that they made sure that "everything that we photographed, everything we used our artistic ability for" was in line with their Christian values.[5] The commission rejected the photographers' constitutional claims, found that they unlawfully discriminated on the basis of sexual orientation, and ordered them to pay attorney's fees of nearly $7,000 to Willock.[6]

Unlike the military draft or pledge of allegiance cases, both sides in the Elane Photography case can wrap themselves in the mantle of conscience. Willock acted on her belief in the moral legitimacy of same-sex relationships by seeking to solemnize her commitment with the same celebratory trappings that have long been part of traditional marriage ceremonies. The Huguenins acted on their belief in the immorality of same-sex relationships by refusing to participate in the celebration of such a relationship. Whereas Willock's critics argue that liberty of conscience should not be interpreted as empowering individuals to force others to assist their morally contested projects, the Huguenins' critics argue that liberty of conscience should not be interpreted as a license for marketplace providers to discriminate against members of historically marginalized groups.

Barnette's warning that the sanctity of conscience forbids the state from compelling allegiance to the flag may offer lessons for today's expanding range of disputes over conscience, but those lessons are far from obvious. A casual observer of America's

---

[5] Barbara Bradley Hagerty, *Gay Rights, Religious Liberties: A Three-Act Story*, NPR Morning Edition (Jun. 16, 2008).

[6] Andrew Webb, *State: It's Discrimination: Photographer Refused to Shoot Gay Ceremony*, Albuquerque J., Apr. 11, 2008, at A1.

cultural and legal landscapes may wonder whether the right of conscience is mor-
phing from a bulwark against government encroachment into a more generally
applicable right to individual autonomy. A central claim of this book is that this
trend is avoidable and should be avoided. We need to expand our understanding of
conscience, not only to support and secure the common good, but also to facilitate
the continuing vitality of conscience itself. Our failure to break conscience out of
its individualist framework affects our understanding of the interplay between the
individual and the state in a variety of intermediate institutions such as voluntary
associations, social service providers, corporations, and even the family.

CONSCIENCE'S RELATIONAL DIMENSION

This book does not aim to overturn the prevailing understanding of conscience as a
person's judgment of right and wrong, but it does aim to bring into focus a dimension
of conscience that is discernible from the term's earliest usage, which is "to denote a
knowledge which can be shared by several people."[7] The concept of conscience as
shared knowledge has been lost amid the individualist clamor of American "rights
talk."[8] There is a clear need to recapture the relational dimension of conscience –
the notion that the dictates of conscience are defined, articulated, and lived out in
relationship with others. Our consciences are shaped externally; our moral convictions have sources, and our sense of self comes into relief through interaction with
others. By conveying my perception of reality's normative implications, my conscience makes truth claims that possess authority over conduct – both my own and
the conduct of those who share, or come to share, my perception. Conscience, by
its very nature, connects a person to something bigger than herself, not only because
we form our moral convictions through interaction with the world around us, but
also because we invest those convictions with real-world authority in ways that are
accessible, if not agreeable, to others. This is the relational dimension of conscience.

Conscience is not just belief, passively held by the individual. It is belief applied
to conduct, an act. To a significant extent, the acting, not the intellectual choosing,
makes up personhood and justifies the state's respect for conscience. As far back as the
writings of St. Paul, conscience was portrayed as a source of authority – not just over
the substance of interior habits of mind, but over a believer's conduct.[9] Indeed, early
Christian usages were telling: Although a person's faculty of apprehension was called
"synderesis," only the faculty of *application* – action derived from apprehension –
received the label "conscientia."[10]

---

[7] Philippe Delhaye, *The Christian Conscience*, 24 (1968).

[8] See generally Mary Ann Glendon, *Rights Talk: The Impoverishment of Political Discourse* (1993).

[9] See, e.g., 1 Corinthians 10 (instructing Christians to forego certain foods if it would offend the
consciences of fellow believers).

[10] Harold J. Berman, *Law and Revolution*, II 74–5 (2004).

As such, conscience cannot be adequately explained as a freestanding individual construct. It might be expressed and defended by the individual, but its substance and real-world implications are relational by their very nature. Cultivating and maintaining the conditions necessary for these relationships to thrive should be a priority for our society if we are serious about freedom of conscience. History is replete with individuals who have tenaciously clung to their claims of conscience from the depths of solitary confinement, of course, but their steadfastness belies the fact that their claims have been relegated, in effect, to a state of suspended animation. Conscience, by its very nature, directs our gaze outward, to sources of formation, to communities of discernment, and to venues for expression. When the state closes down avenues by which persons live out their core beliefs – and admittedly, some avenues must be closed if peaceful coexistence is to be possible – there is a cost to the continued vitality of conscience.

It is not just a vague allegiance to moral pluralism that should underlie our legal system's reluctance to restrict the independence of the myriad associations that make up the vast space between person and state; it is a commitment to freedom of conscience, properly understood. A more robust conception of conscience will also help clarify how our own deeply held moral convictions can foster the sort of thick interpersonal commitments that are one mark of a healthy society.

THE MORAL MARKETPLACE

So what lessons does conscience's relational dimension hold for the Elane Photography case? The problem is that the state, in this and other cases, has chosen sides, effectively giving the individual customer's conscience a trump over the provider's conscience through the imposition of broad nondiscrimination laws. Increasingly, such laws appear aimed not simply at ensuring access to an essential good or service, but at enshrining nondiscrimination as a blanket requirement for providers' participation in the marketplace. Little attention is paid to whether a dissenting provider's discriminatory practice actually threatens access in a significant way.

The problem is compounded by the fact that, too often, the response of those concerned with the erosion of providers' liberty is to champion the recognition of a blanket right of conscience on their behalf. They ask the law to immunize an individual provider's conscience-driven marketplace conduct from state penalty and from employer reprisal. If a photographer (or pharmacist or taxi driver or cashier) has the legal right to make her own decisions about the morally contested goods and services she will provide, it becomes more difficult for institutions to create and maintain their own distinct moral identities. A morally homogeneous landscape of institutional providers makes it more difficult for individuals to gather in venues for the mutual formation, articulation, and living out of shared moral commitments. This problem is more pressing, as we will see, when the state hinders the cultivation of distinct moral identities among religious groups, charities, and other voluntary associations, but venues for conscience are also important in the commercial sphere. Individualized conceptions of conscience – whether espoused by the consumer or the provider – do not hold much promise for resolving the new wave of conscience battles because they overlook the relationships that are key to conscience's long-term flourishing.

This book asks us to step back from the rights-centered rhetoric of current debates and contextualize the public relevance of conscience. In particular, the book outlines the contours of a marketplace in which moral convictions are allowed to operate and compete without invoking the trump of state power. A more deliberate articulation and broader recognition of this "moral marketplace" can enrich our discourse on a range of issues, as the legal system's current response to the competing claims of conscience has afforded little space in which contrasting moral visions might be allowed to flourish in any meaningful way.

The state would prudently support the liberty of conscience by allowing Vanessa Willock and the Huguenins to live out their convictions in the marketplace. Assuming that other wedding photographers are willing and able to shoot a same-sex commitment ceremony, the state should leave the Huguenins to answer to the consumer, not the state, and allow consumers to utilize market power to contest (or embrace) the moral norms of their choosing. Rather than making all photography agencies morally fungible (i.e., freely interchangeable) via state edict, the market allows the flourishing of plural moral norms in the provision of these services. Individual consciences can thrive through overlapping webs of morality-driven associations and allegiances, even while diametrically opposed consciences similarly thrive. At the same time, if the Huguenins cannot find market support for their agency's moral claims, they would not have the right to force other agencies to hire them and accommodate their claims of conscience. They should have the freedom to create an economically viable agency with a distinct moral identity; they should not have the authority to hinder the cultivation of another agency's conflicting, nondiscriminatory moral identity. For the conscience-driven consumer and the conscience-driven provider, the state should not be the primary audience for their moral claims. In the moral marketplace, the zero-sum contest over the reins of state power is replaced by a reinvigorated civil society, allowing the commercial sphere to reflect our moral pluralism.

This is not to suggest that the prospects for civil society are inexorably linked with market economics, but only that where the marketplace provision of certain goods and services is subject to a society-wide battle over moral norms, allowing the contest to proceed may be more conducive to a healthy and engaged public life than the current inclination to enshrine legally one set of moral norms and negate the others. State power is not marginalized in the moral marketplace, but it is constrained, as it is devoted to ensuring a well-functioning market, not to eviscerating the market through the top-down imposition of particular moral norms. This sounds like (and is) a fairly straightforward proposal, but there are few traces of it in the cacophony of voices trumpeting provider (or consumer) rights.

Wedding photographers, obviously, are the very small tip of a very large iceberg. Participants in an exploding array of debates over the provision of goods and services in our society tend to invoke conscience as a freestanding, absolute value without acknowledging – much less articulating – the real-world relationships and associational ties that empower individuals to live out the dictates of conscience. The vibrancy and vitality of these relationships are best facilitated by a state that limits itself to supporting a functioning market (i.e., ensuring access), rather than serving as the marketplace's moral gatekeeper.

As noted, the merits of a flourishing moral marketplace flow from a deeper understanding of conscience than the individualist portrayal that (understandably) dominates American law. Conscience is, as this book will detail, inherently relational: Its claims are formed, articulated, and lived out along paths that transcend the individual. The vibrancy of conscience thus depends on more than the law's protection of individual autonomy; it also depends on the vitality of the associations, such as Elane Photography, against which the right of conscience is currently being invoked. Put simply, if our society is to facilitate an authentic and robust liberty of conscience, it cannot reflexively favor individual autonomy against group authority; it must also work to cultivate the spaces in which individuals come together to live out the shared dictates of conscience.

CONSCIENCE'S NEW BATTLE LINES

To get some sense of the lurking "iceberg" and why the traditional, individual-versus-state conception of conscience is such an unhelpful template for resolving today's conscience battles, try to formulate a coherent and consistent set of solutions to the following roster of recent skirmishes over conscience. First consider the widely publicized "pharmacist wars," in which individuals on both sides claim a right to compel others to honor the dictates of their consciences. Pharmacists in many states have claimed a right of conscience to refuse to dispense any pharmaceutical to which they object morally (typically contraceptives or antidepressants) without fear of government, or even employer, reprisal. At the same time, pharmacy customers have argued – in litigation and before legislatures – that their own rights of conscience entitle them to receive any legal pharmaceutical at any licensed pharmacy with "no hassle, no delay, no lecture." Many states have enshrined one side or the other's claim into their laws. Whose claims should win? Is your answer shaped more by liberty of conscience or by your moral analysis of the pharmaceuticals at issue?

Next consider the recent headline-grabbing battles over conscience that have been sparked by scientific advancements, expanding religious pluralism, rapidly shifting cultural norms, or some combination thereof. Should a physician's right of conscience empower him to refuse to provide reproductive assistance to a patient because she is not married? Does a Muslim taxi driver's right of conscience warrant an accommodation allowing him to avoid transporting passengers carrying alcohol? Should a Muslim cashier be entitled to call over a coworker whenever a customer needs to have pork products scanned and bagged? Should a bus driver be entitled to avoid operating a bus with an advertisement for a gay-friendly magazine? In justifying your answers, note that all of these disputes arose out of marketplace transactions for goods and services. Are these claimants defending their consciences against illegitimate coercion or using conscience as an affirmative weapon by which to force the rewriting of their job descriptions? The state executioner would be hard-pressed to keep his job if he were to invoke conscience as a basis for refusing to participate in the death penalty, but such obvious cases are rare.

Another category of cases involves direct challenges to an organization's moral identity, particularly its religious identity, by individual employees or customers who believe that their own liberty of conscience is threatened by organizational policies. Is it safe to presume that conscience is a relevant concern on the individual's side of the ledger, but not the organization's? Take two recent lawsuits: one filed by employees against the Salvation Army for making religion part of the hiring and retention criteria; and the other by customers against a leading dating web site run by Christians for failing to expand their services to include gays and lesbians. Is the cause of conscience represented by the organizations pursuing distinctive moral identities or by the individuals whose own exercise of conscience may by burdened by the organizational identity?

Some of these challenges to an organization's moral identity are brought by the state itself, purportedly on the individual's behalf. In such cases, the state seeks to compel groups to honor the conscience claims implicit in the morally laden priorities of their employees, prospective members or prospective clients, even when those priorities conflict with the organization's identity. Several years ago, for example, James Dale was excluded from the Boy Scouts based on his openly gay identity, and the state of New Jersey responded by enforcing antidiscrimination law to require his inclusion.[11] Even more recently, state universities have revoked recognition of Christian student groups that exclude non-Christians; state legislatures in California and New York have forced Catholic Charities to cover the cost of contraceptives for employees; and the Massachusetts legislature has required Catholic Charities to place children with same-sex couples as a condition of maintaining its license to perform adoption services, leading to the group's decision to terminate the services. Who should prevail in these cases, and how does our commitment to conscience help us decide who should prevail? Does liberty of conscience favor the dissenting association against the oppressive state or the dissenting individual against the oppressive association?

What if the "oppressive association" in question is a family? A California appellate court recently ruled that parents cannot home-school their children unless the parent is a state-certified teacher.[12] Thirty-five years ago, the Supreme Court was faced with

---

[11] *Boy Scouts of Am. v. Dale*, 530 U.S. 640 (2000).
[12] Mitchell Landsberg, *Ruling Hits Home Schooling*, L.A. Times, Mar. 6, 2008, at 1. The ruling was subsequently reversed on rehearing. See *Jonathan L. v. Superior Court of Los Angeles County*, 165 Cal. App. 4th 1074 (Cal. Ct. App. 2008).

a standoff between the state of Wisconsin and Amish parents who refused to submit to the state's requirement that children attend high school.[13] Both cases present the same question about conscience: To what extend should we, as a society, defer to the consciences of parents when it comes to child rearing? Especially in the years before we recognize an individual as the bearer of a fully formed conscience, who should speak on behalf of the child and her not-yet-formed conscience? Are there limits to parental authority, especially when society perceives that parental prerogative may compromise the child's development? If our protection of conscience aims only to defend the moral autonomy of the individual, where do families fit?

This exercise gets even trickier if we try to discern the extent to which our answers are influenced by the fact that many of these episodes pit our society's deepening commitment to inclusiveness and equality against groups that prioritize other moral claims. In today's climate, these claims are often based on traditional religious views of sexuality or gender. The broader interests at stake, however, do not fall into any single "culture war" category or easily align along the usual conservative-liberal battle lines. To the extent that these cases share a conception of conscience as a sort of trump card to be invoked on behalf of the individual's stated objectives against whatever institution happens to block the path, are you comfortable resolving these cases based on whether you agree with what a particular association is trying to do?

A ROAD MAP

This book seeks to explore conscience's relational dimension and to begin tracing its implications for public policy. Headline-grabbing litigation battles are encompassed within those implications, but they are not the whole story. Reclaiming the relational dimension will bring a depth and nuance to conscience currently lacking from our public discourse, with significant implications for our understanding of prudently ordered relationships among the state, the individual, and the associations standing between them. Recognizing these dynamics of conscience need not denigrate the individual's primacy, but rather aims to honor that primacy by facilitating the relationships that make the individual's conscience possible. In the simplest terms, conscience is the person's interior judge of right and wrong. Its interiority, however, can never be mistaken for self-containment because conscience's formation and operation link the person to the world outside herself.

Although conscience's relational dimension requires some discussion of philosophy, sociology, political theory, and even theology, this is primarily a book about law. Chapter 1 provides a brief overview of the law's treatment of conscience and explains why, despite key points of progress in the legal protection of individual conscience over the course of the twentieth century, the law's support of conscience is unduly narrow. In particular, the law's support tends to be limited to particular instances

---

[13] *Wisconsin v. Yoder*, 406 U.S. 205 (1972).

of conflict between the individual and the state. Those instances are – and should remain – central to the sanctity of conscience in our legal system. But the cause of conscience would be further bolstered to the extent that the law's cognizance of conscience expands beyond points of conflict to encompass paths of formation and expression, beyond the individual-versus-state paradigm to encompass nonstate associations, and beyond purely individualist justifications for liberty of conscience to include justifications grounded in the common good.

The next part of the book lays out three key aspects of conscience's relational dimension. Chapter 2 explores the place of conscience within our conception of the person, tracing the ancient roots of conscience up to Charles Taylor's ground-breaking philosophical work on identity. Because conscience's sources lie outside ourselves, conscience's claims tend to be accessible and intersubjective in a way that claims of preference are not. Our moral convictions provide a framework that allows us to live lives of coherence and integrity; their accessibility and intersubjectivity mean that we tend to construct those frameworks through relationships. Linking the relational dimension of conscience with the nature of the person, I argue, first, that conscience embodies our social nature; second, that conscience is not so much an expression of our identity as an essential means of forming our identity; and third, that conscience is best understood not as a force that binds our will in particular circumstances, but more broadly as a set of truth claims that is perpetually in dialogue with our will.

Chapter 3 focuses more specifically on the inherently self-transcendent quality of conscience's claims. These claims connect the person with the world outside herself because moral judgments are grounded in reality, actual or perceived. The chapter summarizes the tension between objectivist and subjectivist accounts of morality, concluding that even subjectivist accounts make room for conscience's outward orientation. This outward orientation – captured in part by the intersubjective nature of moral language – underscores the importance of communities in which a person's moral identity can be articulated and stabilized and explains how a vibrant community life within a society facilitates the formation of individual conscience, even among those who are not themselves members of a meaningful moral community.

Chapter 4 outlines the connection between conscience and the common good, drawing on a variety of thoughtful perspectives on a just social order, ranging from the nineteenth-century Calvinist theory of sphere sovereignty to the current "cultural cognition" project spearheaded by scholars at Yale Law School. All of the perspectives are bound, to varying degrees, by a shared commitment to decentralized moral authority in society. The chapter concludes that a society committed to the common good presupposes a "bottom up" conversation on contested moral issues, which requires, in turn, ample space for individuals and associations to live out moral identities in tension with – even in open defiance of – the majority's norms.

The book's second half begins to trace the implications of conscience's relational dimension across a range of social settings in which the law and moral claims interact.

Chapter 5 focuses on voluntary associations, emphasizing the importance of the mediating role played by groups to which individuals willingly commit themselves. By providing members with a sense of identity and purpose, a means of expression, and a venue for shared meaning, voluntary associations connect the individual with social power without subjecting her to the collectivizing inclinations of the state. As such, voluntary associations are central to the cause of conscience. This centrality requires a meaningful, but not unlimited, degree of independence from state interference. Determining the prudent degree of independence is no easy task, of course, particularly at a time when many associations are eager to align themselves more closely with the government, or at least to get their share of the government's money. Focusing on the mediating role, and its capacity to support conscience's flourishing, helps clarify the interests at stake.

Chapter 6 examines the role of conscience in the provision of health care, using as an entry point the recent controversy over morality in the pharmacy. On one side, conscience is invoked to justify legislation that would enable individual pharmacists to refuse to fill prescriptions on moral grounds without suffering any negative repercussions, whether in the form of government penalty, employment discrimination, or third-party liability. On the other side, conscience is invoked to justify legislation that would enable individual consumers to compel pharmacists to fill any legally obtained prescription without delay or inconvenience. The chapter proposes a third way, asking the state to allow both sides to live out their convictions in the marketplace, maintaining a forum in which pharmacies craft their own particular conscience policies in response to the demands of their employees and customers.

Chapter 7 uses the pharmacy example to open a broader inquiry into whether corporations in general should be considered venues for the communal expression and implementation of conscience, looking specifically at the capacity of corporations such as Wal-Mart to carve out moral identities that diverge from the norms embraced by the broader society. My inquiry also includes the internal environment of the corporation, exploring the tension between a corporate community's constituent-driven moral identity and the exercise of conscience by dissenting community members, particularly employees. When it comes to facilitating the living out of conscience, I conclude that the relevance of the local church and Wal-Mart are different in degree, not in kind.

Education is the focus of chapter 8. Recent federal court rulings have solidified the authority of school officials to decide what students are taught about contested moral issues and curtailed parents' right to shield students from teachings to which they object. Parental authority over their children's education, courts have reasoned, extends only to the choice of schools. Because many parents do not have a viable choice of schools, however, the state's power over students' moral formation poses a significant threat to conscience. When there is a functioning market of school choice, institutional authority is consistent with – and can actually support – the relational dimension of conscience.

In chapter 9, I use the lens offered by conscience's relational dimension in an attempt to gain a new perspective on the most intimate of social settings: the family. On one hand, the family is the most fertile ground for the formation of conscience; on the other hand, society is rightfully uncomfortable ceding full autonomy to the family in light of the vulnerability of its members and its lack of an exit option, at least for children. Accordingly, we face an uneasy balancing act: wanting to protect the family's freedom to function as a "thick" moral community, but also wanting to protect the well-being of its individual members. There are no bright-line answers to the conundrum, but one key is to avoid expanding the notion of "well-being" to include highly contested visions of the good life, such as individual autonomy. In academic circles and some legal contexts, the expansion is well underway, and this chapter pushes back with a framework made possible by conscience's relational dimension.

In the final chapter, the focus narrows from the law's substance to the law's gate-keepers, contrasting and comparing the proper place for conscience in the work of lawyers and judges. This context illustrates the fact that the contours of conscience's public role are shaped by market dynamics: lawyers are market actors; judges are not. Judges should be discouraged from bringing extralegal moral norms to their work, in deference to their effective monopoly over access to the law. Lawyers, by contrast, should be encouraged to bring extralegal moral norms, as relevant, into their dialogues with clients because, in most representations, the client has an exit option. Lawyers who bring conscience to bear on their professional identities can help expand and enrich the common good by challenging the presumptions of the governing legal paradigm, whether by critically engaging the substance of the positive law or the objectives that the client wishes to pursue through the positive law. Lawyers should still respect the client-directed nature of their work, but authentic respect for the client may warrant entering into a dialogue about the moral considerations that too often remain beneath the surface of the representation.

Conscience is an interior judgment that is oriented outward; it operates, as Sidney Callahan puts it, "in a complex double-directed way" because "[t]here must be an awareness or connectedness with the real outer environment at the same time as an awareness of the inner environment of the self as self."[14] From its beginning, American law has shown a distinctive and evolving commitment to conscience as inner awareness, shielding the sanctum of the mind from state encroachment. The next chapter in the unfolding history of conscience and the law must include a deeper account of conscience's outward orientation, its tendency to flourish in the fertile soil of our relationships, and the corresponding need to protect the venues that are essential to the formation, articulation, and living out of conscience. This book offers such an account.

---

[14] Sidney Callahan, *In Good Conscience*, 41 (1991).

PART I

THE RELATIONAL DIMENSION OF CONSCIENCE

1

Conscience in Law

Conscience is ubiquitous in our law, but it is usually unexamined, functioning as a presumed shared starting point within every citizen's cognitive grasp from which the law can do its work. The law's protection of conscience through a robust defense of individual liberty has been a hallmark of the American experiment, and no one can reasonably contest its success. But individual liberty only tells part of conscience's story. The danger is that a strictly individualized conception of conscience will obfuscate the need for society to defend the myriad relationships that are integral to conscience's full flourishing.

In this chapter, we will explore how modern law's understanding of conscience has provided a formidable bulwark against state encroachment on beliefs that are central to the individual's moral identity. The narrowness of this understanding, however, leaves our legal system ill equipped to handle many of today's disputes in which the cause of conscience is implicated. When viewed through the prism offered by the Supreme Court's most well-known interpretation of conscience, we can see that the law has already laid the groundwork for acknowledging conscience's relational dimension by focusing less on the source of conscience's claims and more on the authority of conscience's claims over the particular individual. In relation, though, the law's deliberately agnostic stance toward the source and nature of conscience's claims – verifying that an individual treats the claims as authoritative but venturing no further – may make it more difficult for the law to protect conscience proactively. Accounting for and evaluating a law's impact on conscience requires discernment of the interplay among a variety of social factors (not just whether an individual's conscience is directly burdened by the law) and mitigating against the law's impact may, in limited circumstances, warrant targeting specific sources of conscience (such as religion) for legal protection. With a deeper understanding of the relationship between law and conscience, it becomes clear that the individual-versus-state paradigm into which we usually force disputes over conscience can be an artificial and unhelpful construct for thinking about these issues.

SEEGER'S LESSONS

The legal exploration of conscience has occurred most famously in a long line of cases setting the boundaries for exemption from compulsory military service. Many cases implicating conscience have arisen under the First Amendment's Free Exercise clause, but the draft cases are more illuminating for our purposes because courts, in the course of separating valid from invalid claims of conscience under the conscientious objection statutes, have been forced to give substance to the content of conscience. In most other settings, courts take "conscience" as a given and focus on the state's asserted justification for the infringement.[1]

Congress originally tied the draft exemptions to an individual's membership in a recognized pacifist sect. In World War II, Congress broadened the exemption to encompass individuals who, by reason of their "religious training and belief," opposed all war. Group membership became unnecessary. Between 1940 and 1948, two federal courts of appeal held that "religious training and belief" did not include philosophical, social, or political views. In 1948, Congress amended the statute to define "religious training and belief" as "an individual's belief in a relation to a Supreme Being involving duties superior to those arising from any human relation, but (not including) essentially political, sociological, or philosophical views or a merely personal moral code."[2]

This legislative background set the stage for Daniel Seeger, a young man from Long Island, who claimed conscientious objector status in 1957. Declaring to the draft board that he was opposed to participation in war because of his "religious" belief, he indicated that he preferred to leave open the question presented on the registration form as to his belief in a supreme being; he could not answer yes or no. He explained, his "skepticism or disbelief in the existence of God" did "not necessarily mean lack of faith in anything whatsoever" because his was a "belief in and devotion to goodness and virtue for their own sakes, and a religious faith in a purely ethical creed."[3] His belief in God was only "in the remotest sense."[4]

The federal district court did not believe that Seeger's understanding of "religion" could be squared with the statute. Seeger's claim for exemption was denied because it was not based on a belief in a supreme being, and he was convicted for refusing to

---

[1] See, e.g., *United States v. MacIntosh*, 283 U.S. 605, 625 (1931) (reasoning that "we are a nation with a duty to survive" in upholding denial of citizenship to applicant who would not swear to bear arms); *United States v. Schwimmer*, 279 U.S. 644, 650 (1929), (upholding denial of citizenship to pacifist because "[w]hatever tends to lessen the willingness of citizens to discharge their duty to bear arms in the country's defense detracts from the strength and safety of the government"); Application of the President and Directors of Georgetown College, Inc., 331 F.2d 1000, 1010 (D.C. Cir. 1964), (authorizing hospital to administer life-saving blood transfusions to nonconsenting Jehovah's Witness based in part on judge's determination "to act on the side of life").

[2] *Seeger v. United States*, 380 U.S. 163, 172 (1965).

[3] *Id.* at 166.

[4] *Id.* at 167.

submit to induction. The court of appeals affirmed the conviction, but the U.S. Supreme Court reversed it.

The Supreme Court's interpretation of the statute – particularly the language "religious training and belief" – was shaped directly by the court's fear that allowing the government to privilege religious believers over their fellow citizens would run afoul of the Establishment clause. As a result, the court looked not to the object of the objector's belief, but to its centrality in the objector's life. The court concluded, "Congress, in using the expression 'Supreme Being' rather than the designation 'God,' was merely clarifying the meaning of religious training and belief so as to embrace all religions and to exclude essentially political, sociological, or philosophical views."[5] Under the court's construction, the statutory test of belief "in relation to a Supreme Being" is "whether a given belief that is sincere and meaningful occupies a place in the life of its possessor parallel to that filled by the orthodox belief in God of one who clearly qualifies for the exemption."[6] This test, the court hoped, would prevent the need for it to function as an arbiter of "authentic" religious belief because the test is "an objective one, namely, does the claimed belief occupy the same place in the life of the objector as an orthodox belief in God holds in the life of one clearly qualified for exemption."[7] Daniel Seeger met that test, and his conviction was overturned.

Seeger remains an emblematic case of our legal system's struggle with conscience, as the justices worked to define and apply the concept in a way that makes sense for a pluralistic society dedicated to the neutral treatment of religious believers and nonbelievers. The reasoning by which the court reached its decision offers three lessons that are central to modern law's struggle with conscience and that provide the backdrop for a deeper exploration of conscience's relational dimension. The *Seeger* court's emphasis on the connection between conscience and authority, its epistemological agnosticism regarding moral claims, and its easy embrace of the individual-versus-state paradigm for settling matters of conscience contributed to a sensible and prudent outcome in the case at hand. The lessons, however, may hold different insights for many of our current disputes.

Lesson 1: Conscience's Authority

The *Seeger* court's focus on religion-like centrality indirectly connects conscience to authority, which, in the process, opens up the potential to see conscience as a set of moral claims that can be shared. The court reasoned that the statute excludes individuals who oppose war "on the basis of essentially political, sociological or economic considerations that war is wrong and that they will have no part of it" because

[5] *Id.* at 165–6.
[6] *Id.* at 166.
[7] *Id.* at 184.

"[t]hese judgments have historically been reserved for the Government, and in matters which can be said to fall within these areas the conviction of the individual has never been permitted to override that of the state."[8] By contrast, in the area of "religious" beliefs, the state's authority bows to the authority of conscience. The lower appellate court had found, in regard to *Seeger*, that "it would seem impossible to say with assurance that [he] is not bowing to 'external commands' in virtually the same sense as is the objector who defers to the will of a 'supernatural power.'"[9]

Early American notions of liberty of conscience shared this emphasis on authority – specifically, the relationship of authority between God and the believer. A claim of conscience was not an exercise of individual will, but an acknowledgment of obligation emanating from outside the self. The substance of that obligation was a matter for individual interpretation; however, the religious roots of conscience entailed self-transcendence. To the extent that we begin to equate conscience with a personal, inscrutable moral code, we lose, as Michael Walzer puts it, a vision of conscience that entails "the sharing of moral knowledge, the sense of Another's presence, the connection of the individual to a universal order."[10] Once conscience enters the realm of the merely personal, it faces "the possibility of moral egotism, which is surely very different from self-dedication to God's law – even if it can be argued that a secular state has no business judging the difference."[11]

With *Seeger*, the Supreme Court undertook the difficult task of constructing a legally meaningful and intellectually coherent view of conscience that made equal space for religious and nonreligious moral convictions. By recognizing conscience as an authority – that is, that it is in relationship with, not coextensive with, the individual will – the *Seeger* court justified the law's deference to conscience. Conscience, in this estimation, is not simply an instinct or preference comprising the will; it is an actor upon the will. This justification also hinted toward conscience's relational dimension. For a moral claim to become a conviction, much less a conviction given authority over the will, the individual must be exposed to and often steeped in that claim. This process by which an individual's conscience comes into authority-wielding relief is an inherently self-transcending process. It is often social, and it always entails the individual's engagement with assertions that are not self-contained. If conscience is a set of moral convictions that transcends the individual will, does its self-transcending nature tend to make it accessible in ways that preference and instinct are not?

Seeger, for example, claimed that he came to his beliefs on war "in a very solitary way."[12] Nevertheless, his worldview could not help but have been shaped by communities. He was a product of a devout Catholic home and school, and although he drifted away from the Church, he explained that he "always remained interested

[8] *Id.* at 173.
[9] *Id.* at 186.
[10] Michael Walzer, *Obligations: Essays on Disobedience, War and Citizenship*, 128 (1970).
[11] *Id.* at 128–9.
[12] Peter Irons, *The Courage of Their Convictions*, 168 (1990).

in philosophical and spiritual questions, and [he] tried to take as many liberal-arts courses as [he could]."[13] Even in the "solitary" phase of his moral formation, his pacifist beliefs were rooted in sources external to himself. Seeger listed Mahatma Gandhi, John Dewey, and Henry David Thoreau as the greatest influences on his decision about the draft. Indeed, it was as a direct result of this reading, he recounts, that he decided that he "wasn't going to serve in the army."[14] It was the beliefs resulting from the course of his life experience – and exposure to the work of these authors in particular – that, in the Supreme Court's estimation, came to "occupy the same place in his life as the belief in a traditional deity holds in the lives of his friends, the Quakers."[15]

The tensions underlying *Seeger* became even starker two years later when the Supreme Court decided the *Welsh* case. The government's conscientious objector form required claimants to declare that their opposition to war arose from their "religious training and belief." Whereas Seeger crossed out the words "training and" and put quote marks around the word "religious," Welsh crossed out "my religious training and," resulting in a declaration that his opposition to war resulted from his "belief," with no "religious" component. Instead, he stated that his beliefs were formed by readings in history and sociology. The court compared Welsh's claim favorably with Seeger's, focusing on the intensity and centrality of the belief in their lives:

> Both strongly believed that killing in war was wrong, unethical, and immoral, and their consciences forbade them to take part in such an evil practice. Their objection to participating in war in any form could not be said to come from a 'still, small voice of conscience'; rather, for them that voice was so loud and insistent that both men preferred to go to jail rather than serve in the Armed Forces.[16]

Once the intensity is established, the court reasoned that the statute's exclusion of individuals whose claims are based on "essentially political, sociological, or philosophical views or a merely personal moral code" should not be read "to exclude those who hold strong beliefs about our domestic and foreign affairs or even those whose conscientious objection to participation in all wars is founded to a substantial extent upon considerations of public policy."[17] Rather, the exclusion must refer to "those whose beliefs are not deeply held and those whose objection to war does not rest at all upon moral, ethical, or religious principle but instead rests upon considerations of policy, pragmatism, or expediency."[18]

By essentially ignoring the requirement of "religious training and belief," the court brought liberalism's conscience problem into sharp relief: Can the epistemologically

[13] *Id.* at 167.
[14] *Id.* at 168.
[15] *Seeger*, 380 U.S. at 187.
[16] *Welsh v. United States*, 398 U.S. 333, 337 (1970).
[17] *Id.* at 342.
[18] *Id.* at 342–3.

neutral state privilege certain sources of moral convictions over others in setting boundaries on the liberty of conscience? By expanding the scope of conscience under the statute – and in deference, no doubt, to the Establishment clause – the court illuminated a defensible and practicable shape of conscience. Welsh had written, in response to the draft board's requirements for exemption, that he believed in the value of human life and that this "belief (and the corresponding 'duty' to abstain from violence toward another person) is not 'superior to those arising from any human relation.' On the contrary, it is essential to every human relation."[19] Although Welsh thereby uprooted his moral claim from conscience's historical grounding in divine authority, he maintained its self-transcendent quality. He opposed war because human life is valuable, a judgment supported by his observation of the human experience. The authority of conscience, in these terms, is accessible and relational. It is not a black box.

Conscience as a "Black Box"

The nature of conscience's authority matters if we aim to understand the conditions necessary for conscience's flourishing, but the topic is rarely explored in our legal system. Most courts and legislatures addressing conscience today do not make the effort to spell out their understanding of conscience's authority, and few bother even to define the term. It is as if legal actors presume that conscience is such a fixed part of our shared vocabulary that it warrants no substantive explication. This was not always the case, however. Consider two sharply contrasting judicial portrayals of conscience from the nineteenth century.

In the 1857 case of *People v. Stewart*, the California Supreme Court held that a juror was improperly excluded for cause for stating that he opposed capital punishment as a matter of "principle." Although the trial judge could have excluded a juror with a conscientious objection to the death penalty, principled opposition was insufficient, in the Supreme Court's view. The court engaged in a lengthy distinction between conscience and principle. Principle, the court explained, "is the result of judgment, is tested by reason, defended by argument, and yields to the decision of an intelligent mind."[20] Conscience, on the other hand, "springs from some internal source of self-knowledge, which acknowledges no superior, bows to no authority, yields to no demonstration, and is governed by no law; it ignores reason, defies argument, and is unaccountable and irresponsible to all human tests and standards; it is a law unto itself, and its scruples, and its teachings are not amenable to human tribunals, but rests alone with its possessor and his God."[21]

This is the "black box" approach to conscience. Not only can the dictates of conscience be difficult to explain fully in rationally accessible terms in the court's

---

[19] *Id.* at 343.
[20] *People v. Stewart*, 7 Cal. 140, 143 (1857).
[21] *Id.*

view, but conscience also "ignores reason" and "defies argument." The *Stewart* court goes so far as to paint conscience as some sort of instinctive and inexplicable personal drive that eludes authority. There is no point in engaging a person whose conscience shapes their viewpoint, for conscience is utterly inaccessible and irrational. The implication is that the legal system's only choice is to accommodate conscience or not.

Beyond the "Black Box"

Compare *Stewart*'s analysis with the work of John Locke, who defended conscience and explained its compatibility with reason. Although divine revelation (via conscience) could confirm the dictates of reason, he wrote, "yet [it] cannot in such Cases, invalidate its Decrees."[22] Defining the bounds of conscience's liberty by reference to the dictates of reason has little appeal today – who among us would favor defining individual liberty by reference to what the majority finds compatible with reason? Locke's point can, however, be expanded: Conscience, as a self-transcending set of moral claims, is naturally situated for interpersonal engagement. Conscience is susceptible to argument precisely because its authority is grounded in the person's conception of reality, rational or not. The law still must decide whether to accommodate the exercise of conscience, but that is not the only relevant question. The necessary conditions for conscience to flourish touch many areas of the law, as will be explored in the second half of this book.

Miller v. Miller, decided by a Pennsylvania court of appeals in 1898, comes closer to this outward-looking conception of conscience. In that case, the court ruled that the trial judge had erred in comments to the jury. The judge, in trying to persuade jurors to reach a verdict, insisted that their disagreement was amenable to resolution because the differences were matters of simple judgment and were not grounded in conscience. The appellate court reasoned that conscience cannot be so easily separated from judgment, for conscience "is that moral sense which dictates to [the juror] right and wrong." As such, the exercise of conscience is unavoidable for a juror:

> Every statute enacted by a legislature, every decision pronounced by a court, every verdict of a jury, is professedly based on a moral sense, prescribing what is right and prohibiting what is wrong. The statement of the learned judge assumed that among the jurors there was no difference of opinion which had its source in the operations of conscience. He says "It is simply a difference in judgment, and no question of conscience whatever in the case." But judgment is only the result or conclusion of conscience, after the latter has performed its office in the different steps leading

---

[22] Noah Feldman, *Divided by God*, 371 (2005) (quoting Locke, *An Essay Concerning Human Understanding*, 693–4).

up to the conclusion; and this conclusion, then, is the very truth to him who has arrived at it by conscientious perception and reasoning.[23]

In one sense, the *Miller* court's view makes conscience more difficult to isolate because it is ubiquitous. At the same time, though, the court makes clear that conscience is not some self-contained or impenetrable box; it comprises convictions about right and wrong in the world of action, and thus is as likely to serve as a path of dialogue as a path of isolation. *Stewart's* definition makes conscience inherently inaccessible, not only to courts, but to anyone else. Although *Seeger's* emphasis on conscience's authority hints strongly at the potential for interpersonal engagement, *Stewart* marginalizes that potential by portraying conscience as some sort of inexplicable and possibly arbitrary individual instinct. If conscience cannot transcend the individual, then the law must accept or reject conscience as a given condition of the individual. The relational dimension falls out of the picture.

The Self-Contained Conscience

Today, elements of both the *Stewart* and *Miller* definitions are apparent in the law's approach to conscience. As in *Miller*, conscience's imprint is seen everywhere. As in *Stewart*, the content of conscience is taken as a given condition of the individual. Both tendencies are displayed in *Planned Parenthood v. Casey*, the Supreme Court's 1992 reaffirmation of the right to abortion originally recognized in *Roe v. Wade*. The *Casey* plurality initially noted that "[m]en and women of good conscience can disagree, and we suppose some always shall disagree, about the profound moral and spiritual implications of terminating a pregnancy, even in its earliest stage."[24] Already, the Court makes clear that conscience is implicated in the decision to have an abortion, even though few women who do so will report feeling obligated by some particular moral conviction to do so. Often, the decision is motivated by practical concerns about finances, relationships, or maturity. In other words, an act of conscience does not always derive from a fixed moral obligation, as it did with Seeger's opposition to war. Perhaps more frequently, the moral content of one's conscience will guide the choice, wrapped up with practical considerations, and may not mandate a single acceptable outcome. A woman faced with an unexpected pregnancy can have the baby or not – either way, unless she decides solely on pragmatic grounds without engaging in any sort of moral reasoning, conscience is in play. On this point, as I will explore in the following chapters, the *Casey* court is correct.

---

[23] *Miller v. Miller*, 187 Pa. 572, 584–5 (1898).
[24] 505 U.S. 833, 850 (1992).

Even though, according to the plurality opinion, some individual justices admittedly "find abortion offensive to our most basic principles of morality," their obligation "is to define the liberty of all, not to mandate our own moral code."[25] And, in what Justice Scalia derisively calls the "sweet-mystery-of-life" passage, the plurality opined that "[a]t the heart of liberty is the right to define one's own concept of existence, of meaning, of the universe, and of the mystery of human life."[26] It is not as though any act of conscience is impervious to state regulation, however. But when it comes to the abortion decision, although it "may originate within the zone of conscience and belief, it is more than a philosophic exercise," for the woman's "suffering is too intimate and personal for the State to insist, without more, upon its own vision of the woman's role, however dominant that vision has been in the course of our history and our culture."[27] Instead, her destiny "must be shaped to a large extent on her own conception of her spiritual imperatives and her place in society."[28] A conscientious decision about abortion is thereby walled off from the moral judgment of society, even if that judgment is deeply rooted in history and has attained broad social consensus.

Grounding the right to abortion in a woman's "right" of conscience contributes to the one-dimensional portrayal of conscience because it appears to elevate and isolate the woman's conscience from all other moral claims. As *Roe* noted, the state has a legitimate interest in the life – actual or potential – of the unborn child. Regardless of the intimacy and importance of the decision from the woman's perspective, critics insist that the stakes of the abortion decision suggest that the law cannot treat the conscience underlying the decision as a black box: inaccessible and beyond debate. Perhaps conscience-as-trump is the only path by which courts can articulate a right to abortion. Whether or not it is a prudent approach in that context, courts must be wary about extending it farther. Conscience's operation is, as *Casey* suggests, ubiquitous in our everyday lives: Recognition of this fact should begin the conversation, not end it.

When the state presumes that conscience is only relevant to individual autonomy and that the law's only responsibility is to decide whether to reject or empower a particular individual's claim of conscience at the point of external conflict, the ongoing moral conversations on which our social fabric depends – and which conscience's authority warrants by its very nature – are vulnerable to being short-circuited. The moral authority wielded by conscience is highly personal, but is not self-contained; even Daniel Seeger's opposition to war emerged from a conscience that possessed an authority made possible by moral claims originating outside himself.

[25] *Id.*
[26] *Id.* at 851.
[27] *Id.* at 852.
[28] *Id.*

Lesson 2: Law's Agnosticism

The *Seeger* court's focus on conscience's authority over the particular individual is a mixed blessing. On one hand, as noted, the exercise of authority connotes a self-transcendence that brings conscience's relational dimension into relief. On the other hand, to the extent that this approach leads to the exclusion of other factors from the inquiry – such as, the source or substance of conscience's claims – the law's protection of conscience may be compromised. In this regard, *Seeger* provided a relatively early glimpse into the epistemological agnosticism that has become a hallmark of modern law's approach to conscience's substance. Through the interpretive contortions that allowed the court to count Seeger's nonbelief in a supreme being as belief in a supreme being, the court signaled the coming challenge of defining conscience without being seen to limit the individual's prerogative to construct her own meaning of the world, including the meaning of morality. The starkness of this challenge is reflected in *Casey*'s admonition, "[a]t the heart of liberty is the right to define one's own concept of existence, of meaning, of the universe, and of the mystery of human life."[29] This agnosticism is understandable given the dangers that accompany government pronouncements of moral truth. This agnosticism can, however, also give rise to a view of conscience as a sort of preformed moral compass that somehow springs into existence ex nihilo. Ignoring the relational nature of conscience – including the moral sources that shape its substance, the relational processes from which it emerges, and its claims' foreseeable impact on the common good – does not bode well for conscience's long-term protection.

Privileging Religion

Our legal system's reaction to conscience is shaped by the impossibility of defining conscience's moral content and epistemological sources within fixed boundaries supported by social consensus. It was the *Seeger* court's understandable reluctance to enforce the contrived boundary between the religious and secular conscience that animated its interpretive gymnastics. In the post-*Seeger* world, the Supreme Court itself acknowledges that liberty of conscience, evolving beyond its religious origins, has become "the central liberty that unifies the various clauses in the First Amendment."[30] So, although the eighteenth-century citizen saw liberty of conscience as a guarantee that he would not be coerced into "performing religious actions or subscribing to religious beliefs that he believed were sinful in the eyes of God," our modern understanding, in Noah Feldman's estimation, "seems to be that every person is entitled not to be coerced into performing actions or subscribing to beliefs that violate his most deeply held principles."[31]

---

[29] *Planned Parenthood v. Casey*, 505 U.S. 833, 850 (1992).
[30] *Wallace v. Jaffree*, 472 U.S. 38, 50 (1985).
[31] Feldman, *supra* note 22, at 424.

Critics contend that courts' reluctance to draw lines has turned the liberty of conscience into nothing more than "the notion of personal existential decision-making."[32] The problem might seem unavoidable in light of the fact that, as Steven Smith has observed, "[a] virtual consensus in the academic community and the courts holds that it would be unacceptable to give constitutional protection to religiously formed conscience, but not to what we call the 'secularized conscience.'"[33] The legal system's epistemological agnosticism toward conscience becomes a reason to prohibit the state from favoring religion-based conscience over other forms of conscience when granting exemptions from generally applicable laws.

Whatever our hesitation about legitimizing religiously derived claims of conscience over other types, a stance of total agnosticism toward conscience from our legal system is deeply problematic. In particular, it remains important not to diminish the importance of accommodating religious convictions, and one effective way of doing so is to address religious convictions specifically. The Establishment clause should not be read to foreclose the law's treatment of religion as a distinct category of conscience-driven claims. On this point, Andrew Koppelman argues that although "[t]he state cannot regard religion as a superior source of moral obligation," what the state "can say is that religion is one of a plurality of goods," and that "religion is not reducible to any other good."[34] As Michael McConnell puts it, "there is no other human phenomenon that combines all [the aspects of religion]; if there were such a concept, it would probably be viewed as a religion."[35] As such, the law may need to privilege religion at a very abstract level to show equal regard to "all of the various categories of morally serious endeavor."[36] The law can privilege moral commitments to the environment or to human equality by legislating on behalf of those commitments; there is no reason why it cannot do so for religious endeavors as well.[37]

Justice Byron White espoused a related approach in a case in which the court struck down a state statute that exempted religious organizations' publications from the sales tax. Although he did not approve a religion-specific exemption, he explained that the state could permissibly "exempt the sale not only of religious literature distributed by a religious organization but also of philosophical literature distributed by nonreligious organizations devoted to such matters of conscience as life and death, good and evil, being and nonbeing, right and wrong."[38] Because serious moral reflection and conversation promote personal accountability and social bonding, the government has a legitimate interest in promoting them. One way to do so is

[32] Marie Failinger, "Wondering After Babel," in *Law and Religion*, 94 (Rex J. Adhar, ed., 2000).
[33] Steven D. Smith, *What Does Religion Have to Do With Freedom of Conscience?* 76 U. Colo. L. Rev. 911, 912 (2005).
[34] Andrew Koppelman, *Is it Fair to Give Religion Special Treatment?* 2006 U. Ill. L. Rev. 571, 593.
[35] Michael McConnell, *The Problem of Singling Out Religion*, 50 DePaul L. Rev. 1, 42 (2000).
[36] Koppelman, *supra* note 34, 597.
[37] *Id.* at 603.
[38] *Texas Monthly, Inc. v. Bullock*, 489 U.S. 1, 27–28 (White, J., concurring).

by protecting religious endeavors from state interference, alongside nonreligious endeavors that facilitate comparable goods. Given the life-and-death stakes of a compulsory military draft, excluding nonreligious objectors from exemption strains our notions of fundamental fairness. In other contexts, such as zoning regulations or hiring decisions, legislative grants of autonomy to religious organizations may be one sensible way to foster the communal life of conscience.

Context Matters

That the legal system should be leery of categorically privileging religious over nonreligious sources of conscience or deeming some sources of conscientious objection to a state imposition more worthy than others does not mean that the law should turn a blind eye to the particulars of a dispute implicating conscience. It is important that lawmakers ascertain what is at stake in a contest over conscience; this requires taking a broad view not only of a claim's authority over the individual, but also of the foreseeable implications that the claim's substance has for the common good. In other words, the social and historical context of the claim matters.

Obviously, the law cannot treat an individual's conscience as a trump over whatever state interests it runs up against, as even the most meager pursuit of the common good will require some claims of conscience to be rejected. This is true whether the claim of conscience belongs to the lone renegade or is shared by a community of like-minded believers. An authentic conception of the common good (as explored in chapter 4), though, warrants a firm presumption in favor of conscience's sanctity. Enforcing this presumption – figuring out when the vital interests of the political community require that the contrary claims of conscience be rejected – requires that the legal system pay attention not only to the substantive claims of conscience, but also to the broader social conversation that has (or has not) preceded the claims and the claims' relationship to the political community's asserted interests.

One obvious instance where the law seems to have dramatically facilitated the common good with little regard for the contrary claims of conscience is the mid-twentieth-century civil rights movement. The Civil Rights Act of 1964 prohibited discrimination based on race (among other grounds) by employers and places of public accommodation, including restaurants and hotels. The legislation came in amid grass roots activism on both sides of the segregation battles. Members of the black community staged lunch counter sit-ins in the South and pressured employers to diversify their workforces. White citizens formed groups such as the People's Association for Selective Shopping to respond by boycotting businesses that employed blacks.[39] If the liberty of conscience demands that we allow individuals to express and live out their moral convictions in the marketplace, permitting them to appeal to like-minded citizens in an ongoing contest over the common good,

[39] Jason Sokol, *There Goes My Everything: White Southerners in the Age of Civil Rights, 1945–1975*, 185 (2006).

the Civil Rights Act is a troubling case. It can be read as having short-circuited the "bottom up" conversation over the good, imposing a collective vision of racial equality on public and private actors alike.

That the Act enshrined a moral vision that was still fiercely contested appears to be an unavoidable conclusion. Senator Barry Goldwater voted against the bill despite opposing segregation, remarking that "you can't legislate morality." The state's coercive power was harnessed to a moral claim that rolled over the claims of dissenting consciences and the communal venues in which those dissenting consciences could find shared meaning and expression, mandating conformity even on the question of how to use one's own property. Ollie McClung, the owner of a previously whites-only restaurant, explained at the time, "We operate our business as a trust to our customers," and an all-white clientele was part of the covenant.[40] Public opinion polls showed that half of the nation thought that President Kennedy was pushing too fast on civil rights before his death.[41]

The conventional wisdom today tells a far different story. The Civil Rights Act is almost universally praised as a vital measure by which America's aspirational ideals became more closely aligned with its reality. Indeed, the widely acknowledged success of assertive lawmaking in this context has emboldened subsequent advocates of social justice to embrace a top-down approach to our nation's moral contests. The lessons of the 1960s can easily be lost or overblown unless lawmakers engage in a nuanced analysis of the apparent tension between the common good to be pursued and the claims of conscience that appear to stand in the way. The analysis must encompass three decidedly nonagnostic questions about conscience.

First, what is the cost of maintaining space in which divergent claims of conscience can operate freely? If the government proposes to shut down the moral marketplace and enshrine one set of claims as binding law, there should have been a deliberate judgment that the continued viability of the dissenting claims exacts too great a cost on the common good. For example, prohibiting discrimination in employment or housing are vastly different propositions than prohibiting discrimination by a Christian fraternity.[42] A business owner whose moral convictions lead him to employ only whites (or men, heterosexuals, etc.) threatens the excluded individuals' ability to function in society by foreclosing economic opportunity. Although there is a job market, determining access to employment is more difficult than determining access to goods and services. It is relatively easy to determine the policy of every pharmacy in town regarding the sale of the morning-after pill, for example, and an individualized inquiry of the affected customer is unnecessary. One can only speculate as to

---

[40] *Id.* at 188.

[41] Nick Kotz, *Judgment Days: Lyndon Baines Johnson, Martin Luther King Jr., and the Laws That Changed America*, 14 (2005).

[42] *See* Jon Sanders, *The College Code*, Wall Street Journal, Aug. 27, 2004 (reporting on the University of North Carolina's decision to revoke recognition of a Christian fraternity for refusing to open membership to non-Christians).

whether a job applicant who was discriminated against by one employer would have found comparable employment elsewhere, and the inquiry will be highly individualized, encompassing many different factors, including the applicant's qualifications and interests, the overlap in timing between the applicant's search and available openings, and the respective compensation and benefit packages associated with those openings. Given the centrality of employment to a person's ability to function in society and the difficulty in implementing a nondiscrimination framework triggered on access, the state is justified in enforcing nondiscrimination norms against employers.

There is also a housing market, but it is not enough that a person has access to a house; for access to be meaningful, there needs to be a meaningful choice of homes and locations. Economic reality and covert discrimination already limit meaningful access, but permitting overt discrimination could quickly worsen the patterns of segregation that already consign historically marginalized minorities to neighborhoods that exacerbate their marginalization. As such, the state prudently excludes certain marginalizing traits of prospective tenants/buyers from the landlord/seller's legitimate consideration. This dynamic is not present in the market for roughly fungible goods and services.

The schooling of our children is a thornier example: On one hand, the education of a child is inexorably linked to economic and political participation as an adult; on the other hand, educational choices are powerful expressions of conscience (as we will explore in chapter 8). Provided that exclusionary private schools do not take on a de facto public identity or crowd out viable nonexclusionary schooling alternatives in a particular community, however, a government mandate of equal access to all private schools is too steep a price to pay in terms of conscience.

Whether or not one agrees with my conclusions about the wisdom of applying nondiscrimination law in these areas, the point is that these are the sorts of observations and arguments that lawmakers should be offering, not simply sweeping rhetoric about the value of equality. The limits of conscience should not be defined categorically. Lawmakers should not shut down the moral marketplace by deciding that its continued operation is not worthy of their respect; they should determine that its operation is incompatible with securing goods that are foundational to participation in our society.

Second, what sort of conscience-driven conversation has preceded the law's intervention? Our nation struggled with the question of race for centuries before the legal system made a concerted effort to make racial equality a reality. A serious conversation on society's treatment of gays and lesbians has only arisen in the last forty years, and the narrower question of equality for same-sex couples reached the headlines only in the past decade or so. A requirement that employers offer the same benefits to same-sex partners of employees as those offered to spouses looks different in 2010 than in 1990. Acknowledging the hardships that result when the law waits for the social conversation to unfold does not negate the fact that the amount of marketplace space demanded by dissenting claims of conscience may change over time. Gauging the appropriate level of deference to conscience is not a popularity contest, but the degree of deference is a function, in part, of the opportunity for majority-defying ideas to be lived out in the marketplace. Political actors will disagree about how long the marketplace conversation should be permitted to proceed; my point is simply that the inquiry preceding state intervention should encompass not just questions of "how" and "why," but "when."

Third, does the proposed legal intervention secure the foundational premises of the common good while it minimizes the coercive impact on conscience? In other words, is the intervention narrowly tailored to achieving the foundational good? It is difficult to imagine how the Civil Rights Act could have accomplished its objective – the dismantling of Jim Crow – without such an aggressive stance. Back in 1944, Sterling Brown had explained, "however segregation may be rationalized, it is essentially the denial of belonging."[43] To be clear, "belonging" as an abstract legal right is dangerous. As will be explored throughout this book, conscience draws individuals into associations grounded on shared commitments, and the vitality of conscience thus presumes the power to exclude. The wisdom of granting a legal entitlement to "belong" depends on the object of the "belonging." Economic, political, and educational opportunities are nonnegotiable building blocks for participation in American society. The Civil Rights Act went far beyond these, targeting theaters, restaurants, and hotels. Context, however, is key. In the 1960s, African Americans in the South faced a society that was hard wired for their subjugation and exclusion. As Risa Goluboff explains, "Jim Crow existed because every day, in ways momentous and quotidian, governments, private institutions, and millions of individuals made decisions about hiring, firing, consuming, recreating, governing, educating, and serving that kept blacks out, down, and under."[44]

Moreover, in terms of the moral contest over integration and racial equality, the marketplace was not functional in any meaningful sense. Voluntary integration was practically impossible because, as the head of the Georgia Council on Human Relations explained, "No one wants to be a martyr or a hero. Everyone wants to make his dollar without disturbance."[45] Even apart from moral claims, bottom-line considerations kept business owners from breaking ranks. As a Mississippi district attorney later commented, "The Civil Rights Act is probably the best thing that ever happened to the south" because "it took us over what was inevitably coming, and it was going to come by violence or bloodshed."[46] It was practically impossible to narrowly target employment discrimination in the Jim Crow south because that was just one element of a tightly woven social web of segregation. More precisely tailored

[43] Quoted in James C. Cobb, *The Brown Decision, Jim Crow and Southern Identity*, 57 (2005).
[44] Risa L. Goluboff, *The Lost Promise of Civil Rights*, 7 (2007).
[45] Sokol, *supra* note 39, at 192.
[46] *Id.* at 195.

legal intervention is possible – and indeed, prudent – in nearly all of the hot-button moral debates today.

The point here is not that our law must reach certain conclusions about certain moral debates (although the book will present some specific policy recommendations as it proceeds). The point is that in figuring out how best to protect conscience without jeopardizing the common good, the law must pay attention to the substance of conscience's claims and to their impact on the state's legitimate pursuit of the common good. Conscience need not be defined by the increasingly strained religious/secular categories, but that does not mean that the state should throw up its hands whenever the term "conscience" is invoked. The basis and content of conscience's claims matter, not because they provide bright-line boundaries of legitimacy, but because protecting conscience in a pluralistic democracy is a messy business, requiring ongoing conversations that are nuanced, widely engaged, and substantive. These may be obvious points with which few will disagree (I hope), but our legislatures and courts must work to identify and articulate more carefully the relationship between a proposed state incursion on conscience and the common good. Of course, this presumes a vision of what the common good actually entails, which is the subject of chapter 4.

Lesson 3: The Individual-versus-State Paradigm

The *Seeger* court was presented with a conflict between the individual as pacifist and the state at war; discerning when one's moral convictions must submit to national need understandably presents an individualized picture of conscience. Focusing on the point of individual-versus-state conflict has been essential to the American legal system's success in maintaining conscience as a bulwark, shielding the individual from the state's coercive power. As noted in the book's introduction, however, conscience's current ubiquity in legal policy debates has spilled far beyond the individual-versus-state paradigm. The paradigm still holds significant sway over the contours of the debates because the dominant conception of conscience lends itself to simplistic portrayals of the interests at stake in the debates. Is it always true that the cause of conscience rests squarely with the individual seeking to rein in group autonomy or authority, even when the group does not wield state power?

The Jury as "Community Conscience"

This is not to suggest that the law never attempts to capture a sense of conscience beyond that of the individual's. These attempts, generally labeled as instances of the "community conscience," are not really about conscience at all. The Supreme Court, for example, has spoken of the jury as embodying the community conscience, protecting defendants against unjust punishment. Our entire system of negligence-based civil liability is founded, according to Kenneth Abraham, on the "notion that the finder of fact represents and reflects the conscience of the community, simply

serving as the vehicle through which norms implicit in everyday behavior are identified and applied."[47] On the criminal side, Justice William Brennan explained,
"[t]he availability of trial by jury allows an accused to protect himself against possible oppression by what is in essence an appeal to the community conscience, as
embodied in the jury that hears his case."[48] Noted federal Appellate Judge David
Bazelon stated it even more directly: "[T]he very essence of the jury's function,"
he wrote, "is its role as a spokesman for the community conscience in determining
whether or not blame can be imposed."[49] Sherman Clark sees the jury acting as the
"conscience of the community" to the extent that it is a vehicle for the exercise of
moral agency in dispensing justice. He believes the jury is "the institution through
which we acknowledge and accept responsibility for our judgments – the institution
through which our individual consciences are implicated in those judgments."[50]

In earlier periods of American history, the law was thought to embody certain
shared moral convictions, making the "community conscience" more comprehen-
sible, if not empirically verifiable. For example, after the Protestant Reformation,
both Lutherans and Calvinists espoused a theological doctrine of the uses of moral
law: first, the moral law's civil use was to restrain people from sinful conduct; second,
its theological use was to condemn sinful persons; and third, its educational use was
to enhance the spiritual development of believers. The doctrine, according to John
Witte, "had ample enough coherence and adherence to provide a common theological touchstone for members of fiercely competing sects," particularly regarding the
purposes of criminal law.[51] The civil, theological, and educational uses of moral law
corresponded to the deterrent, retributive, and rehabilitative purposes of criminal
law.[52] Today, however, the suggestion of a universal, knowable "moral law" is a
nonstarter. There is no agreed-upon catalog of "sins" other than those proscribed by
the positive law. As a result, the only apparent source of the "conscience" embodied
by the jury is the court's instructions on the relevant law. Moral claims beyond those
instructions are idiosyncratic and thus irrelevant.

Even within the positive law, the state cannot presume to enforce any particular
vision of the moral good or to shape the substance of its citizens' visions of the
good; rather, it is to mediate among the citizens' competing visions of the good.
The jury can apply the terms of the law charged to them; extralegal moral convictions may influence the decision of any particular juror or group of jurors, but
such influence tends to be seen as subversive to the rule of law. Federal courts have
remarked on the threat to a defendant's right to a fair trial when jurors use the Bible

[47] Kenneth S. Abraham, *The Trouble with Negligence*, 54 Vand. L. Rev. 1187, 1195 (2001).
[48] *McKeiver v. Pennsylvania*, 403 U.S. 528, 554–55 (1971) (Brennan, J., concurring in part and dissenting in part).
[49] *United States v. Dougherty*, 473 F.2d 1113, 1142 (D.C. Cir. 1972) (Bazelon, C.J., concurring in part and dissenting in part).
[50] Sherman Clark, *The Courage of Our Convictions*, 97 Mich. L. Rev. 2381, 2420 (1999).
[51] John Witte Jr., *God's Joust, God's Justice: Law and Religion in the Western Tradition*, 276 (2006).
[52] *Id.* at 280.

in their deliberations,[53] and although reliance on the Bible raises separate Establishment clause concerns, its prohibition also reflects our worry that extralegal moral sources may cloud the jury's application of the positive law to the facts at issue. A juror's conscience may lead her to keep her Bible at home or to reject a defendant's proffered bribe, but that is a separate matter – the jury's verdict is a determination of the facts in light of the positive law; it is not a statement of conscience in any meaningful sense.

Undoubtedly, a juror's view of the evidence and governing law is shaped by her moral worldview, and the jury room is far from being a morality-free zone. Especially when the case presents an indeterminate legal concept such as "recklessness," the line between law and morality grows fuzzy. As a state-constructed community, however, there is little sense of a deliberately fostered common moral identity, and the group's "conscience" is ultimately expressed in narrow, state-defined terms. The jury verdict is an expression of conscience as random group judgment in that the jury is not self-selected or formed based on jurors' shared beliefs or worldviews. It is a group, not a community, much less a moral community. The verdict may represent the assembled individuals' common answers to the state's question; it is difficult to characterize it as the expression of conscience. So, although the law has affixed the "conscience" label to this assembly of individuals, the jury lacks the authentic relational core of conscience of the type explored in this book.

Still, delegating adjudicative authority to the jury is conducive to the flourishing of conscience within our society to the extent that it is designed to offer some bulwark against the overbearing state, assuming that judges are more likely than citizen-jurors to be loyal to and less detached from the state's viewpoint. A randomly selected group of citizens is less likely to function as a monolithic or oppressive source of top-down norms compared with the state itself.

The State as "Community Conscience"

The jury-as-community-conscience metaphor, although unhelpful, is less pernicious than the state's own assumption of responsibility for articulating the community conscience and enforcing its dictates. In *Bob Jones University v. United States*, for example, the Supreme Court upheld the Internal Revenue Service's (IRS's) denial of tax-exempt status to a Christian university that engaged in racial discrimination. The IRS had determined that the school was not "charitable" under the common-law meaning of that term, and the court agreed. Chief Justice Burger, writing for the majority, reasoned that the exemption is justified by the entity's conferring of a public benefit, and so the entity "must demonstrably serve and be in harmony with the public interest."[54] In the wake of *Brown v. Board of Education*, according to the court, it is "beyond doubt" that "racial discrimination in education violates

---

53 See, e.g., *Robinson v. Polk*, 444 F.3d 225, 226 (2006).
54 *Bob Jones Univ. v. United States*, 461 U.S. 574, 592 (1983).

a most fundamental national public policy as well as rights of individuals."[55] This means that the entity's "purpose must not be so at odds with the common community conscience as to undermine any public benefit that might otherwise be conferred."[56]

Justice Powell, concurring in the judgment, agreed that racial discrimination in education is "sufficiently fundamental" to limit the availability of tax-exempt status,[57] but he was troubled by the "element of conformity that appears to inform the court's analysis."[58] Conditioning tax-exempt status on the organization's "harmony with the public interest" and alignment with "the common community conscience" suggested to Powell that "the primary function of a tax-exempt organization is to act on behalf of the Government in carrying out governmentally approved policies."[59] Powell recognized that the majority's language misconstrues the nature of the tax exemption; it is not a tool with which to "reinforce any perceived 'common community conscience,'" but rather is an "indispensable means of limiting the influence of government orthodoxy on important areas of community life."[60] Although he concluded that Congress "has determined that the policy against racial discrimination in education should override the countervailing interest in permitting unorthodox private behavior," he rejected any notion that the IRS should be authorized to "decide which public policies are sufficiently 'fundamental' to require denial of tax exemptions."[61] Justice Rehnquist, in dissent, agreed that Congress had the power to limit tax exemptions, but found that Congress had not done so in this case.[62]

Racially discriminatory educational organizations do not possess an inviolable right to tax-exempt status, to be sure. If Congress decides to exclude such groups, it can prudently do so given the duration and difficulty of our national conversation on race and the depth of the consensus that has resulted. It is not apparent, however, how or why social consensus could be taken as a form of conscience. The court has never explained how any group (much less a nation) can possess its own freestanding conscience. It is more sensible to say that groups can serve as venues for conscience and that, although the relational nature of conscience makes such groups essential to conscience's flourishing, a group's distinct moral identity is built on the moral content of its members' consciences. Most groups have free rein under the law to carve out their own unique moral identities because dissenting members have an exit option – they can leave and join a group more compatible with their own convictions. When it comes to an entire nation, the exit option is significantly more

---

[55] *Id.* at 593.
[56] *Id.* at 592.
[57] *Id.* at 607 (Powell, concurring).
[58] *Id.* at 609.
[59] *Id.*
[60] *Id.*
[61] *Id.* at 611.
[62] *Id.* at 612 (Rehnquist, dissenting).

tenuous, and thus the nation's imposition of a contested moral claim should be more tentative than a voluntary association's. Public policy positions almost always have a moral dimension, but labeling those positions "conscience" connotes a sanctity and certainty that is problematic. Whether or not an organization should lose its tax-exempt status because of positions that run counter to widely held public opinion, conscience has little to do with public opinion. Indeed, public opinion may prove inimical to conscience's flourishing.

Conscience as Individual Liberty

The legal system's efforts to construct a fictional "community conscience" are a relatively small part of conscience's story in American law. The most obvious reason why the law tends to treat conscience within the individual-versus-state paradigm is the close historical association between conscience and religious liberty. In the American experience, religious liberty was of a distinctly Protestant sort, meaning that one's spiritual standing was a matter for the individual to work out with God, not a matter for the community to determine. Michael Walzer asserts, "[t]o accept the Protestant idea of conscience . . . is to acknowledge the divine ratification of individualism, and that acknowledgment leads necessarily to the political practice of toleration."[63] As Ed Eberle explains, for example, Roger Williams sought to secure the liberty of conscience for his colony of Providence because he believed that conscience was at the core of religion and that the law was the best way to safeguard conscience to the extent that the law could "tame man's natural instinct to control."[64] Conceived as a bulwark against others' control, the right of conscience embarks on an inherently individualistic path.

There were ample resources within the dominant Protestant culture to buttress this orientation, a trend that also served to marginalize the relevance of relationships to the faith journey. To cite just two of the more prominent examples, John Locke famously declared, "[t]rue and saving religion consists in the inward persuasion of the mind."[65] In a letter regularly cited in our time to support the "wall of separation" between church and state, Thomas Jefferson wrote of his belief that "religion is a matter which lies solely between a man and his God, [and] that he owes account to none other for his faith or his worship."[66]

At the time of the Constitution's framing, conscience was understood in suffi-ciently individualist terms that it was guaranteed as an individual right by most early drafts of the First Amendment. Although there is no indication in the record as to why it was dropped from the final version, the widely drawn implication is that

---

[63] Michael Walzer, *Obligations: Essays on Disobedience, War, and Citizenship*, 123 (1970).

[64] Edward J. Eberle, *Roger Williams on Liberty of Conscience*, 10 Roger Williams U. L. Rev. 289, 297 (2005).

[65] Witte, *supra* note 51, at 222.

[66] Letter from Thomas Jefferson to the Danbury Baptists (Jan. 1, 1802) (cited in Witte, *supra* note 51, at 228).

the Free Exercise and Establishment clauses were presumed to cover the necessary ground.[67] Indeed, concern for conscience underlies many of the debates over religious liberty in the intervening years.

Americans more readily connect the liberty of conscience with the First Amendment's requirement that the government not make any law prohibiting the "free exercise" of religion, but equally as important to the cause of conscience is the requirement that the government not make any law "establishing a religion." In fact, Noah Feldman has concluded that liberty of conscience was the central value driving the Establishment clause's enactment. Beyond worries about compulsory church attendance, "the Framers' generation worried that conscience would be violated if citizens were required to pay taxes to support religious institutions with whose beliefs they disagreed."[68] According to Feldman, "[e]ven those who advocated government funding of religion proposed that taxpayers be permitted to designate the denomination of their choice to receive their taxes, or else to opt out of paying those taxes altogether," so that "[b]y the late eighteenth century, almost no one in America thought that government legitimately could compel taxes for religious purposes without offering some possibility of formally opting out of the tax."[69]

Although the Establishment clause has been invaluable to the defense of conscience, it is important to note that its interpretation can exacerbate the marginalization of conscience's relational dimension. Justice Souter, dissenting from the Supreme Court's ruling in *Mitchell v. Helms* permitting certain types of government financial aid to religious schools, opined, "Madison's words make clear that even a small infringement of the prohibition on compelled aid to religion is odious to the freedom of conscience,"[70] and that one purpose of "the establishment prohibition of government religious funding" is "to guarantee the right of individual conscience against compulsion."[71] In *Zelman v. Simmons-Harris*, a case in which the court upheld an Ohio voucher program that allowed students to use state funds to attend religious schools, Souter objected that "every objective underlying the prohibition of religious establishment is betrayed by this [voucher] scheme . . . the first being respect for freedom of conscience."[72]

Justice Souter's approach, whatever its historical merit, can actually hinder the cultivation of relationships that emanate from conscience by making it more difficult for religious groups to compete effectively in the marketplace. When government funding is available to nonreligious groups and is distributed via the independent

---

[67] Noah Feldman, *The Intellectual Origins of the Establishment Clause*, 77 NYU L. Rev. 346, 402-03 (2002); Smith, 76 Colo. L. Rev. at 912 ("[T]he discussions suggest that the framers viewed 'free exercise of religion' and 'freedom of conscience' as virtually interchangeable concepts.").

[68] Feldman, *supra* note 67, at 351.

[69] *Id.*

[70] *Mitchell v. Helms*, 530 U.S. 793, 910 (2000) (Souter, J. dissenting).

[71] *Id.* at 868.

[72] *Zelman v. Simmons-Harris*, 536 U.S. 639, 711 (2002) (Souter, J., dissenting).

choices of individual beneficiaries (e.g., students and their families), rather than according to the government's own preferences, the conscience of the dissenting individual taxpayer does not warrant the categorical exclusion of religious groups. Exclusion under these circumstances is a prime example of the law's propensity to elevate the individual conscience at the expense of the communal venues through which the full flourishing of conscience is most likely to occur. This is not to suggest that the Framers' concern about taxation was misplaced; however, over the ensuing years, the government's role in society has expanded to the point where categorically excluding religious entities from state funds may threaten those entities' marketplace viability, particularly in fields such as health care and education.

Protecting conscience beyond its religious manifestations has required courts to engage in creative constitutional interpretation, although even the most creative interpretations tend to fall squarely within the individual-versus-state paradigm. Lacking a corollary to the religion clauses, the secular conscience appears to operate without explicit constitutional protection. Most commonly, substantive due process has been invoked to protect freedoms that are "so rooted in the traditions and conscience of our people as to be ranked as fundamental."[73] For example, when the Supreme Court upheld a state's stringent evidentiary requirements for permitting family members to terminate the artificial hydration and nutrition of a patient in a persistent vegetative state, Justice Stevens' dissent included his observation that "not much may be said with confidence about death unless it is said from faith, and that alone is reason enough to protect the freedom to conform choices about death to individual conscience."[74]

Justice Stevens is undoubtedly correct to discern conscience's central role in a person's view of death. Again, though, the fact that conscience is implicated in a decision does not end the conversation about its treatment under the law. Discomfort with the increasingly amorphous judicial invocations of conscience does not invariably justify the narrowing of conscience's scope, as though conscience is not implicated by end-of-life decisions or abortion or a myriad of other issues. Instead, we may need to avoid letting our understanding of conscience's relationship with the law be defined by the cases focused only on the point of conflict between state power and individual autonomy. In other words, "conscience" should not be used as legal shorthand for an individual's liberty from government coercion on matters pertaining to her core moral convictions. The cause of conscience encompasses individual liberty from state coercion, to be sure, but it should not be defined solely as such.

Conscience and Coercion

Andrew Koppelman offers one of the more thoughtful attempts to articulate why conscience might justify granting an exemption from the law. He challenges the suggestion made by other scholars that it is conscience, not religious belief per se,

---

[73] *Snyder v. Massachusetts*, 291 U.S. 97, 105 (1934).
[74] *Cruzan v. Missouri Dep't of Health*, 497 U.S. 261, 343 (1990) (Stevens, J., dissenting).

that justifies accommodation. Koppelman identifies as "[t]he most sophisticated justification" the notion that "the person in [conscience's] grip cannot obey the law without betraying his deepest, most identity-defining commitments."[75] For insight, Koppelman mines the concept of "volitional necessity," which describes a situation in which a person "cares about something so wholeheartedly that he cannot form an intention to act in a way that is inconsistent with that care."[76] Because the view of conscience as volitional necessity "need not have any connection to objective value" – that is, I could feel that it is necessary to act in a way that is entirely amoral or wicked – he finds that "it is a poor basis for claims upon other people."[77] Koppelman ultimately concludes that we have to look beyond conscience to justify our practices of religious accommodation and that any justification must "rest on some source of value external to the actor," not just on "the internal psychological makeup of the actor."[78]

For our purposes, it is important to recognize how the conception of conscience as volitional necessity indirectly supports the individual-versus-state paradigm by suggesting that conscience only becomes legally relevant when an individual is being coerced to act in a way that he is incapable of intending to act. Legitimate exercises of such coercive power in our society emanate from the state, and resistance grounded in volitional necessity lies with the individual. Even the individual-versus-state paradigm is overbroad in this regard because volitional necessity demands that we distinguish authentic cases of conscience from cases merely involving moral or religious considerations. For example, in *Employment Division v. Smith*, the Supreme Court held that the Free Exercise clause does not prohibit a state from denying unemployment compensation to claimants fired for work-related misconduct based on their ingestion of peyote as part of a Native American religious ceremony.[79] This is not a case that involves conscience as volitional necessity. One of the claimants, Al Smith, was "motivated primarily by interest in exploring his Native American racial identity," and the other, Galen Black "was merely curious about the Church."[80] Koppelman points out that "[m]any and perhaps most people engage in religious practice out of habit, adherence to custom, curiosity about religious truth, or happy religious enthusiasm, rather than a sense of obligation or fear of divine punishment."[81] Such motivations do not arise from conscience understood as volitional necessity, which "covers only those cases in which the agent feels impelled by a duty that she is capable of performing alone and unaided."[82]

---

[75] Andrew Koppelman, *Conscience, Volitional Necessity, and Religious Exemptions*, 2 (manuscript on file with author).

[76] *Id.*

[77] *Id.*

[78] *Id.* at 34.

[79] 494 U.S. 872 (1990).

[80] Koppelman, *supra* note 75, at 9.

[81] *Id.*

[82] *Id.*

A similar focus on individual obligation underlies much of the Supreme Court's free exercise jurisprudence. In *Lyng v. Northwest Indian Cemetery Protective Association*, for example, the court held that the Free Exercise clause was not violated by the government's construction of a road through a tribe's sacred land. The court reasoned that there was no constitutionally cognizable burden because the construction, although it may make it more difficult to practice their religion, had "no tendency to coerce individuals into acting contrary to their religious beliefs."[83]

The *Lyng* court envisions conscience as a set of nonnegotiable moral obligations, mandates that do not merely guide the will, but dictate its exercise. In the court's telling, as long as the plaintiffs in *Lyng* were not actually forced to violate their beliefs, conscience's sanctity was maintained. A more nuanced view of conscience's operation is set forth by the philosopher Timothy Macklem, who resists the tendency to think of conscience "entirely in terms of the practice of conscientious objection":

> [C]onscience has a role to play in the development as well as in the articulation of our practical reasoning. This means that conscience must be something more than our concluded beliefs on a topic, for it has a part to play in generating those beliefs in the first place. Conscience, it would appear, is a rational resource that we are able to call upon when we want to know what we should do, and the conclusions that we reach with its aid are the conclusions that we subsequently present to the world as the products of our conscience.... [T]he beliefs in question have the content they do only because they have already been shaped, within the process of our reasoning, by the existing claims of that same conscience.[84]

Claims of conscience, as Macklem puts it, "are resistant, though not immune" to the force of other reasons.[85] Even if Daniel Seeger had concluded that he could serve in the military despite his belief that war is immoral, his conscience would still have been operative. Obviously, the process by which he discerned whether military service would violate his conscience itself implicates his conscience. Conscience is moral belief applied through judgment to one's exercise of will; it is not simply the binding of one's will.

Of course, sometimes conscience *will* result in the binding of one's will. Seeger could not participate in war and remain true to his moral convictions. Even in his case, however, conscience is not at stake only at the point of conflict with the state. As a society, we show our concern for Seeger's conscience by providing him with tools to resist state efforts to coerce its violation. These tools would mean little, though, if Seeger was not also able to pursue various paths of conscience formation, to join with others in the process of articulating and living consistently with the dictates of his conscience, and to bring his conscience to bear on matters of public import.

---

[83] 485 U.S. 439, 450 (1988).
[84] Timothy Macklem, *Independence of Mind*, 86–7 (2007).
[85] *Id.* at 101.

In this regard, Seeger's upbringing in the Catholic Church, his exposure to the thought of Gandhi, James, and Thoreau, and his association with the Quakers are relevant to his exercise of conscience – indeed, they are constitutive of his exercise of conscience.

Conceiving of conscience as volitional necessity makes sense when we are talking only about the point of conflict between individual conscience and state power. If Galen Black smoked peyote out of curiosity about the religious dimension of his Native American heritage, that presents, at the point of conflict with state power, a less compelling case for liberty than if he had engaged in the practice out of fear for his soul. (Whether we should trust the law's ability to draw such a distinction is another matter.) To suggest that his curiosity-driven act is irrelevant to the sanctity of conscience would go too far. If our concern for conscience prompts (as it should) concern for the formative power of religious tradition and religious community, we also must take care not to obstruct the points of entry into those traditions and communities, whether entry is motivated by eternal or more pedestrian considerations, like curiosity.

Expanding our vision of conscience is not intended to handcuff the state, as though any matter raising moral considerations amounts to a government "no fly" zone. The vulnerability of an individual's conscience is an important consideration when evaluating state action, not a trump over all competing interests (which often will include competing claims of conscience). We can only fully consider conscience's vulnerability when we have an accurate picture of its relational dimension and that dimension's connection with the law. Part of that connection lies within the Constitution, particularly the principles that are themselves relational, such as the right of association and the due process rights associated with parental authority. More commonly, though, cognizance of the connection will fall within the province of the legislature. A prudential concern for conscience will require a prudential concern for the relational venues in which conscience is formed, articulated, and lived out. These judgments are necessarily contextual, and they are the focus of this book's second half.

THE EVOLVING LIBERTY OF CONSCIENCE

Notwithstanding the ambiguity of *Seeger's* lessons, our law has made great strides over the past century in protecting conscience, and it has done so via the language of individual rights. Two particularly essential developments in the legal treatment of conscience make possible this book's further inquiry into conscience's relational dimension. First, courts have interpreted the Constitution to provide less deference to the legislature's judgment of permissible impositions on conscience. Second, courts have been more skeptical toward arguments that regulating conduct has no impact on conscience, as if there is a clean distinction between action and belief. Both of these developments are more tenuous in some areas of the law than one would think, but they are important enough to provide at least a cursory introduction to their origins.

In the late 1930s, the Gobitis children, aged ten and twelve years, were expelled from their public school for not saluting the flag, as required by state statute. As Jehovah's Witnesses, they had been raised to believe, as a matter of conscience, "that such a gesture of respect for the flag was forbidden by command of scripture."[86] In upholding the state statute, the Supreme Court fully embraced the belief/action dichotomy, explaining that conscience does not relieve "the individual from obedience to a general law not aimed at the promotion or restriction of religious beliefs."[87] Noting society's interest in self-preservation, the court held that the state could "utilize the educational process for inculcating those almost unconscious feelings which bind men together in a comprehending loyalty," as long "as men's right to believe as they please, to win others to their way of belief, and their right to assemble in their chosen places of worship for the devotional ceremonies of their faith, are all fully respected."[88] Even the act of pledging allegiance was relegated to the realm of action despite its stated purpose of fostering loyalty to the nation.

As for deference to the state, the court reasoned that it could not "deny the legislature the right to select appropriate means" for the attainment of national unity, which the court saw as a prerequisite of national security.[89] Indeed, the court's link between national unity and security itself poses significant problems for the viability of conscience. "The ultimate foundation of a free society," in the court's view, "is the binding tie of cohesive sentiment."[90] Because the means of fostering national unity are so uncertain and beyond the court's expertise, it would be improper "[t]o stigmatize legislative judgment in providing for this universal gesture of respect for the symbol of our national life in the setting of the common school as a lawless inroad on that freedom of conscience which the Constitution protects."[91]

Justice Stone, writing in dissent, objected, "there are other ways to teach loyalty and patriotism which are the sources of national unity, than by compelling the pupil to affirm that which he does not believe and by commanding a form of affirmance which violates his religious convictions."[92] Note, however, that Justice Stone's portrayal of the liberty interests at stake was strictly individualist. He was clear about the nature of the conscience interests at stake when he asserted, "[i]t would be a denial of [the Gobitis children's] faith as well as the teachings of most religions to say that children of their age could not have religious convictions."[93] Under his

---

[86] *Minersville School Dist. v. Gobitis*, 310 U.S. 586, 592 (1940).

[87] *Id.* at 594.

[88] *Id.* at 600.

[89] *Id.* at 595.

[90] *Id.* at 596.

[91] *Id.* at 597.

[92] *Id.* at 603–04 (Stone, J., dissenting).

[93] *Id.* at 601.

reasoning, then, the threat to conscience occurs only when the state directly compels the bearer of a fully formed conscience to violate her convictions. Presumably, a kindergartner could legitimately be expelled for failing to salute the flag. The relational dimension of conscience within the family – the parents' right to shape the moral upbringing of their children – is nowhere to be found.

The rule of *Gobitis* was short lived. In 1943 – only three years after *Gobitis* – the Supreme Court reversed itself in the *Barnette* case, which also involved Jehovah's Witness students being expelled from public school for not saluting the flag. Two new appointments to the court, along with a change of mind by three justices, resulted in more serious attention to the liberty of conscience, albeit under the right of free speech. Justice Robert Jackson, writing for the majority, first noted that, unlike many of the conflicts we face today concerning conscience, the students' assertion of freedom "does not bring them into collision with rights asserted by any other individual," as "[t]he sole conflict is between authority and rights of the individual."[94]

Jackson saw through the *Gobitis* majority's attempt to portray the flag salute as conduct not impinging on belief, framing the interest at stake as the "individual freedom of mind."[95] There was no justification for deferring to the government's judgment about the salute's effectiveness in fostering national unity because forcing "an American citizen publicly to profess any statement of belief or to engage in any ceremony of assent to one presents questions of power that must be considered independently of any idea we may have as to the utility of the ceremony in question."[96]

Justice Jackson espoused the prospects of a bottom-up conversation about love of country and loyalty, rather than a top-down imposition of uniformity. The fact that the state could not mandate allegiance to a particular norm did not mean that the norm was not important – indeed, its importance may be the primary reason why allegiance to it should not be mandated. As Jackson more eloquently put it, "[t]o believe that patriotism will not flourish if patriotic ceremonies are voluntary and spontaneous instead of a compulsory routine is to make an unflattering estimate of the appeal of our institutions to free minds."[97]

Jackson then made his famous affirmation of the value of conscience on behalf of the court: "If there is any fixed star in our constitutional constellation, it is that no official, high or petty, can prescribe what shall be orthodox in politics, nationalism, religion, or other matters of opinion or force citizens to confess by word or act their faith therein."[98] This affirmation still guides us, of course, but note its limitations: It applies only to the point of conflict between the individual and state power, and it only applies in the realm of belief. The *Barnette* court was willing to extend conscience's protection, via the Free Speech clause, to an action as belief laden

94 *West Virginia State Bd. of Ed. v. Barnette*, 319 U.S. 624, 630 (1943).
95 *Id.* at 637.
96 *Id.* at 634.
97 *Id.* at 641.
98 *Id.* at 642.

as the flag salute; however, protection for other actions that emanate from belief remain less secure.

On this point, Justice Felix Frankfurter, author of the *Gobitis* majority opinion and the *Barnette* dissent, may still have gotten the last word. He objected to Jackson's analysis on the ground that "[o]ne may have the right to practice one's religion and at the same time owe the duty of formal obedience to laws that run counter to one's beliefs."[99] In Frankfurter's view, the state only "compels" belief if it also denies the "opportunity to combat it and to assert dissident views."[100] Resurrecting the belief/action mantra, Frankfurter insists that the state may, consistent with the Constitution, require citizens to submit "to conformity of action while denying its wisdom or virtue and with ample opportunity for seeking its change or abrogation."[101] In this regard, Frankfurter also embraces the marketplace approach, but with a dramatic difference: Rather than allowing the marketplace of moral norms and ideals to operate free of state coercion, he leaves the dissenting citizen to the mercy of the political marketplace, hinging her freedom of conscience on her ability to enlist enough of her fellow citizens to rein in state power.

Frankfurter asked incredulously whether Jackson's elevation of individual conscience over community norms would threaten accepted practices such as Bible-reading in schools "because of a belief that the King James version is in fact a sectarian text to which parents of the Catholic and Jewish faiths and of some Protestant persuasions may rightly object to having their children exposed?"[102] His concerns were well placed, of course; few contend today that a state system of public education should compel children to pledge allegiance to the flag, participate in teacher-led prayer, or listen to the reading of Scripture as a source of divine truth. Such practices bring the world of action squarely into the world of belief, and our society has settled the contest, at least in this context, in favor of individual conscience against state power.

But Frankfurter was correct in noting that the citizen may still owe a duty of obedience to laws that run counter to his beliefs. Although courts traditionally employed a balancing test to decide a citizen's claim to exemption from a law that required them to violate their religious beliefs, the Supreme Court rejected that approach in 1991, holding that laws of general applicability that are neutral toward religion do not violate the Free Exercise clause, notwithstanding their impact on religious practice. And in an echo of Justice Frankfurter's appeal to the political marketplace, Justice Scalia, writing for the majority in the 1991 case, explained:

> Values that are protected against government interference through enshrinement in the Bill of Rights are not thereby banished from the political process. Just as a society that believes in the negative protection accorded to the press by the First

---

[99] *Id.* at 656 (Frankfurter, J., dissenting).
[100] *Id.*
[101] *Id.*
[102] *Id.* at 659.

Amendment is likely to enact laws that affirmatively foster the dissemination of the printed word, so also a society that believes in the negative protection accorded to religious belief can be expected to be solicitous of that value in its legislation as well.... But to say that a nondiscriminatory religious practice exemption is permitted, or even that it is desirable, is not to say that it is constitutionally required, and that the appropriate occasions for its creation can be discerned by the courts. It may fairly be said that leaving accommodation to the political process will place at a relative disadvantage those religious practices that are not widely engaged in; but that unavoidable consequence of democratic government must be preferred to a system in which each conscience is a law unto itself or in which judges weigh the social importance of all laws against the centrality of all religious beliefs.[103]

It is important to remember that Scalia is talking about a particular form of conscience – religious exercise – that is anchored in the text of the Constitution. Most nonreligious forms of conscience lack constitutional protection unless they can find a foothold in substantive due process, free speech, or the right of association. What we are left with, then, is a legal framework that leaves the liberty of conscience primarily to the legislative process. The rules and rhetoric laid down in *Barnette* and its progeny are secure in our politics, and they are invaluable defenses of conscience in certain narrow contexts. But they are incomplete, reflecting a one-dimensional conception of conscience.

FUTURE CHALLENGES

The predominant view of conscience leaves several pressing questions unanswered. Will our legal system be able to construct a coherent framework for addressing claims of conscience raised by individuals against nonstate associations or by associations against individuals? When such claims are not framed in the language of individual liberty and invoked against the exercise of state power, will they even be recognized as emanating from conscience? Will our commitment to conscience extend past points of direct individual-state conflict to the protection of venues that are essential to the formation, articulation, and living out of conscience? Can our legal system maintain a relevant and coherent definition of conscience without privileging certain sources of conscience's claims over other sources? As developed in the remainder of this book, our society's understanding of conscience – and our law's embodiment of that understanding – must be deepened on several fronts.

First, if we care about an individual's capacity to develop and claim a moral worldview as her own (i.e., her moral autonomy) and her ability to live consistently with that worldview (i.e., her moral integrity), we must break conscience out of the individual-versus-state paradigm. Personal autonomy and integrity are implicated in conflicts between individuals, between an individual and an association of other

---

[103] *Employment Div. v. Smith*, 494 U.S. 872, 890 (1990).

individuals, and between associations. The law has a role in the resolution of these other conflicts, and we must pay attention to the impact of that role on the vitality and viability of conscience.

Given the religious persecution that had afflicted Europe at the time of his journey to the American colonies, it is understandable that Roger Williams focused on the state's physical coercion in his defense of conscience, lamenting "the blood of souls compelled and forced to hypocrisy in a spiritual and soul rape."[104] But, if we do not move past his focus, we can delude ourselves into believing that threats to conscience have been vanquished, once and for all. Granted, most of today's threats are less stark than the hangman's noose, but they are no less real. When nonstate actors collide over conscience, background legal rules on issues as wide ranging as employment discrimination, shareholder profit maximization, the best interests of the child, and equal access to social services are the weapons of choice. The battle lines rarely break down between "proconscience" and "anticonscience" forces, but lessons can still be learned about the interplay among individual identity, group authority, and the cause of conscience.

Second, if we care about individual autonomy and integrity, we must be concerned with conscience beyond the point of conflict – that is, beyond the point where a particular moral claim runs up against a conflicting claim backed by state power. The conditions necessary for conscience's flourishing also encompass the processes of formation, articulation, and implementation, and these will generally occur in the context of relationships. Moral truth claims are inherently relational, as evidenced by the moral and intellectual influence that one self-styled individualist, Henry David Thoreau, had on another, Daniel Seeger. The cause of conscience is supported not only by legal protections against direct state coercion, but by every legal protection that aims "to disperse control of belief formation to all persons in the society, and therefore to extend to every aspect of communication . . . through which persons as equals may express or realize their communicative integrity in conscience formation, exercise, and revision."[105]

By way of illustration, we admire conscientious objectors to the extent that their objections are based on moral convictions that link the objector to others. As Michael Walzer explains, a conscientious objector "cannot simply be true to himself and win our respect; he must also try to be true to his fellow men." That is why describing conscience as "merely personal" is inadequate: conscientious objectors who "continually worry that their objection is a piece of self-indulgence, or who ask over and over again whether they are 'really helping the Movement,' or 'working effectively to stop the war,' or 'hurting their families,' are obviously not acting on the basis of

[104] Roger Williams, *The Bloody Tenent, of Persecution, for Cause of Conscience* (1644), reprinted in Perry Miller, *Roger Williams: His Contribution to the American Tradition*, 143 (1965) (cited in Eberle, *supra* note 64, at 302).
[105] David A.J. Richards, *Toleration and the Constitution*, 169 (1986).

a 'merely personal' code."[106] We may make our moral decisions alone, but, Walzer insists, "the moral code on which such decisions are based" is a "code we almost certainly share."[107] Thus, in our post-*Seeger* age of the secular conscience, "conscience can also be described as a form of moral knowledge that we share not with God, but with other men – our fellow citizens, for example, or our comrades or brethren in some movement, party, or sect."[108]

The moral convictions that make up conscience connect the individual to something outside herself, to a perception of self-transcendent reality. This outward orientation makes our moral claims uniquely susceptible to social engagement and influence. It is important that this relational process be directed by the participants, not by the state or other outside powers. In this regard, the law's responsibility for conscience arises long before (and after) a conscientious objection to a particular law's enforcement is lodged.

Third, our concern for conscience must derive not simply from our commitment to honor the freedom of individual citizens, but from our belief that individuals are most likely to flourish in a certain type of society, one that is oriented to the common good through the operation of a vibrant marketplace of moral ideals and norms. As de Tocqueville observed, "in no country in the world has the principle of association been more successfully used . . . than in America."[109] He viewed American reliance on associations both as a bulwark against tyranny[110] and as an essential inculcator of democratic values,[111] concluding that "if men are to remain civilized, or to become so, the art of association must grow and improve in the same ratio in which the equality of conditions is increased."[112] For associations to fulfill this role, they must maintain their independence. It is not that associations will cease existing when the state begins regulating the moral claims that they make upon and through their members, but they will cease serving their key social function. As Michael Walzer concludes, "no group life of intensity and value is possible if members of the various groups are repeatedly driven into what must seem to them morally degrading performances."[113] The embrace of moral pluralism, not only vis-à-vis individuals, but also vis-à-vis the groups to which they commit themselves, is a foundational genius of American society. We must continue to reject the notion that the "only obligations

---

[106] Walzer, *supra* note 10, at 130.

[107] *Id.*

[108] *Id.* at 131.

[109] Alexis de Tocqueville, *Democracy in America*, vol. 1, 191 (1900 ed.).

[110] *Id.* vol. I at 195 ("There are no countries in which associations are more needed, to prevent the despotism of faction or the arbitrary power of a prince, than those which are democratically constituted.").

[111] *Id.* vol. II at 117 ("Feelings and opinions are recruited, the heart is enlarged, and the human mind is developed by no other means than by the reciprocal influence of men upon each other. I have shown that these influences are almost null in democratic countries; they must therefore be artificially created, and this can only be accomplished by associations.").

[112] *Id.* at 118.

[113] Walzer, *supra* note 10, at 140.

on which a democracy rests, and which its citizens ought to respect, are obligations to itself."[114]

The law's protection of Daniel Seeger's conscience is good for Seeger and for society because it empowers individuals and their associations to act on their moral convictions. It would be even more conducive to the common good if we did not have to rely on the law for its artful but hopelessly imperfect crafting of exemptions.[115] The marketplace of moral claims would open up more widely if the state avoided the need for exemptions in the first place. Writing before the modern volunteer army was a reality, Walzer argued, "[t]he state can survive without a conscript army," and "it will not be a worse state for making itself a testing ground of the quality and reach of the contemporary conscience."[116]

William Galston makes a related point in espousing the virtues of political pluralism, which reflects the fact that "[t]he claims that political institutions can make in the name of the common good coexist with claims of at least equal importance that individuals and civil associations make, based on particular visions of the good for themselves or for humankind."[117] Although this may be "messy and conflictual," if it reflects "the complex truth of the human condition, then the practice of politics must do its best to honor the principles that limit the scope of politics."[118]

It is not always possible or wise to avoid legislating on contested moral norms, of course, and so the cause of conscience demands that exemptions remain part of our legal framework. Foregoing restrictive laws to avoid the need for exemptions is only conducive to the common good if the law itself is not conducive to the common good. As discussed earlier, for example, employment discrimination laws justifiably impose a burden on employers' conscience-driven hiring policies. The 1964 Civil Rights Act exempts religious entities from its ban on religious discrimination in hiring, which sensibly equalizes "religious entities with nonreligious entities that face no comparable statutory impediment to hiring those with ideological loyalty."[119] Similarly, the Fair Housing Act exempts owner-occupied dwellings, which reflects the particular intrusiveness of a state-imposed equality norm in one's own home. The wisdom of regulation and exemption in these areas notwithstanding, the common good, as outlined in chapter 4, will tend to warrant moral humility on the state's part. This restraint includes resisting the temptation to enact sweepingly restrictive

---

[114] *Id.*

[115] See, e.g., Lucas Swaine, *The Liberal Conscience: Politics and Principle in a World of Religious Pluralism*, 104 (2006) ("[A]n accommodation framework proceeds on the assumption that citizens will be subject to laws unless granted exemptions or positive accommodations to the contrary and so does not present a sufficiently solid bulwark against the ravages of overarching regulation.").

[116] Walzer, *supra* note 10, at 145.

[117] William Galston, *Expressive Liberty and Constitutional Democracy: The Case of Freedom of Conscience*, 48 Am. J. Juris. 149, 172 (2003).

[118] *Id.*

[119] Ira C. Lupu, *Why the Congress Was Wrong and the Court Was Right: Reflections on City of Boerne v. Flores*, 39 Wm. & Mary L. Rev. 793, 809 (1998).

legislation and assume that the cause of conscience can always be secured piecemeal by the state acting as moral arbiter, sorting out "worthy" and "unworthy" dissenting moral claims.

Separating the sanctity of conscience from the vitality of the moral marketplace makes both vulnerable to the homogenizing pressure of the law. *Seeger* is an understandable, perhaps even unavoidable, step in the development of the liberty of conscience, but its analysis does not exhaust the field of needed inquiry. The objective of this book's second half is to begin outlining the prudent limits on the moral marketplace by exploring the relationship between particular venues for conscience and the legal order. This exercise, though, requires a deeper understanding of conscience itself, which is the focus of the next three chapters.

2

Conscience and the Person

When Daniel Seeger invoked his conscience as the reason why he should be excused from military service, he made a claim about himself. In fact, his expressed judgment that fighting in the war was incompatible with his moral beliefs may tell us more about Seeger than it does about the war. After all, thousands of other conscripts encountered no moral dilemmas as they joined the same war, and many of them would vehemently disagree with Seeger's conclusions about the war's moral status.

The claim of conscience as self-revelation is familiar territory in our society, where the recognition of overarching moral absolutes has long since given way to the acknowledgment of deeply personal conceptions of moral truth. But while the personal dimension of conscience may be common knowledge, the content of that dimension is not. The "black box" image is apt because, while we remain convinced that conscience is important to personal identity, we know next to nothing about its nature or its function, nor do we believe that such knowledge is realistically attainable.

In the previous chapter, we highlighted how the law's individualist and agnostic stance toward conscience short-circuits a fuller exploration of the relational paths by which conscience contributes to human flourishing. By bringing those paths into sharper relief, we can better understand how the law supports or impedes that flourishing. In this chapter, we will focus on how and why conscience matters to its bearer's sense of identity. Two foundational questions must be addressed: What does conscience tell us about a person, not so much in terms of the substance of her moral convictions, but in terms of the relationship between her moral convictions and personal identity? And what does that relationship tell us about the reasons we honor conscience as a society?

In the long history of conscience, no single set of answers to these questions emerges, but the answers begin to coalesce around certain themes, and these themes are not always reflected in today's tendency to equate conscience with a personal and self-contained moral code. The themes cannot be plucked out of the air, of course; they emerge from centuries of theological and philosophical grappling with the subject.

Admittedly, there are plenty of invocations of conscience from history to support today's individualized view. Cicero memorably captured the essence of this view with his cry, "my own conscience counts for more with me than the verdict of all other people."[1] Our law sensibly privileges Cicero's position, often siding with the individual's conscience when it is subject to coercion by "the verdict of all other people" in the form of state action. Today's use of conscience has expanded beyond the boundaries of Cicero's expression in two ways. First, conscience is invoked not just as a defensive bulwark that allows a person's conscience to count more than society's judgment *for that person*, but potentially as an offensive weapon, which effectively imposes the individual's judgment on the surrounding community. Second, conscience is privileged not just against state action (i.e., "the verdict of all other people"), but against group action by nonstate actors (i.e., the verdicts of some other people).

Cicero's rhetoric proves inadequate to framing today's conscience debates satisfactorily because it fails to account for the extent to which a person's conscience exists in relationships. Fortunately, the individualistic notion of conscience is only one part of the story emerging from history. Themes underlying conscience's relational dimension are oriented internally or externally – that is, we can explain conscience's function by explaining its interaction with other aspects of personal identity (internal) and with the social actors and influences that shape its content (external).

There is nothing novel about either approach. The "internal" orientation of conscience-as-relationship can be analogized to Plato's approach to the soul, which he defined in terms of its component parts. Plato posited that a single thing cannot simultaneously do opposite actions and that if we witness opposite actions, there is more than one "thing" acting.[2] If a man is standing still but moving his hands and head, we cannot say that he is simultaneously at rest and in motion; rather, part of him is at rest and part in motion. If an alcoholic desires a drink, but also has an aversion to it – based on some negative consequence that he foresees – there must be different subjects in play. Because "[t]here is no room for distinguishing different parts of the alcoholic's body for this purpose," we "must posit different parts of his soul."[3] In Plato's estimation, the aversion to the drink emanates from the rational part of the soul, the desire emanates from the appetitive, and a third part is evidenced by our emotions, which sometimes side with desire and sometimes with reason. Plato's three-part classification of the soul does not tell us much about the role of individual

---

[1] Cicero, Ad Att. XII.28.2.
[2] Timothy C. Potts, *Conscience in Medieval Philosophy*, 7 (1980) (discussing Plato, *Republic* (4, 436B-41B)).
[3] *Id.*

conscience within society, but it does support an important lesson about conscience: it is not a self-contained or freestanding set of beliefs, and it is not coterminous with the person; it exists and functions in relationship with things outside itself.

Much of moral philosophy has aimed to relate the dictates of a person's conscience externally – most commonly to a conception of objective truth or to the needs and well-being of the surrounding community. In this regard, Aristotle asserted that all true excellence of character is relational. Our relationships are part of human nature, not just an end of human nature. In Aristotle's understanding, "[t]he solitary life would not only be less than perfect; it would also be lacking in something so fundamental that we could hardly call it a human life at all."[4] Because each of the human excellences, or virtues, is a thing "in relation to others," the person with only solitary concerns is incapable of possessing any of the excellences in their true sense.[5] Perhaps we should expect that conscience, as a major component of the habitual choices that give rise to moral virtue, would also be a thing "in relation to others." The history of conscience, as traced in this chapter, suggests that this is indeed the case.

EARLY CHRISTIANITY

The internal and external aspects of conscience came together in the work of the Apostle Paul, whose epistles loom large in the intellectual evolution of conscience. For one thing, earlier writers had primarily conceived of conscience as possessing what is now referred to as "judicial authority" – the power of conscience to produce a self-condemnatory feeling of guilt after a wrongful act. Paul mentions "conscience" twenty-three times in his epistles; in fifteen of these, he uses it in the sense of judicial authority. Eight other times, he uses the term in the sense of having legislative authority, meaning that conscience can constrain the will before the wrongful act, not just trigger regret in retrospect.[6]

When portrayed in its capacity to bind the will, the interplay between the internal and external aspects of conscience comes into view. Paul reinforced the concept of conscience as an externally rooted judge, linked to a source of knowledge outside the person. In his view, a rightly formed conscience connects to objective truth in the form of divine revelation. At the same time, Paul notes that the conscience can err, being susceptible to disconnection from objective, external truth even while binding the person's exercise of will.[7] In fact, Paul asserts that the conscience can go bad by becoming so corrupted as to be rendered incapable of performing good

---

[4] Martha C. Nussbaum, *The Fragility of Goodness: Luck and Ethics in Greek Tragedy and Philosophy*, 350 (1986).

[5] *Id.* at 351–2.

[6] Eric D'Arcy, *Conscience and Its Right to Freedom*, 8–9 (1961).

[7] *Id.* at 9.

conduct.[8] A conscience can also be "weak."[9] For example, in affirming the propriety of eating meat bought after its use in the worship of idols, Paul nevertheless notes that "some, with consciousness of the idol until now, eat as of a thing sacrificed to an idol, and their conscience, being weak, is defiled." Even though the Christian should know that "food will not commend us to God," Paul cautions not to allow this "liberty of yours [to] become a stumbling block to the weak."[10] These "weak" people labored under a false conscience, but Paul advises that even those with rightly formed consciences should act with deference toward them.[11]

A related example arises two chapters later when Paul advises Christians to abide by the dictates of an unbeliever's conscience when dining at the unbeliever's table:

> Whatever is sold in the butcher shop, eat, asking no question for the sake of conscience, for "the earth is the Lord's, and its fullness." But if one of those who don't believe invites you to a meal, and you are inclined to go, eat whatever is set before you, asking no questions for the sake of conscience. But if anyone says to you, "This was offered to idols," don't eat it for the sake of the one who told you, and for the sake of conscience. For "the earth is the Lord's, and all its fullness." Conscience, I say, not your own, but the other's conscience.[12]

This single passage exhibits both of Paul's key contributions to our understanding of conscience: first, its legislative authority, acting as the moral guide of our dietary decisions, not just as a source of guilt after the fact; second, the respect due its judgments, even when formed in error, as evidenced by the instruction to abide by the terms of the nonbeliever's conscience.[13]

Our attitude toward another's invocation of conscience is determined not by the correctness of its judgment, but by our respect toward the person who invokes it. Of course, Paul hopes that one's conscience will be correctly formed by external sources of moral knowledge (i.e., divine revelation), but our attitude toward an actor's invocation of conscience is determined by the internal relationship between the actor's perception of moral knowledge and her exercise of will. This dynamic foreshadows the subjective dimension of conscience that dominates our understanding of conscience today.

There is a theological aspect to Paul's contribution. The subjective/objective duality of conscience is consistent with the image of God as being simultaneously interior and superior to us. We may believe that we are following God's still small voice within us, but that does not ensure that our perception of God's voice comports with the reality of God's truth. After Paul, conscience stood simultaneously distinct

---

[8] Titus 1:15.

[9] *See* Philippe Delhaye, *The Christian Conscience*, 41 (1968).

[10] 1 Cor. 8:7–9.

[11] D'Arcy, *supra* note 6, at 10.

[12] 1 Cor. 10: 25–9.

[13] See generally D'Arcy, *supra* note 6, at 11–2.

from objective truth and from the individual will; from this point forward, it is understood as a set of moral convictions that may misperceive moral reality, but that nevertheless shape the person's conduct.

Although Paul called for Christians to honor the mistaken consciences of others, this did not mean that a person is morally bound to follow her own mistaken conscience, a question with which later theologians still wrestled. Four hundred years after Paul wrote, Augustine analogized the internal dynamic of conscience to a hierarchical relationship. Just as "the command of a subordinate authority does not bind if it runs counter to the command of a superior in authority," Augustine argued that conscience binds only insofar as its judgment accords with divine law.[14] This point was underscored in the eighth century by John Damascene, who wrote that "God's law enters our mind and draws it to itself by stirring up conscience, which itself is called the law of our mind."[15]

At around the time Augustine was writing, Jerome introduced the concept of "synderesis" to the discussion of conscience (although his discovery of the new term was possibly the result of an error in transcription). Whereas "conscientia" was used to refer to the person's application of moral knowledge to conduct, Jerome used synderesis to designate the person's apprehension of moral knowledge itself. In his commentary on Ezekiel, Jerome analyzed the prophet's vision of four living beings – a man, a lion, an ox, and an eagle – and mentions other writers' interpretations of the vision:

> These writers interpret the vision in terms of Plato's theory of the three elements of the soul. There are Reason, Spirit, and Desire; to these correspond respectively the man, the lion, and the ox. Now, above these three was the eagle; so in the soul, they say, above the other three elements and beyond them is a fourth, which the Greeks call *synderesis*. This is that spark of conscience which was not quenched even in the heart of Cain, when he was driven out of paradise. This it is that makes us, too, feel our sinfulness when we are overcome by evil Desire or unbridled Spirit, or deceived by sham Reason. It is natural to identify synderesis with the eagle, since it is distinct from the other three elements and corrects them when they err.[16]

Note that Jerome did not contend that synderesis automatically or unfailingly corrects the erroneous operation of reason, spirit, and desire. He cautions, "in some men we see this conscience overthrown and displaced; they have no sense of guilt or shame for their sins," and they "deserve the rebuke, 'Still never a blush on thy harlot's brow.'"[17] Conscience, in early Christian understandings, connected a person to objective (divine) truth, but its perception of that truth could be mistaken.

---

[14] Linda Hogan, *Confronting the Truth: Conscience in the Catholic Tradition*, 80–1 (2000) (quoting Augustine, *Sermo vi De Verbis Domini*, cap. 8).

[15] *De Fide Orthodoxa* 4.22 (PG, 94,1199) (cited in D'Arcy, *supra* note 6, at 15).

[16] Jerome, *Commentarium in Ezechielem*, 1,1 (quoted in D'Arcy, *supra* note 6, at 17).

[17] *Id.* (quoting Jer. 3:3).

THE SCHOLASTICS

The period of the Scholastics – extending from the ninth to the fifteenth centuries – saw even deeper theological exploration of conscience. The Scholastics used reason to deepen the understanding of faith and supply it with rational content, and several pushed the concept of conscience in directions that laid the groundwork for more modern understandings. Peter Abelard and Albert the Great, for example, highlighted conscience's subjective dimension. Abelard defined sin as "consenting to that which it is believed ought not to be consented to."[18] Albert asserted that the binding nature of conscience turns not on whether it is true or false, but on the firmness with which it is held.[19]

The most important Scholastic, and the most important figure since Paul for the development of conscience, was Thomas Aquinas. He took Jerome's synderesis and built a framework around the distinction between habitual (synderesis) and actual conscience (conscientia). He asserted that conscientia is neither a faculty nor a habit, but an act – the act of applying knowledge to conduct.[20] But conscientia is not simply the exercise of the will – it is in dialogue with the will, although the will should obey its commands. Like other Scholastics, Aquinas held that the will must be judged by the good as presented by reason, not by the good as it actually exists.[21] He wrote, "every will at variance with reason, whether right or erring, is always evil."[22] As such, in contrast to Augustine, Aquinas held that every dictate of conscience is binding, regardless of its truth or falsity.

It is not always clear whether synderesis, as employed by the Scholastics, was meant to signify a fixed moral knowledge or one that is shaped over the course of time. It is grounded in the natural law, suggesting a correlation with eternal truths. Philip the Chancellor distinguished synderesis and conscientia in terms of specificity and free choice, with synderesis involving general, nondeliberative moral knowledge and conscientia involving the freely chosen application of moral knowledge to particular facts.[23] Under this view, synderesis cannot be mistaken, but conscientia can.[24] This may be jarring to modern sensibilities that tend to view even broad moral principles as objects of belief and so subject to error – rather than knowledge.

Although they viewed synderesis as rooted in moral knowledge, the Scholastics did note that our perception of synderesis can change over time. There is a long tradition

---

[18] Michael Baylor, *Action and the Person: Conscience in Late Scholasticism and the Young Luther*, 27 (1977) (citing Abelard's *Ethica*).
[19] D'Arcy, *supra* note 6, at 85.
[20] *Id*. at 45.
[21] *Id*. at 87–8.
[22] Baylor, *supra* note 18, at 54 (quoting *Summa Theologiae* Ia IIae, q. 19, a.5).
[23] See Timothy C. Potts, *Conscience in Medieval Philosophy*, 16 (1980).
[24] *Id*. at 13, 15.

holding that synderesis can be clouded or stamped out, like a memory.[25] Bonaventure explained, "although synderesis is always right in itself, it is said, because reason and will often go against it – reason by the blindness of error and will by the obstinacy of impiety – to be overthrown, in that its effect and its government of the other deliberative powers is repulsed and broken." He compares synderesis to a soldier "who, so far as it lies in himself, always sits well on a horse but, if the horse falls, is said to be overthrown."[26]

Another way to approach the dual framework of conscience is to view synderesis as a set of rules and conscientia as their application. The rules are still the rules even when we do not accurately perceive their substance or practical import. The gap between rule and application is not necessarily fixed; it may be closed through experience or training. Medieval philosophers were not focused on this potential,[27] but their recognition of the gap helps clarify what is lacking when we characterize conscience as a self-contained moral code that only comes into play at points of conflict between the actor's moral convictions and her surroundings. If conscience consists of both beliefs and the application of those beliefs, the potential disconnect between those two components shows why conscience is subject to continual shaping by the person's experience of and exposure to sources of moral influence. In other words, conscience as a unitary concept is less dynamic than conscience as a relationship between belief and action.

Other Scholastics, such as Bonaventure, buttressed other relational aspects of conscience by asserting that it was not a strictly innate quality of the person. Although Bonaventure insisted that we have "a natural light which is enough to apprehend that one's parents are to be honoured and that one's neighbors are not to be harmed," we do "not have the form of father or form of neighbor naturally impressed" upon us.[28] We naturally possess the knowledge of moral truth, but the circumstances of its application must be learned. The operation of conscience thus depends on knowledge that we acquire.

From the time of Paul, it had been a central tenet of Christian teaching that conscience bears the divine imprint. In the epistle to the Romans, Paul wrote that the Gentiles are able to "do by nature what the law requires" because it "is written in their hearts."[29] In his famous explication of conscience, John Henry Newman expansively described conscience's innate quality:

---

[25] Even today, Pope Benedict XVI teaches that conscience "requires formation and education," and can "become stunted," "stamped out," and "falsified so that it can only speak in a stunted or distorted way." Joseph Cardinal Ratzinger, *On Conscience*, 62 (2007) (from essay originally published in 1984).

[26] Bonaventure, Commentary on Lombard's "Book of Judgements" 2.39 (translated in Potts, *supra* note 23, at 119).

[27] See Potts, *supra* note 23, at 19.

[28] Bonaventure, Commentary on Lombard's "Book of Judgements" 2.39 (translated in Potts, *supra* note 23, at 113–14).

[29] Romans 2:14–15.

That inward light, given as it is by God . . . was intended to set up within us a standard of right and truth; to tell us our duty in every emergency, to instruct us in detail what sin is, to judge between all things which come between us, to discriminate the precious from the vile, to hinder us from being seduced by what is pleasant and agreeable, and to dissipate the sophisms of our reason.[30]

More recently, the Second Vatican Council referred to conscience as the site of "a law inscribed by God."[31]

In emphasizing the acquired component of conscience, Bonaventure expanded on this tradition, but he did not depart from it. Bonaventure would not dispute that conscience has a natural role within every person that preexists environmental influences. That does not mean, however, that the content of conscience is an entirely ready-made, self-executing set of moral directives. Even the traditional portrayal gives space to the ongoing formation of conscience within the believer who listens to God's voice. Pope John Paul II explained, "moral conscience does not close man within an insurmountable and impenetrable solitude, but opens him to the call, to the voice of God."[32] Much of conscience's real-world bite is made possible through the specific knowledge we gain of the human condition, and one primary conduit for this knowledge is our relationships.

In the fourteenth century, William of Ockham actually did depart from earlier Medieval theologians by making no use of synderesis in his exploration of conscience. Although other Scholastics held that it is synderesis that naturally allows us to know the principles that should guide the conscience, Ockham insisted that these principles are known to reason through experience or scripture.[33] He agreed with Aquinas that the will was free in choosing to disregard or follow the principles discerned by reason, but Ockham went one step further in that regard. Aquinas believed that reason had an innate desire for the good. Ockham believed that any innate habits would be incompatible with the will's total freedom, and thus any habits possessed by the will must be acquired.[34]

In the fifteenth century, the so-called last of the Scholastics, Gabriel Biel, reintroduced synderesis, but tried to do so in keeping with Ockham's general approach. He defined synderesis as "the inborn potency or faculty to assent naturally to a practical principle, evident from its terms, which dictates or signifies in universal terms that some action is to be sought or avoided."[35] Synderesis, then, cannot deny

---

[30] Potts, *supra* note 23, at 64 (quoting John H. Newman, *Discourses Addressed to Mixed Congregations*, 89–90 (1849)).

[31] Second Vatican Council, Pastoral Constitution on the Church in the Modern World, Gaudium et spes (1965).

[32] John Paul II, Encyclical letter, Veritatis splendor ¶ 58 (1993).

[33] Baylor, *supra* note 18, at 83.

[34] *Id.*

[35] *Id.* at 95 (quoting Gabriel Biel, Epitome et Collectorium ex Occamo circa quatuor sententiarum Libros, 2 Sent., d. 39, a. 1, E).

self-evident truth. It is a person's inherent rational ability to assent to certain universal and practical principles. This is a departure from earlier figures such as Jerome, who classified synderesis separately from reason; Biel and Ockham both portrayed synderesis in terms of our natural rational ability. Conscience's external orientation, though, remained intact.

THE REFORMATION

Biel died a mere twenty-five years before the Diet of Worms, an event that signaled the emergence of conscience as a defining element of the modern understanding of religious faith. Four years after posting his 95 theses to the door of the Castle Church in Wittenberg in 1517, Martin Luther was summoned by the Holy Roman Emperor to Worms to recant his teachings. The theses had focused Luther's ire on the Church's selling of indulgences, but the Diet of Worms brought out his famous conscience-based defense of his teaching. When authorities insisted that he recant his teaching, Luther responded:

> Unless I am convinced by Scripture and plain reason – I do not accept the authority of the popes and councils, for they have contradicted each other – my conscience is captive to the Word of God. I cannot and I will not recant anything for to go against conscience is neither right nor safe. God help me. Amen.

There is, of course, some truth to the portrayal of Luther as having embraced a more individualistic version of conscience, but the drama of his pronouncement makes it prone to caricature. In reality, Luther's understanding of conscience is more nuanced and less stark in its departure from previous teaching than is widely assumed. Several of Luther's points are especially relevant to our inquiry.

First, Luther expanded the scope of conscience's judgment. It is not simply directed toward the propriety of a particular act, but toward the whole self and its fallen nature. This stems in part from Luther's early belief in a synderesis not only of the reason but also of the will, meaning that the person has some innate knowledge of the good and an inherent desire to do the good.[36] Consequently, in contrast to the Scholastics, who associated conscience with intellectual judgments, Luther saw the experience of conscience as emotional just as much as intellectual.[37] Conscience, in Luther's estimation, is the mechanism by which we evaluate and judge ourselves, in the process helping us realize our need for grace. This led Luther to emphasize the interior virtues over external conduct as the essential objects of conscience.[38]

In a sermon shortly before his appearance at the Diet of Worms, he compared the Tabernacle of Moses with conscience. He equated the Tabernacle's court with

[36] *Id.* at 157.
[37] *Id.* at 173.
[38] *Id.* at 196–8.

a conscience oriented toward external acts, and he warned against those who "hang conscience on these outward things."[39] Instead, he urged:

> Let us go from the court further into the sanctuary, that is into the teaching, work and conscience that is truly good, as namely humility, kindness, mildness, patience, peace, faithfulness, love, discipline, chastity . . . which things are not bound to food and clothing, nor station, nor time, nor person.[40]

It is these interior qualities alone, according to Luther, to which "God's eyes [are] directed" and about which "man should be concerned in his conscience."[41] The sanctuary is not the end of the Christian's journey, for Luther calls the Christian to "crawl to grace and renounce himself," moving from the sanctuary to the holy of holies, where he can have the Holy Spirit.[42] It is here that conscience reaches its full sway, casting judgment not only on external actions, not only on internal motivations and dispositions, but on the whole self and its inescapable need for divine grace. Indeed, synderesis eventually falls out of Luther's analysis because it no longer made sense for him to speak of conscience as the product of the person's grasp of certain principles; conscience became an autonomous "power of making judgments," period.[43]

Second, although Luther emphasized the centrality of conscience to the person's experience of faith, he did not portray a strictly internalized or freestanding conscience. The conscience aimed at works brings self-righteousness and ultimate destruction because it is cut off from God. In Michael Baylor's characterization, "If the conscience is the bearer of man's relationship to God, it is not itself a self-sufficient or self-contained element."[44] Because of our fallen nature, the discernment of our conscience is not infallible. In other words, Luther's negative view of the self requires a negative view of conscience's ability to judge the self.[45] Conscience thus needs to be grounded in a source outside the self – in Luther's case, that source is scripture.

Third, Luther did not mistake the strength of his convictions for evidence of his convictions' truth. Rather, the strength of his convictions was simply the basis for his refusal to submit to temporal authority.[46] On the question of his willingness to retract certain teachings, he reportedly responded that "unless his adversaries by sufficient argument would extricate his conscience, which was captured by those things which they called errors, he would not be able to get out of the nets in which

---

[39] *Id.* at 197 (quoting Martin Luther, "Sermon of the Threefold Good Life to Instruct the Conscience").
[40] *Id.* (quoting "Sermon").
[41] *Id.* at 198 (quoting "Sermon").
[42] *Id.* (quoting "Sermon").
[43] *Id.* at 205 (quoting D. Martin Luthers Werke, *Kritische Gesammtausgabe*, 8, 606, 32–4).
[44] *Id.* at 218.
[45] *Id.* at 239.
[46] *Id.* at 261.

he was entangled."[47] This brings clarity to the interplay between the subjective dimension of conscience and objective truth. Luther did not obey his conscience because he knew that it was true; he obeyed it because of the firmness of his belief in its truth. This is consistent with Aquinas's assertion that the erroneous conscience must be obeyed. Engaging the erroneous conscience should proceed by persuasion, not by coercing the person to defy its dictates. It is no large step from here to honor liberty of conscience – deferring to a person's beliefs because they are believed, not because they comport with some widely held conception of objective truth.

The individual did not feature as prominently in every stream of the Reformation. Calvinism's theory of liberty, for example, was premised on the existence of a covenantal relationship among the people, the rulers, and God.[48] The corresponding web of mutual rights and responsibilities helped check the ascendancy of the decontextualized individual. In general, though, Luther set a new course – one that created tension with the social nature of conscience. His insistence that judgments on the content of morality and faith turn on the persuasiveness of one's own scriptural interpretation ultimately served to weaken the ties between conscience and the community. The experience and motivation of the individual gradually became paramount. Personal well-being was no longer a function of commitments fixed by one's social role.[49] Even so, it is important to recognize that Luther never presented conscience as a self-contained moral code possessed individually. Conscience still extended beyond the self.

THE ENLIGHTENMENT

During the Enlightenment, theories of conscience splintered into so many different directions that any purported overview of the developments is necessarily more cursory than concise. At first glance, the intellectual trends associated with the Enlightenment appear to have obscured conscience's relational dimension. Groundbreaking work in political theory, philosophy, and even theology were premised on the individual's primacy. The era's general skepticism toward authority cast social roles and expectations as a source of oppression more frequently than as a source of self-realization or personal narrative.

Jean-Jacques Rousseau, for example, focused on the individual's capacity to flourish despite, not because of, the surrounding society. In his signature work on education, *Emile*, he praised "amour de soi" (self-love), "which concerns itself only with ourselves, [and] is content to satisfy our own needs." "Amour-propre" (selfishness), on the other hand, "is always comparing self with others." What corrupts us "is a

---

[47] *Id.* at 262 (quoting D. Martin Luthers Werke, *Kritische Gesammtausgabe*, 1, 568, 1–35).
[48] See generally John Witte Jr., *The Reformation of Rights: Law, Religion, and Human Rights in Early Modern Calvinism* (2007).
[49] Alasdair MacIntyre, *A Short History of Ethics*, 125–6 (1966).

multiplicity of needs and dependence on the opinions of others."[50] Because "man cannot always live alone," Rousseau cautioned that it will be hard "to remain good; and this difficulty will increase of necessity as his relations with others are extended."[51] Indeed, "the dangers of social life demand that the necessary skill and care shall be devoted to guarding the human heart against the depravity which springs from fresh needs."[52]

Conscience, in this light, served as a refuge within which the individual could escape the corrupting influence of society. Rousseau taught that "a virtuous man," by following his conscience, can be "his own master and nothing can turn him from the right way."[53] Rousseau did not derive moral duty "from the principles of higher philosophy," but from "the depths of my heart, traced by nature in characters which nothing can efface," meaning that he "need only consult myself with what I wish to do; what I feel to be right is right, what I feel to be wrong is wrong."[54]

Constructing conscience as a bulwark against society is hardly fertile ground for exploring its relational dimension. It is easy to see how Rousseau's portrayal lends itself to a conception of conscience as a "black box" and conversation stopper: One's conscience is what it is, and the only question is whether, and to what extent, the outside world will accommodate its dictates. Even so, Rousseau oriented the well-formed conscience externally, noting that "the good man orders his life with regard to all other men; the wicked orders it for self alone."[55] Rousseau feared the corrupting influence of relationships on the individual's conscience, and that may have led him to portray conscience's formation as a retreat into one's self, rather than as an inescapably self-transcendent process. The social awareness embodied in Rousseau's well-formed conscience, however, suggests that the formation, articulation, and living out of conscience will not be a strictly individualist endeavor, even in his ideal world.

Other leading figures of the Enlightenment, although unquestionably focusing on the individual, highlighted conscience's relational dimension more noticeably. This arose in part from some of the leading theorists' rejection, *contra* Rousseau, of the "innate" quality of conscience. John Locke, for example, viewed conscience as our opinion of the rightness or wrongness of our own action. Such opinions, he observed, can come from education, or social custom, or from the company we keep.[56] As noted earlier, some Scholastics concluded that the existence of morally wayward but guilt-free actors was evidence that one's apprehension of the moral law (synderesis)

---

[50] Jean-Jacques Rousseau, *Emile*, 209 (B. Foxley, trans., 2000).
[51] *Id.*
[52] *Id.*
[53] *Id.* at 489.
[54] *Id.* at 305.
[55] *Id.*
[56] *Cambridge Companion to Locke*, 200–2 (1994).

could become clouded. Locke, however, saw such actors as proof that knowledge of the moral law is not innate, period.

Locke's view of conscience as formed experientially is, without question, the dominant one today. At one level, this view contributes to the modern tendency to treat conscience as an idiosyncratic question of taste or preference, rather than as an objective, or even accessible, source of moral insight. As Austin Duncan-Jones puts it, to the extent that we regard a cognitive power "as not innate, we shall be ready to doubt whether it is reliable."[57] If conscience is not innate, it begins to resemble "our judgments of the sublime and beautiful, which vary so notoriously from age to age."[58]

At a deeper level, though, the experiential view of conscience makes plain the external orientation of its formation. If the dictates of conscience are not simply written on our hearts, the cause of conscience does not consist solely of leaving the individual to her own devices. Moral convictions have sources outside the self, and those sources demand space to operate and have influence. The individual-versus-state paradigm does not adequately explain or defend the need for that space.

Other Enlightenment writers began to cast conscience more as a function of feeling than as an exercise of reason. Adam Smith emphasized sympathy, rather than shared reason, as the foundation of moral consensus. "As we have no immediate experience of what other men feel," he wrote, "we can form no idea of the manner in which they are affected, but by conceiving what we ourselves should feel in the like situation."[59] John Stuart Mill described "the essence of conscience" as the "existence of a mass of feeling which must be broken through in order to do what violates our standard of right, and which, if we do nevertheless violate that standard, will probably have to be encountered afterwards in the form of remorse."[60] Joseph Butler took a more traditional view of conscience than that of many Enlightenment figures, but he still expanded the concept beyond the boundaries of reason, explaining that it is properly seen "as a sentiment of the understanding" and as a "perception of the heart."[61]

David Hume's work is particularly essential to understanding the emotive view of conscience. He believed that passion, not reason, acts as the motivating influence on the will.[62] He famously wrote that "reason is, and ought only to be the slave of the passions, and can never pretend to any other office than to serve and obey them."[63] Reason cannot serve as the foundation of morality because it cannot make

---

[57] Austin Duncan-Jones, *The Notion of Conscience*, 30 Philosophy 131, 133 (1955).

[58] *Id.* at 134.

[59] Adam Smith, *The Theory of Moral Sentiments*, I.I.2 (1790).

[60] John Stuart Mill, *Utilitarianism*, 42 (4th ed. 1871).

[61] Joseph Butler, *The Analogy of Religion, Natural and Revealed, to the Constitution and Course of Nature*, 216–7 (1819) ("Dissertation on the Nature of Virtue").

[62] David Hume, *A Treatise of Human Nature*, book II, part III, sec. 3 (1740); see also A.E. Pitson, *Hume's Philosophy of the Self*, 89 (2002).

[63] Hume, *Treatise of Human Nature*, book II, part III, sec. 3.

moral judgments, which are functions of feeling.[64] It thus makes no sense to speak of the moral quality of an act; the proper object of moral judgment is the actor's motive. Hume explained, "[a]ctions are not virtuous nor vicious, but only so far as they are proofs of certain Qualitys or durable Principles in the Mind."[65] Although reason enables us, in Hume's framework, "to constitute, recognize, and modify our moral feelings," it is feelings that are at the center of our moral convictions.[66]

The "black box" conception of conscience finds fertile ground in Hume's emphasis of feeling over reason. As with Rousseau's fortress-against-society portrayal, Hume's assertion that our moral experience is a function of feeling would seem to render interpersonal moral engagement largely pointless. If our conscience is a product of personal sentiment, there does not seem to be much to talk about as far as the substance of conscience; conscience is what it is, and the focus is on accommodation, rather than on formation grounded in claims of reason that transcend the individual. Emotions might be sparked by prior cognition, but the emotions themselves – rather than the reason to which the prior cognition was directed – provide flimsy grounds for moral conversation. Although Hume insisted on the existence of "some sentiment, so universal and comprehensive as to extend to all mankind,"[67] his explanation holds that the sentiment is simply shared as a matter of fact; he did not pay as much attention to the prospect of interpersonal engagement facilitating the possibility of widely shared moral sentiments. Conscience is still a black box, albeit one that is commonly held. That conscience remains a function of feeling, rather than an exercise of reason, lends an individualist slant to his portrayal. Indeed, Hume observed that the "opinions of men," in matters of morality, "carry with them a peculiar authority and are, in great measure, infallible."[68]

Hume's emphasis on sentiment over reason contributed to our individualist conception of conscience, but his development of the notion of identity as a coherent, self-constructed personal narrative opened new avenues of connection between conscience and human relationships. Hume believed that we convince ourselves that our perceptions are connected in some sort of coherent chain, even though those connections are, in his view, artifices of the mind. Hume explained, "when I enter most intimately into what I call myself, I always stumble on some particular perception or other . . . I never can catch myself at any time without a perception, and never can observe anything but the perception."[69] "[W]hat we call a mind," he wrote, "is nothing but a heap or collection of different perceptions, united together

---

[64] *The Cambridge Companion to Hume*, 163 (David Norton, ed., 1993).

[65] *Letters of David Hume* I: 34 (1932).

[66] David Fate Norton, *David Hume: Common-Sense Moralist, Sceptical Metaphysician*, 109 (1982).

[67] David Hume, *Enquiry Concerning the Principles of Morals*, sec. IX (1751).

[68] David Hume, *A Treatise of Human Nature*, book III, part II, sec. 8 (1740). Note that Hume was not a relativist. He believed that some feelings did not warrant the classification "moral sentiment" because they did not result from a proper view of the attainment of pleasure. Norton, *supra* note 66, at 144.

[69] David Hume, *A Treatise of Human Nature*, book I, part IV, sec. 6 (1740).

by certain relations, and suppos'd tho' falsly, to be endow'd with a perfect simplicity and identity."[70] As A.E. Pitson puts it, "Hume regards our attributions of identity as fictitious products of the imagination."[71]

Put more bluntly, identity is a product of self-delusion to Hume. But that is not to call into question the importance of the self-delusion to a person's sense of herself and her place in the world. Hume insisted that the events of a person's life – or at least a person's perception of those events – are mutually dependent "during the whole period of his duration from the cradle to the grave," and it is not possible "to strike off one link, however minute, in this [chain of events] without affecting the whole series of events which follow."[72]

Hume did not view conscience as a set of discrete, rational claims about right and wrong. It is not as simple as saying, "I believe X, Y, and Z are wrong because reason compels such a conclusion." Instead, conscience is tied up with an ongoing stream of perceptions that our mind cobbles together as a framework of meaning. Our separation of right from wrong emanates from our sentiments about pleasures to be attained or pains to be avoided. More broadly, though, our moral sentiments serve to facilitate our own narratives. These narratives, although highly personal, are self-transcendent; they are possible through relationship, and they call us outside ourselves to something bigger. As Charles Taylor and others will elucidate two centuries later, the narrative-based conception of personal identity that Hume began to sketch is inescapably relational.

Not all Enlightenment figures emphasized feelings over reason in their explanations of morality. Immanuel Kant, most notably, believed that moral beliefs are to be determined through reason. This did not represent a return to Medieval concepts of conscience, though, because the centrality of reason to his moral theory actually pushed conscience to a secondary role. The Kantian conscience is not a moral legislator or arbiter of moral claims; rather, conscience acts as an "inner judge," scrutinizing the actor on two counts, according to Thomas Hill: first, whether "we contravened our own (reason-based) judgment about what is morally right," and second, whether "we failed to exercise due care and diligence in forming the particular moral opinions on which we acted."[73] Conscience's aim is not to foster self-awareness that our action is objectively wrong, but "that we are not even making a proper effort to guide ourselves by our own deepest moral beliefs."[74]

Although this view is geared more toward internal consistency and good faith than toward any external source of moral truth, it still has a social dimension. As

[70] *Id.* book I, part IV, sec. 2.
[71] A.E. Pitson, *Hume's Philosophy of the Self,* 30 (2002).
[72] David Hume, "An Enquiry Concerning Human Understanding," *The Philosophical Works of David Hume* 4: 1, 25 (1854).
[73] Thomas E. Hill Jr., "Four Conceptions of Conscience," in *Integrity and Conscience,* 13, 16–7 (Ian Shapiro and Robert Adams, eds., 1998).
[74] *Id.*

reason-based moral claims should be accessible to others, "consulting with others and taking into account their reasons for the moral judgments must be an important part of the Kantian process of moral deliberation."[75] In this regard, Kant approached the relationship between moral judgment and identity with a different emphasis than Hume. Like Hume, Kant believed that our self-consciousness required an ongoing unity among our mental apprehensions;[76] unlike Hume, Kant focused on our need to step away from our personal narrative in achieving self-consciousness through impersonal abstraction.

Pierre Keller explains that Kant's idea of self-consciousness claims "that we are only able to grasp our own individual identity by contrast with other possible lives that we might have led."[77] More generally, our "capacity for concept formation and use is displayed in judgments and inferences that themselves depend on our capacity for representing ourselves impersonally."[78] That the Kantian moral perspective is impersonal does not mean that it is not relational, for it holds that self-consciousness "involves an awareness of the distinction between me and my representations and other persons and their representations."[79] Getting beyond the personal does not get us beyond the relational, even in a world where reason rules.

MODERN INSIGHTS

The public discourse on conscience today pays relatively little attention to conscience itself. We tend to focus on conscience's function in the modern world, particularly on the degree of deference that society owes to a person's conscience and the circumstances under which the exercise of conscience can be constrained by state power. But the nature of conscience and its relationship to human identity have long since receded into the background. The path of resistance laid out by the Protestant Reformation and developed during the Enlightenment eventually drew attention from the ontological basis of conscience to the political treatment of conscience.

As belief in universal moral truths has faded, most of the attention is now devoted to facilitating rapprochement among those holding divergent conceptions of the good. Much of this effort proceeds along the lines of the pragmatism pioneered by William James, who recommended an "attitude of looking away from first things,

---

[75] *Id.* at 37.
[76] "Now, when I draw a line in thought, or if I think the time from one noon to another, or if I only represent to myself a certain number, it is clear that I must first necessarily apprehend one of those manifold representations after another. If I were to lose from my thoughts what precedes ... there would never be a complete representation. The synthesis of apprehension is therefore inseparably connected with the synthesis of reproduction." Immanuel Kant, *Critique of Pure Reason*, book I, ch. II, sec. 2 (F. Muller, trans., 1907).
[77] Pierre Keller, *Kant and the Demands of Self-Consciousness*, 3 (1998).
[78] *Id.*
[79] *Id.* at 4.

principles, categories, supposed necessities; and of looking towards last things, fruits, consequences, facts."[80] Those who operate in accordance with fixed principles may warrant deference from the surrounding society, but the predominant moral calculus has largely moved past such considerations.

What remains of the effort to define conscience – particularly the Medieval project of locating the conscience within the person – proceeds largely in the field of psychology. Sigmund Freud's explanation of conscience as part of a person's "superego" that originates in the need for parental approval has provided fertile ground for new therapy techniques. Equating conscience with the psychological vestiges of childhood, however, has contributed to the modern tendency to view conscience in strictly individualist terms: The content of a person's conscience may be of interest to her therapist, but otherwise is of little relevance to others unless and until it conflicts with the law or an accepted social norm.

This is not to suggest that modern conversations hold no promise for our understanding of conscience. The locus of the most relevant conversations, however, has shifted from a formal analysis of conscience to broader explorations of personal identity. The importance of personal integrity is now commonly explained in terms of the ability to live one's life as a narrative – as a seamless whole, shaped and directed by one's beliefs. A person's identity is not a mere attribute; it is a source of value that provides a way for maneuvering through life's endless, incommensurable options of value. Identity sets the parameters of a good life.

The segmentation of a person's moral convictions from her conduct can be profoundly unsettling. As Camus described the feeling of absurdity, such segmentation constitutes a "divorce between man and his life, the actor and his setting," creating an existence in which "man feels an alien, a stranger."[81] Modern epistemology casts this battle against absurdity as a quest toward a life of coherence. The "coherentist conception of rationality" offers one "basic test or measure for determining what beliefs it is rational for a person to accept," which is "coherence with whatever else he happens to believe: coherence with beliefs that are presently authoritative for him."[82]

When society prevents a person from acting on the dictates of conscience – whether in the workplace, in school, in the family, or elsewhere – such restrictions often defy the person's efforts to construct a coherent existence. This stems from the fact that, in Christian Smith's words, "we have not really come to terms with human beings – ourselves – until we come to understand human persons as fundamentally moral, believing animals."[83] By this he means that humans "possess a capacity and propensity unique among all animals: we not only have desires, beliefs, and

[80] William James, *Pragmatism*, 54–5 (1907).

[81] Albert Camus, "An Absurd Reasoning," in *The Myth of Sisyphus and Other Essays*, 453 (J. O'Brien, trans., 1955).

[82] Michael J. Perry, *Love and Power: The Role of Religion and Morality in American Politics*, 53 (1991).

[83] Christian Smith, *Moral, Believing Animals*, 4 (2003).

feelings... but also the ability and disposition to form strong evaluations about our desires, beliefs and feelings that hold the potential to transform them."[84] Such "second-order desires"[85] provide "a sense of normative duty to express or perform obligations that are intrinsically motivated," and thus constitute the foundation for collective moral order and action.[86] To the extent that society precludes a person's second-order desires from having an operative effect on her everyday conduct, society challenges the core exercise of the person's morality.

Discerning and maintaining the narrative of one's life is not a passive endeavor – it is not simply a litany of what happens *to* a person. Rather, a narrative is forward looking and aspirational – it not only captures where we have been, but propels us in a particular direction. Alasdair MacIntyre puts it this way:

> When... in the examination of our own past lives we proceed from the narrative structure of those lives, as they have been lived so far, to enquiry about what from now on we are to make of ourselves, we are compelled instead to ask of the universal how it may be particularized, how certain conceptions of the good and of the virtues may take on embodied form through our realization of this possibility rather than that, posing these questions in terms of the specifics of the narratives of our lives. In so doing, we characteristically drew upon resources provided by some stock of stories from which we had earlier learned to understand both our own lives and the lives of others in narrative terms, the oral and written literature of whatever particular culture it is that we happen to inhabit.[87]

Thus, the narratives of our lives are of unsurpassed importance when it comes to any sort of meaningful moral inquiry. This does not mean that narratives are entirely functional, especially when we talk about the core values of a community, for "the center of any collective identity is not instrumental functionality but believed-in ideals and images that are sacred – that are, for the social order, set apart, hallowed, protected, inviolable."[88] But disconnecting the foundational narrative of a person's life and her conduct can impede the cultivation of virtue. MacIntyre warns us that "one of the marks of someone who develops bad character [is] that, as it develops, she or he becomes progressively less and less able to understand what it is that she or he has mislearned and how it was that she or he fell into error," and that "[p]art of the badness of bad character is intellectual blindness on moral questions."[89] What a person needs in this regard, and what a coherent narrative can provide, is a "practically usable answer to the questions 'What is my good?,' and 'How is it to be

---

[84] *Id.* at 9.
[85] Charles Taylor, *Human Agency and Language* (1985) (cited in Smith, *supra* note 83, at 9).
[86] Smith, *supra* note 83, at 10.
[87] Alasdair MacIntyre, "Plain Persons and Moral Philosophy," in *Ethics and Character: The Pursuit of Democratic Virtues*, 47, 53 (1998).
[88] Smith, *supra* note 83, at 76.
[89] MacIntyre, *supra* note 87, at 53–4.

achieved?,' which will both direct us in present-future action and also evaluate and explain past action."[90]

Building on the work of Ronald Dworkin, Kwame Anthony Appiah concedes that not all narratives will empower as sources of identity. For example, one's homosexuality might be a parameter that marks the contours of a meaningful existence, central to the life the person hopes to build. For someone else, homosexuality might function as a limitation that must be overcome to realize life's full value – they would like to build a life in which they do not experience, or at least do not act on, homosexual desires.[91] The person's view of homosexuality as a limitation, though, flows from another source of identity, such as religious belief, that functions as an overarching parameter.

The relationship between one's conscience and one's life narrative may not always be obvious. Take, for example, a person whose sense of identity derives in significant part from his passion for a seemingly conscience-neutral activity, such as surfing.[92] When it comes to narratives built on morally uncharged endeavors, does the state's respect for identity implicate respect for conscience? Even assuming that the state has an interest in facilitating a citizen's ability to maintain a coherent narrative, does that interest necessarily translate into support for the formation and exercise of the citizen's conscience?

I believe that it does, for two reasons. First, even the surfer narrative implicates conscience in meaningful (and even relational) ways, particularly when the conduct on which the narrative is built runs up against conflicting moral claims. For example, suppose that the individual, in building his narrative, commits himself to surfing every Saturday to keep up his skill and stamina. Should that commitment trump other social obligations that he accrues over the years to his spouse, children, or profession? The moral conflicts are not far from the surface. To bring the hypothetical back within the lawyer's purview, suppose that a group of surfers has always surfed a particular section of beach known for its ideal conditions; if that beach happens to be a significant religious site for a Native American tribe, or if the state has designated it for protection because of its fragile ecosystem, then we suddenly have an inescapably moral conflict.[93] The surfers, if they insist on continuing to surf at that spot, will be making their own moral claim as part of their own "surfer" narratives.

Second, few individuals, as dedicated as they might be to surfing, would articulate their life narratives solely in terms of their status as surfers. Surfing may be one component – perhaps a very important component – of their narratives, but a meaningful narrative will include commitments beyond the desire to surf. If a person

---

90 *Id.*

91 Kwame Anthony Appiah, *Ethics of Identity*, 111–2 (2005).

92 Thanks to one of the manuscript's anonymous external reviewers for raising this example.

93 *Cf.* Corneila Dean, "Surfers Deal a Blow to a Beach Dredging Project," *New York Times*, Mar. 9, 2009 (reporting that surfers "succeeded in blocking . . . a strategy widely used against the beach erosion that threatens most of the nation's coast").

defined himself solely by his desire to surf, and by his desire to be perceived as a surfer, we would view such a life as superficial or at least as one-dimensional. Even if the surfing component does not have an obvious moral dimension, these other commitments likely will. At some level, even a surfer's life narrative will implicate conscience.

The surfer narrative, to the extent that it implicates conscience, will do so relationally. If the surfer deems it morally permissible to continue surfing at the contested beach or spending every Saturday surfing – notwithstanding the moral claims demanding that he stop – he is basing his moral judgment on sources external to himself. It might be based on his own experience of the world ("doing this gives me so much pleasure that I am unwilling to sacrifice it for anything or anyone"), on his knowledge of human history ("once again the state is overstepping its proper bounds because state officials are under the thumb of environmental interest groups"), or his observation of others ("parents are more effective when they devote time to their own passions"). These are not just sources of information (as is "I see a brown bird"); when the surfer decides to shape his conduct with their claims, they become sources of authority.

Conscience, in functioning as a person's narrative-shaping moral compass, provides the impetus to link identity to action. In other words, a fully integrated life is not possible unless the dictates of conscience are reflected in action. On a similar theme, Linda Hogan points out that conscience "is more than the sum of particular decisions;" it is "the dimension of one's character that determines the direction of one's moral life, one's self-conscious option for the good."[94] The focus on integrity suggests a more comprehensive relationship between conscience and the person than was contemplated by Medieval theologians, who were "concerned primarily with acts and with specific, unconnected decisions of conscience."[95]

Timothy Macklem recounts a story told by Bernard Williams about a man named Jim who visits a tribal village where government soldiers are about to execute twenty Indians because of recent political protests despite no evidence that they were involved in the protest. The soldier's leader invites Jim to kill one of the Indians, and if he does, the soldiers offer to set the rest free in his honor. We would expect Jim to hesitate before accepting that offer even if he is convinced that the soldiers actually will proceed with the executions if he does not accept. What the story captures, in Macklem's estimation, is the value of personal integrity – in Jim's case, "as a person who does not kill innocent human beings."[96] At the very least, Jim's integrity is a relevant consideration in his moral reasoning. What matters is that Jim not kill, not simply that lives be saved. Whether Jim's integrity as a person who does not kill is worth nineteen lives is another matter. If personal integrity is relevant to the

---

[94] Linda Hogan, *Confronting the Truth: Conscience in the Catholic Tradition*, 129 (2000).
[95] *Id.* at 134.
[96] Timothy Macklem, *Independence of Mind*, 75 (2006).

moral calculus, however, then society should work to protect conscience, which is a primary facilitator of personal integrity.[97]

If conscience's authority extended only as far as reason warranted, it would render its content superfluous in that the rational agent could arrive at the same decision whether or not her conscience was operative. As such, conscience must have the sort of authority that allows it, at least in certain cases, to overrule other reasons.[98] This does not mean that conscience will always trump those other reasons. Macklem gives the example of wanting to go to bed before he finishes grading a stack of papers. His conscience tells him to finish his work, which leads him to question his own reasons and motives for going to bed – whether it is a case of self-indulgence or a need to remain awake and alert the next day. He may still decide to go to bed, but conscience has shaped his decision.[99]

Taking conscience seriously means more than facilitating particular moral acts; it requires space for personal reflection and integration. Macklem points out that, although we can act virtuously "as soon as we learn to act in ways that are capable of manifesting virtue and vice," conscience only comes into play "once we have acquired the developmentally more sophisticated capacity to reflect on our actions."[100] In other words, "action can only be in fulfillment of the claims of one's conscience if and when one sets out to make it so."[101] When action follows moral reflection, the contours of the rational personality come into relief, and this personality "provides us with a rational basis for personal continuity," with conscience acting as its guardian.[102] Further, because personal continuity is a prerequisite for the cultivation of certain values and virtues, conscience also "has the capacity to entrench within the rational personality the moral stabilities that are necessary to be a person of a certain kind."[103]

In Macklem's work, conscience's contribution to the common good lies in its motivational power. Personal commitment separates conscience from "accumulated wisdom," for when the former "reminds us to be moral it is not only for the sake of the reasons that conscience embodies, but for the sake of the self-image and self-respect that adherence to the claims of our conscience gives rise to."[104] When we see "ourselves as people characterized by certain ongoing commitments to what would otherwise be no more than morally permissible in our lives, we may extend the character of those commitments so as to include other objects."[105]

[97] *Id.*
[98] *Id.* at 87–8.
[99] *Id.* at 114.
[100] *Id.* at 103.
[101] *Id.*
[102] *Id.* at 104–5.
[103] *Id.* at 105.
[104] *Id.* at 108.
[105] *Id.* at 112.

These "other objects" bring the social dimension of personal commitment – and personal identity more broadly – to the fore. Anthony Appiah notes, "part of the material that we are responding to in shaping our selves is not within us but outside us, out there in the social world."[106] He does not dispute our capacity for self-criticism but cautions against moving "too quickly from the fact that we sentient creatures have the ability to step back and evaluate our beliefs to the mandate that we actively do so."[107] His observations are not just anthropologically noteworthy. Appiah calls for a politics "that emerges from a consideration not (just) of what we want but of who we are."[108] As persons, "our autonomy ought to be respected," and as "encumbered, socially embedded, selves, we will use our autonomy to protect and preserve a wide variety of extraindividual commitments."[109] The social dimension of identity creates a foundation for state action, particularly in areas such as antidiscrimination law. "Inasmuch as our identities are social things – products of social conceptions and of our treatment by others – a shift in normative stereotype changes who I am." At the same time, Appiah points out, "public actions may change the meanings of social identities without eliminating the possibility of dissent and contestation."[110]

Charles Taylor's work is essential for drawing out this relationship between self-identity and other selves. Taylor shows that the self is inescapably relational because "[a] self can never be described without reference to those who surround it."[111] Human life is dialogical in that we can only understand ourselves and acquire an identity via languages of self-expression, but we enter into these languages only in exchange with others.[112] Taylor is not simply speaking of isolated snippets of spoken language, but of normative moral frameworks within which individuals "can determine where they stand on questions of what is good, or worthwhile, or admirable, or of value."[113] Whether formed by religion, political philosophy, national allegiance, or something else, a person's framework comes into view "when we try to spell out what it is that we presuppose when we judge that a certain form of life is truly worthwhile, or place our dignity in a certain achievement or status, or define our moral obligations in a certain manner."[114]

Even if people no longer see their frameworks as "enjoying the same ontological solidity as the very structure of the universe,"[115] as they might have in earlier ages,

---

[106] Appiah, *supra* note 91, at 21.

[107] *Id.* at 49.

[108] *Id.* at 181.

[109] *Id.* at 211.

[110] *Id.* at 199.

[111] Charles Taylor, *Sources of the Self: The Making of the Modern Identity*, 35 (1989).

[112] "No one acquires the languages needed for self-definition on their own." Charles Taylor, *The Ethics of Authenticity*, 32–3 (1991).

[113] Taylor, *supra* note 111, at 27.

[114] *Id.* at 26.

[115] *Id.*

Taylor insists that "doing without frameworks is utterly impossible for us" because "[t]o know who I am is a species of knowing where I stand."[116] It is not simply that a person is strongly attached to a particular moral framework; the framework is the horizon against which a person is able to make more particular moral judgments, locating herself within the everyday world. Without such a framework, a person "wouldn't know anymore, for an important range of questions, what the significance of things was for them."[117]

The individual's articulation of a framework is itself deeply relational. Taylor points out that "I can identify my identity only against the background of things that matter."[118] Grounding one's moral judgment in nontrivial matters will entail linking to sources outside the self because "to bracket out history, nature, society, the demands of solidarity, everything but what I find in myself, would be to eliminate all candidates for what matters."[119] Significantly, our universe of "what matters" will not always be products of conscious individual choice. This is the point Michael Sandel makes by asking, "Are we as moral agents bound only by the ends and roles we choose for ourselves, or can we sometimes be obligated to fulfill certain ends we have not chosen – ends given by nature or God, for example, or by our identity as a member of a family or people, culture or tradition?"[120]

"What matters" is not necessarily static or self-evident, of course, and the process of discerning "what matters" remains dialogical for its duration, as self-definition requires two groups of interlocutors: first, "those conversation partners who were essential to my achieving self-definition," and second, "those who are now crucial to my continuing grasp of languages of self-understanding."[121] As Timothy O'Connell puts it, "to be human is to be accountable."[122] No matter how individualist our moral framework might be, the process of articulating that framework is not – and cannot be – successfully undertaken by the individual in a vacuum. Making sense of ourselves requires looking beyond ourselves. As a constitutive element of self-identity, conscience is relational.

CONSCIENCE AND THE PERSON

It should go without saying that this cursory review can hardly do justice to more than two millennia of thoughtful and penetrating engagement with questions

---

[116] *Id.* at 27.

[117] *Id.*

[118] Taylor, *supra* note 112, at 40.

[119] *Id.*

[120] Michael Sandel, *Liberalism and the Limits of Justice*, 186–7 (2nd ed. 1998).

[121] Taylor, *supra* note 112, at 36 ("[A]nd, of course, these classes may overlap.").

[122] Timothy O'Connell, "An Understanding of Conscience," in *Conscience*, 25, 26 (Charles Curran, ed., 2004).

surrounding the relationship between conscience and the person. Hopefully, though, even this review has identified some markers across conscience's history that, taken together, shed sufficient light on three themes that have consistently appeared over the centuries, but which seem to have faded from today's debates over society's proper stance toward conscience.

First, conscience corresponds to our social nature. Put more plainly, conscience *embodies* our social nature. Conscience is distinct from preference, which can be unreflective, instinctive, and strictly internal. In many circles today, conscience has been reduced to "a principle of individual self-assertion against social standards," which confuses "the dignity of individual conscience with the absolutizing of individual desires."[123] By contrast, conscience consists of shared moral belief – if not literally shared among persons, at least susceptible to sharing among persons. Because conscience is rooted in sources external to the person, the dictates of conscience call the person outside of herself even while providing a moral center for her own deeply personal values and priorities. This understanding of conscience lends insight into the social nature of the human person. We are relational, including our exercise of conscience. Accordingly, honoring conscience cannot be equated with a presumption favoring the individual's moral convictions over the contrary convictions embodied in a group's institutional identity. The viability of conscience will often depend on the viability of the relationships through which conscience is formed. In other words, if our law is to reflect our concern for conscience, it must also reflect a concern for the groups that embody and facilitate individuals' shared moral commitments.

Second, the exercise of conscience is not just an expression of a person's identity; it is a means by which a person's moral identity may become fully and coherently formed. In this sense, conscience is a two-way street: Its exercise communicates a person's moral convictions to the surrounding society, but it also facilitates personal coherence by bringing her everyday decision making into alignment with her overarching values and priorities. If society pushes a person to sacrifice the unified self for the sake of the greater good, the result is not some sort of dual identity, in Gerald Postema's view, "or some sort of federation of the selves, but no self at all," for "[t]o ignore the demands of unity is to abandon one's self, and the self-concept that includes explicit rejection of this demand is, consequently, incoherent."[124] Of course we value self-expression, but this does not get to the heart of why we honor the liberty of conscience. More fundamental is the value we place on one's ability to live life as a narrative. This rationale is distinct from valuing conscience strictly as a means to individual autonomy, both because a person's narrative will often

---

[123] Germain Grisez and Russell Shaw, "Conscience: Knowledge of Moral Truth," in *Conscience*, 39, 41 (Charles Curran, ed., 2004).

[124] Gerald Postema, "Self-Image, Integrity, and Professional Responsibility" in *The Good Lawyer*, 286, 295 (David Luban, ed., 1983).

unfold along lines not of their own choosing and because the narrative's coherence may turn on the viability of commitments they undertake with others. Narratives are rarely a solitary endeavor.

Third, conscience is not just a discrete binding of the will – it is a never-ending dialogue with the will, and conscience's dictates are in play before, during, and after the moment of choice. In other words, a claim of conscience does not emanate from a prepackaged or fixed personal moral code that becomes operative only when faced with a set of unacceptable choices. These decisions are based not just on what we want, but who we are. We are developing conscience daily, not just at discrete points of conflict and decision. As a result, taking conscience seriously will require more than simply deferring to conscience at the point of conflict between the person and society's expectations. Taking conscience seriously also requires the maintenance of venues where the dictates of conscience can be discerned, articulated, and lived out. Given the importance of personal integrity and a coherent life narrative, prudent lawmakers will recognize that the stakes are higher for an actor whose conscience forbids her from doing X than for an actor whose conscience permits, but does not require, her to do X. That said, focusing only on the point of conscience's "binding" prevents us from seeing the broader context of conscience's operation, and thereby prevents us from accurately assessing the conditions that are most conducive to conscience's flourishing.

One need not accept the existence of the human soul, much less the accuracy of Jerome's classification of its component parts, to recognize the value that he and other Christian scholars brought to our understanding of the maddeningly abstract concept of conscience. By attempting to articulate the nature and function of conscience, they contributed a perspective that is often lacking from current policy debates, which take conscience as a given and focus only on society's response to its operation. But society's response must account for conscience's nature and function. Whether or not we buy into Medieval conceptions of human physiology, we can appreciate the insight that moral decision making does not occur in a vacuum. We can also appreciate the more recent insights of scholars such as Appiah and Taylor who connect our moral decision making to foundational sources of personal identity. Given that conscience has become a placeholder for the convictions that drive moral decision making, we cannot afford to keep these voices out of the conversation.

3

Conscience's Claims

Most students of the human condition today have rejected a belief in conscience as a deposit of absolute and universal moral truth. At the same time, most will intuitively resist the suggestion that conscience is just another expression of personal preference. Exempting Daniel Seeger from the draft remains a troubling proposition for some because of the difficulty in discerning a principled distinction between his justification for not fighting the war and the countless reasons offered by other conscripts as to why they would rather not fight. One popular attempt to draw a distinction is to dress up preference as conscience by focusing on the intensity of one's preference. But the distinction cannot turn on the depth of feeling behind Seeger's opposition to combat. Requests for exemption such as "I don't want to die" or "I don't want to leave my family" could have at least as much depth of feeling as Seeger's claim.

If the scope of conscientious objector status is tied to the personal cost stemming from the request's denial, there is no apparent reason to dismiss the cost faced by those whose preferred life plans did not include military combat. For purposes of conscience, the cost cannot be measured in terms of undesired outcomes. There is a different sort of cost in terms of coerced participation in conduct that is wrong – not just unpleasant or unwelcome, but wrong. By forcing a person to act contrary to what they perceive as a moral obligation, the state jeopardizes the coherence of a life narrative built on certain moral claims, along with a deeper accountability of the person to the source of those claims. That quality of wrongness separates a claim grounded in conscience from a claim based on preference. It is a quality that has fallen into disrepute today, and its shaky status is one reason why the concept of conscience has grown so amorphous.

The last chapter showed how those who have grappled with the concept of conscience over the centuries have consistently portrayed its relevance to personal identity in relational terms. As the Christian tradition emphasizes, conscience is a set of truth claims that is in perpetual dialogue with a person's will; as more modern thinkers emphasize, a person's moral identity – of which conscience is a key formative element – is itself deeply social. Both portrayals mean that conscience connects a person to something beyond herself.

We continue the exploration of the relational nature of conscience in this chapter, with a more particular focus on the self-transcendent quality of conscience's substantive claims. By articulating a practicable distinction between conscience and preference, we can begin to figure out what sort of claims our conscience makes, and why those claims are, by their very nature, oriented toward self-transcendence. The image of conscience as bearing the imprint of God's law has long been out of favor, but that does not mean that claims of conscience do not pertain to something real. Conscience's correlation to reality (actual or perceived) is what makes interpersonal moral accountability possible. The claims of conscience represent a perception and communication of an intersubjective obligation arising outside ourselves. The paths by which the claims are shaped, articulated, and lived out are relational for that very reason. This recognition must inform the law's efforts to protect conscience, particularly as conscience requires the protection of relational venues that do not fall neatly within the individual-versus-state paradigm.

BEYOND PREFERENCE

Most pressing for purposes of our inquiry is the fact that, if conscience is understood as individual preference, its relational dimension becomes even more elusive, as we are not inclined to recognize – much less protect – preference in a way that transcends the individual. If I prefer chocolate ice cream to vanilla, I am not opining that chocolate is better than vanilla. As Emile Durkheim puts it, such judgments "do not attach value to objects but merely affirm the state of the subject."[1] If, however, I ask for chocolate ice cream as a matter of conscience, I am stating, at a minimum, that eating chocolate ice cream is morally superior to eating vanilla. Conscience inescapably involves a truth claim. It may not be a universal truth claim – I am not necessarily pronouncing chocolate to be morally superior to vanilla for everyone in the world – but a truth claim nonetheless: Chocolate is morally superior for me, and I believe that its superiority exists apart from my belief in its existence; my judgment of its superiority corresponds to some perceived state of affairs outside myself.

This distinction between conscience and preference is also essential to justifying the state's respect for conscience. Asking an actor to defy claims of right and wrong that he considers authoritative is problematic for the life narrative project in a way that defying a claim of preference is not. My preference for chocolate ice cream guides my conduct (choosing chocolate over vanilla), but if the state takes chocolate away as an available option, the extent of the harm to me is simply that my preference is not satisfied in that instance. The integrity and coherence on which my life

---

[1] Emile Durkheim, *Sociology and Philosophy*, 80–81 (Free Press ed. 1974).

narrative is based are not threatened beyond that particular denial. If, however, my conduct is being shaped by a moral claim, then forcing me to deny that claim is likely to have a broader "ripple effect" on my sense of integrity and coherence beyond that particular denial. Charles Taylor argues that our age is defined by a fear of "meaninglessness." Experiencing a state-coerced disconnect between my actions and my convictions of right and wrong is more likely to foster a sense of meaninglessness than experiencing a disconnect between a preference and my ability to act on that preference. Preference tends to be instinctive and unreflective, and thus carries less of the life narrative's weight. As Taylor puts it,

> To know who I am is a species of knowing where I stand. My identity is defined by the commitments and identifications which provide the frame or horizon within which I can try to determine from case to case what is good, or valuable, or what ought to be done, or what I endorse or oppose. In other words, it is the horizon within which I am capable of taking a stand.[2]

Claims of right and wrong are the building blocks with which a person's "frame or horizon" is built. Preferences are not. For example, if a person believes that abortion is always immoral and that the morning-after pill causes abortion, it is not sufficient to respond to her claim by pointing out that she is free to choose not to use the morning-after pill. She is not expressing a preference. She is making a truth claim about the pill's moral status, and she does not believe that the pill acquires that status only in the event that she would use it personally. (She may support others' freedom to disagree with her truth claim, but that concession does not negate her belief in the pill's moral status.) If the person is a pharmacist, pharmacy owner, or even pharmacy customer, her truth claim about the pill may shape her views about matters beyond her own choice about whether to use the pill.

Preferences are different. For example, if I prefer chocolate ice cream to vanilla, that does not mean that I will object to your choice of vanilla, and it would be odd for me to be unwilling to hand you a vanilla ice cream cone. If I believe that eating vanilla ice cream is immoral, though, my concern is not necessarily limited to my own choice of consumption. I may not be willing to facilitate your consumption of vanilla, and I may decide to buy ice cream only at parlors that refuse to serve vanilla. This distinction helps explain why respect for conscience demands more than respect for individual consumer choice; it requires venues for living out truth claims more broadly.

None of this is to deny that preferences, like claims of conscience, are often formed in relationship. My preference for chocolate ice cream over vanilla may reflect the fact that my parents bought chocolate, but not vanilla, when I was a child. My taste for baseball may have been shaped by the similar tastes of my neighborhood friends. But without a moral dimension – the judgment that a particular course of

---

[2] Charles Taylor, *Sources of the Self: The Making of the Modern Identity*, 27 (1989).

action is right or wrong – a statement of preference does not have the same quality of self-transcendence as a claim of conscience. A statement of moral judgment is intersubjective because it communicates the speaker's perception of reality in prescriptive terms. There is a corresponding expectation that the speaker can justify a prescriptive statement of conscience (even when the speaker aims only to apply the prescription to herself); this expectation is largely absent from a descriptive statement of preference. For example, it is easy to imagine the following exchange:

"Why do you prefer baseball to football?"
"I don't know. I just do."

A similar exchange about a moral judgment would be off-putting:

"Why is it immoral to play baseball on Sunday?"
"I don't know. It just is."

The second exchange begs for elaboration in a way that the first exchange does not. Conscience, as a claim of perceived truth, is grounded in a source external to the individual. If a person is led to judge a certain choice as morally wrong, that judgment is possible only against a normative background. Preferences, on the other hand, can be unreflective, simply functions of instinctive taste. Both can be rooted externally, but the truth claims embedded in conscience possess an authority that brings the relational dimension to the surface at the stages of articulation and implementation, not just formation. Because my moral claim conveys my perception of reality's normative implications, the process by which I articulate my perception of reality and its implications for my conduct (and the conduct of others who share that perception) will tend to be accessible to others. Preference, by contrast, requires no articulation or conscious awareness of implications. I may have learned to prefer baseball in relationship with others, but from that point on, its influence on my life can function as an unspoken instinct. In other words, preferences can shape my exercise of will, but they need never operate as claims. Conscience, as a set of moral claims, brings us into relationship with others in a way that preference does not.

For religious believers, conscience is a product, in significant part, of truth claims emanating from a faith tradition shared with, accessible to, and debated among fellow believers. When a Catholic pharmacist refuses to dispense emergency contraception, for example, the basis of her refusal – her belief in the sanctity of life – can be readily engaged by others. This relational dimension is relevant not only to the formation of the pharmacist's beliefs, but also to their interpretation and application. In other words, even if my moral conviction regarding the sanctity of life is firm, there is something we can still talk about regarding a particular application of that conviction – for example, does emergency contraception actually function as an abortifacient?

Nonreligious conscience is similarly relational. If my conscience tells me that lying is wrong, even if that judgment does not emanate from my adherence to the tenets of a religious community, it still derives from something outside myself. Most likely, it is based on my perception and evaluation of the social conditions necessary for human well-being. Such a claim is wide open to engagement by others, not only at the point of formation, but also at the point of interpretation and application. There is *still* something to talk about – for example, does my moral opposition to lying hold even when the Gestapo asks whether I am hiding Jews in my attic?

Granted, speakers will not necessarily explain their moral convictions in terms of the social conditions necessary for human flourishing; more likely, they will simply maintain that X is wrong because it violates some broader, more vague moral premise. The fact that the articulation of the basis for their convictions may be elusive does not mean that there is no basis. Indeed, the difficulty of articulating the basis may be another reason to support the relational venues in which moral claims can be engaged and brought to the surface.

On the religious side, there are admittedly some believers who will explain their core moral convictions as products of specific, personal divine revelation. If there is no explanation other than "God told me," the possibility of interpersonal engagement appears slim. The classic stereotype of the zealot confounding society's expectations after hearing God's voice, however, may hold undue sway over our conception of conscience. In terms of formation, most believers who claim to be guided personally by God do not experience that guidance in a vacuum. It arises within a broader faith journey, and that journey usually occurs in community. This individual's interpretation and implementation of God's instruction is ripe for relational engagement. This is not to suggest that a hallmark of conscience is its bearer's willingness to question its claims, but, rather, that the nature of conscience – even the divinely derived conscience – lends itself to interpersonal engagement more than we might think. Imagined or not, the believer's perception of God's voice calls her outside herself, to some moral or spiritual reality, and that reality tends to be embedded in the framework of an overarching worldview made possible by a faith tradition. Rarely does the "still small voice within" speak in isolation.

As noted earlier, a claim of conscience does not always bind the will; often conscience provides the background against which the actor deems a course of conduct morally permissible, but not mandatory. This might seem to make distinctions between conscience and preference more tenuous – after all, my preference for chocolate ice cream also suggests that I find eating chocolate ice cream to be morally permissible. The distinction holds as long as we recognize that most expressions of preference lack any moral component. I never need to make a moral judgment about eating chocolate ice cream because nothing in my life experience even remotely suggests that it might be immoral. Conscience's operation will itself be shaped by social norms in many cases. Deciding to use (or not to use) the morning-after pill carries a corresponding moral judgment in our society. Not everyone will agree on which decisions are morally significant, of course – conceivably, an individual might discern a moral component to the decision of whether to eat vanilla or chocolate ice cream. The point is not whether the moral permissibility is clear or not, it is whether the actor perceives enough of a moral dimension to the decision that she consults her conscience. Conscience, even under the more expansive understanding of its operation portrayed in this book, is conceptually and practically distinct from preference.

As for the law's cognizance of conscience, it is a mistake to presume that an individual's claim of conscience does not become relational unless and until it is opposed by the state. Conscience's relational dimension is broader and deeper: broader because an individual living out the truth claims of her conscience is usually supported and/or opposed by entire webs of conscience claims being exercised by members of the surrounding community, and deeper because conscience's truth claims are relational not just in their lived-out implications, but also in their origins. When we care about conscience, we must also care about the interpersonal paths by which conscience is formed: Our moral convictions emerge from authorities and experiences that, although not always universally or rationally accessible, are susceptible to being engaged by others. Conscience is not a self-contained or isolated construct.

Moral Claims and Reality

This understanding of conscience is premised on the possibility that moral claims purport to pertain to something real. If truth is not even a coherent criterion for evaluating moral claims, then there is no principled distinction between conscience and preference. "I will not fight in that war" and "I would like chocolate ice cream" are distinguishable only by the depth of feeling they inspire. But if conscience represents the person's best effort to discern and abide by the normative implications of reality, then we rightly pay great deference to conscience. Moreover, the person's efforts in this regard connect her to sources of moral belief outside herself, and thus our deference to conscience must encompass the relationships necessary to its realization.

Note that this understanding of conscience does not require us to embrace Emile Durkheim's vision of a scientific morality grounded in "reason supported by the methodological observations of a given reality," which has proved far too optimistic regarding our capacity to articulate – much less agree on – empirically based moral judgments.[3] Most modern philosophers reject the possibility of objective, universal moral truth out of hand. Philippa Foot, for example, explains that "there is no such thing as an objectively good state of affairs" because pronouncements of the good "are used subjectively, to mark what fits in with the aim and interests of a particular individual or group."[4]

---

[3] Durkheim, *supra* note 1, at 61.
[4] Philippa Foot, *Virtues and Vices*, 154 (1978).

It is important, though, to recognize that skepticism about the objectivity of moral truth does not mean that moral beliefs do not transcend the person holding them. Thomas Hobbes argued that moral judgment correlates to the sentiment of the subject making the judgment, rather than to any property of the judgment's purported object.[5] If the statement "fighting in that war is wrong" only asserts something about the speaker's feelings – that is, "I feel that fighting in that war is wrong" – there is no readily discernible connection between the assertion and other moral actors or influences, nor is the assertion inherently accessible to others. If, however, the statement asserts something about fighting in the war – that it is wrong – the assertion is connected to influences outside the speaker and is accessible to others. The former understanding (known as "emotivism") has largely been rejected by philosophers, at least in its most starkly drawn versions, in favor of the latter understanding (known as "cognitivism"). Our legal system's discourse on conscience, though, appears to be stuck in an emotivist conception of conscience.

If our knowledge of conscience was based solely on our knowledge of the law's treatment of conscience, we might justifiably presume that moral discernment is a subjective exercise of the individual, both in terms of process ("How do I decide about X?") and sources ("What are my feelings about X?"). The law's preoccupation with individual autonomy is understandable, but the story must make room for the recognition that moral discernment is relational.

No one reasonably disputes the subjective dimension of moral belief or its importance. John Finnis, today's leading proponent of natural law, agrees with Philippa Foot's characterization of moral pronouncements as deriving from the speaker's perception of her own interests and well-being. He points out, however, "there is no reason to deny the objectivity – i.e. the intelligibility and reasonableness and truth" of statements about "what constitutes someone's well-being."[6] After all, a person's perception of her own interest does not guarantee that she has perceived her interest accurately. "The decisive question always is what it is intelligent to take an interest in."[7]

Human experience gives us a set of moral claims that can be deemed true or false based on their relationship with what has been observed and learned about the conditions necessary for human flourishing. The scope of these claims is limited, of course, but their very possibility allows us to speak of truth that is outside ourselves, even if there is a broad range of views on what that truth warrants in a particular situation.

---

[5] Thomas Hobbes, *Leviathan*, ch. VI (1651) ("For these words of good, evil, and contemptible are ever used with relation to the person that useth them: there being nothing simply and absolutely so; nor any common rule of good and evil to be taken from the nature of the objects themselves; but from the person of the man."). David Hume expanded on this concept in the eighteenth century. *See* David Hume, *A Treatise of Human Nature*, vol. II, book III, part I, sec. 1 (1740).

[6] John Finnis, *Fundamentals of Ethics*, 63 (1983).

[7] *Id.*

The moral claims underlying conscience are not simply statements of individual preference to be tallied politically. There is something to argue about that lies outside those doing the arguing. When we oppose genocide on moral grounds, we are not just marshalling political will, we are marshalling political will in service of moral truth. At the same time, in recognition of the fact that most moral claims are not demonstrably true or false, a society that takes the moral conversation seriously must maintain sufficient space for the diversity and incommensurability of moral claims.

We cannot short-circuit the conversation under the guise of rationality, as Rousseau sought to do when he invoked state power to coerce individuals to act based on their "real self" even if they did not appreciate what rationality supposedly required of them.[8] Many moral claims that are not articulable, or even accessible, in rational terms are not demonstrably false in light of the experience of the conditions necessary for human well-being.

The state must mark off some moral claims as lying beyond the pale of permissibility, at least when it comes to individuals' freedom to act on the claims. The state's humility in setting these bounds is a prerequisite for the moral conversation to proceed. Nonstate actors need not adopt a stance of humility, and often they will not. Even when we are not comfortable, as a society, in ruling a particular moral claim out of bounds, individuals and groups within society will not remain neutral on the claim's truth or falsity. Within the vast range of moral claims that are neither demonstrably true nor false, the claims still offer a judgment about a state of affairs lying outside the speaker.

This state of affairs need not presume the existence of a metaphysical reality. Even Nietzsche passionately defended the viability of truth despite his work toward upending the traditional foundations of truth:

> Truth has had to be fought for every step of the way, almost everything else dear to our hearts, on which our love and our trust in life depend, has had to be sacrificed to it. Greatness of soul is needed for it, the service of truth is the hardest service. For what does it mean to be honest in intellectual things? That one is stern towards one's heart, that one despises 'fine feelings', that one makes every Yes and No a question of conscience![9]

Even in a world that has largely abandoned the idea of a neat, universal hierarchy of moral values, the idea of moral truth still resonates with every claim of conscience. Claims of conscience, by their very nature, call the claimant into relationship with the world outside herself. The claimant may be relating to God, or to the teachings of her community, to critical reflection on her own past experience, or to the opinion of

---

[8] Isaiah Berlin, *Freedom and Its Betrayal: Six Enemies of Human Liberty*, 48–9 (2002).
[9] Friedrich Nietzsche, *The Anti-Christ* ¶ 50 (R.J. Hollingdale, trans. 1968).

the world at large. But such claims cannot be treated as instinctive and individualized statements of personal preference. A moral judgment may be, and often is, highly personal, but it is not self-contained. The person judging makes a statement about the object of her judgment, not just about her interior disposition. The claimant has directed her gaze to something. This is the external orientation of moral judgment that contributes significantly to conscience's relational dimension. We may disagree intensely about the merits of the judgment, but we cannot pretend that there is nothing to talk about.

Moral Claims and Community

Our recognition that moral claims convey a message about their object does not marginalize the importance of the subject. The philosopher Bernard Lonergan explained that truth goes beyond the subject only because "the subject is capable of an intentional self-transcendence, of going beyond what he feels, what he imagines, what he thinks, what seems to him, to something utterly different, to what is so."[10] More than anything else, it is this claim about "what is so" that separates conscience from preference and requires the claimant to fix her moral gaze outside herself. The process of getting to "what is so" is highly subjective to the extent that it entails "teaching and learning, investigating, coming to understand, marshalling and weighing the evidence" – exercises that "are not independent of the subject, of times and places, of psychological, social, historical conditions."[11]

To the extent that subjective experiences of truth lead individuals to dissent from prevailing conceptions of truth, there is no guarantee that their views will be honored, of course. Hegel, for example, defined the ethical life as the subjective will embracing the objective good, arguing that "the state cannot give recognition to conscience in its private form as subjective knowing, any more than science can grant validity to subjective opinion, dogmatism, and the appeal to a subjective opinion."[12]

Today, our embrace of liberty of conscience rejects Hegel's view, but the basis for that embrace is not always clear. The liberty of conscience could arise from our respect for "the dynamics of the advance toward truth,"[13] that is, not rejecting the possibility of truth, but recognizing that the process of discerning truth is complex, messy, and usually indeterminate, requiring substantial space for the free exchange of ideas and robust engagement of conflicting worldviews, processes that often persist without any clear or easy resolution. Alternatively, the liberty of conscience might

---

[10] Bernard Lonergan, *The Subject*, 3 (1975).
[11] *Id.*
[12] G.W.F. Hegel, *Philosophy of Right*, 91 (Knox, trans. 1973).
[13] Lonergan, *supra* note 10, at 4.

reflect a conviction that truth is irrelevant to moral claims and that our respect for conscience derives simply from our respect for individual autonomy. We protect the liberty of conscience because we value the ability of individuals to live consistently with their intensely felt opinions. As should be clear by now, I believe that the latter approach undervalues conscience by rendering it indistinguishable from preference. The former approach, however, can help illuminate how a person's conscience transcends self without resorting to a one-size-fits-all conception of moral truth.

Amy Gutmann avoids equating conscience with preference by defining conscience as "a person's ultimate ethical commitments," which are "ethical precepts that are binding on those who believe in them."[14] Democratic societies should respect conscientious belief because, unlike "people who are ruthlessly interested only in their own welfare, conscientious people try to live up to the ethical precepts or laws that they take to be good and just and therefore binding on their will."[15] This "effort to live according to a sense of goodness and justice constitutes ethical personhood or identity."[16] Gutmann's analysis makes plain the self-transcendent nature of conscience's claims – as beliefs that hold the believer accountable to moral standards that are broader than her own self-interest – although the relational implications are obscured by her tendency to address the liberty of conscience squarely within the individual-versus-state paradigm.[17] She portrays conscience as belief that binds the will (not belief in dialogue with the will), and the state's role in the life of conscience as consisting of the decision whether to exempt a claim of conscience from the law's demands (not the additional function of supporting the relational venues through which conscience flourishes).[18]

By contrast, the work of Stanley Hauerwas brings both the self-transcendence of conscience's claims and the relational implications of that self-transcendence to the foreground. As a theologian, he does not explore the legal treatment of conscience, but his insights advance the legal conversation by supporting the proposition that conscience is formed in and by communities. Hauerwas asserts that members of a particular faith tradition (in his case, Christianity) must serve as witnesses to truth by maintaining their distinctive identity, and his belief in moral truth coexists comfortably with contingency and perspective. Our relentless focus on obligations and rules, according to Hauerwas, "ignores the fact that action descriptions gain

[14] Amy Gutmann, *Identity in Democracy*, 168 (2003).
[15] *Id*. at 170–1.
[16] *Id*. at 171.
[17] *See id*. at 171 ("Respect for persons . . . implies respect both for individual conscience and for the duly constituted laws of a democracy that are the product of people's political freedom."), 172 ("Remove or repress conscientious objectors and tyranny is given freer reign in a nonideal democracy.").
[18] See, e.g., *id*. at 177 ("Conscience is therefore not so special that democratic governments should routinely defer to it, nor is it so ordinary that it should be routinely overridden.").

their intelligibility from the role they play in a community's history."[19] When our moral acts "are abstracted from that history, the moral self cannot help but appear as an unconnected series of actions lacking continuity and unity."[20]

One problem with insisting on the universal accessibility of moral truth, from this vantage point, is that it ignores the fallen state of humanity. In this regard, Hauerwas criticizes natural law, which "confuses the claim that Christian ethics is an ethic that we should and can commend to anyone with the claim that we can know the content of that ethic by looking at the human," and "fails to appreciate that there is no actual universal morality, but that in fact we live in a fragmented world of many moralities."[21] This need not lessen our commitment to moral truth. Hauerwas portrays moral truth as a story to live out, rather than as a set of propositions to be reflected on or debated in terms of perspectiveless rationality. Its viability thus "depends upon vital communities sufficient to live well-lived lives."[22]

Hauerwas does not seek to avoid conversations about the substance of Christian convictions. Instead, he seeks "to enliven the discussion by reminding us of what kind of community we must be to sustain the sort of discussion required by the stories of God."[23] It is thus a deeply contextual vision of moral truth claims, but not a relativist one. Hauerwas would insist that the Christian story is good news for all human beings, but the moral convictions flow from that story and cannot be conceived of or implemented in the abstract, apart from the lived reality of that story. Alasdair MacIntyre would put the point more broadly: moral reasoning involves figuring out what story I am part of.[24] He writes:

> To be a moral agent is [in the modern view] precisely to be able to stand back from any and every situation in which one is involved, from any and every characteristic that one may possess, and to pass judgment on it from a purely universal and abstract point of view that is totally detached from all social particularity.[25]

We cannot separate our moral convictions from who we are, and we cannot separate who we are from our story. Moral philosophers who have tried to do so – Immanuel Kant most notably – end up susceptible to the charge that they have emptied moral truth of its substance, rendering it a formalist template rather than a lived reality. Kant's categorical imperative sought to construct moral claims that are universalizable, unhinged from any consequence, contingency, need, social role, or divine command. The result is a moral framework, critics insist, that can be filled

---

[19] Stanley Hauerwas, *The Peaceable Kingdom: A Primer in Christian Ethics*, 21 (1983).

[20] *Id.* at 21.

[21] *Id.* at 63.

[22] *Id.* at 15.

[23] Stanley Hauerwas, *A Community of Character: Toward a Constructive Christian Social Ethic*, 95 (1981).

[24] Alasdair MacIntyre, *After Virtue*, 201 (1984).

[25] *Id.* at 30.

with any rule articulable at a general enough level of abstraction to satisfy the criterion of universal applicability.[26]

Eschewing the moral relevance of our social and historical contexts gives rise to skepticism toward the "given-ness" of moral truth claims. The moral inquiry begins on a blank slate for every person, as the realization of individual autonomy necessitates the deliberate choosing of one's moral compass. This mindset pervades modern American law, as reflected in the "sweet mystery of life" passage,[27] and helps explain why our legal system can justify such a narrowly drawn, individualist conception of conscience.

The morality-as-self-creation project is ultimately futile. If my moral claim does not purport to convey a truth that exists apart from my belief in its existence or from my desire for it to exist, it is a reflection of myself, nothing more. The modern view of conscience contributes to this project to the extent that we portray conscience's claims as endlessly self-referential. If the statement "I believe doing X is wrong" warrants no meaningful distinction from the statement "I prefer not to do X," we have no meaningful basis for interpersonal engagement. However, if "I believe doing X is wrong" can be located within a larger life narrative, the points of potential engagement expand dramatically because life narratives, no matter how unique, rarely unfold in isolation. The modern view of conscience has tended to deemphasize the breadth of our narratives or to pretend that our narratives are products of our own free choice. In reality, we are always enmeshed in narratives, and much of our narrative is given, not chosen.[28]

The problem is that a community-specific orientation is not easily translated into a publicly accessible vision of morality for a society made up of countless communities, all following their own distinctive narratives. If we look to the defining narrative(s) of our lives as the source of moral truth, instead of attempting to fashion a moral standard that transcends all particular narratives, must not we abandon the hope of meaningful moral discourse?

The community-centered approach appears to face twin obstacles. If we maintain the traditional belief that absolute moral truth exists and is discernible through the exercise of reason, the fact that a given moral claim originates from the shared life of a community appears only marginally relevant to the moral inquiry. On the other hand, if we fall in line with the prevailing skepticism toward the existence and discernibility of absolute moral truth, the community's moral claims are as relevant as any other set of claims, but the prospects for meaningful discourse appear remote. If there is nothing beyond the moral agent to which the agent's moral judgments correspond, any conversation about the judgments is academic. No one is wrong.

---

[26] See *id.*

[27] See *Planned Parenthood of Southeastern Penn. v. Casey*, 505 U.S. 833, 851 (1992) ("At the heart of liberty is the right to define one's own concept of existence, of meaning, of the universe, and of the mystery of human life.").

[28] Hauerwas, *supra* note 23, at 127.

If we want to understand whether and how claims of conscience can be considered claims of truth, we must navigate a path between moral absolutism and moral relativism, both of which can serve to negate the community's moral relevance.

Moral Claims and Value Pluralism

Enter the value pluralists. Value pluralism refers, in Isaiah Berlin's memorable phrasing, to "[t]he conception that there are many different ends that men may seek and still be fully rational, fully men, capable of understanding each other and sympathizing and deriving light from each other."[29] According to Joseph Raz, value pluralism speaks "of the existence of more goods than can be chosen by one person," and of more "virtues than can be perfected by one person," including virtues that are incompatible.[30] Further, values are incommensurable, meaning that they cannot be meaningfully compared or ranked because there is no common measure. For example, how do you compare a beautiful sunset with a Mozart piano concerto? Many of the thorniest disputes about conscience pit the values of equality and liberty against each other: the liberty of a group to exclude individuals versus the equality sought by individuals who protest their exclusion. It is not just that equality and liberty are in tension; they are both foundational values of our society, incapable of being ranked against each other in any sensible way.

Although value pluralism may be seeing a resurgence in popularity in postmodern liberal democracies, it is by no means a new concept, as thinkers since Plato have "understood that many attributes contribute ... to the good life, depending on the abilities and interests of the people seeking the good."[31] The importance of recognizing the plurality of goods became more pressing in the twentieth century. Writing against the background of that century's cataclysm of all-encompassing political ideologies, Berlin warned that the "notion of the perfect whole, the ultimate solution, in which all good things coexist, seems to me to be not merely unattainable ... but conceptually incoherent."[32] Human beings are "doomed to choose" among goods as they structure their lives, and "every choice may entail an irreparable loss."[33]

Berlin did not give up completely on the relevance of moral truth, although he defined moral truth in distinctly modern terms. He rejected the idea of values as a product of "purely subjective judgment," for values are "dictated by the forms of life of the society to which one belongs, a society among other societies, with values held in common, whether or not they are in conflict, by the majority of mankind

---

[29] Isaiah Berlin, *The Crooked Timber of Humanity*, 11 (Henry Hardy ed., 1991).
[30] Joseph Raz, *The Morality of Freedom*, 399 (1986).
[31] J. Michael Martinez and Kerry R. Stewart, "Ethics, Virtue and Character Development," *Ethics and Character: The Pursuit of Democratic Virtues*, 19, 22–3 (1998).
[32] Berlin, *supra* note 29, at 13.
[33] *Id.*

throughout recorded history." Even if there are not universal values, there are values "without which societies could scarcely survive."[34]

Berlin thereby reframes moral truth as deriving from human experience, rather than from divine revelation or some transcendent source. As Bernard Williams puts it, Berlin recognized that "different values do each have a real and intelligible human significance, and are not just errors, misdirections or poor expressions of human nature."[35] There is truth about human nature that has been revealed "in the only way in which it could be revealed, historically."[36] Stuart Hampshire echoes this point, noting that there "are obvious limits set by common human needs to the conditions under which human beings flourish and human societies flourish," and that "[h]istory records many ways of life which have crossed these limits."[37] Michael Moore puts it somewhat differently. He explains, "moral qualities have real world effects, and those effects provide our evidence for the existence of those moral qualities."[38]

It is important to recognize that value pluralism is not value relativism. Meaningful distinctions between good and bad can be rationally and defensibly drawn. What Berlin and his intellectual descendants have done, though, is bring the diversity of moral truths to the center of the moral inquiry. The moral diversity acknowledged (sporadically) in our public discourse is not simply a political convenience, but an empirical reality.

William Galston has helpfully outlined the meanings of "diversity" that might potentially operate in this context. First, borrowing from John Rawls' approach, Galston observes that we might acknowledge moral diversity "as a fact that could be significantly altered only through the employment of unacceptable degrees of state coercion, with unacceptable levels of civil strife."[39] In other words, regardless of the truth value of particular moral claims, attempting to minimize or eradicate moral diversity would carry too high a social cost. Second, we might acknowledge moral diversity as an instrumental value, either because "the existence of visible alternatives enhances the meaning of particular commitment," or because "the multiplication of sects is the surest social obstacle to sectarian tyranny."[40] John Stuart Mill's instrumentalist approach emphasizes the value of diversity in deepening the significance of personal choice; James Madison emphasized the importance of diverse allegiances as a bulwark against the consolidation of power.[41]

A third possibility is one that Berlin and the value pluralists have mined for insight: We might embrace diversity as "an intrinsic value" on the premise that

---

[34] *Id.* at 18.
[35] Isaiah Berlin, *Concepts and Categories: Philosophical Essays*, xviii (1979) (Bernard Williams introd.)
[36] *Id.*
[37] Stuart Hampshire, *Morality and Conflict*, 155 (1983).
[38] Michael Moore, *Objectivity in Law and Ethics*, 122 (2004).
[39] William Galston, *Liberal Pluralism: The Implications of Value Pluralism for Political Theory*, 27 (2002).
[40] *Id.*
[41] See *id.*

"our moral universe is characterized by plural and conflicting values that cannot be harmonized in a single comprehensive way of life," and that therefore "a wide (though not indefinitely wide) range of such goals and conceptions could serve as bases of worthwhile lives."[42] Acting on the diversity of moral values is not a concession to political exigencies; it is coming to grips with reality. This does not mean that value pluralism must be the ultimate answer shaping every moral inquiry, because "to demand that every acceptable way of life reflect a conscious awareness of value pluralism is to affirm what value pluralism denies – the existence of a universally dominant value."[43] It does, however, serve as a useful framework for understanding the public dimension of the moral inquiry. As a society, we must acknowledge the diversity of moral truths without precluding the very possibility that moral truth can be discerned. The process of discernment is necessarily a context-specific one, and that is the subject of this book's second part.

THE INTERSUBJECTIVITY OF CONSCIENCE

One aspect of conscience's relationship with truth concerns the external orientation of the moral claim's substance – making a moral judgment entails looking beyond my instinctive preference. A closely related aspect concerns the intersubjective obligations set forth by moral claims. Put simply, when we make moral claims, we are claiming that we owe obligations to others and they to us.

Both Hauerwas and Berlin share a deep skepticism about the real world's amenability to universalized claims of absolute moral truth, with Hauerwas speaking of our moral "fragmentation" and Berlin of our moral "diversity." Both resist the slide into cynicism about the prospects for meaningful moral discourse by insisting that moral claims refer to something real. And they would affirm that the moral claims shared in community loom large in the ongoing formation of the individual's moral life. They are just two of the influential moral theorists who begin from dramatically different worldviews, yet share an emphasis on the accessibility of moral claims between and among human subjects.

To take another prominent example, Richard Rorty, as a pragmatist, does not condition the truth of a proposition on its correlation with any objective reality, whether temporal or transcendent. Instead, he focuses on whether a proposition helps us solve a problem, and he asserts that we make sense of our lives by connecting ourselves to a human community. He refers to this connection as solidarity.[44] Truth is beside the point:

> [W]hen the pragmatist says that there is nothing to be said about truth save that each of us will commend as true those beliefs which he or she finds good to believe, the realist is inclined to interpret this as one more positive theory about the nature

---

[42] *Id.*

[43] *Id.* at 53.

[44] Richard Rorty, *Objectivity, Relativism, and Truth*, 21 (1991).

of truth: a theory according to which truth is simply the contemporary opinion of a chosen individual or group. Such a theory would, of course, be self-refuting. But the pragmatist does not have a theory of truth, much less a relativistic one. As a partisan of solidarity, his account of the value of cooperative human inquiry has only an ethical base, not an epistemological or metaphysical one.[45]

Giving up claims to objective truth is liberating for Rorty, as he believes that it allows him to connect more intentionally to the needs and concerns of his fellow human beings. He calls pragmatism "a philosophy of solidarity rather than of despair," and traces its development in "Socrates' turn away from the gods, Christianity's turn from an Omnipotent Creator to the man who suffered on the Cross, and the Baconian turn from science as contemplation of eternal truth to science as instrument of social progress," all of which "can be seen as so many preparations for the act of social faith which is suggested by a Nietzschean view of truth."[46] For pragmatists, the quest for human solidarity entails "an endless, proliferating realization of Freedom, rather than a convergence toward an already existing Truth."[47] Our progress is measured by the redirection of our focus from the transcendent to our neighbors in the here and now. Solidarity is to be created, rather than recognized, by trying "to notice our similarities with" those who have been marginalized.[48] Regardless of the merits of Rorty's approach, it is important to recognize that his moral claims remain externally oriented, embodying our efforts to take responsibility for one another.

The intersubjective quality of moral claims is not entirely altruistic. It is also a product of our need for personal coherence. Bernard Williams explains, "[w]e learn to present ourselves to others, and consequently also to ourselves, as people who have moderately steady outlooks or beliefs" because others "need to rely on our dispositions, and we want them to be able to rely on our dispositions because we, up to a point, want to rely on theirs."[49] This gets back to a point raised earlier: When we make moral claims, we are not expressing a fixed opinion as a freestanding agent so much as engaging in a social process of personal formation. Williams urges us to "leave behind the assumption that we first and immediately have a transparent self-understanding, and then go on either to give other people a sincere revelation of our belief from which they understand us . . . or else dissimulate in a way that will mislead them."[50] We are, more fundamentally, taking part in "the social activity of mutually stabilizing our declarations and moods and impulses into becoming such things as beliefs and relatively steady attitudes."[51] Joining others with whom we share

---

[45] *Id.* at 24.
[46] *Id.* at 33.
[47] Richard Rorty, *Contingency, Irony, Solidarity,* xvi (1989)
[48] *Id.* at 196.
[49] Bernard Williams, *Truth and Truthfulness: An Essay in Genealogy,* 192 (2002).
[50] *Id.* at 193.
[51] *Id.*

values allows our beliefs to become steadier, allowing us, in turn, to become what we profess.[52]

The Second-Person Standpoint

There is a stronger intersubjective aspect of morality: Beyond the sentiment of Rorty's solidarity and the social pull of Williams' personal integrity lies the "second person standpoint" developed by Stephen Darwall. Morality is generally approached by asking "What should I do?" (the first-person perspective) or by observing the world and making judgments about its operation, such as judgments about cause and effect (the third-person perspective). The second-person perspective asks a different question: "Under what circumstances am I accountable to you?"

Proponents of the second-person perspective point out that third-person observations of fact are not directly translatable into first-person reasons for action. The fact that something is so does not mean that I must act on it. Our motivations for action are not limited to certain states of affairs that might be produced thereby. We are also motivated by "certain attitudes towards and expectations of specific persons and their conduct, which give rise to a distinctive class of perceived reasons for action in accordance with norms and perceived grounds for criticizing or reacting to their breach in specific ways."[53] When we make a moral judgment, we do more than describe a state of affairs; we claim that a certain state of affairs gives rise to a duty. John Stuart Mill made a similar observation:

> We do not call anything wrong, unless we mean to imply that a person ought to be punished in some way or other for doing it; if not by law, by the opinion of his fellow-creatures; if not by opinion, by the reproaches of his own conscience. This seems the real turning point of the distinction between morality and simple expediency. It is a part of the notion of Duty in every one of its forms, that a person may rightfully be compelled to fulfill it. Duty is a thing which may be exacted from a person, as one exacts a debt.[54]

As Stephen Darwall puts it, "What is wrong is what we can be morally expected not to do, what the moral community assumes the authority to hold us to."[55] A second-person reason must be addressed person to person; authority and accountability between the obligor and obligee are essential.[56] In this way, being "responsible for" certain conduct is tied to being "responsible to" another moral agent to whom the actor relates. Moral responsibility "concerns how, in light of what someone has done, she is to be related to, that is, regarded and addressed (including by herself)

---

[52] *Id.* at 204.
[53] Robin Kar, *Hart's Response to Exclusive Legal Positivism*, 95 Geo. L. J. 393, 447 (2007).
[54] John Stuart Mill, *Utilitarianism*, 72–3 (4th ed., 1871).
[55] Stephen Darwall, *The Second-Person Standpoint: Morality, Respect, and Accountability*, 93 (2006).
[56] *Id.* at 8.

within the second-personal relationships we stand in as members of the moral community."[57]

This departs from philosophers who look to the impersonal reason-giving power of others' interests;[58] instead of looking impersonally *at* one among others, Darwall urges us to adopt the standpoint *of* one among others.[59] The validity of moral demands, then, flows not from the desirability of the action demanded or on the "value of any outcome or state, but on normative relations between persons, on one person's having the authority to address the demand to another." Moral obligation must be "grounded in presuppositions to which you and I are committed when we reciprocally recognize one another as free and equal persons."[60]

Darwall connects the second-person standpoint to the voluntarism espoused by natural lawyers such as the seventeenth-century lawyer–philosopher Samuel Pufendorf, whose theories on sovereignty helped lay the groundwork for the Enlightenment. Natural lawyers believed that physical and moral laws were from God. Intellectualists, such as Aquinas, believed that the laws were a product of God's reason. Voluntarists, such as William of Ockham, believed that they were a product of God's will.[61] For our purposes, it suffices to recognize that voluntarists emphasized the need for accountability in constructing a theory of moral obligation. Pufendorf understood morality as involving accountability to God, by which he did not mean mere submission to God's power, but "an acceptance of an obligation rooted in God's authority."[62] Consequently, accountability "is only possible for free rational agents who are able to hold themselves responsible – who can determine themselves by their acceptance of the validity of the demands, thereby imposing them on themselves."[63]

A similar sense of moral accountability is found in Catholic theology today: A person chooses to accept God's demands because of the person's relationship to God, not as a strategy of self-interest, but in recognition of God's embodiment of truth. Cardinal Joseph Ratzinger (now Pope Benedict XVI) defines conscience as "man's openness to the ground of his being, the power of perception for what is highest and most essential," rejecting what he sees as the modern conception of conscience "as subjectivity's protective shell, into which man can escape and there hide from reality."[64] The nature of the accountability represented in conscience entails "the transparency of the subject for the divine," rather than a "mechanism

---

[57] *Id.* at 69.

[58] See *id.* at 102 (citing Thomas Nagel, *The Possibility of Altruism* (1970)).

[59] *Id.*

[60] *Id.* at 103.

[61] See e.g., Terence Irwin, *The Development of Ethics*, 304 (2008); Edmund Leites, *Conscience and Casuistry in Early Modern Europe*, 33–5 (2002); Margaret J. Osler, *Divine Will and the Mechanical Philosophy*, 18–29 (1994).

[62] Darwall, *supra* note 55, at 105.

[63] *Id.*

[64] Joseph Ratzinger, *On Conscience*, 16 (2007).

for rationalization."[65] Ratzinger maintains the belief in the innate quality of conscience – although he drops the term synderesis, preferring Plato's term "anamnesis," which suggests a "capacity to recall." Even the innate quality is externally oriented, requiring "assistance from without so that it can become aware of itself."[66] As with the Scholastics, Ratzinger acknowledges the subjectivity of accountability to the extent that "the conviction a person has come to certainly binds in the moment of acting," but culpability still arises from "having stifled the protest of the anamnesis of being" in the process of reaching those convictions.[67] Note that the accountability spoken of by Ratzinger and other natural lawyers today remains inescapably in the second person, as is Darwall's. Ratzinger emphasizes that "[a]s far as the fixed character of the natural laws is concerned, morality means the free 'yes' given by one will to another, in this case, the conformity of man to the will of God and the consequent correct perception of things as they really are."[68]

A claim of conscience is not just an expression of the agent's accountability to moral truth. It is an expression of accountability to those who are the source of the demand to recognize the moral truth, whether that is another person, a community, God, or one's self. As Darwall puts it, being under moral obligation "is not simply a matter of standing under categorical oughts, but, as well, of being obligated to (answerable to) someone for complying with these oughts."[69] The obligated actor does not accept the demand in the sense of appreciating it from the other person's perspective; she subjectively makes the demand of herself by being able to share the other's perspective.[70] She takes ownership of the demand through a relationship of accountability.

In practice, this means we have to break out of the usual categories of human motivation as being either altruistic or selfish. The motives underlying moral obligation, according to Robin Kar, "are better characterized as deontological attitudes, which allow us to take the perceived fact that something is right or required as a sufficient reason to act."[71] Obligations are subjective to the extent that they are "agent-centered" – that is, the agent must "fulfill a given requirement, even if by failing to do so he or she could cause two or more others to fulfill the requirement in equally weighty circumstances."[72] For example, Kar points out that a person could not fulfill a moral obligation to act respectfully to her friend at an important social gathering by acting like such a fool that she motivated two other people to act respectfully toward their friends.[73] When I breach a moral obligation to you, my acceptance

[65] *Id.* at 21–2.
[66] *Id.* at 32, 34.
[67] *Id.* at 38.
[68] *Id.* at 52.
[69] Darwall, *supra* note 55, at 108.
[70] *Id.* at 112–3.
[71] Robin Bradley Kar, *The Deep Structure of Law and Morality*, 84 Tex. L. Rev. 877, 918–9 (2006).
[72] Robin Bradley Kar, *Hart's Response to Exclusive Legal Positivism*, 95 Geo. L. J. 393, 429 (2007).
[73] *Id.*

of responsibility must be second personal. If you ask, "How could you have done this to me?," my response could be first and third personal if I say "sorry" only because otherwise I will "never hear the end of this" in light of my perception of your state of mind.[74] Your question, however, was not just to provide information about your state of mind, it was meant to address me directly and to call me out for the breach, and thus my apology must be from me to you and must be based on my recognition that I owe you the apology "for it to function as a genuine apology."[75] Moral obligations cannot be understood solely as first- or third-person deliberations.[76] From the second-person standpoint, we are addressing problems that have an "inherently relational aspect; we are engaging in forms of interpersonal address that allow us to negotiate, manage, repair, and sometimes dissolve, our social relationships with one another."[77] Conscience's authority does not emerge as a set of impersonal abstractions at one extreme or inexplicable individual instinct at the other. Its authority is subjective but not self-contained; conscience connects a person's perception of reality with demands spoken from one moral agent to another.

Conscience and Accountability

Because our claims of conscience are premised on accountability, the community to which one is accountable has an essential role in supporting conscience's vitality. This is true as a descriptive matter – we hold ourselves accountable by adopting the moral demands of those with whom we share fundamental truth commitments – but also as a normative matter – conscience's identity-shaping function is tied up with the mutual accountability of communities. As Hauerwas puts it, "[t]he 'otherness' of another's character not only invites me to an always imperfect imitation, but challenges me to recognize the way my vision is restricted by my own self-preoccupation."[78] As such, "the kind of community in which we encounter another does not merely make some difference for our capacity for agency, it makes all the difference."[79]

 Conscience's operation draws individuals out of themselves to some object of their moral deliberation. Although conscience is rooted in our innermost core, its gaze is fixed outward, making judgments about right and wrong against a background formed by the personal perception of and conclusions about the human experience. The myriad communities that make up society are not just venues for the expression of an individual's conscience, they are venues for the formation of conscience – indeed, a perceived moral obligation is generally rooted in accountability to

[74] *Id.* at 427.
[75] Kar, *supra* note 71, at 941.
[76] Kar, *supra* note 72, at 430.
[77] *Id.*
[78] Stanley Hauerwas, *The Peaceable Kingdom*, 45 (1983).
[79] *Id.*

someone. The community built on shared moral claims, in this regard, is inseparable from the content and very nature of conscience. Accountability is a social
dynamic.

But not always. Occasionally we are confronted with Thoreau, a moral agent
seemingly accountable only to himself. For the self-consciously atomistic agent,
intersubjective accountability recedes into the background, but the accountability to
one's own convictions still supports the relational dimension of conscience because
the convictions point to something beyond the self. In Thoreau's case, for example,
the object of his moral discernment was not his own self; it was the question of a
citizen's proper response to an unjust government and his resulting claim of moral
truth – that the proper response is noncooperation, even at risk of incarceration –
was accessible far beyond the bounds of his physical isolation on the shores of
Walden Pond. Gandhi's later reliance on Thoreau testifies powerfully to the outward
orientation of conscience.

The moral discernment of the hermit and the community member are more
similar than different. Accountability is not about bowing to group power or the
wishes of the majority. It is about internalizing moral demands, whether the demands
originate with a group, with God, or simply with your perception of reality's truth.
When the moral agent has adopted a demand and claimed it as her own obligation,
she now has a reason for action that trumps competing reasons for action such as
preference or desire. This does not mean that conscience only becomes implicated
at the point when the obligation arises or encounters resistance from some outside
power; the processes by which moral obligations are formed and discerned fall within
conscience's province.

Spheres of Intersubjectivity

If communities are important to a fulsome understanding of moral discourse's
inescapable intersubjectivity, we need to be precise about what sort of communities we are talking about. The accountability between subjects – and, more importantly for our purposes, the conversations that can give rise to that accountability –
look quite different depending on the nature of the membership on which the
accountability is premised. Rainer Forst's navigation of the ongoing debates between
liberalism and communitarianism is helpful in drawing some needed distinctions
in this regard. Here is the gist of Forst's thesis, in his words:

> The analysis of the debate between supposedly "context-forgetful" liberal-
> deontological theories and "context-obsessed" communitarian theories thus leads
> to a differentiation of four normative contexts in which persons are "situated" as
> members of various communities; that is to say, they are intersubjectively recog-
> nized and are authors and addressees of validity claims in various communities:
> communities of ethical, constitutive bonds and obligations; a legal community that
> protects this "ethical identity" of a person as a free and equal legal person; a political

community in which persons are the authors of law and mutually responsible citizens; finally, the moral community of all human beings as moral persons with the right to moral respect. A theory of justice is at the same time context-bound and context-transcending insofar it takes these normative dimensions into consideration, without absolutizing any particular one. According to this theory, the society that unites these contexts in the appropriate manner can be called just.[80]

Forst defines ethical questions as "questions of the good life of a person as a member of particular ethical communities, with whose history the unique life history, the narrative of the self – its past, present, and future – is connected."[81] He resists the atomistic view of the individual that can creep into liberal theory, that is, he explains that "I share with [the people who belong to the core of my identity] a particular ethical world that forms the framework for strong evaluations without which I cannot understand myself."[82] At the same time, he avoids the marginalization of the individual that can occur in some strands of communitarian theory and that stands in considerable tension with a social order that honors conscience. He explains, "I justify myself to myself and to others against the background of values important to us; but they are important only because each individual person considers them important: their validity does not have categorical force."[83]

Forst nicely captures the need for the political community to adopt a stance of humility when it comes to enforcing moral norms on ethical subcommunities. Echoing the lessons of value pluralism, he emphasizes that "'reasonable' persons recognize the possibility of a plurality of ethical answers to questions of the good life – answers that are reasonable insofar as they are neither irrational nor immoral," and they further recognize "the significance of such answers to persons and respect them even if they regard them as ethically unsatisfactory answers."[84] Even an outsider to a particular life narrative must acknowledge the importance of that life narrative to those situated within it, and they thus should resist the temptation to use legal or political norms to shut down the claims of ethical communities simply because they are in conflict with the claims of other ethical communities. In other words, although there is nothing wrong with attempting to persuade others that certain values would enrich their lives, it is morally unacceptable to restrict "ethical forms of life with reasons other than those reciprocally and generally justified." Put simply, "[r]espect for ethical identity is . . . morally required."[85]

The challenge is to identify and articulate the boundaries between a prudent respect for ethical identity and an imprudent license of conduct that violates the

[80] Rainer Forst, *Contexts of Justice: Political Philosophy Beyond Liberalism and Communitarianism*, 5 (2002) (originally published as *Kontexte der Gerechtigkeit* (1994)).

[81] *Id.* at 258

[82] *Id.* at 259.

[83] *Id.*

[84] *Id.* at 45.

[85] *Id.*

moral norms that should be deemed nonnegotiable for society. Part II of this book explores how legal norms can and should be used to create space for divergent ethical norms, particularly when those ethical norms are viewed by adherents as moral norms. The even trickier question is whether there are circumstances under which the law should effectively enforce a perceived moral norm as an actual moral norm, that is, as a binding norm of universal applicability that will trump conflicting ethical norms.

Forst and I might disagree about how to categorize or prioritize particular claims, but he describes the moral-ethical–political-legal tensions insightfully: "The validity of a legal norm ('this is legally permitted or forbidden') can collide with an ethical conviction ('this is not consistent with my beliefs'), with a political end ('this ought to be regulated differently'), or with a moral norm ('nobody may demand this')."[86] In all of these spheres, Forst reminds us, we must recognize each other as both an individual and "a communal being." We cannot fully understand community or the intersubjectivity of human relationships without accounting for the different spheres.

Although this is a book about law, the legal sphere must reflect a cognizance of the other spheres. The individual-versus-state paradigm is not helpful in this regard, as it ignores the intermediate communities that bring the ethical-moral distinction into relief. (Even when elucidating the boundaries between what "nobody may demand" and the permissible range of divergent beliefs, I will, for simplicity's sake and in reflection of common usage, continue to use "moral," rather than "ethical," to describe most judgments about right and wrong.[87]) Usually concern for conscience focuses on the moral convictions of the individual, and the operative question is one-dimensional: Should the state defer to those convictions or not? We need to widen the field of inquiry, asking what type of society will support the sort of community life that is best suited to nurturing and sustaining conscience. The inquiry begins to take shape once we recognize that our communities' normative conversations do not proceed exclusively, or even primarily, through law or politics. Tracing the paths by which this recognition can be implemented is the concern of chapter 4.

CONSCIENCE'S CLAIMS

Whether undertaken individually or in a group, the ultimate end of a given normative deliberation will not be universally agreed on or even accessible, so making space

---

[86] *Id.* at 265.

[87] As a practical matter, it is not always easy to decipher whether a particular community understands its normative claim as potentially applying to all rational people (moral claims) or as being limited to those who are connected to the community because of their "unique life history" and "narrative of the self" (ethical claims). Further, such a distinction is of limited relevance to the law's treatment of the claim – that is, whether a community believes that the claim is applicable to all rational agents does not tell us much about whether the state should treat the claim as applicable to all rational agents.

for the free operation of conscience places us squarely in the province of value pluralism. Just as "[a] belief quite rational for one person might be quite irrational for another," "a belief rational for one community, given the other beliefs shared by members of the community, or by most of them, might be irrational for another community."[88] Because "the agent is constrained by the commitments she has made over her lifetime in the process of constructing herself as a unique individual," some options may not be morally permissible for her that would be for others.[89]

As noted previously, this does not mean that all moral claims are of equal validity. Michael Perry points out that a belief "might eventually come to be seen as rationally unacceptable," meaning that "the belief might be false, that it might not get it right, even if, so far as we can now tell, the belief is fully adequate to our interests and projects."[90] In other words, the coherentist conception of rationality "leaves room for the possibility that our beliefs can be inadequate to the world," and thus "is in no way inhospitable to self-critical rationality."[91] The key inquiry for the second part of this book is figuring out how and when the state should act to rule actions derived from certain beliefs to be out of bounds as "inadequate to the world."

Conscience separates itself from preference through the authority that it conveys as a claim of truth. This does not mean, however, that authentic claims of conscience are invariably premised on the existence of absolute or objective moral truth. It is true that most people of reason and good faith will agree that certain conduct is immoral, and that its immorality is not solely a function of the person's belief in the immorality. We can argue about how far that category of conduct extends beyond acts such as genocide or racism, but few would dispute that moral judgment is capable of transcending the subjective in a way that preference is not. I do not claim that conscience can only legitimately be invoked regarding matters akin to genocide. On the contrary, conscience is in play in the myriad decisions we make every day that are touched by our conceptions of right and wrong. It might be that no one on earth agrees with our particular moral judgment, or that we ourselves acknowledge that our moral judgment is the product of historically or culturally justified conventions, rather than a universal moral order. The key for conscience is that we are basing the judgment on principles, criteria, or observations. We are looking outside ourselves.

Because conscience's sources lie beyond the self, conscience's claims exhibit an accessibility and intersubjectivity that claims of preference do not. As a result, the moral frameworks that allow us to live lives of coherence and integrity tend to take shape through relationships. (This links the relational dimension of conscience and the social nature of the person, which was the focus of chapter 2.) My conscience makes truth claims that possess authority over conduct – both my own and the

---

[88] Michael J. Perry, *Love and Power: The Role of Religion and Morality in American Politics*, 53 (1991).
[89] W. Bradley Wendel, *Value Pluralism in Legal Ethics*, 78 Wash. U. L. Q. 113, 119 (2000).
[90] Perry, *supra* note 88, at 60.
[91] *Id.* at 61.

conduct of those who share, or come to share, my perception. My moral convictions do not just describe, they govern. Because of their accessibility and authority, moral claims naturally promote shared endeavors centered on those claims. Although the individual ultimately must take ownership of the moral claims on which she builds her life narrative, the ongoing formation, articulation, expression, and living out of those claims are relational endeavors.

The self-transcendence of moral judgment has practical implications for our understanding of conscience. First, communities are not secondary to the individual as the locus of the moral life, and the importance of the community cannot be fully grasped as a mere collection of individual agents expressing their own freestanding moral identities. Whether it is a church, political association, student club, family, or place of business, our communities are inherently moral enterprises that facilitate the articulation and stabilization of their members' moral convictions. When the individual looks outside herself, it is often the community where she finds and forms her moral direction. The viability of conscience requires venues in which we can connect with others around shared conceptions of moral truth.

Second, the language of conscience is inherently relational because it is premised on the existence and articulation of intersubjective obligations. It is not just that communities help create the content of our consciences. Communities are the natural fora in which we express the dictates of conscience because it is there that the concept of duty takes on practical meaning. Conscience is not easily expressed in timeless or placeless abstractions; it is a moral claim made on one's conduct by another.

Third, for the individual who has managed to construct her own moral convictions apart from any community, and whose convictions give rise to duties owed only to her self, the vibrancy of community life still serves as a resource for her own formation of conscience. Even Thoreau's gaze turned outward in matters of moral judgment. No moral agent operates on a blank slate, for we are all shaped by the moral marketplace in which we find ourselves. If the marketplace were populated only by individual moral agents and the collective state, it would be no marketplace at all, but simply an assortment of individuals under varying degrees of state coercion. The viability of conscience requires venues in which conversations regarding the substance of moral truth can proceed. When the state shuts down those venues, the external orientation of moral judgment does not disappear; it simply shifts its gaze to the levers of collective power, the only remaining locus of conscience's relational dimension. The vitality of intermediate associations embodies the distinction between the common good and the collective good, a subject to which we now turn.

4

Conscience and the Common Good

Conscience's orientation toward action contributes to its relational nature by drawing the believer beyond the boundaries of her mind and into her social environment. When Daniel Seeger sought an exemption from military service based on his conscientious opposition to war, he defied any effort to equate conscience with belief. If the government had responded to his claim by assuring him that the United States would never coerce him to abandon his belief that war is immoral, the gesture would have been properly ridiculed as absurd. Defining freedom of conscience as freedom of belief avoids the tough questions (how often does the state attempt to compel belief today?), but it eviscerates the power of conscience, which is more properly understood as moral belief applied to conduct.

This understanding of conscience, however, does not always prevail. Both houses of the British Parliament recently issued a report analyzing new regulations prohibiting discrimination against gays and lesbians in the provision of public services. The report addressed whether the prohibition was problematic as applied to religious providers, particularly as applied to religious schools that were now forbidden from teaching that homosexuality is immoral. What is noteworthy is not so much that the government approved the regulations, but that it did so by explicitly equating conscience with belief:

> [T]he scope of the [religious] exemption in the [sexual orientation regulations] gives adequate protection to the absolute right . . . to freedom of conscience and religion. Nobody is required by the Regulations not to have beliefs about the morality of different sexual orientations, or its compatibility with the tenets of one's religion, or punished or subjected to any other disadvantage for having such beliefs. In our view, the prohibitions on discrimination in the Regulations limit the manifestation of those religious beliefs and that limitation is justifiable in a democratic society

for the protection of the right of gay people not to be discriminated against in the provision of goods, facilities and services.[1]

At one level, this strategy is understandable, as it removes a highly charged issue from the reach of groups that do not embrace the emerging social consensus, while at the same time it appears to maintain a longstanding commitment to religious freedom. There is a temptation to believe that the way around the "culture wars" is to separate belief from action, leaving untouched the idiosyncratic and seemingly archaic worldviews of individuals and groups while avoiding the tangible harms that arise from actions driven by those worldviews. If we can honor conscience while we maintain a modicum of social harmony, what is not to like?

As it turns out, plenty. In the previous two chapters, I have established conscience's relational dimension by showing how its dialogical and social functions support personal identity (chapter 2) and how its substantive claims are by nature intersubjective (chapter 3). If our society is committed to facilitating the flourishing of conscience, it makes sense for the law to account for conscience's true nature. In this chapter, I go a step further and argue that the law should aim to foster conscience's relational dimension, not just because it comports with the reality of conscience, but because it represents a vision of the social order that is conducive to the common good. In particular, I will endeavor to show that both premises of the belief/action separation are mistaken. First, categorically excluding action from conscience's ambit does not honor conscience because it cuts the connection between conscience and personal integrity. Second, ordering society based on the false model of conscience-as-belief is not the path to true social harmony because it represents the imposition of the collective good, rather than the cultivation of the common good. The law supports both conscience and the common good by maintaining space for the cultivation of distinct moral identities among associations, empowering them to function as venues for conscience-driven action.

CONSCIENCE AS ACTION

Conscience is not just belief, passively held by the individual. It is belief applied to conduct, an act. Saint Paul portrayed conscience as a source of authority over a believer's conduct, and Thomas Aquinas continued that theme. Early Christian sources were also key in establishing the extrinsic authority of conscience by grounding it in the relationship between God and the believer. If conscience emanates in significant part from a moral sense instilled (or revealed) by God, it is imbued with authority that transcends the individual. Christianity also developed the notion that

---

[1] House of Lords–House of Commons Joint Committee on Human Rights, *Legislative Scrutiny: Sexual Orientation Regulations, Sixth Report of Session 06–07* (Feb. 26, 2007) (http://www.publications. parliament.uk/pa/jt200607/jtselect/jtrights/58/58.pdf)

conscience can function independently of temporal authority, revealing the possibility of disconnection between legal obligation and the dictates of conscience. This disconnection was not simply embedded in the life of the believer's mind; it was an impetus for civil disobedience, exploding from the moment of the crucifixion, which was grounded in the chasm between the moral and legal orders.

The conduct-centered essence of conscience is not limited to religious believers. Our society in general distinguishes conscience from belief. The point does not need intricate theoretical defense; it is plain from the lives of those who occupy conscience's pantheon of heroes. Thomas More would not swear an oath recognizing the King of England as head of the universal Christian church and was beheaded. If conscience were simply a belief, he would have been free to sign his name without compromising his integrity. Martin Luther King Jr. could have grasped with certainty the evils of segregation, but he ended up in a Birmingham jail because his cognitive grasp of those evils led him to march. Henry David Thoreau's conscience took form, not through his views on government, but through his refusal to pay taxes based on those views. Conscience becomes relevant, not in the sphere of belief, but on the question of whether the person holding the belief is "willing to conform their conduct – or at least their public expression – to some civil requirement."[2]

Of course, there are no guarantees that conscience will always be associated with conduct. Thomas Hobbes, for one, advised that "the law is the public conscience, by which [the citizen] hath already undertaken to be guided."[3] When "private consciences," in all their diversity, are given legitimacy outside the realm of personal belief, Hobbes predicted, "no man dare to obey the sovereign power."[4] It is important to note, however, what is lost if our conception of conscience slides into the privatized sphere of belief. As David Richards explains, erecting a wall between belief and action "shrivels conscience itself when conscientious belief cannot shape the experiences of our lives."[5]

If our focus is only on belief, conscience has very little to do with personal integrity, which requires a unity of action and belief. Protecting conscience-as-action is an essential component of ensuring that individuals' lives can unfold in narrative form. The moral coherence on which a personal narrative is built requires an ability to integrate the various strands of life into a relatively seamless story, as explained in chapter 2.

Discerning and maintaining the path of integration is not a passive endeavor – it is not simply what a person believes about what is happening *to* her. Rather, it must be prescriptive – it not only captures where we have been, but propels us in a

[2] Steven D. Smith, *What Does Religion Have to Do With Freedom of Conscience?*, 76 U. Colo. L. Rev. 911, 922 (2005).
[3] Thomas Hobbes, *Leviathan*, 239 (1660).
[4] *Id.*
[5] David A.J. Richards, *Conscience, Human Rights, and the Anarchist Challenge to the Obligation to Obey the Law*, 18 Ga. L. Rev. 771, 778–9 (1984).

particular direction. Liberty to act on belief – the exercise of conscience – may bring conflict and condemnation in a society in which the dictates of conscience vary so widely. But an externally oriented conscience is "preferable to the privatized, personalized conscience that amounts to meaninglessness."[6] When the state encroaches on the venues in which people live out their core beliefs, the cause of conscience suffers. It is no answer to point out the state's self-restraint in intruding on the inner sanctum of the mind; conscience cannot easily or prudently be separated from action.

CONCEPTIONS OF THE COMMON GOOD

Although concern for personal integrity cautions against the belief-action disconnect, so do the interests of society and the human freedom it serves. The external orientation of conscience underlies much of the other-regarding conduct engaged in by individuals. Maintaining space for conscience-driven action furthers the common good to the extent that individuals' moral beliefs motivate their participation in the myriad associations that stand between the individual and the state. Such participation is essential to social stability, to a prudently limited state, and to the prospects for human flourishing. These facets of the common good help capture the social value of conscience. Deciphering what the common good entails (and what it does not) is thus one path by which to bring the practical implications of conscience to the fore.

References to "the common good" may have achieved a new ubiquity in the 2008 presidential election,[7] but their traces stretch as far back as Aristotle. Today's invocations are often unhelpfully vacuous, but Aristotle got to the heart of the matter by linking social welfare with the possibility of conflicting values – a nascent embrace of value pluralism. In contrast to Plato, who attempted to eliminate potential grounds of conflict such as private property and exclusive sexual relations, Aristotle defended the importance of interpersonal bonds. In Martha Nussbaum's words, Aristotle saw in the "good city" that the "contingent conflict of values" is a "condition of the

---

[6] See Charles Taylor, *Sources of the Self: The Making of the Modern Identity*, 18 (1989).

[7] See e.g., Barack Obama, *Presidential Inauguration speech* ("The success of our economy has always depended not just on the size of our gross domestic product, but on the reach of our prosperity; on the ability to extend opportunity to every willing heart – not out of charity, but because it is the surest route to our common good."); Thomas L. Friedman, *Finishing America's Work*, New York Times, Nov. 5, 2008, at A35 ("[Obama] will only succeed if he is able to articulate a new politics of the common good," quoting Harvard professor Michael Sandel); Jane Lampman, *'08 Race has got Religion, Is that Good?* Christian Science Monitor, May 28, 2008, at 1 ("The voters care more about the common good than the culture wars," quoting sponsor of Compassion Forum debate between presidential candidates); Editor's Desk, Newsweek, Apr. 14, 2008, at 4 ("Politics being politics, big reforms requiring economic sacrifice and devotion to the common good are not easy to accomplish."); CNN Larry King Live, Feb. 13, 2008 ("We are going to be able to win . . . on an appeal to the common good," remarks of Democratic strategist David Wilhelm).

richness and vigor of civic life itself."[8] Particular bonds and loyalties among citizens provide civic life with "sources of motivation and concern that could be found in no other way."[9] Put simply, "personal separateness" is "an essential ingredient of human social goodness."[10]

Viewed from the perspective of the common good, state deference to conscience does not simply represent a laissez-faire judgment that individual liberty should be maximized for its own sake. A robust liberty of conscience actually bolsters the type of decentralized social bonding that has been lauded as a hallmark of American life; there is a close relationship between social health and the maintenance of a robust web of nongovernmental, freely chosen human associations known as "civil society."

This chapter's portrayal of the common good requires us to step back from our dominant rights-driven political theory – today shaped in significant part by the work of John Rawls[11] – in which persons are conceived of as "free and independent selves, unencumbered by moral or civic ties they have not chosen."[12] To an extent, this entire book seeks to answer questions posed by Michael Sandel in his own efforts to push back against rights-oriented liberalism with insights gleaned from the republican tradition:

> How might our political discourse engage rather than avoid the moral and religious convictions people bring to the public realm? And how might the public life of a pluralist society cultivate in citizens the expansive self-understandings that civic engagement requires?[13]

Sandel may not agree with every conclusion drawn in this book's second half, but we start with similar concerns, as do other writers, such as Charles Taylor, Michael Walzer, and Alasdair MacIntyre, who frequently bear the "communitarian" label.[14] Indeed, conscience's relational dimension can be understood as a lens through which to bring our citizens' "expansive self-understandings" into clearer focus. It is the self-transcendence of our myriad moral claims that, when given social space to flourish, contributes powerfully to the common good.

To begin to paint a picture of the relationship between conscience and civil society requires cognizance of the distinction between the common good and the collective good. Ordering society according to the collective good has marked the

---

[8] Martha Nussbaum, *The Fragility of Goodness: Luck and Ethics in Greek Tragedy and Philosophy*, 353 (1986).

[9] *Id.*

[10] *Id.*

[11] See John Rawls, *Political Liberalism* (1993); John Rawls, *A Theory of Justice* (1971).

[12] Michael J. Sandel, *Democracy's Discontent: America in Search of a Public Philosophy*, 6 (1996).

[13] *Id.* at 7.

[14] Challenging the depiction of a person as a "free and independent self" is a common theme of these writers, but my engagement with their work does not rely on the "communitarian" label, both because their work fits uneasily within any unified characterization and because they themselves have expressed discomfort with the label.

range of totalitarian regimes across history, but a fixation on the collective good can also operate more subtly, not so much as the chosen end of civilization, but as the chosen means of securing laudable goals. The French Revolution famously enshrined the ideals of liberty and equality by imposing them on the society in an unmistakably top-down manner, insisting that "[t]he principle of all sovereignty resides essentially in the nation," and that "[n]o body nor authority may exercise any authority that does not proceed directly from the nation."[15]

A single source of authority is inimical to the common good, as is the opposite extreme of casting each individual as a self-sufficient, atomistic sovereign. The French philosopher Jacques Maritain explains, "[t]he common good is common because it is received in persons, each one of whom is a mirror of the whole."[16] In Maritain's work, as elucidated by Patrick Brennan, "the common good is not the collection or a summation of private goods; neither is it the good of a whole such that the goods of the components are sacrificed to the good of the whole."[17] Rather, it is "the shared life of a political community of free persons living oriented toward justice, friendship, and the transcendent."[18]

The state, as society's only legitimate purveyor of coercive force, must act with deference toward the dimension of the common good that is not defined by the collective will. This is why it is so important that the state recognize and respect the rights needed to protect the human person from overbearing state incursions on individual and associational autonomy. The state's self-restraint helps ensure that the common good is not defined and imposed from above as either a uniform, fixed norm or as an idiosyncratic product of office-holders' own moral claims, but is instead realized from the bottom up, constituted by the conscience-driven decisions and day-to-day actions of individuals and the communities to which they belong.

The state's self-restraint cannot be absolute, of course, for the common good requires a level of social justice and order that only state authority can ensure. But the exercise of state authority must be premised on a vision of society that is not always apparent in today's rights-based discourse. The common good's correlation with state self-restraint is expressed well in Stephen Carter's work focusing on the need for society to embody diversity, difference, and dialogue. He cautions, "the idea that the state should not only create a set of meanings, but try to alter the structure of institutions that do not match it, is ultimately destructive of democracy because it destroys the differences that create the dialectic."[19] Associations formed via the impetus of conscience possess an independent normative authority, empowering

---

[15] *Declaration of the Rights of Man* (1789).

[16] Jacques Maritain, *The Person and the Common Good*, 49 (1966).

[17] Patrick Brennan, "Jacques Maritain," in *The Teachings of Modern Christianity on Law, Politics and Human Nature*, 75, 94 (Witte and Alexander, eds., 2006).

[18] *Id.* at 95.

[19] Stephen L. Carter, "Liberal Hegemony, Religious Resistance," in *Christian Perspectives on Legal Thought*, 25, 33 (2001).

citizens through a shared sense of identity, purpose, and meaning to participate in projects that are bigger than themselves – a hallmark of a vibrant civil society.

At the same time, focusing on the relationships necessary to pursue the common good is not to subvert the individual. Indeed, a robust system of individual rights, prudently focused in purpose and scope, promotes both the individual and the common good as a wonderfully diverse whole. It is not just the maximization of individual choice that we aim to protect through a framework of rights, but the promotion of meaningful social interactions over questions of the good. Even the sheer exercise of conscience can provide an interpersonal bridge as a common moral experience "capable of being accessed . . . from a wide variety of differing belief systems."[20] If we hope to facilitate shared conceptions of the good, we must acknowledge that the facilitation is itself a deeply relational process. As Alasdair MacIntyre explains, "we learn what our common good is, and indeed what our own individual goods are, not primarily and never only by theoretical reflection, but in everyday shared activities and the evaluations of alternatives that those activities impose."[21]

The common good does not lend itself to easy definition or fixed criteria, but five different perspectives informed by philosophy, theology, and sociology help fill out its content and clarify its connection with conscience. All five aim to justify the decentralization of social power, including moral authority. Although they share an unmistakable commitment to individual liberty, it is noteworthy that their justifications are not grounded in a reflexive enshrinement of individual rights. The following five perspectives underscore the extent to which the common good requires us to recognize the social dimension of freedom: subsidiarity, sphere sovereignty, organic solidarity, the moral marketplace, and cultural cognition.

1. Subsidiarity

Although the principle has now been embraced across the political spectrum – for example, by both the European Union and the George W. Bush Administration – subsidiarity was first articulated explicitly in the late nineteenth century by the Catholic Church as it struggled to define its vision of the social order in a way that avoided the twin pitfalls of individualism and collectivism. The Church needed to find a way to express the dignity of the person without abandoning the proposition that humans are inescapably social creatures. Subsidiarity is thus premised on the empowerment of individuals and groups to meet the needs around them, with the state acting, not as the primary locus of social action, but in a supportive, secondary role. This dispersal of social authority represents the "bottom up" ordering of society in which needs are met, where possible, by the moral agents who are closest to them.

---

[20] W. Cole Durham Jr., *Religious Liberty and the Call of Conscience*, 42 DePaul L. Rev. 71, 72 (1992).

[21] Alasdair MacIntyre, *Dependent Rational Animals: Why Human Beings Need the Virtues*, 136 (1999).

The person in need should be cared for first by her family; if the family cannot do so effectively, then her neighborhood or church should step in; if they cannot, then her town should act, and so on up the chain. Only if the lower bodies cannot address a problem effectively should the higher bodies step in. The importance of the free, meaningful, and efficacious operation of lower bodies presents the "most weighty principle" of subsidiarity, as Pope Pius XI explained:

> Just as it is gravely wrong to take from individuals what they can accomplish by their own initiative and industry and give it to the community, so also it is an injustice and at the same time a grave evil and disturbance of right order to assign to a greater and higher association what lesser and subordinate organizations can do. For every social activity ought of its very nature to furnish help to the members of the body social, and never destroy or absorb them.[22]

Subsidiarity pushes back against the temptation to view the individual as a decontextualized rational agent by reminding us that the human person is, above all, relational – not just as an empirical description, but as a normative claim. And this relational nature must shape not only our theoretical vision of society but our practical responses to everyday social problems. Saint Augustine's thought is just one notable example, as explicated by Jean Bethke Elshtain:

> We cannot 'combine many relationships' in one single self; rather, our 'connections should be separated and spread among individuals, and that in this way they should help to bind social life more effectively by involving in their plurality a plurality of persons.... Thus affection stretches over a greater number.' The social tie radiates out from kinship groups to ever widening circles of sociability; near and far, distant and intimate. There is something mysterious about all this, about what Augustine calls an 'inherent sense of decency.' Any society that loses this sense of decency is a society in very big trouble, indeed. It is a society that has repudiated, whether tacitly or explicitly, the ground of human being and of human being-among-others.[23]

The doctrine of subsidiarity embodies a recognition of the "human being-among-others," and it reflects the conviction that the individual's relationship to others cannot be captured simply by conceiving of her as a preference-expressing participant in the political process or the free market.[24] Instead, the human person "is realized in various intermediary groups, beginning with the family and including economic, social, political and cultural groups which stem from human nature itself and have

---

[22] Pius XI, Encyclical Letter, Quadragesimo anno ¶ 79 (1931).
[23] Jean Bethke Elshtain, "Augustine and Diversity," in *A Catholic Modernity?*, 99 (James L. Heft, ed., 1999).
[24] John Paul II, Encyclical Letter, Centesimus annus ¶ 49 (1991) ("[I]t seems as though he exists only as a producer and consumer of goods, or as an object of State administration.").

their own autonomy, always with a view to the common good."[25] These institutions operate not through power, as political society does, but through "affinities, voluntary alliances and natural forms of solidarity."[26] This fundamental ordering "must be respected" because "needs are best understood and satisfied by people who are closest to them and who act as neighbours to those in need," a perception that derives, in turn, from the fact that "certain kinds of demands often call for a response which is not simply material but which is capable of perceiving the deeper human need."[27]

Casting social action as the responsibility of those who are in the closest proximity to a given problem reconfigures the modern citizen as a proactive moral agent, not simply as a reactive subject of higher authority. Contrary to its more conservative interpretations, subsidiarity does not foreclose a role for centralized authority, for often local problems are not susceptible to effective remedy without society's collectively channeled attention. For example, in today's market economies, subsidiarity clearly contemplates effective labor unions and a vigorous antitrust enforcement regime, both of which require legislative action and oversight by a central government authority. But subsidiarity does reframe our image of the modern state, envisioning it as a resource for localized empowerment and coordination, rather than as the arbiter and provider of the social good. This preference for the local puts individuals and their relationships at the center of the social order, ensuring the efficacy of their conscience-driven commitments.

2. Sphere Sovereignty

While subsidiarity functions along a vertical axis, pushing authority down to more local levels, the concept of "sphere sovereignty" introduces a horizontal axis to a pluralist social order. Closely associated with the nineteenth-century Dutch pastor and statesman Abraham Kuyper, sphere sovereignty limits state authority to the political sphere, while it carves out parallel spheres of authority for other areas of social life such as family, education, the arts, science, and business. Kuyper never provided a detailed blueprint for allocating power among the spheres, but his framing of sovereignty in these terms provided the vision of a social order in which voluntary associations are dependent on the state for neither their legitimacy nor authority. Sphere sovereignty has had enormous impact on Americans – particularly on many Protestant intellectuals; for our current inquiry, its significance lies in its emphasis on the connection between the common good and the maintenance of multiple sources of authority in society.

[25] *Id.* ¶ 13.
[26] Pontifical Council for the Family, The Family and Human Rights ¶ 64 (1999).
[27] John Paul II, Encyclical Letter, Centesimus annus ¶ 48 (1991).

Kuyper was motivated by the oppressive sameness that he saw emerging in the Netherlands. He went so far as to call "false uniformity the curse of modern life" in that "it disregards the ordinances of God revealed not only in Scripture but throughout his entire creation."[28] Conceding that "corporate bodies" had "oppressed the individual" in the past and thus needed to be "pulled down," he wondered whether the individual was "freer now or rather defenseless and helpless when faced with the all-devouring super-corporation of the State?"[29]

As a Calvinist, Kuyper's theory of the common good was as much a statement of theology as it was of politics or sociology. Two Calvinist tenets were especially important for him. First, Calvinism emphasizes that, in light of original sin, man is totally depraved. As a consequence, his view of the state has an eye toward human sinfulness more than toward the potential for human greatness. John Calvin had embraced the republican form of government in light of our sinfulness, because "it is safer and better to let several people together steer the ship of state so that one may restrain the other when the lust for power might degenerate into tyranny."[30]

Second, Calvinists believe in God's total sovereignty, even to the point of God foreordaining from eternity who will be saved. According to Reformed theologian Richard Mouw, Kuyper believed that "God created a macroordering of diverse spheres of cultural interaction, and he gave to each of the individual spheres its own unique internal orderedness."[31] In contrast to other Protestants such as Luther, who viewed the created cosmos as ordered but society as human-created chaos, Kuyper believed that there was order to be discerned in all of creation, including society. This is important because it shifts his focus from the instrumental value of nonstate entities to their embodiment of "diverse patterns of human interaction that are important elements in God's structuring of the creation."[32] As a result, these entities no longer bear the burden of justifying their existence or liberty to the state; they stand shoulder to shoulder with the state as coparticipants in the divine plan.

Although our fallen nature cautions against the consolidation of authority, God's sovereignty suggests that the social order is subject to a divine plan. On these two bedrocks, Kuyper built his principle of sphere sovereignty. Observing that "the individual exists only in groups, and only in groups can the whole become manifest," he urged Christians to recognize that:

> [T]here are in life as many spheres as there are constellations in the sky and that the circumference of each has been drawn on a fixed radius from the center of a unique principle, namely the apostolic injunction ["each in its own order" from

---

[28] *Abraham Kuyper: A Centennial Reader*, 35 (James D. Bratt, ed., 1998).
[29] *Id.* at 282.
[30] *Id.* at 285 (quoting Calvin's Institutes at IV/20/8).
[31] Richard J. Mouw, "Some Reflections on Sphere Sovereignty," in *Religion, Pluralism, and Public Life: Abraham Kuyper's Legacy for the Twenty-First Century*, 87, 95–96 (Luis E. Lugo, ed., 2000).
[32] *Id.* at 91.

1 Corinthians 15:23].... Just as we speak of a 'moral world,' a 'scientific world,' a 'business world,' the 'world of art,' so we can more properly speak of a 'sphere' of morality, of the family, of social life, each with its own domain. And because each comprises its own domain, each has its own Sovereign within its bounds.[33]

To be sure, Kuyper was not the first to link Calvinism with a robust liberty for associations. Nearly three centuries earlier, Calvinist philosopher Johannes Althusius (1557–1638) noted that "families, cities, and provinces existed by nature prior to realms, and gave birth to them,"[34] and that a law's propriety depends on the nature of the association to which it is applied. (Contrast this Calvinist theme with the political theory of Aristotle, for whom "the polis was the most supreme community in which human beings achieve the ultimate destination and perfection of their lives."[35])

Kuyper's distinctive contribution lies in his adaptation of Calvinist insights to modern society, laboring to hem in not only the overreaching state but also the overreaching church. Perhaps because of his unique vantage point as scholar (he founded the Free University of Amsterdam), pastor, journalist, and statesman (he served as prime minister), he appreciated the dangers of infringement from any number of spheres. No sphere, in his estimation, was privileged to stand in judgment on the rest of society. This may have served to immunize his framework from secularist challenges, despite its explicit theological foundation.

This is not to suggest that the boundaries of Kuyper's spheres were impermeable, although the degree of permeability remains somewhat unclear in his writing. Kuyper conceded that absolute autonomy for each sphere was not possible given the capacity for tyranny within a group and between groups. Indeed, Kuyper's work was used to justify separate ethnic cultures within South African apartheid ideology.[36] Kuyper was not opposed to state authority by any means; he saw the state as "the power that protects the individual and defines the mutual relationships among the visible spheres."[37] As such, the government has both the right and duty 1) to adjudicate disputes between spheres, 2) to defend the weak against the strong within each sphere, and 3) to exercise coercive power to ensure that citizens "bear personal and financial burdens for the maintenance of the natural unity of the State."[38] Still, Kuyper insisted that the state "does not confer but acknowledges" the authority of other spheres, and in defining laws governing the relationships among the spheres,

---

[33] Kuyper Reader, *supra* note 28, at 467.

[34] Johannes Althusius, *Politica*, ch. XXXIX (1614).

[35] Henk E.S. Woldring, *Multiform Responsibility and the Revitalization of Civil Society* in Kuyper 175, 180 (citing Aristotle, Politics).

[36] T. Dunbar Moodie, *The Rise of Afrikanerdom: Power, Apartheid, and the Afrikaner Civil Religion*, 153–74, 215–33 (1975) (cited in Mouw, *supra* note 31, at 106).

[37] Kuyper Reader, *supra* note 28, at 468.

[38] Mouw, *supra* note 31, at 89 (quoting Kuyper, Lectures on Calvinism 97 [Eerdmans 1931]).

"is bound by the choice of a Higher will, as expressed in the nature and purpose of these spheres."[39]

Some students of Kuyper have insisted that sphere sovereignty provides a much stronger bulwark against the overbearing state than subsidiarity does. Herman Dooyeweerd, for example, sees subsidiarity as only a pragmatic limitation on state authority, calling for lower bodies to remain autonomous to the extent prudent.[40] He portrays sphere sovereignty, by contrast, as more than a "hands off" policy; its boundaries are natural, embedded in the divine plan.[41] It is not a case of the state permitting authority to reside in lower bodies; it is a case of the state abiding by the natural order. James Skillen and Rockne McCarthy approach the distinction from another angle, asserting that although the Catholic tradition sees the state as "the inherent natural development of a higher unity in human society," for Kuyper it is more like "a dike against the flood of chaos produced by the brokenness of sinful human beings."[42]

Whether these distinctions have much practical import is another matter. As noted, Kuyper acknowledged that the state must act to protect individuals and to adjudicate disputes among the spheres. Identifying when state action is justified within these categories is not discernibly different from subsidiarity's instruction that the state should act when lower bodies cannot address a problem effectively. Both principles require a healthy dose of prudence in application.

Indeed, given the difficulty in reaching agreement on when individual well-being or social conflict warrant state interference with a sphere's autonomy, violations of sphere sovereignty will not always be clear. But sphere sovereignty provides a lens that brings the danger of some modern tendencies into relief. For example, when Mario Cuomo memorably referred to all Americans as a "family," Kuyper's cautions loomed large. As Jean Bethke Elshtain explained, "to call a modern nation-state a family, in the interest of connecting us to one another, should be faulted because it too easily transforms citizens into Big Children."[43]

For our purposes, what sphere sovereignty contributes is a vision of society that is ordered around individuals and the communities to which they commit themselves. As John Witte observes, Kuyper's social spheres – ranging from churches, families, schools, unions, guilds, plantations, clubs, and convents to corporations – "depend upon the voluntary association and activity of private parties."[44] Perhaps even more strongly

---

[39] Kuyper Reader, *supra* note 28, at 468.

[40] Mouw, *supra* note 31, at 93 (discussing Dooyeweerd, Roots of Western Culture: Pagan, Secular, and Christian Options 127).

[41] *Id.*

[42] Paul E. Sigmund, "Subsidiarity, Solidarity, and Liberation," in *Religion, Pluralism, and Public Life: Abraham Kuyper's Legacy for the Twenty-First Century*, 205, 219. (quoting James M. Skillen and Rockne McCarthy, *Political Order and the Plural Structure of Society*, 401 [Scholars Press 1991]).

[43] Jean Elshtain, *Mario Cuomo Isn't Your Daddy*, New Oxford Review (Dec. 1996) at 26 (cited by Mouw, *supra* note 31, at 108).

[44] John Witte Jr., "The Biography and Biology of Liberty," in *Religion, Pluralism, and Public Life: Abraham Kuyper's Legacy for the Twenty-First Century*, 243, 246.

than subsidiarity does, sphere sovereignty does not ask the state to grant space to the wide array of conscience-driven commitments. Rather, it offers a three-fold reminder to the state: first, that its authority is limited not just by the interests and liberties of its citizens as individuals, but by the interests and liberties of its citizens in relationship; second, that these relationships are centered in endeavors that are not within the state's purview; and third, that the boundaries of this purview are not of the state's choosing.

3. *Organic Solidarity*

Both subsidiarity and sphere sovereignty are premised on certain theological claims about the human person and society. With the rise of the social sciences, normative assertions regarding the value of decentralized authority have just as frequently been secular in outlook. The most prominent of the early pioneers of this trend is Emile Durkheim, the father of sociology. The nature of "society" took on an almost mystical status in his work, as he resisted the tendency to see society as a material entity lying outside the person. For Durkheim, according to Robert Bellah, society "is something deeply inner, since . . . it is the source of morality, personality, and life itself at the human level. It is something on which we all depend whether we know it or not."[45]

Much of Durkheim's work was driven by his categorization of social solidarity as either mechanical or organic. Mechanical solidarity resulted from "likeness" and was found in early societies "characterized by a common conscience enforced by coercive or repressive sanctions."[46] As a society grows more complex, organic solidarity emerges from "a system of cooperative relations based on the division of labor and characterized by restitutive sanctions."[47] So while the simpler societies produce cohesion based on similarities, modern societies achieve "the same end through the interdependencies induced by individual differences."[48] The division of labor looms large in organic solidarity because specialized functions produce mutual dependence, which means that "everyone has his own sphere of action even as he remains inseparable from everyone else."[49]

The division of labor would not, on its own, produce a just social order absent the rise of communities corresponding to that division. A society of unorganized individuals would require a "hypertrophied State," which would result in a "veritable sociological monstrosity."[50] Durkheim explained that the collective activity on which society and its members depend "is always too complex to be able to be expressed through the single and unique organ of the State."[51] If community is limited to the

45 Emile Durkheim, *On Morality and Society*, ix (Robert Bellah, ed., and intro., 1973).
46 *Id.* at xxiii.
47 *Id.*
48 Emile Durkheim, *On Institutional Analysis*, 11 (Mark Traugott, intro., 1978).
49 *Id.* at 206.
50 Emile Durkheim, *The Division of Labor in Society*, 28 (Free Press ed., 1947).
51 *Id.*

state, individuals will "inevitably lose contact, become detached, and thus society disintegrates."[52] Consequently, Durkheim insisted on the importance of mediating structures – those "secondary groups near enough to the individuals to attract them strongly in their sphere of action and drag them, in this way, into the general torrent of social life."[53]

With the division of labor, in Durkheim's view, comes a division of moral commitments and obligations. He believed that morality cannot be entirely self-regarding, and thus that "[m]oral life begins with membership of a group, however small the group may be."[54] Durkheim also embraced moral particularism, not in the context of individual morality, but in the affairs of a group, especially in the area of professional ethics. He called for the establishment of professional associations not only to stand between individual workers and the state, but also to help fashion a workable moral framework based on the function and responsibilities of each particular profession.

Durkheim was not opposed to the use of collective power in the service of moral norms. Believing that only "collective power" can "stand . . . above the individual" and "legitimately make laws for him," he insisted that a "system of morals is always the affair of a group and can operate only if this group protects them by its authority."[55] He went so far as to suggest that this group-based framework of professional ethics should be attached to the state.[56] He believed that the expansion of state power is compatible with the primacy of the individual, asserting that "the functions of the State may expand, without any diminishing of the individual" because "history gives sound authority for this relation of cause and effect as between the progress of moral individualism and the advance of the State."[57] Society, in his view, is what created moral individualism and made itself the servant of the individual.[58] In other words, "[w]hat lies at the basis of the right of the individual is not the notion of the individual as such, but the way in which the society conceives the right and the valuation it puts on it."[59]

In retrospect, it is easy to accuse Durkheim of being overly optimistic about social progress and the edifying forces of collective, impersonal ideals. For example, he likened morality to science, both of which "imply that the individual is capable of raising himself above his own peculiar point of view and of living an impersonal life."[60] Nevertheless, his focus on social roles and functions allowed him to recognize empirically that an awareness of society itself "forces the individual to transcend

---

[52] *Id.*
[53] *Id.*
[54] Emile Durkheim, *Sociology and Philosophy*, 52 (D. Pocock, trans., 1953).
[55] Emile Durkheim, *Professional Ethics and Civic Morals*, 6–7 (C. Brookfield, trans., 1958).
[56] *Id.* at 39.
[57] *Id.* at 57.
[58] Emile Durkheim, *Sociology and Philosophy*, 59 (D. Pocock, trans., 1953).
[59] Emile Durkheim, *Professional Ethics and Civic Morals*, xxxix (Georges Davy, intro., 1958).
[60] Emile Durkheim, *The Elementary Forms of the Religious Life*, 445 (2nd ed., 1976).

himself and to participate in a higher form of life."[61] As noted, he was not oblivious to the dangers of state power, believing in the need for secondary groups to act as counter balance. Such groups are useful for the specific interests they are created to serve and for the wider purpose of forming a condition "essential to the emancipation of the individual."[62] A working democracy allows for the protection of individual rights and the recognition of individual dignity, but only to the extent that citizens can transcend their own self-interest. For this, according to Durkheim, we need associations. Not only are they necessary to "prevent the State from tyrannizing over individuals," but they are "equally essential to prevent individuals from absorbing the State."[63] After all, adherence to "some thing that goes beyond the individual, and to the interests of the group he belongs to, is the very source of all moral activity."[64]

Durkheim pioneered the sociological basis for defending conscience's relational dimension. Any suggestion of a "collective conscience" as a set of moral norms believed and enforced by the society as a whole is a nonstarter for students of modernity. At the same time, the Enlightenment's elevation of the individual conscience as the locus of moral discernment proved unhelpfully feeble in facilitating the sort of discourse on which any moral community depends. Durkheim's concept of organic solidarity bridges the individual and the collective, demonstrating why modernity did not invariably signal the demise of community. The modern moral life is one grounded in difference, not sameness. The division of labor spawns dependencies and commitments that are more personal and meaningful than the all-encompassing coercion of mechanical solidarity. Durkheim's work maintains the modern concern for the individual, but shows that real concern for the individual must include concern for the relationships on which the individual's moral life depends.

4. The Moral Marketplace

Writing in the early twentieth century, British political theorist Harold Laski was concerned with the nature and function of state authority. Like Durkheim, Laski was committed to the moral primacy of the individual. While Durkheim sought to describe the individual's place within a vast framework of social relationships, Laski's analysis was focused much more closely on the individual's relationship with the state. As one of the first theorists to invoke "pluralism" as the organizing label of modern society, Laski's work sheds light on how the very nature of state authority presupposes a vibrant landscape of nonstate associations.

Laski's political theory was premised on individuals' plural memberships, allegiances, and affinities. As he memorably put it, "[w]hether we will or no, we are bundles of hyphens."[65] Although we are shaped by our associations, we are not

---

[61] Emile Durkheim, *Sociology and Philosophy*, 93 (D. Pocock, trans., 1953).
[62] Emile Durkheim, *Professional Ethics and Civic Morals*, 63 (1958).
[63] *Id.* at 106.
[64] *Id.* at 24.
[65] Harold Laski, *The Foundations of Sovereignty*, 170 (1921).

absorbed by them.[66] Just as the individual rises above the authority of any single association, she also rises above authority understood as the brute exercise of state power on its own terms. Laski embraced a consent theory of law, arguing that "[t]here is no sanction for law other than the consent of the human mind."[67] The authority of the state's claims, then, is contingent on our acceptance of its claims as binding on us. Our acceptance depends on the context and nature of the claim and on the nature of our conflicting allegiances that might be relevant in that context. After all, in Laski's view "the State is only one of the associations to which [the individual] happens to belong, and [she] will give it exactly that pre-eminence – and no more – to which on the particular occasion of conflict, its possibly superior moral claim will entitle it."[68]

Echoing the realist view of his friend Oliver Wendell Holmes, who wrote that the law is simply a prediction of what judges will do, rather than a freestanding set of principles, Laski rejected the notion that the state embodies some sort of unified will. Instead, "the mind of society" is "merely a metaphorical way of describing a course of action which is made valid by translation into fact."[69] Individuals do not obey the state simply because it is the state; they judge the state "from the angle of satisfactions they think it should provide."[70] In other words, the state is just one more participant in the marketplace of moral claims, each seeking to attract the individual's allegiance in a given scenario.

This "pluralistic theory of the State" dissolves "the inherent claim of the State to obedience," and "insists that the State, like every other association, shall prove itself by what it achieves."[71] In this regard, Laski espoused a more individualistic view of social authority than the ones represented by sphere sovereignty and subsidiarity. Unlike sphere sovereignty, Laski's theory "does not try to work out with tedious elaboration the respective spheres of State or group or individual," instead leaving the question "to the test of the event."[72] Unlike subsidiarity, Laski's theory does not order social actors hierarchically in terms of their proximity to human need. Rather, all groups compete for the allegiance of individuals. If the state is to succeed, it must persuade the individual to support its cause, and it will persuade them only to the extent that it respects them. The state's respect for conscience, then, is driven by prudent concern for its own authority: as Laski puts it, whatever "concerns the conscience of man, whatever brings its activity into operation, must, for the state, be sacred ground."[73]

This concern for conscience has two practical implications for the state. First, the state's authority must support the exercise of responsibility by individuals. Laski

---

[66] Harold Laski, *Authority in the Modern State*, 65 (1919).
[67] Harold Laski, *Studies in the Problem of Sovereignty*, 14 (1917).
[68] *Id.* at 19.
[69] Harold Laski, *Liberty in the Modern State*, 28–9 (1930).
[70] Harold Laski, *The State in Theory and Practice*, 5 (1935).
[71] Harold Laski, *Studies in the Problem of Sovereignty*, 23.
[72] *Id.* at 23–4.
[73] Harold Laski, *Authority in the Modern State*, 57.

found it pointless to criticize an individual for being "uninterested in politics:"; what individuals are interested in is "anything which nearly touches their lives, provided only that they have a share in its application."[74] Accordingly, society must guard against "the concentration of power."[75]

Second, the state supports the exercise of responsibility by individuals by supporting the autonomy of associations. Laski lamented, "[n]othing is more stupid than for the state to regard the individual and itself as the only entities of which account must be taken, or to suggest that other groups live by its good pleasure."[76] To do so is to assume mistakenly "that the activities of man in his relation to government exhaust his nature."[77] Laski went so far as to describe a person's freedom "to combine with his fellows for joint action in some realm in which they have a kindred interest" as "the essence of liberty."[78] Writing during World War II, he saw no meaningful difference between the partition of Poland and a state's suppression of a Communist party because each is "an attack upon a corporate experience – a wrong attack because it does not persuade those who share that experience to abandon its implications."[79]

This takes Laski back to his marketplace theme. The state must, in a sense, appeal to customer demand. Associations may conflict with the state's intentions, but suppression of associations will only succeed if "the need they supply is, in some equally adequate form, answered by the state itself."[80] And "there are many such interests that the state cannot serve."[81] Laws can shape the individual, but they cannot absorb her. A person will not obey a law that conflicts with her fundamental beliefs. Whatever the wisdom or folly behind the belief, a person will not "feel free unless they can act by their own moral certainties."[82] Some, in fact, will "deliberately decide that an anarchy in which they seek to maintain some principle is preferable to an order in which that principle must be surrendered."[83]

The moral marketplace serves a "checking" function on state efforts to instill conformity in matters governed by contested moral norms.[84] This seeming resistance to majority rule actually is in keeping with democratic values because it limits the contexts in which citizens are defied by their government. The moral marketplace contemplates a bottom-up, rather than top-down, approach to contentious

---

[74] *Id.* at 91.

[75] *Id.*

[76] *Id.* at 56.

[77] *Id.*

[78] Harold Laski, *Liberty in the Modern State*, 121.

[79] *Id.* at 239.

[80] Harold Laski, *Authority in the Modern State*, 56.

[81] *Id.*

[82] Harold Laski, *Liberty in the Modern State*, 71.

[83] *Id.*

[84] See Vincent Blasi, *The Checking Value in First Amendment Theory*, 1977 Am. B. Found. Research J. 521, 539 ("Because no concentrated force is available to check it, government misconduct may properly be regarded as a more serious evil than misconduct by private parties who are subject to the checking power of government.").

social issues. The tolerance valued by the moral marketplace is not the placing of artificial boundaries around each individual, beyond which their own moral claims are rendered powerless; rather, it means, as William Galston puts it, "the principled refusal to use coercive state power to impose one's views on others, and therefore a commitment to moral competition through recruitment and persuasion alone."[85]

The moral marketplace has been effectively shut down in some of the more controversial state actions that are the focus of this book's second half. In its place stands the fully autonomous individual, empowered by the state to overcome the group's authority to obstruct her chosen path – even if that path directly contradicts the group's own moral claims. Laski's work is a cautionary reminder that restricting the authority of associations to embody their own distinct – even deviant – moral identities is not necessarily a tool that enhances legitimate state authority; when such maneuvers serve to marginalize the moral convictions of a group's members, state authority dissipates. There are times when an association's activities threaten a level of harm that is unacceptable, but a consent-based vision of democracy mandates that the coercion of associations be a narrow exception in a moral marketplace built on the art of persuasion. Conscience drives allegiance in the moral marketplace, and a concern for conscience warrants deference to other market actors.

5. Cultural Cognition

Building on previous work linking culture and risk perception,[86] Yale law professor Dan Kahan has developed and explored the concept of "cultural cognition." His work mounts a cognitive challenge to liberalism's premise that the state can remain neutral on ultimate questions of the good, so that individuals are free to pursue their own visions of the good. The state's capacity for neutrality presumes the citizenry's capacity for neutrality, and that presumption is highly problematic. In Kahan's view, "we lack the psychological capacity . . . to make, interpret, and administer law without indulging sensibilities pervaded by our attachments to highly contested visions of the good."[87]

When applied to public policy debates, these moral sensibilities lead us to "instinctively trust those who share our values" even if they are biased in a certain direction by emotion or dissonance avoidance.[88] Because we are "inclined to associate with

---

[85] William A. Galston, *Expressive Liberty and Constitutional Democracy: The Case of Freedom of Conscience*, 48 Am. J. Juris. 149, 151 (2003).

[86] See, e.g., Mary Douglas and Aaron Wildavsky, *Risk and Culture: An Essay on the Selection of Technical and Environmental Dangers*, 9 (1982) ("We choose the risks in the same package as we choose our social institutions. Since an individual cannot look in all directions at once, social life demands organization of bias. People order their universe through social bias.").

[87] Dan M. Kahan, *The Cognitively Illiberal State*, 60 Stan. L. Rev. 115, 116–117 (2007).

[88] *Id.* at 117.

those who share our cultural outlooks," there are "highly uniform views of societal harms among persons of shared cultural persuasions."[89] When behavior violates our own moral norms, we are likely to view that behavior "as endangering public health, undermining civil order, and impeding the accumulation of societal wealth."[90] This insight undercuts the utility of John Stuart Mill's famous "harm principle," which holds that individual liberty should be restricted only as necessary to prevent harm to others.[91] The principle is rendered essentially meaningless with the realization that individuals tend to perceive as harmful any threat to their own moral convictions.[92] As Kahan and Donald Braman explain, "[i]t's not comforting – indeed, it's psychically disabling – to entertain beliefs about what's harmless and what's harmful that force one to renounce commitments and affiliations essential to one's identity."[93]

Because our moral convictions color our beliefs about facts, we tend to "perceive the state's adoption of instrumental policies, no less than its adoption of symbolic ones, as adjudicating the competence and virtue of those who adhere to competing cultural outlooks."[94] For example, individuals who oppose drug criminalization and antisodomy laws tend to support gun control even though all three types of laws pose significant restrictions on personal liberty and target behavior that defies certain cultural norms. Gun possession, unlike drug use and sodomy, defies egalitarian and communitarian norms, "the holders of which despise guns as symbols of patriarchy and racism, indifference and distrust."[95] Even though lawful activities such as backyard pool ownership and alcohol consumption are each much more deadly than guns, Kahan concludes that gun control advocates "selectively accept evidence of the need and feasibility of gun control because gun ownership, unlike swimming in backyard pools and drinking beer, offends their values."[96]

Kahan does not mine cultural cognition to mourn the impossibility of liberalism; he uses it to chart a course beyond the "culture war" tenor of much of our public discourse. In particular, Kahan faults the modern insistence – popularized by John Rawls and others – on conducting our political life exclusively through "public reason," using secular terms accessible across the spectrum of cultural and moral identities. Kahan believes that this amounts to "a form of false consciousness that compounds the impulse to enforce a moral orthodoxy by enabling its agents to deny (to themselves even more than to others) that this is exactly what they are

[89] *Id.* at 121.
[90] *Id.* at 117.
[91] John Stuart Mill, *On Liberty*, 80 (D. Bromwich and G. Kateb, eds., 2003).
[92] Kahan, *supra* note 87, at 117.
[93] Dan M. Kahan & Donald Braman, *Cultural Cognition and Public Policy*, 24 Yale L. & Pol'y Rev. 149, 155 (2006).
[94] Kahan, *supra* note 87, at 130.
[95] *Id.* at 134.
[96] *Id.* at 136.

doing."97 For example, in *Roe v. Wade*, the Supreme Court trumpeted its own above-the-fray agnosticism on the question of personhood and unborn life, as though the result could somehow be portrayed in morally neutral terms. Judging by the response to *Roe* that has unfolded over the ensuing decades, the court's claim to neutrality only embittered those who were already inclined to oppose the holding on moral grounds. It is no answer to the problem of moral disagreement "to think that denuding the law of cultural resonances is the best way to assure citizens that the law respects their identities."98

In the place of public reason, Kahan offers "expressive overdetermination" to bring cultural values into the center of our legal and political discourse, and, in fact, to "self-consciously [multiply] the cultural meanings that laws are susceptible of bearing."99 Proponents of public reason are correct to focus on discourse norms, but they reach the wrong conclusion. If we are serious about mitigating "the problem of cognitive illiberalism," we should encourage citizens to "strive to infuse law [with] as many diverse and competing cultural meanings as it can possibly bear – [that] is the best way to mitigate (if not solve) the problem of cognitive illiberalism."100

"Expressive overdetermination" is a strategy that bears promise for the vitality of individuals and the associations to which they commit themselves. The very concept of cultural cognition recognizes that "individuals process information in a manner that protects their group-based identity."101 Kahan does not, however, mistakenly assume that valuing one's group-based identity invariably spawns a group-based moral imperialism. His research suggests that most people are "expressive moderates" who "react defiantly when they perceive that adoption of a law would denigrate their cultural worldview," but as "long as they can see evidence that the law in fact affirms their outlooks, they do not demand that the law be framed in a way that denies persons of an opposing cultural persuasion the opportunity to experience the same sense of affirmation."102

In France, for example, law does not make abortion available "on demand," but only "for a reason" – that is, a condition of "emergency" sufficient to overcome the fetus's "right to life."103 In terms of legal outcomes, the language is of marginal importance because the woman's own certification of "emergency" is dispositive. In terms of citizens' reaction to the law, the language affirms the values of each side in the debate, allowing both sides to embrace the meaning most supportive of their values. The alternative of requiring law to be justified in secular terms does not "spare dissenters the perception that they are being forced to abide by laws that

97 *Id.* at 118.
98 *Id.* at 142.
99 *Id.* at 118.
100 *Id.* at 142.
101 *Id.* at 148.
102 *Id.* at 149.
103 *Id.* at 146 (citing Mary Ann Glendon, *Abortion and Divorce in Western Law* (1987)).

reflect an antipathy toward their ways of life."[104] Instead, it "enrages them by forcing them to endure the smug insistence of their adversaries that such policies reflect a neutral and objective commitment to the good of all citizens."[105]

Obviously, Kahan's proposal is not a remedy for all of our society's deep-seated moral disagreements. Clashes of conscience are not just about language. Many citizens' consciences would not be assuaged by permissive abortion laws, even if they placed a rhetorical value on life. But the insight of cultural cognition for a society intent on taking conscience seriously is deeper than language. Because we see public policy questions through the lens of our moral convictions, a government that wants its citizens to buy into its policy proposals must join the moral conversation. For those who fear that the state's entry signals the conversation's end and a particular moral claim's enshrinement into law, cultural cognition suggests that particular policy outcomes can supportively engage multiple moral claims simultaneously. Further, because of the trust we place in those who share our worldviews and moral premises, the state's moral engagement must make space for the relational dimension of conscience. In other words, it is not enough to say that we encounter public policy as individuals who have been shaped by our moral communities. More than that, our encounter of public policy is itself shaped – and is perpetually being shaped – by our communities. As such, our conversation about the common good cannot transcend our various particular commitments and associations via some sort of moral Esperanto; it must proceed through them, in acknowledgment of their claims on our lives.

CONSCIENCE AND THE COMMON GOOD

In seeking to protect conscience and foster the common good, the distinction between the state and society must be understood and defended. The state's actions and omissions can make it more or less difficult for conscience's dictates to be expressed and lived, but the primary responsibility for conscience's day-to-day vitality within society lies with nonstate actors. Today, the separation between the state's judgment and the citizenry's well-being is uncontroversial, but for someone like Plato, "it would not have occurred to him that the government needed to consult the citizens' conceptions in order to decide what was best for their souls."[106] It was Thomas Hobbes' failure to appreciate the distinction between the state and society that renders his analysis so inimical to individual liberty when viewed with modern sensibilities. While most modern political theorists have rejected these aspects of Plato's and Hobbes' work, there is no consensus regarding an affirmative vision of

---

[104] *Id.* at 144.
[105] *Id.* at 144–5
[106] Kwame Anthony Appiah, *The Ethics of Identity*, 156 (2005).

the state's relationship with and responsibility for the broader society, particularly in matters of conscience.

The question is, in the realm of conscience, how should the state operate in light of its conceptual and practical separation from society? There is no formulaic answer, but several lessons emerge from the perspectives on the common good discussed in this chapter.

First, state actors must appreciate that the human person is inherently social. As a consequence, they must acknowledge the social dimension of freedom. Group power is not invariably aligned against individual freedom. Group power is often the vehicle by which individual freedom is realized. As Will Kymlicka emphasizes, liberal freedoms are geared to allowing individuals to revisit and reformulate their ideas of the good through social interaction.[107]

Second, in light of the "bottom up" nature of moral discourse underlying the common good, the state must permit individuals and the groups to which they belong broad discretion to pursue moral identities that are not favored by the majority or contemplated by the premises of liberalism. The marketplace of moral claims is essential to the common good. This does not preclude the exercise of the state's coercive power, but it does mean that such exercise should be geared primarily toward preventing harm and maintaining the marketplace's viability. Discerning what constitutes actionable "harm" or illegitimate market interference, of course, is no easy matter, and the book's second half will be devoted to exploring these questions in light of the social interests at stake in particular fields. When the state seeks to interject its own favored moral claims beyond these objectives, it should do so with awareness of its own market-trumping power and should aim to make moral claims as another market participant, not as a moral arbiter.

Third, the state's commitment to equality need not preclude the partiality that invariably arises in meaningful human relationships, although some tension is unavoidable. To keep the tension manageable, the state should focus its equality initiatives on ensuring access to goods and services, not on enshrining equality as a nonnegotiable requirement for marketplace participation. When the market is not providing access, state intervention may be appropriate. When it comes to goods that are foundational to social participation and for which a marketplace approach is problematic (employment and housing),[108] the state will prudently act more aggressively in rooting out and guarding against discrimination. In other areas of social life, the state's categorical imposition of equality carries too high a cost in terms of group autonomy and the empowerment of individuals' moral claims. Partiality and particular affinities built on shared worldviews, among other factors, are inescapable in a society committed to the shared pursuit of the common good.

---

[107] Will Kymlicka, *Liberalism, Community and Culture*, passim (1989).
[108] These are discussed more fully in chapter 1.

Fourth, embracing moral pluralism does not preclude the building of social consensus on issues of common importance. The lessons of moral pluralism, though, caution against the presumption that consensus must always be built from shared principles. Our lived experiences will produce points of agreement even among people who operate from different moral frameworks. Public policies in areas such as the environment, employment discrimination, and family life are ripe for consensus reached via starkly different moral frameworks. When policy positions are wrapped up with overarching moral claims, the likelihood and depth of disagreement and alienation increases. This is not to suggest that overarching moral claims should never be part of the public discourse – for example, the Civil Rights Act might not have been possible without such claims – only that, as Anthony Appiah observes, "we can identify points of agreement that are much more local and contingent than" claims emanating from a shared worldview.[109]

So, to return to our entry point for exploring the law's stance toward conscience, what does Daniel Seeger's invocation of conscience – and its recognition as a legitimate ground for avoiding military service – have to do with the common good? After all, the prosecution of war seems the paradigmatic case in which the collective good and the common good are one and the same. Even in this case, the two are not coextensive. A blanket imposition of the moral claims inherent in waging war would be antagonistic to the common good, which requires us to protect both the individual's moral agency and the society's bottom-up orientation.

As for the individual, the common good does not allow him to be subsumed within the interests of the collective. This does not mean that the individual should be granted veto power over every state imposition on his autonomy, but it does mean that the individual's moral convictions, as part of his self-conception, should be included in the state's evaluation of an exemption's prudence. The common good calls a person to take stock of interests beyond her own, but it is still that person who is primarily responsible for undertaking the moral analysis and acting accordingly.

In terms of the social order, an exemptionless imposition of the draft shuts down the moral marketplace, failing to honor the autonomy of groups that have built their moral identities on claims that reject war. When limited exemptions are allowed for groups and individuals with demonstrable antiwar moral identities, the common good is furthered to the extent that such identities serve as a critical and prophetic witness to the truth claims embodied in the underlying convictions.

But the common good and conscience are related in more fundamental, if subtle, ways. The common good presumes that individuals are social beings, and that their myriad forms of relationship should be free to shape, express, and implement the moral identities of their participants. From the perspective of the common good, even more important than Daniel Seeger's resistance to the draft are the relationships in his life that drove him to resist the draft. The precise point of conflict is only a

[109] Appiah, *supra* note 106, at 253.

sliver of the story. If we believe that our moral commitments should be brought to bear on the course of our lives, we will honor the relationships through which that occurs. And we will resist the collective imposition of norms that short-circuit that process. In some cases, of course, the collective imposition of norms facilitates the process by expanding social participation and mitigating or preventing the identity-squelching harms of certain relationships. Discerning the lines between prudent and imprudent state action is no easy task and thus is the subject to which the book's second half is dedicated.

PART II

IMPLICATIONS

5

Voluntary Associations

It is no accident that America's political commitment to freedom of conscience has coincided with an equally distinctive sociological commitment to voluntary associations. Nearly 170 years ago, Alexis de Tocqueville famously declared, "in no country in the world has the principle of association been more successfully used . . . than in America."[1] However, just as the law tends to force conscience into an individualist framework, the law often fails to recognize associations as anything more than an assembly of individuals. We tend to formulate legal interests, rights, and obligations in terms that are easily classified between the individual on one side and the state on the other. Even though associations defy either category, we try to force disputes involving associations into a close approximation of this bipolar framework. As our legal system wrestles, for example, with the Salvation Army's implementation of faith-driven hiring practices,[2] the Boy Scouts' exclusion of openly gay scoutmasters,[3] or Catholic Charities' refusal to allow same-sex couples into the pool of prospective adoptive parents, observers gravitate toward one of two perspectives. Generally, those who favor the association's side in a particular controversy frame the dispute as one pitting the freedom-loving association against the oppressive state. By contrast, those who oppose the association frame the dispute as one pitting the equality-seeking individual against the oppressive association. Both characterizations have elements of truth, but they give rise to an unnaturally and unhelpfully segmented view of associations.

A deeper understanding of voluntary associations and their symbiotic relationship with conscience is possible if we view associations in their relational context. The value of associations derives, in significant part, from the extent to which associations stand in tension with the individual on one side and the state on the other.

---

[1] Alexis de Tocqueville, *Democracy in America*, 191 (Renaissance ed., Colonial Press, 1900) (1835).
[2] See *Lown v. Salvation Army*, 393 F. Supp.2d 223 (S.D.N.Y. 2005).
[3] *Boy Scouts of Am. v. Dale*, 530 U.S. 640 (2000).

Like conscience, associations are important relationally, as their relationships with the individual and the broader society equip them to fulfill a mediating role.[4] As explored in the preceding chapters, one's conscience is at the same time deeply personal and inescapably social. Associations embody this dynamic because they contribute to a member's self-conception while connecting her to the world outside herself. This role allows associations to serve as bridges between the individual and the surrounding society, but it also injects tension into the association's relationships with the individual and the state. Where any single anchor of the association in relationship (individual versus association versus state) is given unfettered authority to pursue its own interests at the expense of the other, the resulting disparity eviscerates the association's mediating values, thereby threatening to negate the very reasons we seek a vibrant associational life in the first place.

Recognizing the mediating tension of associations provides a more nuanced functional justification for the association's robust (but not unfettered) resistance to individualist and collectivist pulls – even when that resistance culminates in the widely polarized, frequently vitriolic associational landscape of the culture wars. This does not negate our concern over the social harm inflicted by certain associations, but it does give us a sense of what is at stake when we seek to remedy that harm by curtailing the free operation of the associational marketplace.

When afforded their natural vitality and vibrancy, associations are the vehicle by which we transcend our individual, atomistic existences and carve out a communal role for ourselves that is distinct from and often in opposition to the identity of the state. Voluntary associations can overcome an individual's self-alienation by connecting her with other individuals in a freely chosen community, thereby infusing her with a sense of purpose, place, and meaning. Associations bridge the gap between an individual and the state by giving her a voice and connecting her to social power. All of these functions implicate and are implicated by the dictates of a person's conscience. Our joining is shaped, in significant part, by what we believe, and the mediating functions made possible by our joining matter to us because we do, in fact, believe.

How exactly do associations mediate between the individual and the state, and how does that process, in turn, benefit both the individual and social aspects of our existence? I propose three mediating "values" that allow voluntary associations to serve as bridges between the individual and the state and that capture the essence of the benefits derived from associations by individual participants and the surrounding society. Put simply, the mediating values are *identity*, *expression*, and *purpose*. These

---

[4] Mediating structures are "those structures standing between the individual in his private life and the large institutions of public life." These large institutions, or "megastructures," include the state, as well as the "large economic conglomerates of capitalist enterprise, big labor, and the growing bureaucracies that administer wide sectors of the society, such as in education and the organized professions." Richard J. Neuhaus and Peter Berger, "To Empower People: The Role of Mediating Structures in Public Policy," in *The Essential Neoconservative Reader*, 213, 214 (Mark Gerson, ed., 1996).

values not only help bridge the gap between the individual and the state, but, in doing so, they place the association in significant tension with both the individual and the state. The paths by which this process occurs – that is, the pursuit of identity, expression, and purpose – flow into each other, inform each other, and must each be accounted for to appreciate the support associations provide to conscience's relational dimension.

ASSOCIATIONS AND IDENTITY

Voluntary associations mediate between an individual and the state by allowing individuals to join together to pursue or maintain a common identity. One key function for all mediating structures is their ability to connect people to people. To fulfill this role, associations must have the freedom to reflect their members' values and views, even when they conflict with the state's. After all, associations are not simply miniature versions of the state, but rather communities based on members' common adherence to a distinct set of beliefs. As a mediating value, the common identity fostered by associations is essential both to participants and to the state.

The common identity that is chosen through the act of associating gives individual members a sense of place in the world. Protecting an association's ability to pursue and maintain its common identity gives greater efficacy to an individual's identity-driven membership decision. Individuals benefit in the sense that they are empowered to carve out, along with like-minded others, a common identity of their own choosing in the face of an anonymous and alienating collective. The resulting sense of place stems not simply from a desire to transcend an individual's limited sense of self, but from the fact that an individual's sense of self is, to a significant extent, determined by her relationship with the surrounding world, as discussed in chapter 2. An individual's identity can be influenced by relationships in a manner that fosters a sense of belonging (by affirmatively choosing to associate with others in ways that one finds meaningful) or a sense of alienation (by interacting with others as a necessary condition of life in modern society, but nothing more). Voluntary associations are a primary vehicle for choosing the former over the latter, particularly when the decision to join is a function of one's moral convictions.

An association's ability to foster a common, conscience-shaped identity also has clear benefit for the surrounding society in that it socializes an increasingly isolated and atomized citizenry. Associating with other individuals as a function of free choice, rather than by government fiat, is essential to this common identity. There are two positive aspects of this freely chosen socialization. First, as individuals associate themselves among the seemingly infinite number and type of groups, the variety of resulting loyalties – some agreeable to the state, some disagreeable to the state – itself is a boon to society, as associations become "wrenches in the works of whatever hegemonizing ambitions government might be tempted to indulge."[5]

---

[5] Richard W. Garnett, *The Story of Henry Adams's Soul: Education and the Expression of Associations*, 85 Minn. L. Rev. 1841, 1853 (2001).

Second is the "social capital" outgrowth of associational life.[6] Relating to one another in a freely chosen common forum increases levels of cooperation and trust among members, enabling the collective purposes of the group to be achieved more easily, especially relative to a group constructed according to government mandates on membership. Further, many would argue that participation in an association increases attitudes of trust and cooperation toward citizens in general, making participants more inclined to participate in broader societal projects.

Identity and the Power to Exclude

The nagging problem with all of this, of course, is that even for those of us who favor, as a general proposition, a thriving associational life, the "identity" of many real-world associations that make the headlines is not as noble or as social minded as the theoreticians' lofty language suggests. Indeed, it seems that some of the groups that are most obsessed with their chosen identities are the most corrosive of widely accepted social values and norms. In particular, groups whose identity is based, at least in part, on the categorical exclusion of certain segments of the population call into question the social capital component of the purported benefit because such groups are unlikely to foster trust or cooperation between those inside the group and those who are excluded or who oppose the exclusion. Put simply, why should we value the ability of the Ku Klux Klan to give white supremacists a conscience-driven common identity and greater sense of place in society?

By way of background, the primary tool by which voluntary associations seek legal protection of their identities is the freedom of association under the First Amendment. Associational identity gains constitutional protection as an outgrowth of associational expression. Specifically, courts protect the ability of associations to establish and maintain their unique identities when they show deference to associations' stated objectives and expressions of identity; courts should be hesitant to second-guess the sincerity of such expressions. This notion is reflected most famously in *Boy Scouts of America v. Dale*,[7] in which the Supreme Court held, by a five–four vote, that applying New Jersey's antidiscrimination law to require the Boy Scouts to allow openly gay scout leaders would violate the group's right of association.

Two aspects of the *Dale* majority's analysis are essential to an association's pursuit of a unique identity. First, the court recognized that "[i]t is not the role of the courts to reject a group's expressed values because they disagree with those values or find them internally inconsistent."[8] Rather, the court gave deference to the Boy Scouts' expression of its beliefs and values.[9] Second, the court held that "[a]s we give deference to an association's assertions regarding the nature of its expression, we must

---

[6] Robert D. Putnam, *Bowling Alone: The Collapse and Revival of American Community*, 19 (2000).
[7] 530 U.S. 640 (2000).
[8] *Id.* at 651.
[9] See *id.* ("We accept the Boy Scouts' assertion.").

also give deference to an association's view of what would impair its expression."[10] These twin aspects of deference allowed the Boy Scouts to maintain its mediating tension. By refraining from second guessing the sincerity or legitimacy of the group's exclusionary policy, the court effectively upholds the tension between the Boy Scouts and the state – the Boy Scouts' policy pitted against New Jersey's collective judgment that excluding gays is impermissible.

By accepting at face value the Boy Scouts' contention that allowing Dale to serve as an openly gay leader would impede their efforts to rear "morally straight" young people, the court is upholding the tension between the Boy Scouts and the individual – the particular decision to terminate Dale as a scout leader pitted against Dale's interest in remaining as a leader. This association-individual tension will virtually always be present to some degree when it comes to an association's identity because the ability to pursue a common identity entails the ability to exclude individuals who fall outside the defined traits of that common identity. There is nothing inherently nefarious about this aspect of the tension because even exclusions that are based on an individual's willful choices (a pro-life group excluding a member who advocates abortion on demand), rather than his status (a country club excluding an African-American) potentially subvert the desires of the individual to the will of the association.

In *Dale*, these twin forms of deference together allow interested parents to associate themselves – albeit through the participation of their children – for the pursuit of various skill- and character-building activities without the influence of openly gay leaders. The mediating value to participants is clear: In a world that appears increasingly antagonistic to their conception of a "morally straight" upbringing, like-minded parents have at least one forum in which their views hold sway, giving them an unmistakable sense of place and connection to others. The mediating value to the collective is less obvious, as the further marginalization of gays – especially when institutionalized by groups charged with the development of young people – hardly befits our common self-conception as an egalitarian democracy devoted to fostering respect for the dignity and worth of all people. Nevertheless, the alternative to the mediating tension of the Boy Scouts is the trump of the individual and/or the state; as shown by Justice Stevens' dissent, it is a remedy that is worse than the ailment.

Justice Stevens' dissent would significantly diminish the Boy Scouts' mediating tension, effectively giving both the individual (Dale) and the state a judicial trump over the Scouts' efforts to maintain its chosen identity. Justice Stevens challenged the sincerity of the Boy Scouts' stated policy on gays, concluding, "there is no evidence that this [antihomosexual] view was part of any collective effort to foster beliefs about homosexuality."[11] In terms of an association's ability to maintain its chosen

---

[10] *Id.* at 653.
[11] *Id.* at 675.

identity, even the presumed relevance of this assertion is problematic (although Justice Stevens was by no means the first to make such a presumption).[12] To be entitled to constitutional protection, why must the association show that it is engaged in efforts to "foster" certain beliefs – why is it not enough simply to hold those beliefs and express them through the make-up of its membership?[13] Skepticism pervades Justice Stevens' analysis. Not only does he fail to show any deference to the Boy Scouts' stated belief regarding gays, but he goes so far as to criticize the underlying motivation for that policy, opining that the "harm [resulting from antigay discrimination] can only be aggravated by the creation of a constitutional shield for a policy that is itself the product of a habitual way of thinking about strangers."[14] This progression of reasoning – casting doubt on the sincerity of an association's stated beliefs, and then making value judgments about the beliefs themselves – suggests that, in the absence of deference to an association's stated beliefs, the state's values fill the void. As Dale Carpenter observes, this approach "would likely be systematically unfavorable to unpopular groups, including gay civil rights groups," as it would put such groups "at the mercy of legislative majorities who have their own, often hostile, conception of the good life."[15]

Questions of associational identity generally arise from state efforts to forbid certain grounds for excluding members and/or an individual's utilization of those legislative efforts in his own quest for inclusion. As such, when a court invalidates the association's identity-based defense to the state/individual challenge, it is the state/individual's expressed values taking the place of the association's expressed identity. Participants lose their distinct sense of place, occupying instead a state-sanctioned space that connects them only to society's general notions of acceptability, rather than the personal convictions, beliefs, or priorities of fellow participants. The state, despite its short-term vindication of its inclusiveness norm, may lose the long-term benefits of a citizenry connected in wildly divergent – but meaningful – ways.[16]

This dynamic has become almost comic at several state universities, as Christian groups have been pushed off campus for not opening their leadership positions to

---

[12] See, e.g., *New York State Club Ass'n v City of New York*, 487 U.S. 1 (1988) (holding, in an opinion by Justice White, that a group must demonstrate that it was "organized for specific expressive purposes" to fall within the right of expressive association).

[13] See Dale Carpenter, *Expressive Association and Antidiscrimination Law After Dale: A Tripartite Approach*, 85 Minn. L. Rev. 1515, 1542 (2001); see also Seana Valentine Shiffrin, *What is Really Wrong With Compelled Association?*, 99 Nw. U. L. Rev. 839, 846 (2005) ("Groups who tolerate or encourage within their ranks internal dissent, experimentation, or critical re-examination are more likely to lose control over their membership than those who adopt a posture of unyielding stridency.").

[14] *Dale*, 530 U.S. at 700.

[15] Carpenter, *supra* note 13, at 1517–18.

[16] *See* Shiffrin, *supra* note 13, at 873 (defending freedom of association on the ground that "sites in which people can identify with what they say and who they are surrounded by" generates "character virtues of sincerity, earnestness, and mutual trust that are essential to successful cooperative and democratic culture and in particular to a thriving, meaningful free speech culture").

non-Christians.[17] With the state's growing sensitivity to discrimination, it has grown more resolute in defining and enforcing fixed boundaries to the marketplace of norms and ideals. For the prospects of conscience, the boundaries have become particularly problematic to the extent that they require all campus groups to open their membership and leadership to all interested students. These policies are not constitutionally mandated,[18] nor are they compelled by the state's role as market actor. When a state university permits a student group to have access to campus facilities despite the group's defiance of antidiscrimination norms, the university acts as a market facilitator. As market actor, the university can still espouse the importance of nondiscriminatory membership and even criticize the group's policy, but closing off the group's access to the university marketplace is a different prospect. A group's ability to use the normative claims embodied in its moral identity as membership criteria is essential to its mediating role. Especially in higher education – where the marketplace of ideas should be at its most robust – this boundary can have a crippling effect on the viability of conscience venues.

For example, Southern Illinois University revoked its recognition of the Christian Legal Society (CLS) because of the group's refusal to accept as members individuals who engage in or approve of homosexual conduct. CLS brought suit, and the court observed that the university policy's enforcement was not simply to facilitate attendance at meetings by nonmembers, but to "induce CLS to alter its membership standards," and that "this change would impair its ability to express disapproval of active homosexuality."[19] Given that CLS's "beliefs about sexual morality are among its defining values," the court found that "forcing it to accept as members those who engage in or approve of homosexual conduct would cause the group as it currently identifies itself to cease to exist."[20] Significantly for our purposes, the court recognized that the university's interest in "eradicating or neutralizing" CLS's antihomosexual belief was not a sufficient ground constitutionally for pushing the group out of the university's marketplace of ideas.[21]

Contrast this with the University of California at Hastings' similar exclusion of CLS from campus. The district court in that case upheld the school's action, reasoning

---

[17] See, e.g., *Christian group drops challenge to college's anti-discrimination policy*, Associated Press, April 13, 2003 (reporting on settlement between Rutgers University and InterVarsity Christian Fellowship after the school banned the group for excluding non-Christians from leadership); *Every Nation Campus Ministries v. Achtenberg*, 597 F. Supp.2d 1075 (S.D. Cal. 2009) (upholding exclusion of Christian student group for discriminating against non-Christians and "unapologetic homosexuals").

[18] See *Rosenberger v. Rector & Visitors of Univ. of Va.*, 515 U.S. 819, 833–34 (1995) (explaining difference between government funding of private groups to communicate government message and government funding of private groups to encourage diversity of views from private speakers).

[19] *Christian Legal Society v. Walker*, 453 F.3d 853, 863 (2006).

[20] *Id.*

[21] *Id.* (citing *Hurley v. Irish-American Gay, Lesbian & Bisexual Group of Boston*, 515 U.S. 557, 579 (1995) ("While the law is free to promote all sorts of conduct in place of harmful behavior, it is not free to interfere with speech for no better reason than promoting an approved message or discouraging a disfavored one, however enlightened either purpose may strike the government.")).

that "Hastings did not withhold recognition of CLS because of CLS's views, but because CLS refused to comply with the Nondiscrimination Policy."[22] The court distinguished between a group's philosophy and its activities, and CLS's refusal to admit to membership individuals who approved of or engaged in homosexual conduct fell onto the activity side of the ledger.[23]

Such reasoning ignores the "lived out" dimension of conscience. Conscience, to reiterate, is not easily separated from action. By forcing CLS to separate its beliefs from its membership policy, the court's reasoning reflects a constrained – and hopelessly artificial – vision of conscience. As Stephen Carter remarked about Yale Law School's rejection of CLS's request to recruit on campus while hiring only Christians, "The basic response of liberal theory to religiosity is to try to speak words that seem to celebrate it (as a part of the freedom of belief, or conscience, or the entitlement to select one's own version of the good) while in effect trying to domesticate it . . . or, if that fails, to try to destroy it."[24] The state need not be sidelined as a market actor when it comes to promoting its vision of the good, but it must resist the temptation to conflate the promotion of its vision of the good with the foreclosing of competing visions.

Limits on the Power to Exclude

This is not the end of the inquiry, however, for the maintenance of the mediating "tension" on which conscience's relational dimension depends presumes that there is resistance on both sides, that is, associations cannot enjoy an automatic trump over individual and state interests. Showing deference to an association's expressions of identity allows the association to maintain its mediating role – in tension with the individual to be excluded and the state whose collective values and norms are flouted – but it does not mean that associations are thereby given license to run roughshod over all individual rights and collectively held values.

Two factors limit the potentially tension-negating impact of such deference. First, allowing an association to invoke its right to association – taking its allegations of protected associational activity at face value – does not preclude judicial regulation of its conduct. Although a court should not second guess an association's stated reason for being, whether that reason for being trumps the governmental interest at issue is another question. Thus, judicial deference to an association's expressions of identity does not preclude the application of nondiscrimination statutes to all associations. Where the association excludes certain segments of society from access

---

[22] *Christian Legal Society v. Kane*, No. C 04–04484, 2006 WL 997217, at *20 (N.D. Cal. May 19, 2006), aff'd, No. 06–15956, 2009 WL 693391 (9th Cir. Mar. 17, 2009).

[23] *Id.* at *16 (citing *Healy v. James*, 408 U.S. 169, 188 (1972)).

[24] Stephen L. Carter, "Liberal Hegemony, Religious Resistance," in *Christian Perspectives on Legal Thought*, 25, 29 (2001).

to employment, for example, the statute should still be enforced, as explained in chapter 1.[25]

The call for courts to show deference to an association should not be equated with the call for courts to abdicate their role in monitoring the exclusionary impulses of the majority. The difference is not easily encapsulated into categorical legal principles, but there is line drawing to be done. One example of defensible line drawing is shown by contrasting *Dale* with a case like *Roberts v. Jaycees*,[26] in which the Minneapolis and St. Paul chapters of the Jaycees were held subject to state antidiscrimination law and effectively forced to admit women to their previously male-only ranks. The majority held that the Jaycees did not establish that their message or purpose would be significantly burdened by admitting women. The Jaycees already admitted women as nonvoting members, and the court refused "to indulge in the sexual stereotyping that . . . by allowing women to vote, application of the Minnesota Act will change the content or impact of the organization's speech."[27] This reasoning lacks deference to an association's own understanding of what will impair its expressive activity, but a firmer potential foundation for the court's holding is found in Justice O'Connor's concurrence.

Justice O'Connor argued that the inquiry turns not on the Jaycees' evidentiary showing, but on the different levels of constitutional protection afforded to commercial associations and expressive associations. She concluded that the state "has a legitimate interest in ensuring nondiscriminatory access to the commercial opportunity presented by membership in the Jaycees."[28] This approach takes into account the need to balance an association's interest in maintaining its chosen identity against the state's interest in ensuring an individual's access to the building blocks of American life. One area in which state and individual resistance to an association's ability to maintain its chosen identity must be accounted for, then, is where the association provides economic opportunities to citizens. Justice O'Connor's analysis would have been more persuasive if she could have addressed, as a factual matter, the degree to which the Jaycees served as a gateway to economic opportunity in Minneapolis and St. Paul. Her general point remains valid, though: In our free-market system, where the government depends on private companies to provide individuals with the means to support themselves, we cannot afford to shut out entire classes of individuals from securing those means. If the Jaycees functioned as a male-only business network with significant market influence, the state would have a legitimate

---

[25] Subject to exemptions ensuring that religious organizations can hire employees who support and believe in the organization's mission, just as secular organizations do. See Ira C. Lupu, *Why the Congress Was Wrong and the Court Was Right: Reflections on City of Boerne v. Flores*, 39 Wm. & Mary L. Rev. 793, 809 (1998) (comparing "religious entities with nonreligious entities that face no comparable statutory impediment to hiring those with ideological loyalty").

[26] 468 U.S. 609 (1984).

[27] *Id.* at 628.

[28] *Id.* at 640.

interest in regulating the organization to promote women's access to economic opportunity.

The second factor making deference to an association's expressed identity more palatable is the realization that associations are equipped to serve as countervailing forces against messages emanating from other associations. When an association has chosen to pursue an identity that conflicts with one's deeply held conception of the social good, there are effective and enriching responses short of trumping, as a matter of law, its ability to engage in such pursuits. In this regard, state action is not the only – or even necessarily the most effective – means of countering the detrimental impact of associations whose identities are rooted in the exclusion and marginalization of other segments of society. Pursuant to their mediating function, voluntary associations provide a tool for members' collective views and values to influence the broader society – including other associations. For those who are members of the association with which they take issue, the most obvious path is leaving the association. Others may join with similarly minded individuals to engage in private forms of collective actions (boycotts, picketing, meetings, publicity campaigns, etc.). Not only will these often prove effective in countering the harmful message, but they also avoid the association-squelching fallout that often accompanies judicial or legislative pronouncements. In fact, collective countervailing action often leads to, as Abner Greene puts it, "the bonding among the challengers and the increased confidence in their ability to affect the conditions of their lives."[29] Often, the best weapon against the corrosive mediating function of one association is the mediating function of another association. Where associational identity has been degraded in pursuit of individual or state interests, a pressing danger is the absence of such counterweights.

ASSOCIATIONS AND EXPRESSION

Associations give individuals a voice in the world by expressing their members' views and values. Much of an association's day-to-day value for its members derives from its ability to disseminate the members' views to the broader, impersonal world. By providing a collective voice to sentiments that likely would go unheard if left to be expressed by an individual standing alone, associations serve as a megaphone for members' most deeply held beliefs and opinions, including, of course, the moral convictions that make up conscience. The value derived by individuals from associational expression goes beyond the tangible member benefits realized through the association's communications (e.g., lobbying) because the act of collective communication itself gives members a sense that they and their views matter. Bringing individuals together to form a common voice is a mediating function in its purest form.

---

[29] Abner S. Greene, *Civil Society and Multiple Repositories of Power*, 75 Chi.-Kent L. Rev. 477, 482 (2000).

In facilitating the mediating value of expression, courts must ensure that associations have the freedom to communicate their members' messages to the public – in particular, courts must ensure associations' access to any public forum established by the government. A primary way to do so is to ensure that the viewpoint discrimination inquiry under the First Amendment focuses on the subject addressed, not the manner in which it is addressed. Maintaining access for the messages of all associations recognizes the tension inherent in the mediating value of expression. First, access exerts tension on the relationship between the association and the individual, especially when the individual also occupies the space to which access is granted; the individual often will find the association's message to be disagreeable, offensive, or contrary to her most deeply held values. Second, access exerts tension on the relationship between the association and the state because the association's message often will conflict with the state's judgment over the proper use of the facilities to which access is sought.

The mediating tension that arises from a court's proper understanding of the viewpoint discrimination inquiry is most readily apparent in the Supreme Court's analysis in *Good News Club v. Milford Central School*,[30] in which the Supreme Court required a public school that had opened itself to after-hours meetings held by various civic groups to allow a religious club for children to use the school's facilities as well.[31] Writing for the five–four majority, Justice Thomas noted that groups devoted to discussing morals and standards of behavior were allowed to meet at the school. He then concluded that the Good News Club simply wanted to discuss morals and standards from a religious viewpoint, and thus the club's exclusion amounted to unconstitutional viewpoint discrimination by the school.[32]

Justice Souter, writing in dissent, took issue with the majority's broad reading of "viewpoint." He reasoned that the Good News Club did not simply seek to discuss an otherwise permissible topic from a religious point of view, but rather it sought to conduct an "evangelical service of worship calling children to commit themselves in an act of Christian conversion."[33] Writing separately, Justice Stevens argued that the school's decision to allow discussions of morals did not require opening the school to "worship" or "proselytizing."[34]

The dissenting Justices' approach to viewpoint discrimination effectively allows the state's judgments about appropriate messages to trump the association's interest in accessing an otherwise available public forum. This trump negates the mediating tension inherent in associational expression. Further, the substance of the dissent's analysis hinders the vitality of associational life, as its analysis hinges not on the subject addressed at the Good News Club's meetings, but on the means chosen by

[30] 121 S. Ct. 2093 (2001).
[31] *Id.* at 2097.
[32] *Id.* at 2100.
[33] *Id.* at 2117 (Souter, J., dissenting).
[34] *Id.* at 2113 (Stevens, J., dissenting).

the club to address an otherwise permissible subject. Because the particular means objected to – worship and proselytizing – are by definition utilized only by religious groups, the dissent would deny access on grounds that have an impact only on religious associations. No nonreligious groups would be barred under the worship/proselytizing prohibition. Given the overbreadth of the terminology, religious groups would likely be barred even when they attempt a permissible debate or discussion of an issue. By way of illustration, what if a church group held an open meeting at the school to discuss parenting from a religious perspective, but at the end asked if people wanted to join the church – does that qualify as impermissible proselytizing? What about a Catholic discussion group that closed its meeting with a prayer – does that qualify as an impermissible worship service?

The carve out of worship and proselytizing as materially different from other, more acceptable forms of expression on a given subject not only singles out religion for exclusion, but its open-endedness threatens a whole range of otherwise permissible religious activities. As a practical matter, this approach imposes a heavier burden on individuals who seek a collective voice for their religiously derived consciences than on those who seek a voice for other types of conscience. This disparity in burdens not only runs counter to the First Amendment, but it also hinders the mediating function of religious associations. Once the government establishes a public forum for activities and discussions on a range of subject areas, it must give access to all groups who wish to express a message on those subjects – whether the form of their expression is lecture, debate, worship, or witnessing to boys and girls.

Admittedly, *Good News Club* is a factually sympathetic case, for most Americans take little offense from the prospect of boys and girls engaged in Christian worship or instruction. More troubling is the specter of a white supremacist group, such as Matthew Hale's brand of religion-tinged racism,[35] using the protection of viewpoint neutrality to avail themselves of public school facilities. Obviously, if exceptions to this call for equal access were to be carved out for groups with unsavory social agenda, the mediating value of associational expression to both individuals and the state would be rendered largely meaningless because the messages would simply function as outgrowths of sentiment acceptable to the majority. The alternative – public schools filled with after-school Matthew Hale membership rallies – may not be as dire as it would seem. First, judicial prohibitions on viewpoint discrimination do not preclude the enforcement of broadly applicable criminal laws, and thus to the extent groups use their right to access as a means to effectuate aims that are punishable by the state, access need not translate into unfettered discretion to realize the association's objectives. Second, as discussed earlier, one of the essential attributes of a vibrant associational life is competition for the hearts and minds of potential adherents. The government may not be in a position to block Hale from

---

[35] See Anti-Defamation League, *Extremism in America: Matt Hale*, http://www.adl.org/learn/ext_us/ Hale.asp?xpicked=2&item=6 (accessed July 28, 2009).

using public facilities, but that does not mean that other associations need stand idly by while he pursues his corrosive agenda.

This once again reflects the broader notion that mediating *tension* presumes resistance on both sides of the relationship. An association does not have absolute authority to express its message in any way it sees fit. There are limiting principles to the notion of access that avoid an associational trump over individual and state interests. Most obviously, if a public space has not been designated (implicitly or expressly) as a public forum, access need not be granted. Even in the public forum context, however, individuals and the state have the tools to resist an association's message, even if they do not have the capacity to preclude access altogether.

Further, an association's message is not allowed to hold sway completely over an individual's conflicting values and views given that the association does not enjoy a monopoly over the public forum – the association's access is never exclusive. This may be an obvious proposition from the standpoint of free speech doctrine, but its impact is not limited to that context. A meaningful application of the Establishment clause also demands that government-controlled spaces not be captured by any single religious message or messenger. To do so eviscerates the mediating function of religious associations by giving a single messenger (whether an individual or group) a state trump over competing messengers, negating the tension that is key to their mediating role and to the cause of conscience more broadly.

In *Santa Fe Independent School District v. Doe*,[36] for example, the Supreme Court held as unconstitutional a Texas high school's practice of allowing a student chosen by the student body to offer a prayer over the public address system before football games. Even apart from the constitutional inquiry, this holding was proper as viewed from the interest of voluntary associations. This case was not about a group seeking access to a public forum, but was an example of the government, by virtue of its decision to grant access to a single religious message, effectively becoming the vehicle for the expression of a particular religious message into a forum that was not open to other religious (or nonreligious) messages. Allowing the government to co-opt a message that could otherwise be expressed in other ways by religious groups does not enhance the vitality or viability of associations. If anything, it diminishes associations. This diminishment takes two forms. First, the government-sanctioned expression renders moot the mediating function of some associations to the extent their message is already communicated in the government-controlled forum. Second, it negates the mediating function of other associations to the extent their message is trumped by the government's adoption of a competing message. To protect the conscience-expressive function of associations, religious messages should not be given access to a forum that is closed to competing messages.

Although courts' recognition of the nonexclusive nature of the access enjoyed by associations helps maintain the mediating tension between the individual and the

[36] 530 U.S. 290 (2000).

association, tension between the association and the state is maintained when courts recognize the distinction between government-provided access and government promotion. That is, the government must ensure that associations have access to a public forum, but the government is not required to join in the promotion of that message. This avoids giving the association a trump where the government's own legitimate interests run counter to the association's message. The aftermath of the Supreme Court's ruling in *Dale v. Boy Scouts of America* provides a good example of the access/promotion distinction. With *Dale* bringing publicity to the Boy Scouts' ban on gay scout leaders, a school board in Florida barred the Boy Scouts from using school facilities because the ban on gays violated the school district's antidiscrimination policy.[37] The district court judge ruled that this violated the Boy Scouts' right of expressive association because several gender- and race-specific groups were also in violation of the antidiscrimination policy, but the school board had made no attempt to prohibit their use of school facilities.[38] Accordingly, the school board had to allow the Boy Scouts to use the facilities to the same extent as other groups.[39]

The court, however, ruled that the school board could terminate a partnership agreement it had entered into with the Boy Scouts, under which the district's schools, including teachers, were obligated to make special efforts to promote scouting. The court ruled that the Boy Scouts' discriminatory policy was good cause for the agreement's termination.[40] The court seems to have struck a good balance. The school board had an interest in its own antidiscrimination message and so could not be required to promote the Boy Scouts' contrary message; at the same time, the board could not deny the Boy Scouts otherwise available access simply because the board disagreed with the Scouts' message.

Voluntary associations require access – they do not require promotion of their message by the government. Such promotion not only poses constitutional problems in some contexts, but it also threatens the mediating tension between the association and the state. Blurring the line between associational and governmental interests not only makes it more difficult for the government to pursue its own proper interests within the moral marketplace, but, ultimately, it eviscerates the association's capacity to function as a vehicle for conscience by turning it into an arm of the state.

ASSOCIATIONS AND PURPOSE

Associations attract and keep members by allowing them to join together in pursuit of a common purpose, often a purpose that springs from and is shaped by members' shared dictates of conscience. The ability of many associations to serve their chosen

[37] *Boy Scouts of America v. Till*, 136 F. Supp.2d 1295 (S.D. Fla.).
[38] See *id.* at 1303–04.
[39] See *id.* at 1311.
[40] See *id.* at 1308.

purposes can be significantly enhanced or stifled by the state. This is especially true of religious associations, which traditionally have been subject to greater restrictions than secular associations when it comes to accessing government resources used to advance an association's chosen purpose. My focus here is on religious associations that bring members together, at least in part, to address a problem of broader public concern – essentially any area that is a legitimate subject for direct state action.

An association's pursuit of its chosen purpose benefits the state when it leads the association to perform a function valued by the state, that is, when the apparatus of government has endeavored to pursue the same purpose as the association or at least has expressed the desirability of obtaining an objective embodied in the association's chosen purpose. Obviously, this overlap is not present where the association is dedicated to a purpose that is not valued by the state (e.g., collecting comic books) or where the purpose is antagonistic to the state's expressed values (e.g., establishing the racial superiority of white people). But, in a wide array of contexts – such as education, substance abuse, or poverty – the overlap is clear.

In a broader sense, however, society derives benefits even when an association's chosen purpose does not readily correlate with an identifiable state-valued function. When individuals work together toward one common purpose, it facilitates future cooperation toward other common purposes. In this regard, the pursuit and the attainment of an association's purpose is circular: The pursuit of a common purpose gives rise to associations, and the associations in turn make the pursuit of common purposes in a community more feasible in the future. As Robert Putnam explains, "[n]orms of generalized reciprocity and networks of civic engagement encourage social trust and cooperation because they reduce incentives to defect, reduce uncertainty, and provide models for future cooperation."[41]

Individual members benefit from an association's pursuit of a common purpose to the extent that they are empowered to realize that purpose and to bring about (or resist) change to a degree that would have been impossible for any individual member standing alone. In other words, associations mediate by connecting individuals to social power. The tendency is to focus on small, inward-looking associations in a sentimental way, but "humanizing also requires a sense of participation in ultimate social power."[42] If people are alienated from social power, the relief found in group life is akin to Marx's opiate of the masses. Whether seeking to maintain the social status quo or effectuate affirmative change, individuals seek the mediating function of associations as a means to have an impact on the world.

An association's ability to mediate by bringing individuals together to tackle a given social problem is tied to government policy, not simply because associations want as much public money as possible (although, not surprisingly, many do), but

---

[41] Robert D. Putnam, *Making Democracy Work: Civic Traditions in Modern Italy*, 177 (1993).
[42] J. Philip Wogamon, "The Church as Mediating Institution: Theological and Philosophical Perspective," in *Democracy and Mediating Structures*, 69, 71 (Michael Novak, ed., 1980).

also because the government's domination of the social service arena makes it more difficult for an association to attract members to the pursuit of an objective that is increasingly seen as a government function. This is reflected in the transformation of America's associational landscape over the past thirty years. Robert Putnam has famously (and controversially) concluded that, in contrast with a generation ago, today's thriving associations "are professionally staffed advocacy organizations, not member-centered, locally based associations."[43] These groups "focus on expressing policy views in the national political debate, not on providing regular connection among individual members at the grass roots."[44] In other words, the government is seen as the organ by which we collectively meet needs, and associations simply influence the priorities reflected in government action.

The Bush administration, building on the Clinton administration's work, advocated for the government to become more of a partner in helping associations – especially religious associations – fulfill their chosen service-oriented purposes, and President Obama has pledged to continue that partnership.[45] The availability of government funds does not necessarily mean that the prudent association should accept such funds. Proponents of neutrality often overlook the corrosive effect government funds may have on the mediating function of religious associations. Unlike the values of expression and identity, the mediating tension inherent in an association's pursuit of its chosen purpose is threatened not just by an overly intrusive state, but also by an overreaching association, that is, an association that unwittingly eviscerates its own mediating function by becoming reliant on government largesse.

Many of today's battles emanate from the privatization trend in public services over the last two decades. My purpose here is not to evaluate the trend itself, but to take it as the premise against which the relationships between nonstate entities and the government must be analyzed. The goal of Charitable Choice – making it easier for religious organizations to receive government funding without sacrificing their distinctive religious identities – is laudatory, but the devil is in the details. If the government is required to fund religious providers without regard to the manner in which they provide the public service, we marginalize the government's own role as market actor, subverting public values in the process. At the same time, if heavy-handed regulations accompany all public funds, the government threatens the viability of the marketplace, eroding organizations' capacity to function as mediating structures and turning them into state agents. One key factor in determining the nature and scope of the regulatory strings attached to funding is whether the money is directed to the organization by the state itself or by individual beneficiaries via vouchers.

---

43 Robert D. Putnam, *Bowling Alone: The Collapse and Revival of American Community*, 51 (2000).
44 *Id*.
45 See Amendments to Executive Order 13199 and Establishment of the President's Advisory Council for Faith-Based and Neighborhood Partnerships (Executive Order dated Feb. 5, 2009).

Direct Funding

When the state selects private entities to provide essential services with public funds, the state is acting as a market participant, unavoidably making normative claims with its funding decisions. There is no reason to disqualify the state from pursuing certain values through its market participation and no obligation that the state should embrace values that defy those embraced by the public as embodied in government policy. This stems primarily from the inescapable moral dimension of the funding decision – there is no morally neutral way of dispensing a limited amount of funds to a potentially limitless number of providers. There is no morally neutral resolution of the bitterly contested debate over whether or not the federal government should fund embryonic stem cell research. If the Department of Defense awards a construction contract to a company that has never employed racial minorities, the moral dimension is inescapable, regardless of the company's compliance with the technical specifications of the work. In a democracy, the state acts as moral agent of the people. When the state makes funding decisions, it is supporting, or withholding support from, a particular type of provider, acting as a consumer on behalf of the citizenry on whose behalf it speaks. In constitutional terms, the government has substantial discretion to attach strings to its funding, even to take moral positions vehemently opposed by the institutions funded.[46]

Obviously, the state is no ordinary consumer. Given its size, in many fields the state is not subject to the relevant market dynamics; rather, it determines the relevant market dynamics through its expenditures. The state must be sensitive to the impact of its participation, because it can effectively close down the marketplace by funding certain groups but not others, particularly in fields where the funds represent a significant portion of available revenue (ranging from health care, to scientific research, to social services such as "welfare to work" employment training). This realization should affect how aggressively the state imposes contested moral values through its funding decisions.

Accountability, not conformity, should guide the state's relationship with funded organizations. The tools of accountability should be geared toward ensuring that the public purpose underlying the funding is actually being met.[47] If a nonprofit corporation running a faith-based program for recovery from drug addiction proves to have less (measurable) success than available secular programs, cutting off funding

---

[46] See *Rumsfeld v.* Forum for Academic and Institutional Rights, Inc., 547 U.S. 47, 69 (2006) (holding that law school's associational rights are not burdened by law requiring military recruiters to have same access to campus as other recruiters because they do not become "members of the school's expressive association").

[47] Martha Minow, *Public and Private Partnerships: Accounting for the New Religion*, 116 Harv. L. Rev. 1229, 1239–40 (2003) (discussing changes to GI Bill that "restricted redemption of the G.I. benefit to state-approved schools and provided for stricter oversight by the Veterans' Administration" after veterans were victimized by unscrupulous practices by proprietary schools that did not deliver on promises).

is not a case of religious discrimination. It is a case of the state acting as agent of the people in furthering the objectives of the funding program. This may be obvious, but the public rhetoric on this issue should reflect recognition that equal funding to religious and secular providers is not a stand-alone public value underlying funding decisions; it is a secondary attribute of a funding decision that otherwise carries out the purposes of the program effectively.

The process by which private actors fulfill public objectives is not a value-free zone, but the "process" values to be imposed should be minimal, widely held, and fundamental to the American vision of an open, democratic society. For example, forbidding a government-funded homeless shelter from refusing shelter to individuals on the basis of race hardly bespeaks of a state bent on eradicating moral diversity. Such measures ensure that the process by which the public objective is met is accessible to everyone. In many cases, it is not much of a stretch to transfer the antidiscrimination principle from a provider's beneficiaries to a provider's employees. It is difficult to build a logical case for making public funds available for hiring only whites to staff a homeless shelter, particularly in a society in which the racial composition of the staff has no readily discernible connection to the provider's ability to serve the public purpose.

Beyond relatively easy cases like these, the inquiry quickly gets thorny. An expansive application of public values – even antidiscrimination values – poses a significant obstacle to associational autonomy. This is most obvious for groups that accept funds with strings attached; however, less direct threats face unfunded groups forced to compete against funded groups.[48] Religious discrimination in hiring by a religious organization that receives public funds is the most fertile ground for exploration, as evidenced by its centrality to the real-world political debates in this area.[49]

Hiring policies at the Salvation Army ("the Army") have provided the grist for the most widely publicized of these conflicts, beginning from news reports in 2001 that the Army had reached a deal with the Bush Administration to allow employment discrimination against gays by religious organizations in exchange for the Army's public support of the President's faith-based initiatives.[50] The ensuing controversy helped derail the proposed legislation, but the Army soon found itself under fire again for practicing religious discrimination as a federally funded nonprofit corporation.

---

[48] Thomas C. Berg, *The Voluntary Principle and Church Autonomy, Then and Now,* 2004 B.Y.U. L. Rev. 1593, 1605 (2004) ("Religious organizations . . . may be pressured to become wholly secular in order to receive aid on a level playing field. Or they may be pressured to alter their programs and messages in order to attract more private support – not the level of support that their original messages would attract, but the extra support necessary to compete against government-favored secular institutions.").

[49] The major legislative obstacle to expanding Charitable Choice was the battle over "government financing of religious discrimination," or "hiring rights." Ira C. Lupu and Robert W. Tuttle, *The Faith-Based Initiative and the Constitution,* 55 DePaul L. Rev. 1, 9 (2005); see also Jeff Zeleny and Michael Luo, *Obama Seeks Bigger Role for Religious Groups,* N.Y. Times, Jul. 2, 2008, at A1 (reporting on Sen. Obama's proposal to forbid employment discrimination by recipients of federal funding).

[50] Dana Milbank, *Salvation Army, Bush Work to OK Hiring Ban on Gays,* Wash. Post., Jul. 10, 2001.

The story of Mary Jane Dessables, a former director of the Army's Social Services for Children agency (SSC) in New York City, makes plain the tension between the Army's officers, who have ultimate authority over the organization and are strongly committed to the religious beliefs underlying its mission, and the front-line employees, who tend to be professional social workers.[51] When Dessables worked at the Army's office in Buffalo, for example, she recalls that before sending a job candidate's resume to the officers for approval, "my boss took the second page off because she had listed that she was a member of the Pro-Choice Action Network," and "that would not be a good thing for the officers to see."[52] At SSC in New York City, by contrast, she asserts that the Army's officers tolerated agency practices that diverged from the Army's religious beliefs, including the provision of birth control and facilitation of abortions. Dessables attributes this inconsistency to the SSC's determination "that we were going to do best practices of social work, and if that conflicted with the Salvation Army structure, we were still going to do best practices of social work."[53] This was a relief to Dessables, who acknowledges that "[w]ithin the social work world, it is fairly well known that the Army is a church with strong religious beliefs on contraception, abortion, and homosexuality."[54] Indeed, according to Dessables, "[i]n graduate school, I had to defend the SSC all the time, saying that we are not like that. We are not counseling against abortion. We are not withholding birth control. We are not discriminating against gays."[55]

Dessables' comfort that her agency's practices were not consistent with the sponsoring organization's conservative religious beliefs dissipated as the Army initiated efforts to integrate more fully the religious dimension of its mission with its ground-level operations. Labeled a "One Army Concept," the reorganization plan sought to ensure that "a reasonable number of Salvationists along with other Christians [will be employed] because The Salvation Army is 'not a Social Service Agency [but] a Christian Movement with a Social Service program.'"[56] Although the previous employee manual had guaranteed "equal employment without unlawful discrimination as to . . . creed," the Army introduced a new manual providing for "equal opportunity for employment . . . except where prohibition on discrimination is inconsistent with the religious principles of the Salvation Army."[57] SSC employees were now required to acknowledge and support the Army's religious mission, which is to "preach the Gospel of Jesus Christ."[58]

---

[51] See *Lown v. Salvation Army*, 393 F. Supp.2d 223 (S.D.N.Y. 2005).

[52] Fred Scaglione, *The Battle of 14th Street*, New York Nonprofit Press, at 8 (May 2004).

[53] *Id.*

[54] *Id.*

[55] *Id.*

[56] 393 F. Supp.2d at 229.

[57] *Id.* at 231 n.5.

[58] *Id.* at 230.

The plan directed the Secretary of Social Services for Greater New York to "conduct all activities of his office with a view to accomplishing the Army's fundamental purpose of proclaiming Jesus Christ as Savior and Lord, which purpose must find expression in both the message proclaimed and the ministry of service performed."[59] Much of the effort focused on personnel, as the Army asked the SSC supervisors to gather information from employees' ministers about their church attendance and standing.[60] When one longtime director resisted, he was escorted off the premises by security.[61]

This is not just a case of a religious organization clamoring to reclaim its roots. It is the case of a religious organization that subsists on public funds clamoring to reclaim its roots. SSC receives 95% of its $50 million annual budget from government entities.[62] This funding was a centerpiece of the lawsuit brought by Dessables and other employees against not only the Salvation Army, but the federal government. The claims were steeped in the language of conscience, asserting that "Plaintiffs cannot, as a matter of conscience and professional responsibility, sign a form stating that they would acknowledge and support The Salvation Army's Evangelical Christian teachings."[63] The court dismissed most of the claims against the federal government, reasoning that there was no basis for concluding that "the employment practices of the Salvation Army may properly be attributed to the government defendants."[64] The court found no intent to discriminate by the government in choosing to fund the Salvation Army because "the contracts existed before the Salvation Army initiated the Reorganization Plan and they included provisions mandating that the Salvation Army not engage in unlawful employment discrimination."[65]

The facts of this case underscore the tension faced by the state when it chooses to fund certain organizations to provide social services. By hiring without reference to religion, the Army hired employees who apparently felt greater loyalty to their fellow social work professionals than to the contrary moral claims that animated the Army to enter the field (and hire them) in the first place. At the same time, supporting such discriminatory practices with taxpayer dollars strikes many as beyond the pale. To critics, tolerating such intrusive and exclusionary employment practices is one thing; financially empowering them with public funds is quite another.

---

[59] *Id.*

[60] According to Dessables' complaint, the Salvation Army began requiring that employees "in the social services and child welfare programs must fill out a form on which they a) identify their church affiliation and all other churches attended for the past decade and b) authorize their religious leaders to reveal private communications to the Salvation Army." Compl. ¶ 6.

[61] *Id.* ¶ 9.

[62] 393 F. Supp.2d at 228.

[63] Compl. ¶ 9.

[64] 393 F. Supp.2d at 235.

[65] *Id.* at 236.

It will always be tempting to use the strings attached to funding as a way to enlist private actors in public projects.[66] As Jody Freeman points out, private actors need not be viewed simply as "menacing outsiders whose influence threatens to derail legitimate 'public' purposes," for they are "also regulatory resources capable of contributing to the efficacy and legitimacy of administration."[67] Freeman is remarkably candid in acknowledging that she sees privatization, not "as a means of shrinking government," but as "a mechanism for expanding government's reach into realms traditionally thought private."[68] The "public/private engagement" can enhance "state power while simultaneously augmenting private power," as "agencies may extend their influence to matters and actors that they could not otherwise lawfully reach."[69]

The problem is that this state aggrandizement, however noble its aims, threatens to marginalize the religious and moral convictions on which a private provider's devotion to the common good is based. To the extent that the strings attached to state funding render providers morally fungible, the cost cannot be measured simply in the number of providers who choose autonomy over the level of public service made possible by funding, but must also count the providers who choose the path of homogeneity, valuing continued funding over autonomy. These providers essentially make themselves accountable to the collective norms pursued by the state, rather than the conscience-driven norms of their constituents.

As noted previously, state funding decisions are laden with moral claims, and nothing in this book should be read as presuming that the state is wedded to a position of moral neutrality. Rather, this book is premised on a more nuanced question: Under what circumstances can the state assert moral claims as a marketplace actor without shutting down the marketplace itself? When the state funds an organization that includes as part of the public service a moral claim that conflicts with an essential public value, the message can easily be attributed to the state based on its decision to fund that particular provider.[70] If the moral claims expressed by the provider are tangential to the public service, there is less reason to deny funding because there is less risk of attribution.

For example, the Salvation Army's theological views, which include a belief that homosexuality is immoral, should not categorically preclude its affiliated social service agencies from receiving government funds. However, if the Salvation Army were to operate an AIDS hospice in which residents were asked to repent from any homosexual conduct as part of making peace with God, the government would not be overreaching morally to deny funding to such a program. In its role as a marketplace

---

[66] Jody Freeman, *The Private Role in Public Governance*, 75 N.Y.U. L. Rev. 543, 548 (2000).

[67] *Id.* at 548–9.

[68] Jody Freeman, *Extending Public Law Norms Through Privatization*, 116 Harv. L. Rev. 1285, 1285 (2003).

[69] *Id.* at 671.

[70] If the message is religious, Establishment clause problems may arise.

actor embodying public values, the state can ensure that its functions are carried out in keeping with those values. But, in its concurrent role as marketplace facilitator, the state overreaches if it requires all funded organizations to conform their overall moral identities to public norms. Obviously, it will not always be easy to distinguish between the moral claims made as part of a provider's public function and the moral claims otherwise embedded in the provider's identity, but the demarcation is essential for maintaining venues of conscience without rendering the state an amoral shell.

The state may also ensure that the social service providers it chooses to fund allow equal access to those funds – whether by individuals who need the funded services or by individuals who seek the funded employment. Although the state's legitimate interest in ensuring access does not justify heavy-handed state requirements that the organization promote messages that are in tension with its mission,[71] the state can require that formal barriers to access be removed. If this makes it more difficult to compete in the marketplace for certain discriminatory groups who must give up funding because they reject the equal access norm, so be it. Conscience's vitality requires the maintenance of venues in which countercultural convictions can find shared expression and purpose; it does not require that those venues be given state-subsidized platforms. The vitality of conscience must be measured by an organization's freedom to remain faithful to their mission, not by their marketplace success. If the Ku Klux Klan were somehow able to open and operate an effective homeless shelter that served and was staffed by whites only, it should not expect to receive public funds.

As a marketplace actor, the state is free to include within its moral claims a prohibition on funding the Salvation Army pursuant to the equal access norm. However, in light of the principled distinction between the Army's hiring discrimination and other forms of hiring discrimination, and given the importance of mission-sensitive hiring to a vibrant marketplace of social service providers, the state should decline to do so. Religious discrimination in hiring should not preclude public funding of religious organizations because allowing religious organizations to consider religion in hiring does not stack the deck in favor of religion. An exemption in this case gives religious organizations the same ability to pursue their missions that secular organizations enjoy. Planned Parenthood will not, and should not, lose access to public funds by requiring employees to affirm the cause of reproductive rights. Amnesty International should not lose funding by declining to hire a pro-death penalty advocate. The Ku Klux Klan should not receive public funds with a whites-only hiring requirement, but a requirement that all employees indicate support for the Klan's mission (including a belief in the racial superiority of whites) should not be similarly

---

[71] For example, a government council in the United Kingdom temporarily cut off funding to a Christian nursing home because the group would not ask its residents – all of whom are over 80 years old – "about their sexual orientation four times a year" or "use elderly gay, lesbian, bisexual and transgender people in its leaflets." David Harrison, *Christian care home victorious in gay dispute*, Daily Telegraph, Feb. 7, 2009.

disqualifying.[72] The Salvation Army should be able to hire employees who share its commitment to proclaiming "the Gospel of Jesus Christ." Conditioning funds on an organization's willingness to sacrifice its identity as a community of shared belief unnecessarily excludes the groups that place the highest value on their shared beliefs and unwisely homogenizes the rest.

Religious organizations are exempt from Title VII's prohibition on religious discrimination in hiring, and their acceptance of public funds does not negate the rationale for that exemption. If anything, the rationale is even stronger when public funds are involved. As the state pushes more of its functions to nonstate entities, its funding decisions can reshape entire fields and determine a given organization's competitive viability. If only secular organizations are permitted to hire consistently with their missions and maintain funding eligibility, the marketplace in those fields could quickly skew against religious organizations. The state, in its conscience-friendly role as marketplace facilitator, should permit funded organizations to hire individuals who share the moral or religious claims that motivate the organization's entry into the public service arena in the first place.

The importance of this specific exemption notwithstanding, the state does not overreach by imposing more general nondiscrimination hiring and service norms, demanding effective and efficient performance of the publicly valued task, and distancing itself from moral claims that conflict with public values. An association may find it difficult to thrive in the marketplace without public funding, but it should proceed cautiously, counting the cost of becoming more reliant on – and responsive to – the state, rather than the constituents whose moral claims provide the association's very reason for existence.

Indirect Funding (Vouchers)

The conscience-squelching dangers of direct government funding are partly alleviated through a voucher system, presently used for services such as childcare, substance abuse recovery, and education. When individual beneficiaries of government programs are allowed to choose where to spend government funds, the state is acting as a marketplace facilitator. Rather than entrusting the state with the responsibility of selecting particular providers that most deserve funding, individuals are empowered to bring the dictates of their own consciences to bear on the choice of provider. Within broad limits, the supply of state-funded providers should be allowed to reflect individuals' moral and religious preferences.[73]

---

[72] Another caveat: given the state's legitimate expectation that funded services will not include moral claims that conflict with public values such as equality, the shelter could not include any discernible indication of the Ku Klux Klan's mission, which would probably also mean that the shelter would have to be operated under a name that did not indicate a connection with the Klan.

[73] See *Simmons-Harris v. Zelman*, 122 S. Ct. 2460 (2002) (holding that Cleveland's school voucher program did not violate Establishment clause because the program did not favor the participation of

Three factors make voucher programs more amenable to conscience than direct funding programs. First, the relationship between the state and the funded provider is more attenuated, and attribution of the provider's moral claims to the state less likely, when the beneficiary chooses the provider. There is thus less danger that individuals will perceive their moral claims as being opposed or rendered superfluous by the monolithic state's espousal of public norms. Second, the state's actual impact on the marketplace is not as stark when responsibility to direct the funds is dispersed among many individual moral agents. With vouchers, prospects for conscience do not rely as squarely on the state's capability of self-restraint; market mechanisms will more naturally bring the moral identities of providers in closer conformity with the moral identities of beneficiaries. Third, when providers are dependent on being selected by individual beneficiaries, grass roots accountability develops; that is, the organization's moral identity is defined from the bottom up, which is the benchmark of an effective mediating function. The most serious threat posed by a direct funding program – that providers become morally homogeneous agents of the government rather than venues for the living out of divergent moral convictions – becomes less pressing.

The state's role is not completely erased, however. In approving an organization as an eligible recipient of vouchers, the state must ensure that the organization will accomplish the public purpose effectively. Because government funds are involved, the government should have reasonable discretion to inject its own view of effectiveness into those requirements. Unlike the direct funding context, the state should not be as concerned with the substantive moral claims expressed by a provider in a voucher system, even when the claims are part of the service provided. If the operators of an otherwise effective AIDS hospice held bible studies for residents in which they expressed theologically conservative views on scriptural passages discussing homosexuality, the state's role as marketplace facilitator counsels in favor of maintaining the hospice's eligibility for voucher funds. This assumes that 1) the voucher program includes viable alternative hospices at which such bible studies would not occur; and 2) beneficiaries are informed of the moral claims reflected in a hospice's operation prior to selecting one. If options are lacking, of course, then the empowerment promised by vouchers is illusory.

The "process" values – those public norms governing the openness and accessibility of a funded program – remain relevant even with vouchers. Such values do not define the substance of the services eligible for funding; instead, they forbid funded providers from negating citizens' eligibility to act as market participants. As with direct funding, providers' resistance to those norms will become more heated with the norms' expansion.

---

religious schools over nonreligious schools); McCallum II, 214 F. Supp. 2d 905 (W.D. Wis. 2002), aff'd 324 F.3d 880 (7th Cir. 2003) (upholding state funding of faith-intensive substance abuse treatment for individuals on probation or parole).

Consider the case of the adult day care center in Minnesota operated by a conservative church and funded in part by government money. A transgendered individual was turned away from the center on the ground that his presence was inconsistent with the church's beliefs.[74] Government officials wisely ended their funding of the center based on the nondiscrimination requirements of the funding legislation. It makes no difference whether participants are excluded by an organization funded directly by the state or as part of a voucher program. Either way, the individual has been excluded from publicly funded services for reasons deemed illegitimate by the public. Deferring to these expressions of the collective conscience does not elevate the state as moral arbiter, but simply sets the ground rules of a functioning, publicly funded marketplace.

The differences between vouchers and direct funding should not be understated. Vouchers provide a more fertile ground for conscience because as part of a viable market, they entail the voluntary and mutual embrace of mission by beneficiaries and providers. In this regard, vouchers reflect the communal nature of conscience while avoiding the mistake of equating communal formation with collective imposition. With vouchers in hand, beneficiaries can become part of a conscience-shaped community in a way that is not feasible when funding decisions rest exclusively with the state.

Regulation Absent Funding

In the absence of funding, government regulation of an association's pursuit of a shared moral purpose becomes most dangerous because it represents the removal of a particular moral claim from the marketplace completely. Moral claims, as divergent from the mainstream as they might be, provide the foundations for venues in which conscience can be lived out. Unhinged from funding, the state's naked assertion of authority over morally divergent groups becomes a straight power play. It is no longer a question of taxpayers subsidizing practices that create tension with foundational public norms; it is a question of the state using a failure to adhere to those public norms as justification for shutting down a group's market participation entirely. Especially when state regulation is not limited to guaranteeing access to essential public goods and services,[75] the viability of conscience is imperiled.

One noteworthy recent example of this is the enforcement of a Massachusetts law requiring that adoption agencies not discriminate against same-sex couples as

---

[74] David Peterson, *Faith and law collide in St. Francis: A church's refusal to care for a woman who was once a man highlights a national battle over faith-based social programs*, Mpls. Star-Trib., Apr. 11, 2006, at A1.

[75] That is, if there is a functioning market, access is not at issue, and the case for state regulation is considerably weakened. See Robert Araujo, S.J., *Conscience, Totalitarianism, and the Positivist Mind*, 77 Miss. L.J. 571, 594 (2007) ("If the legislature has the competence to say the Governor is the head of the state, why should the citizen be required to swear in a public oath that this is indeed the case?").

potential parents for placement purposes. Rather than include same-sex couples in its adoption services, Catholic Charities decided to end its services in light of binding Church teaching. In enacting this law,[76] the state was not acting as market participant, seeking to influence Catholic Charities' moral identity through the provision or withholding of funds.[77] Nor was the state acting as a check to ensure that public services are performed competently. There was no allegation that Catholic Charities' discrimination against same-sex couples had compromised the quality or effectiveness of its adoption work – unless the failure to abide by the nondiscrimination norm is, by definition, equated with a lack of competence. It is not as though the exclusion of same-sex couples from the pool of adoptive parents compromised the pool's quality to such an extent that there was a meaningful impact on the best interests of adopted children.

Provided that birth parents were informed of the organization's discriminatory policy, and that they could have chosen other agencies that did not exclude same-sex couples, the state should have allowed the marketplace to function. Note that this does not mean that Massachusetts officials needed to remain on the sidelines completely; they could have publicly criticized Catholic Charities' policy while continuing to ensure that no state funding made its way to the organization. The legislature could have prohibited discrimination by the state's own adoption agency, sending a powerful message and perhaps recalibrating the industry norm as the largest adoption services provider. Other citizens and the myriad associations to which they belong could have boycotted, protested, and otherwise brought attention to the discrimination in hopes that Catholic Charities would eventually change its position. Such a bottom-up approach to social change provides even more avenues for individuals to act on conscience. Instead, Massachusetts shut down any potential market-driven moral interaction by elevating its nondiscrimination norm as a collective trump. Instead of Catholic Charities responding to the demands of its constituents, it was left to pay heed to the dictates of the state.

Admittedly, certain state dictates are prudent in an endeavor as undeniably public as the placement of children with adults other than their biological parents. For example, suppose that Catholic Charities excluded not same-sex couples as adoptive parents, but nonwhite couples. Leaving this moral stance to operate freely within the marketplace would ignore the fact that the public discourse on race

---

[76] The Code of Massachusetts Regulations requires that adoption agencies, as a condition of obtaining a state license, not "discriminate in providing services to children and their families on the basis of race, religion, cultural heritage, political beliefs, national origin, marital status, sexual orientation, or disability." 102 Mass. Code Regs. 1.03(1) (2007). According to Martha Minow, "[t]his provision dates back to at least 1989, when Massachusetts amended its antidiscrimination statute dealing with employment, housing, and government services to include sexual orientation as one of the forbidden grounds of discrimination." Martha Minow, *Should Religious Groups Be Exempt From Civil Rights Laws?*, 48 B.C. L. Rev. 781, 832 n.301 (2007).

[77] Catholic Charities Boston did receive state funds, but the funding was not the basis of the state's exercise of authority.

has extended over many years and has resulted in what can readily be perceived as a broad consensus on the moral illegitimacy of racial discrimination. No comparable conversation on sexual orientation has yet occurred. In other words, the normative claim for freedom of conscience on sexual orientation is qualitatively different than a similar claim on race given the degree to which moral claims related to sexual orientation remain contested.[78] It is not that the state should not stake out positions on moral controversies until they are conclusively resolved; it is just that they should resist shutting down opposing view points so early in the conversation.

More glaring examples of the state's moral overreaching came recently in California and New York, where the legislatures enacted measures requiring all employers to include contraceptives in their employee health care coverage. An exemption for religious employers was drawn so narrowly that Catholic Charities fell outside its scope. The law was upheld by the courts,[79] and thus employers in that state are required to subsidize the use of products that they find fundamentally immoral. In this regard, the legislation embodies the hollowed-out vision of conscience that dominates today's discourse and obliges the state to favor the individual in any contest against group authority. It is, of course, a woefully simplistic view of the conditions necessary for conscience to flourish. Catholic Charities did not foreclose the use of contraceptives by any individual: If an employee desired to use them, she could have paid for them herself; if she considered it important not to have to pay for them, she could have chosen another employer. On this point, the New York Court of Appeals asserted, "when a religious organization chooses to hire nonbelievers it must, at least to some degree, be prepared to accept neutral regulations imposed to protect those employees' legitimate interests in doing what their own beliefs permit."[80]

Left unaddressed is the organization's interest in serving as a communal embodiment of a distinctive set of beliefs. It is not as though the statute protects the individual against being *coerced* in her exercise of conscience; it goes much farther and protects the individual against being *inconvenienced* in her exercise of conscience, but at the cost of erasing another venue where countercultural moral claims can be integrated into the life of the community. The state does not honor conscience simply by empowering individual preference; in its relational dimension, conscience requires a recognition that group authority matters and that the authority of individual preference cannot be unfettered.

---

[78] For a fuller discussion of the considerations underlying our law's apparent lack of deference to dissenting consciences on the matter of racial discrimination, see chapter 1.

[79] See *Catholic Charities v. Serio*, 859 N.E.2d 459 (N.Y. Ct. App. 2006); *Catholic Charities of Sacramento, Inc. v. Superior Court of Sacramento County*, 85 P.3d 67 (Cal. 2004); Susan J. Stabile, *State Attempts to Define Religion: The Ramifications of Applying Mandatory Prescription Contraceptive Coverage Statutes to Religious Employers*, 28 Harv. J.L. & Pub. Pol'y 741 (2005).

[80] *Serio*, 859 N.E.2d at 468.

CONSCIENCE AND ASSOCIATIONS

In extolling the virtues of associations, Tocqueville may not have foreseen their central role in some of the most wrenching battles that have shaken American society over the years. "In a country like the United States," he naively explained, "in which the differences of opinion are mere differences of hue, the right of association may remain unrestrained without evil consequences."[81] Even so, that does not mean that he was somehow deluded into thinking that associations would limit themselves to uncontroversial community functions such as barn raisings and church potlucks. Even at the time of his American journey, voluntary associations were already staking out combative positions on slavery and other divisive issues. Our national history is replete with instances of individuals banding together to pursue priorities that unmistakably heightened social tensions and in many cases tore at the very fabric of society itself.

Illiberal associations may stand out more starkly today than in earlier eras because of our society's growing recognition of human diversity and our growing commitment to inclusive values such as equality and tolerance. As our increasingly pluralist society spawns ever more social cleavages, causes, and fringes to which individuals and groups are drawn to plant their respective ideological flags, there is a temptation to conclude that our association-friendly legal and political climate has finally outlived its utility. But conscience's relational dimension demands space for relationships built around shared values, beliefs, and priorities: It demands space for voluntary associations. Maintaining such space requires us to account for several core truths about the mediating role of associations.

First, associations are uniquely capable of carving out a shared identity that is valued by the individual. This identity is defined, in significant part, in relation to others and to the state, and places the association in tension with both. Tension presumes resistance in both directions; in the case of the exclusionary association, this means that associations must have the latitude to define themselves, but it does not mean that the resulting definition trumps all conflicting state interests.

Second, associations provide a voice to individuals who, absent collective expression, would not be heard above the din of modern America. The mediating tension arising from the exercise of this shared voice requires the maintenance of resistance on all three fronts of the association in relationship: The association must be ensured access to the public forum on an equal basis with other speakers; the dissenting individual must be assured that the access is not exclusive to any particular association; and the state must be permitted to identify and maintain the crucial distinction between access and promotion.

---

[81] Tocqueville, Democracy in America, 204. See also John Inazu, The Forgotten Freedom of Assembly 157–60 (2009) (unpublished Ph.D. dissertation, University of North Carolina) (on file with author).

Third, associations empower individuals to pursue common objectives that would otherwise be beyond their reach and that may not be shared by those around them or by the state. The importance of purpose demands that religious associations be allowed to compete for state funds on an equal basis with nonreligious associations, but the potentially corrosive effect of such funding on the association-state tension demands caution, if not resistance, on the association's part.

Fourth, any mediating role played by associations presupposes a degree of autonomy that is sufficient to allow the association to facilitate shared meaning among its members. The degree of autonomy is not boundless, as it is properly subject to the tension of the association in relationship. For the well-being of individual participants in an association that flouts traditional norms of due process and democracy, the degree of autonomy afforded must be a function of the voluntariness of participation, that is, members' acceptance of the intersubjective obligations that are at the base of moral claims. For the well-being of the state, autonomy cannot extend to all circumstances where the state has a pressing interest, such as where an association threatens significant harm to those outside the association or to nonconsenting participants.

Together, these mediating pathways allow the individual to transcend herself, to shape an existence that is bigger than her own yet substantively distinct from the conforming and alienating pressures of the state. Significantly, this function demands that associations operate within limits, for allowing associations to operate with unfettered discretion not only threatens important individual and state interests, but also threatens the tension on which the association's mediating role is based. As bridges between the individual and the state, associations are, by their very nature, informed by and comprise both the individualist and collectivist aspects of our existence. To a more limited extent, they may be held accountable to both.

This accountability is best expressed as an effort to maintain the mediating tension by acknowledging as legitimate the dual pressures exerted on associations by the individual and the state and giving those pressures the force of law in those limited instances when an association has gone beyond its proper mediating role. The mediating value of associations, then, is, in large part, a function of the associational marketplace, that is, the extent to which society creates and protects a common space in which associations can pursue their chosen identities, expressions, and purposes. It is essential to recognize that the space cannot be cultivated on an association-by-association basis. To the extent we seek to squelch associations that embrace social agendas contrary to generally accepted conceptions of the common good, we threaten to replace the associational marketplace with the will of the state.

Tocqueville's confident pronouncement of this country's unparalleled "success" with associations thereby takes on a new emphasis. This notion of success does not mean that every association must produce undisputed, tangible benefit to our society. Success depends not on the eradication of unsavory associations, but on individual Americans' continued willingness to join together with like-minded others in pursuit of the good, however unpopular their conception of the good might be. It is conceivable that individuals and the associations to which they belong would give up that struggle, instead ceding to the state the sole power to construe and construct a common good. In this regard, it is the *absence* of controversial groups from the associational landscape that would cast our "success" in a more doubtful light. Such groups show that individuals continue to connect themselves in meaningful, efficacious, and wildly unpopular ways, and that nearly two centuries after Tocqueville's observations, associations remain at the center of the national story because they are a primary means by which Americans define themselves and the world in which they live. In a very real sense, voluntary associations embody conscience's relational dimension. As such, the law should reflect the recognition that a vibrant associational landscape is vital evidence of conscience's flourishing.

6

Pharmacies

Given the morally controversial nature of developing medical technologies and the centrality of health care decisions to virtually all modern conceptions of individual autonomy, it is no surprise that health care is a primary battleground in today's conscience wars. Health care consumers are understandably concerned at the prospect of a provider's moral qualms limiting the available range of treatment options, even if the consumer finds the treatment to be morally permissible. Providers are understandably concerned at the prospect of the state, acting on the consumer's behalf, compelling them to violate their own moral convictions. Both consumer and provider seem to have conscience on their side. Little attention has been paid to the nature, much less the importance, of the relational dimension of these conscience claims.

This omission is exemplified glaringly by the well-publicized battle over the extent to which pharmacists may allow their religiously shaped moral judgments to narrow the range of services they offer. Both sides beseech the state to enshrine collectively a particular vision of the individual's prerogative.[1] On one side, conscience is invoked to justify legislation that would enable individual pharmacists to refuse to fill prescriptions on moral grounds without suffering any negative repercussions, whether in the form of government penalty, employment discrimination, or third-party liability. On the other side, conscience is invoked to justify legislation that would enable individual consumers to compel pharmacists to fill any legally obtained prescription without delay or inconvenience. For the most part, legislatures have embraced the zero-sum terms in which the combatants have framed the contest. Academics have done little to change the course of the conversation. As with most legal scholarship,

---

[1] See Rob Stein, *Citing Religious Beliefs, Some Pharmacists Refusing to Fill Prescriptions*, Wash. Post, Mar. 28, 2005, at A1 (reporting that battle over pharmacists "has triggered pitched political battles in State Houses across the nation as politicians seek to pass laws either to protect pharmacists from being penalized or force them to carry out their duties").

the proffered resolutions are grounded in the law's coercive power: in the guise of insurmountable individual right, nonnegotiable state trump, or both.

The relational dimension of conscience asks us to step back from these two-dimensional terms of engagement and to contextualize both the pharmacists' and customers' moral claims. Taking conscience seriously suggests that the state should allow all sides in the pharmacist controversy to live out their convictions in the marketplace, maintaining a forum in which pharmacies craft their own particular conscience policies in response to the demands of their employees and customers. If a pharmacy wants to require all of its pharmacists to provide all legal pharmaceuticals, or to forbid all of its pharmacists from providing certain pharmaceuticals, or to leave it within the pharmacist's individual moral discretion whether to provide certain pharmaceuticals, so be it. The pharmacy must answer to the employee and the customer, not the state, and employees and customers must utilize market power to contest (or embrace) the moral norms of their choosing. Rather than making all pharmacies morally fungible via state edict, the market allows the flourishing of plural moral norms in the provision of pharmaceuticals.

PHARMACISTS ON THE FRONT LINES

In July 2002, Wisconsin pharmacist Neil Noesen rejected a college student's prescription for birth control pills and refused to refer her to another pharmacy.[2] A devout Roman Catholic, Noesen considered the facilitation of contraceptive use to be immoral. The state pharmacy board voted to discipline Noesen and required, as a condition of maintaining his license, that he provide written notice to prospective employers of the pharmaceuticals he declines to dispense and the steps he will take to ensure that a patient's access is not impeded.[3] He was also required to pay for the costs of the proceeding (amounting to as much as $20,000) and to undergo six hours of continuing pharmacy education.[4]

A New Culture War Battleground

One's view of Noesen's conduct and subsequent punishment is a good indication of how one will view the broader controversy over pharmacists and conscience. In Wisconsin, the Noesen episode is frequently cited as a galvanizing impetus on both sides of the debate.[5] For some, Noesen is a courageous figure standing against the

---

[2] See Charisse Jones, *Druggists refuse to give out pill*, USA Today, Nov. 9, 2004, at 3A.

[3] Apparently, Noesen had reached a verbal agreement with his supervisor to avoid filling birth control prescriptions, but had not provided written notice to the pharmacy itself. *Legal battle over pharmacists' obligations is joined in Illinois*, Chain Drug Rev., Jun. 6, 2005, at 248.

[4] See *id.*

[5] See, e.g., Stacy Forster, *Lawmakers push for conscience clauses*, Milw. J. Sentinel, Mar. 5, 2005, at B1 ("The Noesen case has pushed the issue of a pharmacists' 'conscience clause' to the forefront.").

onrushing tide of unfettered and self-centered reproductive choice. Although Noesen's refusal to dispense birth control pills failed to win legislative backing, his case
helped drive both houses of the state legislature to pass a bill forbidding employment
discrimination, state disciplinary action, or third-party liability based on a pharmacist's refusal to dispense drugs used for sterilization, abortion, the destruction of a
human embryo, or euthanasia.[6]

From the opposite vantage point, Noesen is seen as a paternalistic zealot using
his state-licensed power over pharmaceuticals to demean women and hinder lawful
access to health care. In vetoing the bill, Governor Jim Doyle reflected this perspective, explaining, "you're moving into very dangerous precedent where doctors make
moral decisions on what medical care they'll provide."[7] The governor's allies on
the issue subsequently sought to enshrine their own consumer-driven moral claims,
introducing legislation requiring "every pharmacist" to "administer, distribute, and
dispense" all FDA-approved contraceptives unless a patient will be harmed.[8] One
of the bill's sponsors explained that a physician "must be assured that his or her
medical judgment will not be overruled by a pharmacist's personal moral or religious beliefs."[9] Even if a woman's overall access to contraceptives is not jeopardized,
another sponsor insisted that she should not "have to go through the humiliation of
being denied her legal, safe contraception at the pharmacy counter."[10]

As any casual observer of recent news coverage can attest, Noesen's story is not
unique, and every reported incident of a pharmacist refusing to dispense FDA-
approved drugs and/or being punished for such refusal is quickly assimilated by the
culture war armies and unfurled as a battle flag to rally the troops. Eighteen states have
laws that explicitly address the question of pharmacists and conscience.[11] Four states
have enacted conscience clauses specifically protecting the exercise of conscience
by pharmacists,[12] and other states encompass pharmacists within the conscience

---

[6] Assemb. B. 67, 95th Leg., Reg. Sess. (Wis. 2003), S.B. 155, 95th Leg., Reg. Sess. (Wis. 2005).

[7] Stacy Forster, *Women's Health Debate Intensifies*, Milw. J. Sentinel, Apr. 21, 2004, at B1.

[8] Assemb. B. 532, 97th Leg., Reg. Sess. (Wis. 2005). The opposing side introduced more narrowly
tailored conscience legislation – covering only drugs believed by the pharmacist to cause abortion or
other death – in an effort to overcome the governor's veto. See S.B. 155, 95th Leg., Reg. Sess. (Wis.
2003).

[9] *Democratic Leaders Announce Birth Control Protection Act*, Press Release of State Senator Judy Robson,
Jun. 7, 2005.

[10] Judith Davidoff, *Democrats Unveil Their Bill on the Pill*, Capital Times, Jun. 7, 2005, at 3A (quoting
state senator Christine Sinicki).

[11] National Women's Law Center, *Pharmacy Refusals: State Laws, Regulations, and Policies* (Jan. 2009)
(available at http://www.nwlc.org/pdf/PharmacyRefusalPoliciesJanuary2008.pdf) (accessed Feb. 16,
2009).

[12] The states are Arkansas, Georgia, Mississippi, and South Dakota. See Ark. Code Ann. § 20–16–304;
Ga. Comp. R. & Regs. § 480–5-.03(n); Miss. Code Ann. § 41–107–5; S.D. Codified Laws § 36–11–
70. As this book went to press, Idaho was on the verge of enacting similar legislation. See Simon
Shifrin, *House Passes Bill to Give Idaho Pharmacists Conscience Protections*, Idaho Bus. Rev., Mar.
30, 2009.

protection afforded health care providers in general.[13] Mississippi's statute is held up as a template by the conscience movement because it protects pharmacists[14] from being held "civilly, criminally, or administratively liable for declining to partici-pate in a health care service that violates his or her conscience," and forbids any employment discrimination based on such exercises of conscience.[15]

Other states have pursued rights claims from the opposite angle, enacting laws aimed at ensuring customer access to all drugs for which they have a valid prescrip-tion. California law forbids a pharmacist from refusing to fill a prescription on moral or religious grounds unless she notifies her employer in writing of her objections and the employer is able to ensure the patient's "timely access to the prescribed drug."[16] New Jersey requires a pharmacy to fill all lawful prescriptions for drugs that it carries, notwithstanding an employee's moral or religious objections. If a pharmacy does not carry a drug, it is required to help the customer locate another pharmacy that does carry the drug.[17] As of 2009, fourteen states have some type of law aimed at ensuring that pharmacists' conscience claims do not threaten customer access. Other states have considered, or are considering, similar measures.[18]

State action on this issue is not waiting on the legislature. The Washington State Pharmacy Board, under pressure from the governor, has adopted a rule requiring pharmacies to fill all legally valid prescriptions on site, effectively ending a practice by which pharmacists could decline to fill a prescription on moral or religious grounds and refer the customer to another pharmacy. Now, an individual pharmacist can exercise a right of conscience, but only if another pharmacist is present to fill the prescription in question.[19]

---

[13] See, e.g., O.R.S. § 127.625 (Oregon law shielding health care providers from being required to participate in the withdrawal or withholding of life-sustaining procedures); Colo. Rev. Stat. § 25–6–102(9) (Colorado law providing that "[n]o private institution or physician, nor any agent or employee of such institution or physician, shall be prohibited from refusing to provide contraceptive procedures, supplies, and information when such refusal is based upon religious or conscientious objection"); Fla. Stat. Ann. § 381.0051(6) (statute "shall not be interpreted so as to prevent a physician or other person from refusing to furnish any contraceptive . . . for medical or religious reasons"); Wyo. Stat. § 42–5–101(d) (protecting refusals to offer "family planning and birth control services"); Tenn. Code § 68–34–104(5) (same as Colorado).

[14] The statute covers all "health care providers," which is explicitly defined to include pharmacists. See Miss. Stat. Ann. § 41–107–3.

[15] Miss. Stat. § 41–107–5(2), (3).

[16] Cal. Bus. & Prof. Code § 733.

[17] N.J. Stat. § 45:14–67.1.

[18] For example, Missouri's legislature considered a bill that would require a pharmacist to fill all prescriptions unless her employer could accommodate her objections without undue hardship to the consumer; "undue hardship" is defined in part as an inability to fill the prescription in "the equivalent time period" as the pharmacy fills other prescriptions of in-stock medications. Mo. Senate Bill No. 458 (2005).

[19] In late 2007, a federal district court temporarily enjoined implementation of the new rule on the ground that its enforcement would violate the free exercise rights of pharmacists. *Stormans, Inc. v. Selecky*, 524 F. Supp.2d 1245 (W.D. Wash. 2007). The ruling was overturned by the Ninth Circuit. See *Stormans, Inc. v. Selecky*, 571 F.3d 960 (9th Cir. 2009).

In response to two incidents in Chicago in which pharmacists refused to dispense birth control pills, Illinois Governor Rod Blagojevich ordered all pharmacies serving the public[20] to dispense "all FDA-approved drugs or devices that prevent pregnancy" to the patient "without delay, consistent with the normal time frame for filling any other prescription."[21] The governor's stated justification for the order was pitched in the language of individual rights, albeit those of the customer, not the pharmacist.[22] A significant motivation seemed not so much a perceived threat to contraceptive access itself but potential inconvenience and aggravation.[23] Efforts by pharmacy chains to carve out their own policies on the issue were immediately squelched.[24]

This is a battle that has exploded in only the past few years, which shows no signs of abating. Indeed, as therapies utilizing embryonic stem cells become widely available, the conflict promises to escalate dramatically. In the states that have not taken up the issue, observers believe that "it is only a matter of time."[25]

And in a predictable turn, the battle was joined on the national stage. Competing bills were introduced in Congress. One bill, premised on honoring the consciences of individual pharmacists while requiring that every pharmacy ensure that all legal prescriptions are filled, would have guaranteed that all of the nation's pharmacies dispense all legal pharmaceuticals.[26] A more narrowly focused approach was taken by the proposed Workplace Religious Freedom Act, under which a

[20] The order applies to Division I Pharmacies, defined as "any pharmacy that engages in general community pharmacy practice and that is open to, or offers pharmacy service to, the general public." Pharmacy Practice Act, 68 ILCS 1330.5.

[21] *Governor Blagojevich moves to make emergency contraceptives rule permanent*, State of Illinois, Department of Financial and Professional Regulation, Official Press Release, Apr. 18, 2005.

[22] "Filling prescriptions for birth control is about protecting a woman's right to have access to medicine her doctor says she needs. Nothing more. Nothing less. We will vigorously protect that right." *Id.* (press release).

[23] Dirk Johnson and Hilary Shenfeld, *Swallowing a Bitter Pill in Illinois*, Newsweek, Apr. 25, 2005, at 28 (reporting Blagojevich's assertion that women should be able to fill birth control prescriptions "without delay, without hassle and without a lecture").

[24] See *Four Pharmacists Suspended Over Morning-After Pill*, Chi. Trib., Dec. 1, 2005, at 7 (reporting Walgreen's suspension of pharmacists for failing to comply with governor's rule); *Legal Battle Over Pharmacists' Obligations Is Joined in Illinois*, Chain Drug Rev., Jun. 6, 2005 (reporting on claim that Albertson's accommodated a pharmacist's religious beliefs by having him "refer patients seeking emergency contraceptives to another pharmacy less than 500 yards" from the store "until it was required to comply with the governor's rule"). A legal challenge filed by pharmacists was still making its way through the courts as this book went to press. See *Morr-Fitz, Inc. v. Blagojevich*, No. 104692, 2008 WL 5246307 (Ill. Dec. 18, 2008) (ruling that pharmacists have standing to bring claim, but not reaching merits).

[25] Caryn Tamber, *Conscience Clauses for Pharmacists Is Controversial Topic in MD and Other States*, Daily Record, Jun. 10, 2005.

[26] Edward Epstein, *Boxer Eyes Prescription Protection: Bill Would Secure Birth Control Rights*, S.F. Chron., Apr. 19, 2005, at A1; Monica Davey and Pam Belluck, *Pharmacies Balk on After-Sex Pill and Widen Fight*, N.Y. Times, Apr. 19, 2005, at A1 (reporting that "bills requiring all legal prescriptions to be filled have been introduced in recent days [in both the Senate and the House]").

pharmacy would accommodate the religious objections of a pharmacist by ensuring that another pharmacist is on duty to dispense the drug in question.[27]

The national debate received a high-profile jolt when President George W. Bush issued a new conscience regulation in the closing days of his administration. The rule cut off federal funding from state and local governments, hospitals, health plans, or other entities that do not accommodate health care personnel – including pharmacists – who refuse to participate in research or services that are contrary to their religious beliefs or moral convictions.[28] As a condition of continued funding, more than 584,000 health care organizations were given until October 1, 2009, to provide written certification of compliance.[29] Supporters insisted that the regulation merely implemented existing law[30] and was necessary "to ensure that health-care professionals have the same civil rights enjoyed by all Americans."[31] Opponents claimed that the rule threatened patients' rights and women's health, and that it would "cause chaos among providers across the country."[32] Seven states and two family-planning groups sued to block the rule,[33] and the rule's critics pressured President Obama to revoke it.

The Pharmacist Wars in Context

So how and why did pharmacists so suddenly take center stage in our collective culture war drama? Conscience clauses have been common since *Roe v. Wade*, as the reigning political judgment since then has held that health care providers not be compelled to participate in a procedure as morally wrenching as abortion. Such clauses remain fairly uncontroversial as applied to physicians, but the advent of "Plan B" emergency contraception has driven pharmacists to seek the same protection enjoyed by physicians. Plan B prevents pregnancy for up to three days after intercourse, and some pharmacists believe that it functions as an abortifacient by blocking the fertilized egg's implantation in the uterus.[34] Coupled with pharmacists'

---

[27] Senators Santorum and Kerry explain that under their Workplace Religious Freedom Act, a "pharmacist who does not wish to dispense certain medications would not have to do so long as another pharmacist is on duty and would dispense the medications." See Letters, N.Y. Times, Apr. 12, 2005.

[28] *See* 45 C.F.R. § 88.4(d) (2009).

[29] Rob Stein, *Rule Shields Health Workers Who Withhold Care Based on Beliefs*, Wash. Post, Dec. 19, 2008, at A10; see also David G. Savage, *"Conscience" Rule for Doctors May Spark Abortion Controversy*, L.A. Times, Dec. 2, 2008 (reporting that proposed regulation would cover 4,800 hospitals, 234,000 doctor's offices, and 58,000 pharmacies).

[30] *See, e.g.*, 42 U.S.C. § 300a-7 (2000).

[31] Rob Stein, *supra* note 29, at A10.

[32] *Id.*

[33] Rob Stein, *Lawsuits Filed Over Rule That Lets Health Workers Deny Care*, Wash. Post, Jan. 16, 2009, at A4.

[34] It is not clear whether Plan B actually does block the implantation of a fertilized egg. See, e.g., James Trussel and Elizabeth Raymond, *Emergency Contraception: A Last Chance to Prevent Unintended*

gradually expanded discretionary role as gatekeepers to pharmaceutical care,[35] the widespread availability of Plan B brought the issue to a head. It has now spilled over to the dispensation of the more common birth control pills, and in a few documented incidents, to other medications such as antidepressants.[36] As pharmaceutical technology encompasses moral hot potatoes such as genetic screening tools, research derived from embryonic stem cells, or race-specific medications,[37] the stakes and passions will ratchet up accordingly.

That these emerging moral tensions have resulted in clumsily and rigidly drawn lines in the sand within the political arena may be understandable given the public discourse surrounding the issue. From one side of the cultural divide, objecting pharmacists appear as religious zealots seeking to turn the clock back on women's reproductive rights. A *New York Times* editorial, for example, pronounces any refusal by a pharmacist to dispense contraceptives to be "an intolerable abuse of power," and asks that such pharmacists "find another line of work."[38] Other commentators label the conscience movement a thinly veiled attempt by pharmacists to "be the arbiters of morality for their customers."[39] Nationally syndicated columnist Ellen Goodman attempts to resolve the issue with the simplistic reminder that "the pharmacist's license [does] not include the right to dispense morality."[40] Other newspaper editorials call the pharmacists' actions "a clear and simple abuse of power," urge pharmacists who "do not want to fill legal prescriptions [to] quit" their jobs,[41] and conclude that "[m]oralizing and dispensing medications don't mix."[42] An official from the National Organization of Women labels pharmacists who will not dispense

---

Pregnancy (Oct. 2008) (available at http://ec.princeton.edu/questions/ec-review.pdf) (accessed Feb. 16, 2009).

[35] Pharmacists do not function as clerks, especially in recent years, as the legal system has imposed on them a counseling role in many contexts. Alan Meisel, *Pharmacists, Physician-Assisted Suicide, and Pain Control*, 2 J. Health Care L. & Pol'y 211, 231 (1999); see also Molly M. Ginty, *Pharmacists Dispense Anti-Choice Activism*, Women's Enews, May 4, 2005 ("Today, [pharmacists] hold more power over our medical decisions than ever before.") (quoting Adam Sonfield of the Adam Guttmacher Institute); William L. Allen and David B. Brushwood, *Pharmaceutically Assisted Death and the Pharmacist's Right of Conscience*, 5 J. Pharmacy & L. 1, 1 (1996) ("Pharmacists see themselves as drug managers whose duty it is to assure that patients' best interests are promoted.").

[36] See Tresa Baldas, *Fighting Refusal to Treat: Conscience Clauses Hit the Courts*, Nat'l L.J., Feb. 7, 2005, at 1, 17.

[37] Nicholas Wade, *Race-based Medicine Continued*, N.Y. Times, Nov. 14, 2004, § 4 (Magazine), at 12 ("Researchers last week described a new drug, called BiDil, that sharply reduces death from heart disease among African-Americans . . . But not everyone is cheering unreservedly. Many people, including some African-Americans, have long been uneasy with the concept of race-based medicine, in part from fear that it may legitimize less benign ideas about race.").

[38] Editorial, *Moralists at the Pharmacy*, N.Y. Times, Apr. 3, 2005, § 4, at 12.

[39] *Governor Dispenses with Pharmacists' Nonsense*, Chi. Sun-Times, Apr. 5, 2005, at 37; see also Eric Ferkenhoff, U.S. News & World Report, Apr. 25, 2005, at 18.

[40] Ellen Goodman, *Pharmacists and Morality*, Bost. Globe, Apr. 14, 2005, at A14.

[41] Editorial, *Just Fill the Prescription*, Palm Beach Post, Jun. 29, 2005, at 14A.

[42] Editorial, *Morals and Medicines Cause Bad Reactions*, Greensboro News & Rec., May 1, 2005, at H2.

contraceptives as "extremists... [who] are arrogantly playing the role of doctor and God."[43]

From the other side, critics see the monolithic state attempting to stifle freedom of religion in the service of the sexual revolution. In response, the conscience movement asks the monolithic state to ensure that individual pharmacists can act without the possibility of negative consequences, by effectively removing the pharmacist from the marketplace. The consumer's moral claim, we are repeatedly told, pales in comparison to the pharmacist's because allowing "one person's convenience [to] trump another person's moral conscience" is "obnoxious, offensive and un-American."[44] After all, if Plan B is the evil its opponents claim, "[t]he only thing the pharmacist is objecting to is being forced to kill and being forced to do harm."[45] Requiring an objecting pharmacist to refer the customer to a pharmacy where the drug in question is available is viewed by many within the conscience movement as a moral nonstarter. Karen Brauer, president of Pharmacists for Life, describes such referral requirements as forcing the pharmacist to say "I don't kill people myself but let me tell you about the guy down the street who does."[46] Once health care providers are forced to disconnect their own moral judgments from their professional roles, we have, it is feared, embarked on the path infamously forged by Dr. Mengele.[47] The state must step in.

Unfortunately, academic commentators have fallen into the same two-dimensional template – presuming that the controversy is resolvable only with the rights-driven language of state power. State action is warranted given the unjustified oppression of the consumer or the pharmacist, depending on the commentator's perspective. Noted ethicist Anita Allen urges, "the medicine counter is no place for ad hoc moralizing," insisting that pharmacists must "withhold their moral judgments at work."[48] Health law specialists Susan Fogel and Lourdes Rivera urge that health care entities "should not be able to refuse, on religious or 'moral' grounds, to honor patients' informed health care decisions, or to provide medically appropriate services (including drugs, devices and procedures), as defined by the applicable standard of care."[49]

---

[43] Kirsten Singleton, *Governor's Directive to Pharmacists Gets Support at Statehouse Rally*, State J.-Reg., May 17, 2005, at 28.

[44] Sheila G. Liaugminas, *Pharmacists Battling Lawsuits Over Conscience Issues*, Nat'l Catholic Register Feb. 13–19, 2005, at 1.

[45] Shari Rudavsky, *Pill Raises Concerns Over Ethics*, Journal-Gazette, Jun. 12, 2005, at 7C (quoting Karen Brauer, president of Pharmacists for Life).

[46] Editorial, *Prescription Politics Hard to Swallow*, Balt. Sun, Apr. 22, 2005, at 13A.

[47] See Letters, Phila. Daily News, Apr. 19, 2005, at 16 ("I wonder how many of Buchenwald's victims were village pharmacists who refused on moral grounds to provide cyanide or other deadly poisons to local Nazi functionaries for 'official use.'").

[48] Anita L. Allen, *Rx for Trouble: Just Give Us the Medicine, Please*, Newark Star-Ledger, May 8, 2005, at 1.

[49] Susan Berke Fogel and Lourdes A. Rivera, *Saving Roe is Not Enough: When Religion Controls Health Care*, 31 Fordham Urb. L.J. 725, 748 (2004).

Moreover, like the popular discourse, the academic debate pays scant attention to the middle ground between the individual and the state: The prospect of institutional autonomy in these matters is given short shrift. Bioethicist Bernard Dickens has even equated efforts to protect hospitals' religious autonomy as "ethically doubtful legal protection of religious fundamentalism." "While conscientious objection is an important human right," according to Dickens, "it is not a right that institutions can invoke" because "hospitals and clinic corporations are artificial legal bodies that have no eternal soul that they may claim an entitlement to protect."[50] In Fogel and Rivera's terms, "[w]hile it is appropriate for individuals to decide what role religion will play in their personal health care decisions, it is not appropriate for corporate health care entities to impose those beliefs on physicians and patients and the communities they serve in a manner that supplants sound medical decision making and patients' rights."[51]

This is true even of those who favor conscience legislation. A leading conservative scholar in the field, Lynn Wardle, has drafted model legislation providing that no one may:

> discriminate against, penalize, discipline, or retaliate against any individual in employment, privileges, benefits, remuneration, promotion, [or] termination of employment . . . because of his or her refusal or unwillingness to counsel, advise, pay for, provide, perform, assist, or participate directly or indirectly in providing or performing health services that violate his or her conscience."[52]

Another scholar insists that legislation is needed to provide pharmacists "with protection against efforts to conform their actions to the employers' views."[53] On both sides, the individualist terms of the debate are amenable only to a resolution grounded in a rights-based conception of autonomy. Contestants urge that priority be placed on one conscience or the other – the consumer's or the pharmacist's – presuming together that such priority is to be realized through the bestowal of state power.

Such is the landscape against which the pharmacist controversy rages. The choices are stark: Favor the pharmacist and bring state power to bear on any entity that would retaliate against the pharmacist's conscience-shaped professional conduct, or favor the consumer and bring state power to bear on any entity that would stand in the way of their conscience-shaped health care decisions.

[50] Bernard M. Dickens, *Reproductive Health Services and the Law and Ethics of Conscientious Objection*, 20 Med. & L. 283, 291 (2001).

[51] Fogel and Rivera, *supra* note 49, at 748–9.

[52] Lynn D. Wardle, *Protecting the Rights of Conscience of Health Care Providers*, 14 J. Legal Med. 177, 228 (1993).

[53] Alan Meisel, *Pharmacists, Physician-Assisted Suicide, and Pain Control*, 2 J. Health Care L. & Pol'y 211, 236 (1999).

THE PHARMACY IN THE MORAL MARKETPLACE

As explained in chapter 4, the state honors the claims of conscience by ensuring the conditions necessary for the moral conversation to continue, not by imposing one set of claims over another. In seeking to protect their moral autonomy through state action, both the pharmacist and the pharmaceutical consumer are unnecessarily short-circuiting the conversation, isolating themselves in the process. In making their rights-based claims, the pharmacist and consumer have made the state the only relevant audience for moral persuasion. If both were instead left to operate within the moral marketplace, their sustenance would come from targeting the hearts and minds of their neighbors, joining together in common cause. Rather than short-term political advocacy aimed at one-time legislation, the moral marketplace enlists actors in an ongoing competition over the good. Pushing moral ideals upward through employment and consumer transactions fosters social ties in ways that the top-down enforcement of state-enshrined rules cannot.

Defining Liberty in the Pharmacy

Failing to recognize the hyperindividualist slant of our public discourse emanates, at least in part, from our broader failure to distinguish between positive and negative liberty in setting our expectations of the law's function in the social order. Negative, or "freedom from," forms of liberty recognize claims of entitlement to noninterference with one's pursuit of the good, however the good is defined by the pursuer. Positive, or "freedom to," forms of liberty contemplate claims of entitlement to affirmative support from the surrounding society for the pursuit of a particular good. In our morally pluralist society, individuals' conceptions of the good will often conflict, and thus attempts by the state to embrace all conceptions of positive liberty would be contradictory and self-defeating. Just as the state cannot support equal distribution of wealth and the right to private property, for example, the state cannot support an unfettered right among pharmacists to conscience along with an unfettered right among customers to all legal pharmaceuticals on demand. As a result, positive liberty usually requires the state to adopt certain conceptions of the good and reject others.

In the current dispute, the predominance of positive liberty is evident in the advocacy of both the consumers and the pharmacists. On the consumer side, the cause of reproductive rights has evolved from one of negative liberty – seeking to prevent the state from criminalizing abortion or contraception – to an extreme form of positive liberty – asking not only to have the full range of legal pharmaceuticals available at every pharmacy, but to insist on their availability with "no hassle, no delay, no lecture."[54] The problem, in a society that values pluralism, is that positive

---

[54] *Governor Blagojevich moves to make emergency contraceptives rule permanent*, State of Illinois, Department of Financial and Professional Regulation, Official Press Release, Apr. 18, 2005.

liberty claims conflate legality with universal availability. The fact that the state does not forbid a drug's sale is taken to mean that every licensed pharmacist must sell that drug to every customer legally entitled to purchase it. This conflation renders the moral convictions of pharmacists and the moral identities of pharmacies irrelevant. The individual consumer does not just coexist with the morally divergent views of the provider; the individual, backed up by state power, trumps the provider. All pharmacists are enlisted in the service of a lowest-common-denominator approach to professional morality: All legal drugs are deemed morally permissible, and providers have no standing to object. The individual preference has become the collective norm. By no means is this to suggest that consumer access to morally controversial pharmaceutical products is not an important public value; the point is to emphasize that requiring universal provision of all pharmaceuticals, rather than meaningful access to all pharmaceuticals, imposes significant burdens on other public values, most notably a sense of moral agency among pharmacists.

On the provider side, the desire to exercise moral agency has led pharmacists to seek more than a negative liberty to protect themselves against coercive state requirements that they dispense certain drugs; they also seek a positive liberty to restrain nonstate private employers from punishing them for the professional byproducts of their moral convictions. In effect, pharmacists ask the state to shield them from the marketplace fallout that would otherwise accompany their marketplace conduct. The importance of professional space to exercise moral agency is beyond dispute, both in its public and personal aspects. As with consumer access, there are costs to an absolutist defense of a professional's moral agency. One's conscience cannot always be given authority over the contours of one's role; certain roles are not suited for certain consciences, and no one is compelled to become a pharmacist.

A path to resolution must acknowledge more nuance than is shown in either of these positions. Yes, a consumer's access to legal pharmaceutical products is, on balance, beneficial to society, as is a pharmacist's ability to take moral responsibility for her professional conduct, but the legal order's collective enshrinement of either quality is not. One essential element of a healthy civic life is acknowledging the relevance of our links to one another even (or especially) when those links are partial or embodying normative ideals that are opposed by other segments of society. The legal status of the individual should be a primary concern of, but not constitutive of, our ongoing conversations regarding the good.

Of course, the common identity that is facilitated by a for-profit pharmacy shaped in part by moral norms is hardly the stuff of Tocquevillian dreams. Our nation's robust history of associational life conjures up images of the Knights of Columbus or United Farm Workers, not monthly runs to refill a prescription. But the fact that consumers and pharmacists drawn to a particular moral stance on controversial pharmaceutical products are unlikely to give rise to "thick" communities does not negate the value of the collective life they do create. Ronald Dworkin gives the example of an orchestra's limited collective life, in which "[a]lthough the members view some of their individual activities as expressive of and constituted by the larger entity, they do not view all or indeed most of their individual activities that way."[55] Pharmacy patrons might be pulled in several different directions. A Roman Catholic might choose a pharmacy that sells the morning-after pill despite what she hears from her bishop, as "different communities could each exert claims over different parts of the individual's identity and sometimes exert conflicting claims over the same ones."[56] Most of today's associational life is messier and more complex than the straightforward, all-encompassing enclaves of the Amish, as most of us do not belong to a single community, but rather lie "at the intersection of many different ones."[57] Even with the partial loyalties fostered by a morality-driven pharmacy landscape, the moral discourse is reinvigorated, and individuals become active participants in cultivating their own moral environments, not just constituents asking that their chosen norms be imposed on the whole.

To many, the travails of individualism do not pose a threat nearly as dire as the one posed by opening up pharmaceutical access to market forces. Transcending individualism is a fine idea, the skeptic concedes, but not at the price of commodifying something as personal as health care, especially because the most controversial pharmacy issues center on women's reproductive health care, and because the commodification takes the regulation of the issues out of a politically accountable central authority. As lawyer and bioethicist Alta Charo remarked at the prospect of some pharmacies declining to offer contraceptives, "We're talking about creating a separate universe of pharmacies that puts women at a disadvantage."[58] In this regard, institutional liberty appears more threatening than individual liberty; as the American Civil Liberties Union recommended in a report advocating for laws requiring pharmacies to satisfy any lawful request for birth control, "institutions, when operating in the public world, ought to play by public rules."[59]

Further, the benefits to civil society may seem attenuated, as the cultivation of moral autonomy among what are primarily large corporations strikes modern sensibilities as being of dubious importance.[60] Indeed, generally "commercial entities are not included within the purview of civil society."[61] After all, unlike relationships that are "glued together by notions of reciprocal obligations and visions of common

55 Ronald Dworkin, *Law's Empire* (discussed in Daniel R. Ortiz, *Categorical Community*, 51 Stan. L. Rev. 769, 782–83 (1999)).
56 Ortiz, *supra* note 55, at 806.
57 *Id.*
58 Rob Stein, *"Pro-Life" Drugstores Market Beliefs*, Wash. Post, Jun. 16, 2008, at A1.
59 ACLU Reproductive Freedom Project, *Religious Refusals and Reproductive Rights: Assessing Birth Control at the Pharmacy* (2007).
60 "Clearly, corporations do not have the same kind of moral autonomy that humans do, and it would be a mistake to 'anthropomorphize' corporations for purposes of ethical analysis." Don Mayer, *Community, Business Ethics, and Global Capitalism*, 38 Am. Bus. L.J. 215, 254 (2001).
61 Miriam Galston, *Civic Renewal and the Regulation of Nonprofits*, 13 Cornell J.L. & Pub. Pol'y 289, 294 (2004).

destinies . . . [c]ommodified relationships . . . are instrumental in nature."[62] Relationships centered in the pharmacy transaction may seem inescapably instrumental, especially because most large pharmacy chains are ill suited to function as mediating structures that would foster deeper connections or a sense of reciprocal obligation among consumers.

It is true that the moral discourse fostered by pharmacies' profit-driven identities cannot match the richness of the discourse nurtured within thicker communities such as families, churches, and voluntary associations organized deliberately around a set of normative claims. That is not to say that the moral discourse occurring in the marketplace is somehow nonexistent or inauthentic. Timothy Fort's work has pointed out that although "businesses do not necessarily nourish solidarity, compassion, empathy, and respect for others," "[s]aying that businesses are not necessarily mediating institutions does not mean . . . that they cannot become mediating institutions."[63] Indeed, as Harold Laski famously put it nearly 100 years ago, a corporation has "a personality that is self-created, and not state-created," and corporations are "in relations with the state, a part of it; but one with it they are not."[64] This personality "follows from the corporation's mediating function: through incorporation individuals can achieve a sanctioned object, whether economic, moral or intellectual."[65] The place of the corporation in a society that takes conscience seriously is the focus of the next chapter. For now, suffice to say that if we understand civil society as "an inherently moral term that implies the existence of social and moral obligations that exist independent of the individual and operate upon him,"[66] there is no reason that a pharmacy landscape defined in part by moral convictions cannot be encompassed within its reach.

If the state stays out of the battle over pharmacists and conscience, pharmacies – from small mom-and-pop operations to national chains such as CVS and Walgreen's – will have the space to build moral claims into their corporate identities. Customers and employees alike will have the opportunity to come together in support of a moral stance with which they agree. For the employee pharmacists, this coming

---

[62] Jeremy Rifkin, *The Age of Access: The New Culture of Hypercapitalism, Where All of Life is a Paid-for Experience*, 11–12 (2000) (quoted in Mayer, *supra* note 60 at 235); Don E. Eberly, *America's Promise: Civil Society and the Renewal of American Culture*, 22 (1998) ("[C]ivil society self-consciously serves public purposes as it calls people beyond the minimalist obligations of the law and the narrow self-interest of the market's bottom line to a higher plane of social cooperation and generosity.").

[63] Timothy L. Fort and Cindy A. Schipani, *Corporate Governance in a Global Environment: The Search for the Best of All Worlds*, 33 Vand. J. Transnat'l L. 829, 862 (2000); see also Eberly, *supra* note 62, at 23 ("Civil society . . . might include the economies of the local grocer, dentist, and shopkeeper, but probably not the international corporate conglomerate" because the latter are less likely, "by virtue of their scale, ownership, and function, to permit local loyalties to affect the bottom line.").

[64] Harold J. Laski, *The Personality of Associations*, 29 Harv. L. Rev. 404, 413, 425 (1916).

[65] Joel Edan Friedlander, *Corporation and Kulturkampf: Time Culture as Illegal Fiction*, 29 Conn. L. Rev. 31, 39 (1996).

[66] Nancy L. Rosenblum, "The Moral Uses of Pluralism," in *Civil Society, Democracy and Civic Renewal*, 255, 266 (R. Fullinwider, ed., 1999).

together will be significant, dissipating the tension between their personal beliefs and professional calling. For customers, although the coming together will occupy only a small segment of their identities, it will represent a mediating function that is now largely absent. By supporting a pharmacy based at least in part on the pharmacy's treatment of controversial drugs and/or treatment of its pharmacists' moral qualms about such drugs, the customer's day-to-day existence will become more closely aligned with her beliefs and values, even if only incrementally. Especially to the extent that the pharmacist's and customer's beliefs and values are not predominant in the wider community, the pharmacy performs a mediating function in the purest sense, serving as a vehicle for shared expression, purpose, identity, and meaning. The distance between traditional civil society stalwarts and commercial health care providers dealing in morally charged products is not as great as it might seem.

The Moral Marketplace and Collective Power

Just as individual autonomy should not be the sole object of our conversations regarding the good, the state should not be the exclusive audience for, or arbiter of, those conversations. We must recognize that "[w]hen mediating and moderating associations collapse, human passion asserts itself through power, not reasoned argument and consensual interaction."[67] In this regard, there is a necessary corollary to our recognition of the moral marketplace's power to transcend the domain of the atomistic individual: The moral marketplace does not subjugate the individual to the collective will. If anything, it creates space for individual human flourishing by reining in attempts to harness collective power to a particular conception of individual well-being.

Replacing collective political determinations with market determinations is not an obvious path to ideal policy outcomes. James Boyd White, for example, cautions us "not to abandon our collective powers of judgment, as the marketplace metaphor invites us to do," because "[d]espite what we say about the 'marketplace of ideas,' we also know, if we allow ourselves to reflect on it, that we simply cannot trust any such process to winnow out the bad and promote the good."[68]

Nor can we rely on the marketplace to winnow out the false and promote the true, at least when it comes to religious and moral convictions. Justice Holmes, who pioneered the marketplace approach to free speech in his famous dissent in *Abrams v. United States*, presumed that "the best test of truth is the power of the thought to get itself accepted in the competition of the market."[69] The relative marketplace

---

[67] Eberly, *supra* note 62, at 173.

[68] James Boyd White, *Free Speech and Valuable Speech: Silence, Dante, and the "Marketplace of Ideas,"* 51 UCLA L. Rev. 799, 813 (2004).

[69] 250 U.S. at 630 (Holmes & Brandeis, JJ., dissenting); Stanley Ingber, *The Marketplace of Ideas: A Legitimizing Myth,* 1984 Duke L.J. 1, 3 ("This theory assumes that a process of robust debate, if uninhibited by governmental interference, will lead to the discovery of truth, or at least the best perspectives or

successes of pharmacies that do or do not offer the morning-after pill, or that do or do not force their employees to dispense the morning-after pill, will do little to bring consensus as to the "truth" of the moral claims made regarding the pill or the sanctity of pharmacists' consciences. As Stanley Ingber observes, "if the possibility of rational discourse and discovery is negated by [individuals'] entrenched and irreconcilable perceptions of truth, the dominant 'truth' discovered by the marketplace can result only from the triumph of power, rather than the triumph of reason."[70] The ends of this market power are not always noble. After all, market forces catapulted "shock jock" Howard Stern to the heights of cultural influence; do we really want those same forces unleashed with respect to health care? Which values, in the end, will rule the marketplace, and which values will be marginalized once stripped of support from collective ordering?

One reassurance stems from the fact that the current project is not directed toward the establishment of communes devoted to the all-encompassing embodiment of a contested norm. Pharmacies are not equipped or positioned to transform wholly the worldviews of their customers. As such, the constraints on a pharmacy's mediating function are also constraints on the corrosive effects of a pharmacy's embrace of any particular norm. But a more fundamental reassessment of the marketplace threat requires us to recognize that the current trend toward collectively enshrining individual autonomy as an absolute value (on the consumer or pharmacist side) already reflects normative claims of dubious social value. The problem is that this trend merges the atomistic individual with the collective power of state authority, effectively barring divergent (i.e., nonindividualist) conceptions of meaningful autonomy. The pharmacist's conscience must be honored, period. The pharmacy customer must have maximum access to all legal pharmaceuticals, period. The space between the individual and the collective has been swallowed up.

This intermediate space is where the moral marketplace does its work, and much of that work is aimed at constructing bulwarks against the encroachments of the state. That this work may not result in a broader discernment of truth is immaterial because the state's elevation of a single contested conception of individual autonomy also has little relation to truth. Morally distinct pharmacies give individuals room to experience and act on divergent worldviews and priorities, whether or not their aim is to reach any consensus via the political apparatus of the collective.

Contrary to popular conceptions of the phrase's origins, Justice Holmes never actually used the phrase "marketplace of ideas," in his landmark *Abrams* dissent, and his actual phrase, "competition of the market," may suggest a concern not with markets' "celebration of discretionary choice, but rather [with] the harsh fact that

---

solutions for societal problems. A properly functioning marketplace of ideas, in Holmes's perspective, ultimately assures the proper evolution of society, wherever that evolution might lead.").

[70] Ingber, *supra* note 69, at 15.

economic actors and their products are pitted against one another."[71] Vincent Blasi extrapolates from this to draw out the lesson for free speech theory:

> An unregulated marketplace of ideas encourages free thought not so much by determining the equilibrium of the moment as by keeping low the barriers to entry, barriers that take the form not only of coercive sanctions but also social and intellectual peer pressures toward conformity. The sheer proliferation of ideas in a free market complicates perceptions in a manner that helps to weaken such barriers. In addition, the market metaphor makes a statement about the dynamic and chronically incomplete character of understanding and the value of intellectual contest and innovation.[72]

Although pharmacists traffic in products, not ideas, our society's struggle with the moral dimension of modern pharmaceuticals displays a similar capacity for benefiting from a well-functioning and diverse marketplace. Understanding this diversity to warrant that a full range of consumer choices is available in every pharmacy eviscerates the concept because it presumes that the only relevant decision-maker in the provision of pharmaceuticals is the individual, and that the efficacy of individuals' moral convictions should extend no farther than themselves.

The widespread disregard of the moral marketplace in the pharmacist debate stems, at least in part, from a misunderstanding of pluralism – in particular, a failure to draw distinctions among different types of authority. The imposition of particular moral claims by nonstate actors cannot be held to the same normative standard to which the state's imposition of similar claims is held. Bernard Dickens, for example, asserts that "[g]overnments that enforce one version of conscience, such as [a health care institution's] prohibition of medically indicated sterilization or abortion, are ethically and in human rights law indistinguishable from those that enforce another, such as involuntary sterilization or forced abortion."[73] If pluralism means anything, it means that a local pharmacy's decision not to sell the morning-after pill cannot be equated with the state's decision to prosecute criminally anyone found in possession of the morning-after pill. To disempower nonstate institutions from defying prevailing norms effectively disempowers individuals, exacerbating the problem of having "large numbers of people [who] do not participate in decisions that determine the conditions of their everyday lives, relying instead upon government officials, government institutions and government-funded institutions, and other outsiders to provide for their well-being."[74]

The checking power of the moral marketplace also is a function of the fact that pressure to conform emanates not just from the state, but from a marketplace stripped of ideological or moral diversity. There is something to be said for allowing

---

[71] Vincent Blasi, *Holmes and the Marketplace of Ideas*, 2004 Sup. Ct. Rev. 1, *24.

[72] *Id.* at *27.

[73] Bernard M. Dickens, *Reproductive Health Services and the Law and Ethics of Conscientious Objection*, 20 Med. & L. 283, 293 (2001).

[74] Miriam Galston, *supra* note 61, at 297.

institutions to promote a type of second-order diversity,[75] which also can be thought of as interinstitutional diversity rather than intrainstitutional diversity, by adopting distinctive morality-driven policies, even if those policies have the effect of repelling certain segments of the potential employee and customer pool.

To be sure, sprawling pharmacy chains will not always function as mediating structures. Any corporation can acquire sufficient power to oppress, particularly vis-à-vis its employees, and sometimes with greater efficiency than the state. Navigating the tension between the corporation's moral identity and the dissenting employee's conscience is a primary topic of chapter 7. Even beyond the employment relationship, it is not always obvious why replacing state power with corporate power will improve prospects for conscience in the pharmacy. Especially compared with small, owner-operated pharmacies,[76] a large nationwide pharmacy chain may not be a promising vehicle for accurately reflecting customers' moral convictions in pharmacy counter policies and practices. Nevertheless, state action shuts down those morally distinct owner-operated pharmacies; the existence of Walgreen's does not, even if it can make their market viability more precarious. Even large chains make meaningful moral claims that could be relevant to a customer's choice of pharmacy.[77]

Pharmacies, as moral venues, are far from perfect; nevertheless, they are integral to the cause of conscience. Robust public discourse regarding the moral claims embedded in current and future pharmaceutical controversies will be fostered more directly by pharmacies representing a range of perspectives than by the current system in which the adherents to various moral perspectives are scattered randomly and anonymously among morally fungible pharmacies. Individuals are equipped to withstand the homogenizing force of uniform market norms when they can associate with like-minded others, which requires the accessibility of diverse associations. Again, the moral marketplace reflects the social reality of human beings and a reminder that those concerned with the cause of individual autonomy must do more than harness collective power to its realization; they must, to a certain degree, disconnect the individual and the state, rediscovering the social space between the two.

The State as Market Actor

Recognizing the relational dimension of conscience need not become some recycled libertarian take on the culture wars, for recognizing the importance of the market in our "culture war" debates is not meant to suggest an embrace of all market

---

[75] *See* Heather K. Gerken, *Second-Order Diversity*, 118 Harv. L. Rev. 1099 (2005).

[76] Rob Stein, *"Pro-Life" Drugstores Market Beliefs*, Jun. 16, 2008, Wash. Post, at A1.

[77] *See* Dean Olsen, *Walgreen's Joins Suit Against Blagojevich*, Springfield State J.-Reg., Jul. 23, 2006, at 5 (reporting that Walgreen's "hopes the judge allows the company to reinstate its 'pharmacist conscience clause,' which would allow pharmacists to decline to dispense emergency contraception but requires the pharmacists to refer patients to another pharmacist or pharmacy").

outcomes. The state's primary role will be to address market failure. As do traditional economic markets, markets composed of commercial firms trafficking not just in goods and services, but also in moral claims, will also fail. One essential safeguard is for individuals to be given the information necessary for their active and knowing participation in the market: the moral marketplace will not function as such unless consumers and employees know the moral claims on which the pharmacy's identity is based. If the state allows pharmacies to stake out their own positions on controversial drugs and pharmacists' obligations, it would be justified in requiring those positions to be publicized.[78]

Markets also run into problems with externalities "when the full quantum of social costs generated by an activity cannot practically be observed, measured, or assessed against those who engage in the activity."[79] The most glaring externality in the pharmacy debate stems from the individuals who might lack access to the pharmaceuticals they desire. In a given community, sufficient market power might reside with those who favor restrictions on contraceptives, for example, so as to block their availability even for those who seek to use them. Especially in rural areas, there might be so few individuals seeking contraceptives that economic incentives are insufficient to motivate a contraceptive-dispensing pharmacy to enter the market. Under these circumstances, individuals holding the minority view will be precluded from market participation because there is no pharmacy option reflecting their own moral claims.

But we must recognize the limited scope of the access problem, and the correspondingly limited scope of the justified government response. In most areas, rural or otherwise, access to widely relied on pharmaceuticals such as contraceptives will not be a problem. Most Americans support the availability of such products, and the market will reflect that.[80] The fact that individuals might have to drive across town, or switch pharmacies, or use a (potentially) higher-cost alternative does not necessarily mean that the market has failed. (Given the current lack of professional safeguards, it is arguable whether the widespread availability of drugs via the Internet should be considered a suitable measure of access.) If moral discourse regarding controversial

---

[78] California, for example, is the "first state to require managed care organizations and insurance companies to warn consumers that some physicians and hospitals restrict access to covered reproductive health services and to offer consumers information about those restrictions." Fogel & Rivera, *supra* note 49, at 741. Note, however, that the provision of information should not be turned into a government shaming mechanism. See, e.g., Chain Drug Rev., Apr. 18, 2005 ("Any drug store that employs a pharmacist unwilling on moral, not medical, grounds to fill certain prescriptions must identify that pharmacist by name by posting a sign at the pharmacy, in the store's front window, or in both locations, so that all patients know, in advance of bringing a prescription to the pharmacy counter, that the pharmacist has in the past taken it upon himself or herself to determine not to fill certain prescriptions for certain patients.").

[79] Blasi, *supra* note 71, at 6–7.

[80] See Belden, Russonello and Stewart, *Religion, Reproductive Health, and Access to Services: A National Survey of Women Conducted for Catholics for a Free Choice*, Apr. 2000 (available at http://brspoll.com/Reports/CFFC-cons%20clause%20report.pdf) (accessed Feb. 16, 2009).

pharmaceuticals is going to take place, we must discern between market-driven inconvenience and market-driven lack of access. The latter warrants state intervention; the former does not.

The distinction is reflected in the recent litigation battle over the Washington state rules requiring that all pharmacies dispense all legal pharmaceuticals, particularly the "Plan B" emergency contraception pill, which was the focus of the dispute. Two pharmacists and a family-owned pharmacy brought suit, claiming that their "rights of conscience" under the Constitution were violated by the rules' enforcement. The federal district court granted a preliminary injunction against the state, ruling that the plaintiffs had demonstrated a likelihood of success in proving that their free exercise rights were violated.[81]

In light of binding Supreme Court precedent, the district court was on shaky ground in finding a constitutional violation.[82] As expected, the Ninth Circuit vacated the injunction, finding that the rules at issue were neutral and reasoning that "The Free Exercise Clause is not violated even though a group motivated by religious reasons may be more likely to engage in the proscribed conduct."[83] As a policy matter, the vitality of conscience is not necessarily strengthened by dressing up conscience claims in the workplace as constitutional rights. As misguided as the district court's reasoning might have been, the pharmacy board's rules were even more so, particularly when viewed through the lens offered by conscience's relational dimension.

Most legal commentators disregard this dimension. Marci Hamilton, for example, objected to the district court's ruling because we are dealing with a "right to obtain contraceptives free of state interference."[84] It is not clear how such a right is at stake here. The state interference is coming at the request, not of the pharmacies and pharmacists, but of those who wish to obtain contraceptives, and it is not clear that the state needs to intervene in the marketplace unless the goal is to ensure that Plan B is available at every single pharmacy. If we embrace the more modest goal of access to Plan B, there should be a greater showing that state intervention is needed in a particular geographical area.

Hamilton also noted that "the woman seeking contraception has a set of religious beliefs, too, and they permit the use of contraception," so it is not obvious why "the licensed pharmacist's beliefs get to trump the patient's beliefs." She is undoubtedly correct that the pharmacist's beliefs should not trump the patient's, but they only function as a trump when the market is not providing alternative access points to the

[81] *Stormans, Inc. v. Selecky*, 524 F. Supp.2d 1245 (W.D. Wash. 2007).

[82] See *Employment Div. v. Smith*, 494 U.S. 872 (1990) (law upheld if it is neutral on the subject of religion and is of general applicability).

[83] *Stormans, Inc. v. Selecky*, 571 F.3d 960, 983 (9th Cir. 2009).

[84] Marci Hamilton, *Why A Federal District Court Was Wrong to Apply Strict Scrutiny to a Washington State Law Requiring Pharmacies, But Not Individual Pharmacists, to Fill "Plan B" Prescriptions* (Nov. 15, 2007) (http://writ.news.findlaw.com/hamilton/20071115.html).

pharmaceutical at issue. Consider the five women who intervened in this litigation in support of the regulations:

- One woman who was out of town visited a pharmacy that did not carry Plan B; the pharmacist there indicated generally the location of another pharmacy for her to try, but did not provide specific directions. The woman returned home early and obtained Plan B at a pharmacy with which she was familiar.
- A second woman was refused Plan B by one pharmacist, but then another pharmacist on duty at the same pharmacy apologized to her and filled the prescription.
- A third woman obtained Plan B on two occasions from Planned Parenthood because she had "heard numerous accounts of pharmacists who refuse to fill emergency contraception prescriptions or otherwise act in a hostile or harassing manner to those seeking such prescriptions."
- A fourth woman did not use Plan B, but participated in a Planned Parenthood testing program designed to identify pharmacists who refused to stock or distribute Plan B. She found that in the town of Wenatchee (population: 27,000), she could obtain Plan B at two of five pharmacies.
- The fifth woman had never used Plan B, but wanted to join the suit to ensure that "all women in Washington can get timely access to emergency contraception . . . without harassment or hostility."

These accounts do not provide much evidence that the market has failed. As the Ninth Circuit observed in denying the state's motion to stay the injunction pending appeal, "there is no evidence that any woman who sought Plan B was unable to obtain it."[85] A survey cited by the court showed that only two percent of pharmacies in Washington state did not stock Plan B because of personal, moral, or religious reasons.[86] Although not correcting for any apparent market failure, the regulations do preclude pharmacies from staking out any distinctive claim on the propriety of offering morally contested products and services, short-circuiting any possibility that pharmacies can function as venues for conscience. To reiterate, this does not mean that pharmacies should somehow be shielded from the marketplace fallout of their conduct. Prior to the adoption of the regulations, in fact, the family-owned pharmacy that ultimately brought suit was the target of a boycott because of its refusal to stock Plan B. We do not need to give pharmacists a constitutional right to make unilateral decisions about what services they will offer; we also do not need to make all pharmacies morally fungible via state edict absent a specific showing that access has been compromised.

Access cannot be trotted out as a bogeyman every time a pharmacy decides to carve out an identity for itself that diverges from the model of unlimited consumer

---

[85] *Stormans, Inc. v. Selecky*, 526 F.3d 406, 409 (9th Cir. 2008).
[86] *Stormans, Inc. v. Selecky*, 571 F.3d at 965.

choice. If the marketplace is going to be relevant, the state must restrain its regulatory ambition. Intervention should be precisely targeted. The state should be legislatively empowered to declare a market failure with respect to particular pharmaceuticals and to require, as a condition of licensing, the provision of those pharmaceuticals by pharmacies operating within that market. But the fear of market failures should not be invoked as the basis for constraining the moral marketplace before it has the chance to operate.

As a market actor, the state can do more than guard against market failure; the state can pursue its own normative claims, though self-restraint again is in order. The obvious mechanism is through licensing requirements and funding programs (e.g., the state-level equivalents of Medicare and Medicaid).[87] The marketplace's prospects turn on the substance and expansiveness of those normative claims. Stephen Macedo argues that a "liberal society . . . need not guarantee that its institutions and policies provide a level playing field for the different groups that compete for members in society,"[88] but, as David Cole has recognized in the First Amendment context, the danger of government-funded speech laden with coercive "strings" lies not "in the coercive effect of the benefit on speakers, but in the indoctrinating effect of a monopolized marketplace of ideas."[89] The question of such regulation is a thorny one because "of the paradoxical nature of such speech: it is both necessary to and potentially subversive of democratic values."[90]

As an actor within (not over) the moral marketplace, the state must resist the tendency to regulate in favor of the least objectionable norms, which often results in the imposition of a lowest-common-denominator approach to contested values, ensuring that unfettered individual choice becomes the universal norm. Cole focuses on the federal government's abortion-related "gag rule" in advocating for a "spheres of neutrality" approach, which calls us to consider the role that certain institutions play in public debate and in checking government indoctrination. "Only by barring government control of the content of speech in critical public institutions," Cole writes, "can the first amendment ensure an 'uninhibited, robust, and wide-open' public debate."[91] He focuses on public fora, the press, and public universities, while also acknowledging that institutions "such as medicine, education, and the law" are "critical to individual autonomy and choice."[92] Cole also wants government neutrality to

---

[87] "[R]evenue sources of religious[ly] controlled health systems are not significantly different from those of any other private corporate interests in the health care industry," as in 1998, "the combined Medicare and Medicaid funding for religiously-controlled hospitals accounted for roughly half of their revenues." Fogel and Rivera, *supra* note 49, at 742.

[88] Stephen Macedo, *The Constitution, Civic Virtue, and Civil Society: Social Capital as Substantive Morality*, 69 Fordham L. Rev. 1573, 1592 (2001).

[89] David Cole, *Beyond Unconstitutional Conditions: Charting Spheres of Neutrality in Government-Funded Speech*, 67 N.Y.U. L. Rev. 675, 680 (1992).

[90] *Id.* at 681.

[91] *Id.* at 711.

[92] *Id.* at 716.

reign in fiduciary relationships such as "doctor-patient," given that "a counselee is the paradigmatic 'captive audience,' particularly vulnerable to indoctrination," and "[o]ne of the first amendment's principal aims is to ensure that individuals are free to choose their own destinies free of the government's ideological intrusion."[93]

The need to guard against the government's "ideological intrusion" is equally applicable to the pharmacist controversy. Although Cole might resist the moral marketplace's deemphasis of an individualist understanding of moral autonomy, a similar impetus for a "'wide-open' public debate" on the provision of morally controversial pharmaceuticals exists in this context. As such, the normative claims pursued by the government should not impose particular substantive outcomes on the moral debate – the nonnegotiable sanctity of the pharmacist's conscience or the nonnegotiable sanctity of consumer choice – but should be geared toward facilitating participation within the market. The state is a facilitator, not an arbiter.

The professional provision of pharmaceuticals should not be regulated out of independence, co-opted by the collective will. As with other professions, pharmacists can be regulated "as a means of fostering the existence and integrity of the institution," but also must be protected "from ready destruction at the hands of the State, whether by direct regulation or by selective funding."[94] Organizations of pharmacists, especially when committed to common ideals and norms, can mediate "the isolated endeavors of individuals and the collective political decision making of universalizing government institutions."[95] The normative claims to be pursued by the state as market actor thus boil down to questions of access. Whether to remedy market failures or to overcome deliberately exclusionary practices by key economic gatekeepers, the state's objective is not to impose a certain vision of the good, but to promote the public conversation(s) regarding the good.

CONSCIENCE AND HEALTH CARE

The operation of the moral marketplace, of course, is not limited to the pharmacy. A more deliberate effort to create space for the coexistence of plural and competing moral norms holds out hope for mitigating the alienation and intransigence fostered by the rights-driven, state-imposed solutions sought by culture war combatants on a range of contested issues. In much of our heated public discourse, the mere invocation of individual conscience does not bring clarity, much less the clarity presupposed by the zero-sum terms in which resolutions are framed.

To take another hot-button health care example, in the debate over the institutional autonomy of religious hospitals, the overriding concern has become patient choice and employee freedom, with little credit given to the societal benefits that

---

[93] *Id.* at 743.
[94] Daniel Halberstam, *Commercial Speech, Professional Speech, and the Constitutional Status of Social Institutions*, 147 U. Pa. L. Rev. 771, 873 (1999).
[95] *Id.*

divergent organizational identities might bring. Once the value of organizational identity is removed from the equation, the stakes of the public debates over controversial health care issues – emergency contraception, abortion, genetic screening, end-of-life treatment – can be communicated only in terms of the individual employee's or patient's interests. If all hospitals are morally fungible, then the state's judgment that a given treatment should be available is equivalent to a judgment that the treatment should be available everywhere. Physicians, administrators, nurses, patients, and financial donors who lose the public debate do not just face a community that makes available a treatment that defies their moral convictions, but they are precluded from even maintaining a subcommunity that enables them to live out their convictions. As the state increasingly requires that certain controversial treatments be made available at all hospitals, public and private, dissenting moral claims are effectively negated, and the moral marketplace is shut down.

In some contexts, however, a hospital's moral claims carry sufficient market power that state intervention may be appropriate. It is not enough to show that no other provider serves a particular community. For example, suppose that a Catholic health care provider operates the only medical facility in a community, but they would cease operations if forced to offer abortion services. Certainly there is no functioning market of abortion providers, but if the state acted to remedy that, there may very well be no functioning market of health care services, period. The state's market intervention is not guaranteed to expand choice in every circumstance, and tolerating some limits on morally controversial services may serve to maintain a health care presence in an otherwise underserved area.[96] There is a different set of considerations when the state is asked to permit a merger, for example, between a Catholic provider and a secular provider where the merger would result in the curtailment of controversial services. In those situations, the state may be justified in withholding permission for the merger if it threatens a currently viable market.

Regardless of the policy resolutions reached in a specific health care dispute, it is important to reorient the conversation toward what is at stake. The conscience-driven practices of providers are not inherently less legitimate than the conscience-driven needs and preferences of health care customers, provided that goods and services to meet customers' needs and preferences are accessible in the moral marketplace. In a functioning marketplace, the viability of conscience requires us to give providers and like-minded customers an opportunity to live out their ideals. If Tom Cruise wants to enter the pharmacy business without selling (highly profitable) antidepressant medications, the state should stand aside and let him. It is one thing for a true believer to try out his moral convictions in the public sphere and find them incapable

[96] Similar forbearance by the state would not be as justified in the pharmacy context. Given that the cost of market entry is not as high for pharmacies as for hospitals, it will be easier – and, in all likelihood, more financially attractive given the established market demand – for another pharmacy to fill the void left by pharmacy owners who would cease operations if forced to provide a pharmaceutical that they find objectionable.

of attracting sufficient interest and support to be viable; it is quite another for the state to forbid him from even trying. By more steadfastly defending space in which individuals and groups can live out the dictates of their consciences, even when those dictates have been rejected by the majority, we may reduce the bright-line vitriol and widespread alienation that has defined the culture wars and gradually introduce a more nuanced, contextual understanding of conscience and its role in our public life.

In health care as elsewhere, recognizing conscience's relational dimension equips us to resist the temptation to construct abstract visions of "conscience" and pit them against each other in a winner-take-all struggle for power in our legal system. Instead, we can place greater focus on the vital human associations that allow an individual's conscience to enjoy real-world traction. More often than not, this will require the state to step back and narrow its function to ensuring a vibrant and accessible marketplace. Making space for the unpopular exercise of conscience is an American tradition, but that tradition cannot be relegated to the Amish-style enclave and isolated military conscript; the tradition must extend to the heart of the American experience, where our moral convictions and daily existences intersect. If conscience is going to matter in today's society, it should matter at Walgreen's.

7

Corporations

Imagining a role for pharmacies in the flourishing of conscience opens a broader inquiry: Are corporations, as a category, positioned to support the relational dimension of conscience, and if so, how should the law facilitate that function? Corporations occupy a significant segment of the vast space between the intimacy of the family and the anonymity of the state. This chapter explores the broad implications that conscience's relational dimension has for our understanding of corporations and their role in society. The first part examines whether for-profit corporations may properly be considered venues for the communal expression and implementation of conscience, looking specifically at the capacity of corporations such as Wal-Mart to carve out moral identities as marketplace actors that diverge from the norms embraced by the broader society. In the second part, I shift the inquiry to the internal environment of the corporation, exploring the tension between a corporate community's constituent-driven moral identity and the exercise of conscience by dissenting community members, particularly employees.

CORPORATE CONSCIENCE IN THE MARKETPLACE

As a marketplace actor, the corporation is a moral agent with the capacity for exercising a robust institutional conscience – not in the sense that the corporation actually exists as a conscience-wielding being, but in the sense that the corporation serves as a venue and vehicle for the sharing of conscience-driven claims among its constituents. The moral identities of nonprofit corporations generally find fertile ground in the marketplace because they attract constituents through a distinct mission, not through the allure of financial gain. The moral identity of the for-profit corporation remains a largely untapped resource. To realize the for-profit corporation's potential for serving as a venue for the communal exercise of individual constituents' moral convictions, we must transcend competing conceptions of the corporation as either a profit-maximizing amoral entity or a public actor bound to reflect collective moral norms.

Two seemingly unrelated announcements by Wal-Mart in 2006, considered together, lend insight into the thorny question of a corporation's moral identity. Over the summer, Wal-Mart announced that it had hired a former nun as "senior director of stakeholder engagement" to help steer the company's policies on the environment, labor relations, and health care,[1] and detailed an ambitious $500 million sustainability plan, aiming to increase the efficiency of its vehicle fleet by 25%, eliminate 30% of the energy used in its stores, and reduce solid waste from stores by 25%.[2] Earlier in the year, the company announced that it would begin to offer the Plan B "morning-after" emergency contraceptive pill at its pharmacies, citing legal pressure in various states as the reason to reverse its previous policy.[3]

The mammoth discount chain was widely applauded for taking steps to shore up its stewardship of the environment and for deciding to sell the morning-after pill. In reality, the two decisions stand in stark tension. Undertaking the sustainability campaign, notwithstanding criticism that it would prove to be a "costly distraction,"[4] is an example of the corporate conscience in action. But so was the policy of *not* dispensing the morning-after pill, especially to the extent that it conformed to Wal-Mart's self-perception of having based its decisions "on the values of Scripture" in selling sanitized versions of CDs, declining to sell racy men's magazines, and concealing other magazine covers.[5] Buckling to state coercion may have produced an outcome – increased availability of Plan B – that is pleasing to many Americans, but the broader view reveals it as another step toward a morally homogeneous corporate landscape, where the corporate conscience dissipates, replaced by a top-down imposition of collectively enshrined norms.

The Nature of the Corporation

Any evaluation of the feasibility or prudence of a corporation's cultivation of a distinct moral identity requires jumping into the debate over the nature of the corporation. Corporate law, as Michael Novak observed, "opened human history to the action of social institutions freely entered into."[6] The corporation's rise is inexorably connected with the relational dimension of conscience because the corporation depends "on ideas that are powerful and clear enough to organize thousands of persons around common tasks" and that "are strong enough to endure for years, so that individuals who commit themselves to them can expect to spend

---

[1] Kim Hart, *A Bid to Get Religion? Wal-Mart Hires Ex-Nun*, Wash. Post, July 18, 2006, at D3.

[2] Marc Gunther, *Wal-Mart sees green*, Fortune, Aug. 7, 2006.

[3] Michael Barbaro, *In Reversal, Wal-Mart Will Sell Contraceptive*, N.Y. Times, Mar. 4, 2006, at C4.

[4] Gunther, *supra* note 2.

[5] Jeff Sellers, *Deliver Us From Wal-Mart?* Christianity Today, May 2005 ("Is Wal-Mart a Christian company? No," said former Wal-Mart executive Don Soderquist at a recent prayer breakfast. "But the basis of our decisions was the values of Scripture.").

[6] Michael Novak, *Toward a Theology of the Corporation*, 5 (1981).

thirty to forty years working out their vocation."[7] It is no stretch to observe that the set of ideas around which a given corporation is organized may include ideas derived from the moral convictions of the organization's constituents. The corporation can be a powerful device for channeling the dictates of individual conscience into a shared moral purpose, identity, and expression within the marketplace.

This view is counterintuitive to many. Taking a stand on widely contested moral issues is the province of individual citizens, not corporations. Skepticism toward the corporate conscience is grounded in the purpose of the corporation itself, understood widely as the maximization of shareholders' profit. The debate over the propriety of corporations taking on tasks beyond profit maximization has been raging for years, particularly in light of the corporate social responsibility (CSR) movement. CSR is a loose affiliation of advocates and scholars seeking, through both moral suasion and calls for legal reform, to make corporate management accountable to constituencies other than the shareholders. Critics claim that it actually stands for corporate "irresponsibility" because "[t]he modern corporation is meant to be a vehicle to create wealth for its shareholders, and that is what CEOs must always keep in mind."[8]

Some seek to have it both ways, suggesting that serving the community will also benefit the bottom line. United Nations Secretary General Kofi Annan, for example, asked members of the U.S. Chamber of Commerce to combat AIDS "because AIDS affects business," and "there is a happy convergence between what your shareholders pay you for, and what is best for millions of people the world over."[9] The problem with this sort of appeal is that, for most businesses, it is simply not true. As Reuven Avi-Yonah points out, "[i]t is hard to show that combating the AIDS crisis in Africa will have any discernible impact on the bottom line for shareholders of an office equipment manufacturer in Kalamazoo, Michigan."[10]

The fact that there is not a direct relationship between combating AIDS in Africa and the manufacture of office equipment in Kalamazoo does not mean that the former endeavor cannot coexist with the latter in a financially viable firm. Some shareholders will be attracted to a company willing to expend resources battling a disease that does not directly threaten its operations or market viability, as evidenced by the recent successes of socially screened mutual funds. According to a recent study by KPMG, "corporate stakeholders, customers, and workers are pushing a trend toward nonfinancial performance reporting" because of "their concerns about environmental management, worker relations, and social responsibility."[11] Some

---

[7] *Id.* at 41

[8] Philip Kotler and Nancy Lee, *Corporate Social Responsibility: Doing the Most Good for Your Company and Your Cause*, 12 (2005) (quoting Arthur Laffer).

[9] Quoted in Reuven Avi-Yonah, *The Cyclical Transformations of the Corporate Form: A Historical Perspective on Corporate Social Responsibility*, 30 Del. J. Corp. L. 767, 768 (2005).

[10] *Id.*

[11] Ronald R. Sims, *Ethics and Corporate Social Responsibility: Why Giants Fall*, 35 (2003).

companies practice "triple-bottom-line" reporting in which economic, environmental, and social performance (e.g., labor practices, human rights, gender, ethical concerns) are included for shareholders' consideration.[12]

This is not to suggest that the propriety of socially responsible corporate conduct turns on its ability to attract enough shareholders to further the profit maximization objective. The American Law Institute provides the background rule for those who resist profit maximization as the unitary corporate objective:

> Even if corporate profit and shareholder gain are not thereby enhanced, the corporation, in the conduct of its business: (1) is obliged, to the same extent as a natural person, to act within the boundaries set by law; (2) may take into account ethical considerations that are reasonably regarded as appropriate to the responsible conduct of business; and (3) may devote a reasonable amount of resources to public welfare, humanitarianism, educational, and philanthropic purposes.[13]

Even proceeding under the American Law Institute's framework, the status of the corporation's moral identity remains murky. Where in this framework does Wal-Mart's decision not to sell the morning-after pill fall, assuming that it could have been financially profitable for it to do so and that it would normally fall within its existing pharmacy business?[14] Would it be considered "reasonably appropriate to the responsible conduct of business?" Is it a "humanitarian" or "public welfare" concern? The categories become more elusive when the corporation's action is driven by a moral judgment that is widely contested in society.

The Corporation and Collective Norms

The problem is the tendency to collectivize the social norms of which the responsible corporation may take heed. The implicit presumption is that corporate decision making that does not maximize profit will serve some moral norm that is widely accepted within society: The corporation's decision to sacrifice profit is motivated, at least in part, by the pressure of social and moral sanctions. Einer Elhauge employs this logic to argue that the gap between shareholder interest and public interest is illusory. He asserts, "even patent exercises of the power to sacrifice profits in the public interest will enhance shareholder welfare by furthering what most shareholders view as the public interest."[15] If we allow corporate management "to respond to social and moral sanctions," instead of focusing simply on profit, this "will move corporate behavior in the right direction, assuming our society's social and moral

---

[12] *Id.* at 60.

[13] Quoted in Einer Elhauge, *Sacrificing Corporate Profits in the Public Interest*, 80 N.Y.U. L. Rev. 733, 763 (2005) (comment indicates that last prong includes operational decisions such as keeping unprofitable plant open to allow employees to transition to new work, providing pension for former employees, or other decisions that take into account the social costs of corporate activities).

[14] Wal-Mart has suggested that business concerns motivated the decision, without specification.

[15] Elhauge, *supra* note 13, at 739.

norms correctly identify which direction is right."[16] Elhauge recognizes the difficulty in defending an "objective" version of the public interest; accordingly, he defines the public interest broadly to cover cases "where managers are sacrificing corporate profits in a way that confers a general benefit on others, as opposed to conferring the sorts of financial benefits on themselves, their families, or friends that courts police under the duty of loyalty."[17] That gap between the shareholders and the public closes to the extent that "our social and moral sanctions have enough general accuracy that they overall move us closer to the outcomes that society deems desirable rather than being affirmatively counterproductive."[18]

Note what is left out of the conversation: the possibility that a corporation will sacrifice profit, not as a reaction to the pressure of moral norms widely held by society, but as a proactive stance on contested moral norms. It is as if the corporation is to reflect, not shape, the norms prevalent in society. In much of the CSR literature, the alternative to serving profit is serving "the society as a whole"[19] and "the general interest"[20] through the implementation of a "universal system of values"[21] and a "world standard."[22] Corporations are to commit to meeting or exceeding the "ethical, legal, commercial, and public expectations that society has of business."[23] The CSR controversy centers on the notion that the corporation should divert its attention from profit maximization;[24] the substance of its nonprofit-maximizing duties

---

[16] *Id.* at 740.

[17] *Id.* at 744.

[18] *Id.*

[19] From the early 1970s, "[t]he thesis of the movement was that in order to solve the ills of society – thought in large part to be the product of corporate behavior (in turn, thought to be the result of the separation of ownership from control) – some sort of government intervention was necessary to make large corporations and their managers again accountable, if not to the owners of such corporations, then to the society as a whole." Douglas M. Branson, *Corporate Social Responsibility Redux*, 76 Tul. L. Rev. 1207, 1211 (2002).

[20] See Phillippe de Woot, *Should Prometheus Be Bound? Corporate Global Responsibility*, 101 (2005) ("[F]irms must look beyond profit and explicitly consider the general interest. They must act in the long-term interest of the common good, which market forces do not entirely define.").

[21] See *id* at 111 ("In a globalizing economy we can no longer define the purpose of the firm and the market economy without reference to a sufficiently universal system of values."), at 117 ("In a globalizing world, deciding what type of society we wish to build should be based on values that are as universal as possible.")

[22] The influential Caux Round Table's "principles for business" "aims to express a world standard against which business behavior can be measured." Also see the Global Reporting Initiative, Global Sullivan Principles, Social Accountability 8000, Interfaith Center on Corporate Responsibility, Sunshine Standards for Corporate Reporting to Stakeholders, and the Keidanren Charter for Good Corporate Behavior for similar approaches.

[23] Philip Kotler and Nancy Lee, *Corporate Social Responsibility: Doing the Most Good for Your Company and Your Cause*, 3 (2005) (quoting Business for Social Responsibility standards).

[24] "[T]he basic question of corporate social responsibility is not whether we wish to compel or forbid certain kinds of corporate conduct by legislative command . . . but rather whether it is socially desirable for corporations organized for profit voluntarily to identify and pursue social ends where this pursuit conflicts with the presumptive shareholder desire to maximize profit." David L. Engel, *An Approach to Corporate Social Responsibility*, 32 Stan. L. Rev. 1, 3 (1979).

is often taken for granted, as though reasonable folks will share a conception of the responsible corporation.[25] Many CSR advocates seem to presume that the state (or a multinational organization[26]) is well positioned for the task of articulating the interests to be served by the "socially responsible" corporation.[27] Sacrificing profit, in this sense, becomes a collective endeavor.

Faced with the alternative of corporate moral stances based on the whims of management, perhaps the collectivist inclination is understandable. To the extent that one aim of CSR advocates has been to construct a legal framework in which management is permitted to consider nonshareholder interests, the project is laudable (and remarkably successful).[28] The movement has, however, devoted insufficient attention to bringing the lessons of moral pluralism to bear on our understanding of social responsibility. One consequence of this oversight is a corporate moral landscape in which unmistakably noncontroversial issues prevail. Whether it is Nike taking an overdue stand on child labor, Nestle finally buckling to public pressure regarding its marketing of infant formula in developing countries, Starbucks selling "fair trade" coffee, Home Depot ending its sales of products from old growth or endangered forests, Shell addressing human rights issues with its investments in developing countries, or McDonald's adopting the European Union's restrictions on the use of growth-promoting antibiotics for its beef and chicken suppliers, the moral claims embedded in American corporate policies tend to be reactive and largely uncontested in terms of public opinion.[29] Only a few companies make up the diminutive (and constantly cited) universe of counter-examples as being

[25] Ronald R. Sims, *Ethics and Corporate Social Responsibility: Why Giants Fall*, 47 (2003) (giving examples of the "four distinct organizational approaches to social responsibility: illegal and irresponsible [e.g., dumping toxic waste], illegal and responsible [e.g., Greenpeace blocking nuclear tests], irresponsible and legal [e.g., beer companies targeting teens], and legal and responsible [e.g., Patagonia giving 10% of pretax profit to charity]").

[26] The Global Compact is a United Nations initiative that "relies on public accountability, transparency and the enlightened self-interest of companies, labour and civil society to initiate and share substantive action in pursuing... universal environmental and social principles." *See* United Nations Global Compact (http://www.unglobalcompact.org/AboutTheGC/index.html) (accessed Feb. 27, 2009).

[27] Stephen M. Bainbridge, *Community and Statism: A Conservative Contractarian Critique of Progressive Corporate Law Scholarship*, 82 Cornell L. Rev. 856, 887 (1997) (noting that progressive corporate law movement proposes "a set of honorable or trustworthy conduct to which corporate actors will be expected to adhere" and suggesting statist answer to the question of who gets to define the standard of conduct).

[28] Lyman Johnson notes, "approximately thirty states in the 1980s enacted statutes expressly empowering boards of directors to consider an array of interests other than shareholders," and that "[n]o statute, by way of contrast, mandates that only shareholder interests are to be advanced." Lyman Johnson, *Faith and Faithfulness in Corporate Theory*, 56 Cath. U. L. Rev. 1, 9 (2006).

[29] Philip Kotler and Nancy Lee, *Corporate Social Responsibility: Doing the Most Good for Your Company and Your Cause*, 1–2 (2005). One notable exception is the issue of gay rights. Most large corporations forbid discrimination on the basis of sexual orientation and many provide benefits to domestic partners, significantly outpacing government initiatives in this area. Marc Gunther, *Faith and Fortune: The Quiet Revolution to Reform American Business*, 26 (2004).

aggressive in trying to shape, rather than reflect, prevailing moral norms on issues such as global warming[30] and animal testing.[31]

Corporate Identity and the Market

The obvious rejoinder to any suggestion that the corporation should be more aggressive in staking out morally controversial matters is to invoke market dynamics. Why would a company seek to shape society's moral norms when they are still hotly contested, potentially alienating customers and shareholders? The answer lies in the malleability of the market and in the largely untapped potential of a distinct corporate moral identity. Success stories abound in which a corporation ignores existing knowledge about customer preferences, for "while customers shape markets, so do companies."[32] A corporation taking a moral stand may lose some constituents who oppose the truth claim embedded therein, but it may attract additional constituents and solidify the support of other existing constituents who find a forum for living out the dictates of conscience. Further, the moral identity, as a set of truth claims, cannot be evaluated simply in terms of profit and loss. If the morning-after pill is immoral, then Wal-Mart's decision not to sell it promotes the good in a way that may not be ascertainable in the balance sheet. To be clear, its promotion of the good does not depend on the objectivity of the morning-after pill's moral status; it is a function of providing space for the convergence of those whose consciences bear out shared convictions of its moral status.

In contrast to the moral homogeneity of the American corporate landscape, deliberately cultivated communal identities allow individuals to bring their normative frameworks to bear on their lived experiences. They function, in other words, as venues for the relational dimension of conscience. Charles Taylor argues that authenticity requires "creation and construction," and will frequently entail "opposition to the rules of society and even potentially to what we recognize as morality."[33] Postmodernists and deconstructionists excel at exploring this dimension of authenticity but, as Taylor points out, they neglect the dimension of authenticity that "binds us to others,"[34] particularly the requirement that authenticity be steeped in dialogue and exhibit an "openness to horizons of significance."[35] Without a cognizance of such horizons, "the creation loses the background that can save it from insignificance."[36]

---

[30] This issue was pursued early on, perhaps most famously, by Ben & Jerry's. See Kotler and Lee, *supra* note 29, at 49.

[31] The Body Shop's founder relentlessly advocated against animal testing, even after taking the company public and incurring the objections of significant shareholder groups. See *id.* at 69.

[32] Marc Gunther, *supra* note 29, at 105 (recounting the history of Starbucks ignoring market dogma that customers would not pay a premium for coffee).

[33] Charles Taylor, *The Ethics of Authenticity*, 66 (1992).

[34] *Id.* at 67.

[35] *Id.* at 66.

[36] *Id.*

The background moral frameworks through which individuals make sense of their lives and shape their surroundings require communities of meaning such as families, churches, and voluntary associations. There is no reason that corporations cannot play a supporting role. As Stephen Bainbridge explains, "even if virtuous citizens are developed solely by smaller institutions with roots in the local community, the corporation still can act as a vital counterweight against the state – an alternative island of power within the community."[37]

Contract or Community?

To a certain extent, allowing corporations to function as venues for conscience transcends the CSR debate. One foundational distinction driving that debate hinges on rival contractarian and communitarian conceptions of the corporation. The former is espoused by scholars such as Bainbridge, who asserts that "[t]he firm is simply a legal fiction representing the complex set of contractual relationships between [the firm's] inputs," and thus "the firm is not an individual thing, but rather a nexus or web of explicit and implicit contracts establishing rights and obligations among the various inputs making up the firm."[38] Communitarians are concerned that this approach marginalizes constituents whose interests are not so readily protected by contract,[39] and they seek to ground management's "obligation on a rich foundation of mutual trust and interdependence rather than limiting it to the bare bones of actual contractual terms [which rests, in turn] on a vision of the corporation as a community rather than a mere aggregation of self-seeking individuals whose relationships are defined solely by contract."[40] Communitarian critics see contractarianism as an extension of American individualism in which "organizations serve solely to further the ends of the participants and have no independent or transcendent meaning."[41] Perhaps it is not surprising, then, that a strand of the communitarian critique is grounded explicitly in religion. Susan Stabile, for example, challenges the prevailing view of corporate law as being grounded in a vision of "an individual independent and separate from others, motivated by self-interest, and possessing an entitlement to all that is in the world."[42] She proposes a religious view of the corporation that "sees the communion and interrelatedness of all beings and that sees the things of the world not as an entitlement, but as a gift."[43]

---

[37] Stephen M. Bainbridge, *Catholic Social Thought and the Corporation*, 1 J. Cath. Soc. Thought 595, 598 (2004).

[38] Stephen M. Bainbridge, *Community and Statism: A Conservative Contractarian Critique of Progressive Corporate Law Scholarship*, 82 Cornell L. Rev. 856, 859 (1997).

[39] David Millon, "Communitarianism in Corporate Law: Foundations and Law Reform Strategies," in *Progressive Corporate Law* 1, 1 (Lawrence Mitchell, ed., 1995).

[40] *Id.* at 4.

[41] Roberta Romano, *Metapolitics and Corporate Law Reform*, 36 Stan. L. Rev. 923, 933 (1984).

[42] Susan J. Stabile, *Using Religion to Promote Corporate Responsibility*, 39 Wake Forest L. Rev. 839, 839 (2004).

[43] *Id.*

The transcendent meaning of corporations does not rest comfortably in the communitarian critique, which is premised on an understanding of "corporations as more than just agglomerations of private contracts; they are powerful institutions whose conduct has substantial public implications."[44] The problem lies in the remedy that flows from communitarians' "strong skepticism toward the baseline presumption that contract alone should specify the terms of corporate governance relationships."[45] This skepticism becomes an invitation for state action.[46] Because they focus on our interdependence and our "responsibility for the quality of the lives of all community members," communitarians insist that the "state acts appropriately when it enforces such duties" against corporations.[47] In particular, although communitarians "share the contractarians' commitment to individual autonomy and choice as foundational moral values," they "insist that meaningful choice requires a social framework that cannot itself be constructed entirely out of private, bilateral transactions."[48]

On one hand, maintaining social obligations that are not captured in contractual terms can help restore the webs of mutual trust on which a vital associational life depends, and contractarians' tendency to celebrate profit maximization as the only legitimate interest of the corporation has its own homogenizing effect on the corporate moral landscape. But, to the extent that communitarians cede to the state the power to define and enforce social obligations to nonshareholder constituents, the project threatens the autonomy on which a vital associational life also depends. Especially with a benchmark as elastic as "meaningful choice," state intervention can easily subvert the corporation's potential mediating role, rendering it accountable to majoritarian norms rather than the conscience-driven convictions of constituents. Many identity-squelching state intrusions into the corporate sphere are justified as ensuring the "meaningful choice" of individuals, such as the state actions forcing pharmacies to dispense the morning-after pill. Instead of focusing on unmistakable problems of consumer access – such as in rural communities where Wal-Mart may have state-like power in that its decision not to provide a product would effectively preclude availability – access has been trotted out as a rhetorical trump card based on Wal-Mart's decision to carve out an identity for itself that diverges from the model of unlimited customer choice.

Even those sympathetic to communitarian goals note that "the process by which governments determine what behavior is consistent with the common good is not always reliable, and there is no guarantee that the mandates put in place are in

---

[44] David Millon, *Communitarians, Contractarians, and the Crisis in Corporate Law*, 50 Wash. & Lee L. Rev. 1373, 1379 (1993).

[45] *Id.* at 1381

[46] Bainbridge, *supra* note 38, at 884–5 (noting that the differences between contractarians and communitarians "come to a head in contrasting attitudes towards the proper role of state").

[47] Millon, *supra* note 44, at 1382–3.

[48] *Id.* at 1383.

fact consistent with the common good."[49] Indeed, as discussed in chapter 4, the state's role in facilitating the common good is necessarily limited. Otherwise, the line between a healthy concern for the common good and a stifling imposition of the collective good quickly blurs. There must always be room for the integration of moral virtues into corporate identity, but, if the corporation is to serve as a space for the communal exercise of conscience, the integration whenever possible should proceed bottom-up as a constituent-driven endeavor, not via the top-down trump of state power.

In other words, conscience flourishes when like-minded individuals are able to join together in communities that embody moral claims, which requires that the state resist the impulse to dictate the substance of those claims. As a bottom-up endeavor, of course, the market will determine the moral contours of the corporate landscape. The state still has a role in ensuring a functioning market and as a market actor to further its own interests, but it should avoid serving as the arbiter of moral norms.

Reimagining the corporation as a venue for conscience could easily become a flight of fancy if disconnected from the mundane realities of the constituent relationships that make up the corporation. Most mutual fund investors, even conscientious ones, could not identify the corporations they own, much less articulate the compatibility between their own moral convictions and the decision making of corporate management. Most consumers shop at Wal-Mart because of its proximity or price, not because of its decisions not to sell racy magazines, vulgar music, or the morning-after pill. Given the attenuated nature of the relationships on which it is built, it is not credible to speak of a corporation as a robust community.

The corporation does not, however, need to constitute a robust community to serve its mediating role. We cannot expect investors or customers to find fulfillment through the meager personal relationships occasioned by the corporate form. But the corporation can serve as a venue for conscience without serving as a conduit for meaningful relationships. The former function is made possible whenever the corporation stakes out a moral claim on an issue that draws together constituents who support that claim, particularly when the claim is somehow distinctive.

In this regard, the contractarian's skepticism toward statist solutions and the communitarian's greater openness to objectives beyond profit maximization both contribute to the conscience project. When the corporation is governed by a single moral norm (profit maximization) or answerable to a single source of moral norms (the state), its capacity to serve as a venue for conscience is drastically curtailed. Morally distinct stances become more difficult to the extent that the state requires all corporations to reflect an overarching normative value, particularly when – as the recent spate of controversies reflects – the value imposed is the maximization of consumer choice.

At the same time, no one can pretend that the corporation is composed of actual contracts created by arms-length negotiations among interested individuals. As Lyman Johnson clarifies, the insistence that "positive corporate law is contractual" is not "about actual bargains, but only about derived, deduced, and imputed bargains," which "are based on the theoretical workings of economic principles in various imperfect markets."[50] Background legal rules always shape the decision making of corporate constituents. Espousing a bottom-up approach to a corporation's moral identity represents a difference in degree, not in kind, from the CSR advocates who seek to inject their moral claims into the law's substance, for the legal system will always have something to say about the way corporate life unfolds. The question is, how aggressive should the law be in imposing particular values on the corporation?

Further, the contractarians' tendency to define the corporation's purpose exclusively as profit maximization may reflect an overly narrow understanding of shareholders' interests. Amy Domini, a pioneer of socially responsible investing, explains, "My wallet is not me."[51] In terms of fostering loyalty among shareholders, customers, and employees, prudent managers may be led to make nonprofit-maximizing decisions that support the corporation's moral identity. Lyman Johnson, critiquing the law-and-economics movement, observes that "[t]he dignity, inherent worth, and enormous energy and initiative of the individual are rightly valued, but to conceive of human existence solely as a vast collection of individuals is to fail to explain many of our existing social arrangements and interactions and to provide no solid moral foundation for genuinely selfless behavior."[52]

Their occasional rhetoric aside, contractarians already make at least some room for morality-driven corporate management. Larry Ribstein points out that "[m]anagers can promote shareholders' interests without maximizing profits to the extent that shareholders have some objective other than profit maximization."[53] More broadly, corporate law scholars across the ideological spectrum agree that "directors and officers possess very broad decision-making latitude, a latitude only imperfectly constrained by markets, norms, and law," which means that "senior decision-makers have significant freedom in charting how modern corporations behave and whose interests they advance."[54] As such, the question posed by the CSR movement is not "whether the parties in a firm may contract to take society's interests into account" – no one reasonably asserts that they cannot – but rather "the extent to which the law should mandate contracts intended to produce more socially responsible governance

[50] Lyman Johnson, *Individual and Collective Sovereignty in the Corporate Enterprise*, 92 Colum. L. Rev. 2215, 2226 (1992) (book review).
[51] Gunther, *supra* note 32, at 219.
[52] Johnson, *supra* note 50, at 2248.
[53] Larry E. Ribstein, *Accountability and Responsibility in Corporate Governance*, 81 Notre Dame L. Rev. 1431, 1433 (2006).
[54] Lyman Johnson, *Faith and Faithfulness in Corporate Theory*, 56 Cath. U. L. Rev. 1, 4–5 (2006).

or prohibit contracts that constrain socially responsible management."[55] The contractarian approach transforms the shareholder wealth maximization norm "from a right incident to private property into a mere bargained-for contract term."[56] As explained by Frank Easterbrook and Daniel Fischel,

> An approach that emphasizes the contractual nature of a corporation removes from the field of interesting questions one that has plagued many writers: what is the goal of the corporation? Is it profit (and for whom)? Social welfare more broadly defined? . . . Our response to such questions is: 'Who cares?' If the *New York Times* is formed to publish a newspaper first and make a profit second, no one should be allowed to object. Those who came in at the beginning actually consented, and those who came in later bought stock at a price reflecting the corporation's tempered commitment to a profit objective. . . . Corporate ventures may select their preferred "constituencies."[57]

Left to the market, the question of the corporation's purpose becomes less pressing because the answers become (potentially) less uniform.

Supporting the Corporation's Moral Identity

Viewing the corporation as a nexus of contracts should not cloud the degree to which background legal rules determine the contracts' default terms and permissible range of deviation from those default terms. These background rules can bolster the corporation's moral identity in tangible ways. First, transparency is essential. If the market is the vehicle by which to facilitate a morally diverse corporate landscape, transparency allows constituents to account for the moral dimension of corporate identity in their decisions to support the corporation.[58] As such, disclosure of morality-driven management decisions may bolster the corporation's mediating function.[59] However, because there will be considerable overlap between decisions made for moral reasons and those made for economic reasons, mandatory disclosure of morality-driven decisions would be practically unworkable. The corporation's moral identity will likely be articulated as a result of the directors' discernment of constituents' values

55 *Id.*
56 Stephen M. Bainbridge, *The Case for Limited Shareholder Voting Rights*, 53 UCLA L. Rev. 601, 605 (2006).
57 Frank H. Easterbrook and Daniel R. Fischel, *The Corporate Contract*, 89 Colum. L. Rev. 1416 (1989).
58 "As long as the corporation's CSR activities are adequately disclosed to the shareholders . . . it is not clear that they have a right to complain." Reuven Avi-Yonah, *The Cyclical Transformations of the Corporate Form: A Historical Perspective on Corporate Social Responsibility*, 30 Del. J. Corp. L. 767, 815 (2005).
59 Cf. Cynthia A. Williams, *The Securities and Exchange Commission and Corporate Social Transparency*, 112 Harv. L. Rev. 1197, 1295 (1999) ("Expanded social disclosure seeks to provide greater information to shareholders concerning these actions so that shareholders can determine the extent to which they approve of the trade-offs management has made between economic returns and social and environmental effects.").

(as may have happened with "red state" Wal-Mart), which has implications for the corporation's economic well-being. In other words, a blanket requirement that the corporation articulate the moral basis of a given decision wrongly presumes that such bases can be articulated apart from economic considerations. When possible, though, if there is a moral message to be communicated by the decision – "Wal-Mart does not believe that offering the morning-after pill is consistent with the company's values" – alerting the public enhances the mediating function and strengthens the case against state intervention.

Second, robust enforcement of the business judgment rule facilitates the corporation's moral identity. The rule prohibits courts from substituting their "own notions of what is or is not sound business judgment,"[60] as long as "the directors of a corporation acted on an informed basis, in good faith and in the honest belief that the action taken was in the best interests of the company."[61] This prohibition becomes especially helpful under Bainbridge's interpretation. He argues that the rule should not be viewed as a substantive standard of liability by which courts judge directors' actions. Instead, Bainbridge portrays the rule as a doctrine of abstention under which courts refrain from "reviewing the substantive merits of the directors' conduct unless the plaintiff can rebut [the rule's] presumption of good faith."[62]

For example, when Philip Wrigley refused to install lights in Chicago's Wrigley Field baseball stadium, a shareholder challenged the decision on the ground that the club's financial losses resulted from, in part, the lack of nighttime games, which generally brought larger crowds. In dismissing the complaint, the court noted that it "will not undertake to control the policy or business methods of a corporation although it may be seen that a wiser policy might be adopted and the business more successful if other methods were pursued."[63] The court speculated that Wrigley might have been concerned with the effect of night baseball on the neighborhood, and the neighborhood's viability is one factor in evaluating the long-term interests of the corporation. Absent allegations of fraud, illegality, or self-dealing, Wrigley's motivation was none of the court's business.[64] By carving out space for corporate directors to operate based on their own understanding of the corporation's long-term interests – not simply profit maximization – the business judgment rule is one linchpin of a legal system that values morally autonomous corporations.

The business judgment rule is not an absolute shield, of course, and the board's authority over the corporation's moral identity also demands a measure of accountability to shareholders. If the directors of General Motors are presented with evidence of their vehicles' impact on the environment, for example, the directors may invoke

---

[60] *Aronson v. Lewis*, 473 A.2d 805, 812 (Del. 1984).

[61] *Sinclair Oil Corp. v. Levien*, 280 A.2d 717, 720 (Del. 1971).

[62] Stephen M. Bainbridge, *The Business Judgment Rule as Abstention Doctrine*, 57 Vand. L. Rev. 83, 90 (2004).

[63] Shlensky v. Wrigley, 237 N.E.2d 776, 778 (Ill. App. Ct. 1968) (applying Delaware law).

[64] Bainbridge, *supra* note 56, at 97.

moral claims to justify an aggressive pursuit of lower-impact technology. If the directors decide to cease all vehicle production until the new technology is operational, their pursuit of a moral identity has resulted in the abdication of their responsibility to protect the company's ongoing profit-making capacity. Similarly, Wal-Mart's directors should not face liability if they, in keeping with their sense of the company's moral identity, decline to sell the morning-after pill despite FDA approval of the drug. The availability of the pill is a morally laden question that had not presented itself before, and Wal-Mart's refusal to sell the pill does not stand in tension with any other dimension of the company's moral identity. If the directors decide, on strictly moral grounds, to terminate all supply relationships with China, shareholders may have cause to complain. Because Wal-Mart has never displayed moral qualms about importing goods from China – and indeed, has built itself on the strength of such imports – taking such a step would defy investors' expectations while seriously damaging the company's ability to maintain the low costs that drive its market success. A newfound moral conviction is more difficult to implement than an ongoing one, especially if there is not a corresponding business rationale. Maintaining an existing moral identity is less problematic because investors are on notice; the only new developments concern the implementation of the existing identity in light of changing circumstances. Newfound moral convictions are not impossible, but they will face greater limitations when they conflict with the business model that has shaped shareholder expectations.

Third, maintaining the primacy of directors in corporate governance is more likely than shareholder empowerment to be the path most conducive to a distinct moral identity for the corporation. Shareholder voting rights are limited to a few key contexts under Delaware law,[65] and except for the election of directors and the amendment of bylaws, director approval is required before shareholder action is possible.[66] Supporting the corporation as a venue for conscience does not mean that the myriad decisions comprising the boundaries of the corporate venue can or should be made by shareholders directly. The sheer number of shareholders and the complexity of corporate decision making warrant the delegation of authority to a board of relatively independent directors.[67] Directors are also better positioned than

---

[65] See Matthew T. Bodie, *AOL, Time Warner, and the False God of Shareholder Primacy*, 31 J. Corp. L. 975, 977 (2005).

[66] Stephen M. Bainbridge, *The Case for Limited Shareholder Voting Rights*, 53 UCLA L. Rev. 601, 616 (2006).

[67] Stephen M. Bainbridge, *Director Primacy and Shareholder Disempowerment*, 119 Harv. L. Rev. 1735, 1749 (2006) ("Active investor involvement in corporate decisionmaking seems likely to disrupt the very mechanism that makes the widely held public corporation practicable: namely, the centralization of essentially nonreviewable decisionmaking authority in the board of directors."); Stephen M. Bainbridge, *Director Primacy: The Means and Ends of Corporate Governance*, 97 Nw. U. L. Rev. 547, 561 (2003) ("[A] unique attribute of the modern public corporation is the ever-increasing use of independent board members who typically lack both day-to-day management power and any significant equity stake in the corporation.").

shareholders to account for the views of employees and other constituents, who also should have a role – although not a dispositive one – in the ongoing formation of the corporation's moral identity.

Director primacy is particularly essential because the majority vote of shareholders may be more vulnerable to the lure of short-term profit at the expense of other corporate values. For example, Time, Inc., always portrayed itself as having cultivated a distinctive corporate culture in which the foremost value was journalistic integrity. In the late 1980s, while Time was exploring merger possibilities with Warner Communications, Time's board was careful to insist on measures designed to keep Time's culture intact.[68] When Paramount made a surprise takeover bid just before the merger was to go through, Time's board changed the deal with Warner in a way that avoided the necessity of a shareholder vote.[69] The board was fearful that the shareholders would jump at Paramount's bid, and that Paramount's profit-driven priorities would threaten the viability of Time's culture.[70] The Delaware courts refused to enjoin the Time Warner deal. Chancellor Allen noted that Time had shown "a desire to maintain an independent Time Incorporated that reflected a continuation of what management and the board regarded as [a] distinctive and important 'Time culture.'"[71] The Delaware Supreme Court affirmed, reasoning that "[d]irectors are not obliged to abandon a deliberately conceived corporate plan for a short-term shareholder profit unless there is clearly no basis to sustain the corporate strategy."[72]

Critics claim that, by changing the deal with Warner, Time's directors "eliminated the need for shareholder approval in order to cram the transaction down the shareholders' throats."[73] Perhaps in some settings, though, preventing shareholders from taking an immediate profit is essential both to long-term corporate well-being and to the viability of a distinct corporate identity. Out of the disaster of the more recent AOL-Time Warner merger, one lesson stood clear: the Time Warner ethos triumphed over AOL's propensity to worship "the false god of share price."[74] Maximizing shareholder value is still the overarching purpose of the corporation, but that value must be measured over the long run and it must encompass factors that are not always reflected in the short-term share price. Moral claims are among such factors.

Under a director primacy approach, the board is not a mere agent of the shareholders; the board "is a *sui generis* body – a sort of Platonic guardian – serving

---

[68] Nina Munk, *Fools Rush In: Steve Case, Jerry Levin, and the Unmaking of AOL Time Warner* (2004) (cited in Bodie, *supra* note 65, at 983).

[69] See *id.*

[70] See *id.*

[71] *Paramount Commc'ns Inc. v. Time, Inc.*, Civil Action Nos. 10866, 10670, and 10935, 1989 WL 79880, at *4 (Del. Ch. July 14, 1989) (cited in Bodie, *supra* note 65, at 984).

[72] *Paramount Commc'ns Inc. v. Time, Inc.*, 571 A.2d 1140, 1154 (Del. 1989) (cited in Bodie, *supra* note 65, at 984).

[73] Julian Velasco, *Structural Bias and the Need for Substantive Review*, 82 Wash. U. L.Q. 821, 890 (2004).

[74] Bodie, *supra* note 65, at 1001.

as the nexus for the various contracts comprising the corporation."[75] Admittedly, the directors' ability to steward the corporation's moral identity over the long term may be compromised to the extent that a significant portion of the directors' own compensation is tied to stock performance, and thus companies for which such stewardship is important should resist that trend. Although share price cannot be the exclusive barometer of well-being for the morally distinct corporation, there is still a place, at the margins, for accountability to the shareholders[76] – most obviously when shareholders move their money to another corporation, but more power-fully, for instance, when shareholders are given the chance to approve a takeover bid in response to mismanagement.[77] As Bainbridge observes, "shareholder voting is properly understood not as an integral aspect of the corporate decision-making structure, but rather as an accountability device of last resort to be used sparingly, at best."[78]

The looming issue in corporate governance, as Ken Goodpaster puts it, "is not whether corporations (and other organizations) should be 'unleashed' to exert moral force in our society but rather how critically and self-consciously they should choose to do so."[79] The powerful influence of corporations does not favor moral disen-gagement, but moral awareness.[80] Such awareness comes with the mediating role, through the cultivation of moral values among the corporation's constituents and their expression in the marketplace.

If we embrace this vision of the corporation as a moral endeavor, not just an economic enterprise, we will lament corporations' move toward moral homogeneity, especially when the move is the result of state action rather than the morally self-aware decisions of management. How many corporations will take this idea of a more proactive moral identity seriously? Perhaps very few, but if we take conscience seriously, we need to make space for those few because they serve a very important function. A corporation that serves as a venue for living out the dictates of conscience will practice a form of authentic self-definition that Charles Taylor discerns in the modern artist. "If we become ourselves by expressing what we're about," Taylor explains, "and if what we become is by hypothesis original, not based on the pre-existing, then what we express is not an imitation of the pre-existing either, but a new creation."[81]

---

[75] Stephen M. Bainbridge, *Director Primacy: The Means and Ends of Corporate Governance*, 97 Nw. U. L. Rev. 547, 549 (2003).

[76] *Id.* at 565 ("[M]ost theories of the firm agree, shareholders own the residual claim on the corporation's assets and earnings. The ownership of that claim explains why the set of contracts comprising the corporation treats the shareholders as the beneficiaries of director accountability.").

[77] Robert C. Clark, *Corporate Law*, 95 (1986).

[78] Bainbridge, *supra* note 67, at 627.

[79] Kenneth E. Goodpaster, *Conscience and Corporate Culture*, 164 (2007).

[80] *Id.*

[81] Charles Taylor, *supra* note 33, at 62.

CORPORATE CONSCIENCE FROM THE INSIDE

The corporation's moral identity, as expressed in its marketplace conduct, may create tension with its internal environment to the extent that the exercise of employees' own consciences is fettered by the boundaries of the institutional conscience. This tension may actually be productive, not paralyzing. As a community of workers, both the for-profit and nonprofit corporations must foster an atmosphere in which individual consciences can flourish within the broad limits necessary for maintaining the corporation's moral agency. The ongoing process of articulating those limits has the potential to promote both a robust institutional conscience and a more carefully crafted environment for employees' own exercise of conscience.

Corporate Culture and Personal Integrity

The disconnection between a corporation's moral identity and the moral convictions of its employees is pervasive and easily discernible across the American corporate landscape. Consider the infamous case of the late former Enron CEO Ken Lay, a donor to hundreds of charitable causes who was lauded at his funeral as a devoted follower of Jesus Christ.[82] After his criminal conviction for fraud, Lay paraphrased St. Paul in asserting that "all things work for good for those who love the Lord," and explained that "we love our Lord."[83] The obituary posted on his web site asserted that Lay "exemplified" the personal qualities cited in Paul's epistle to the Galatians: "But the fruit of the Spirit is love, joy, peace, patience, kindness, goodness, faithfulness, gentleness, self-control."[84] Indeed, one eulogist recalled talking to a custodian at the courthouse in which Lay's trial was held. Lay had approached her on the first day of trial to commend her for the job she did cleaning the courtroom floor. According to the custodian, "I've been working here for years. He is the first man in a suit ever to look me in the eye and say anything kind."[85]

If there is even a kernel of truth in these characterizations, how did Lay preside over a corporation that unraveled through a web of schemes that, according to prosecutors, "boils down to lying, cheating, and stealing?"[86] Enron's rise to the top was fueled by dubious transactions orchestrated by Lay and his colleagues, reflecting several distinct moral claims: that profit trumps principle, that public perception of profit is a matter for advocacy and manipulation, that the corporation's only duty

---

[82] Sylvia Moreno, *Lay Eulogized in Glowing Terms at High-Profile Houston Funeral*, Wash. Post, Jul. 13, 2006.

[83] Mary Flood, *Ex-Enron Bosses Closer to Prison*, Hous. Chron., May 26, 2006, at A1.

[84] Galatians 5:22.

[85] Mike Tolson, *Lay Praised and Defended by Family and Friends*, Hous. Chron. Jul. 13, 2006.

[86] Carrie Johnson, *Judge Lets Enron Jurors Consider Whether Defendants Turned a Blind Eye*, Wash. Post, May 11, 2006.

to its shareholders is the maximization of share price, and that it owes no duties to the public at large whatsoever. That Lay appears to have paid homage to a panoply of Christian values in his personal affairs makes his company's marketplace conduct more glaring. The relentless pursuit of profit is the only value discernible in Enron's institutional identity, and evidence of any contrary convictions among its key managers is not easily discerned.

If corporate culture exhibited a presumption that managers' own deeply held values should be integrated with their professional decision making, could that have made a difference at Enron? More than fifty years ago, Adolf Berle observed that, in light of "the legal presumption in favor of management, and the natural unwillingness of courts to control or reverse management action save in cases of the more elementary types of dishonesty or fraud," the only real control on corporate action is the "philosophy of the men who compose" management.[87]

Faith in the Workplace

We may never know if Lay's personal philosophy could have changed the outcome, but the question has become more pressing since Enron's demise seems to have contributed to a "spiritual awakening" in the American workplace, "as executives look[ed] for ways to bring their faith into the office after a turbulent year."[88] The traditional divide between spirituality and work has encountered a challenge from a "diverse, mostly unorganized mass of believers – a counterculture bubbling up all over corporate America."[89] The organizational infrastructure has been slow to catch up with the grass roots initiatives among workers, but has now exploded.[90]

Bolstered by evidence of collateral damage from the movement in the form of a 30% increase in religious discrimination claims filed since 2000,[91] skeptics will insist that conscience is best protected by keeping deeply held, contested moral

[87] Adolf A. Berle Jr., *The 20th Century Capitalist Revolution*, 180 (1954).
[88] Victor Godinez, *Some Corporate Execs Follow Spiritual Beliefs*, Dallas Morning News, Dec. 25, 2001.
[89] Marc Gunther, *God and Business*, Fortune, Jul. 9, 2001.
[90] In 1995, there were 25 workplace ministries; as of 2005 more than 900, not including "thousands of Bible and prayer groups that meet regularly in workplaces." Faith in the Workplace, Religion & Ethics Newsweekly (Jan. 28, 2005). See, e.g., The CEO Institute (described as an "organization of CEO's and Presidents who are Christians who help each other solve a myriad of problems that will positively affect their company's bottom line as well as increase their spiritual significance and eternal rewards") (www.ceoinst.com/pages/who_we_are); Legatus (1300 Catholic CEOs); Neela Banerjee, *At Bosses' Invitation, Chaplains Come Into Workplace and Onto Payroll*, N.Y. Times, Dec. 4, 2006, at A1 ("From car parts makers to fast food chains to financial service companies, corporations across the country are bringing chaplains into the workplace.").
[91] Religion & Ethics Newsweekly; see also Laura M. Johnson, Note, *Whether to Accommodate Religious Expression That Conflicts with Employer Anti-Discrimination and Diversity Policies Designed to Safeguard Homosexual Rights: A Multi-Factor Approach for the Courts*, 38 Conn. L. Rev. 295, 301 (2005) ("[T]he total number of religious discrimination cases filed with the agency has increased by twenty-seven percent since 2000. In contrast, the number of race and sex discrimination cases have actually decreased since that year.").

convictions out of the corporate environment. Indeed, the workplace is where an imprudently empowered conscience seems to threaten the viability of conscience as traditionally understood. Two distinct tensions underlie this concern. First, the institutional embodiment of conscience seems to run up against individual conscience, as the coherent moral identity of the corporation presumes the authority to ensure that employees support – or at least do not undermine – any given claim on which the identity is built. Second, even when an employee's workplace exercise of conscience does not threaten the corporation's moral identity, its unfettered exercise may interfere with the ability of coworkers to live out the dictates of their own consciences.

Institutional Conscience versus Employee Conscience

The authentic integration of the employee's own convictions with her workplace environment is not the predominant theme of many workplace spirituality programs. Instead, discussions often center on the introduction of an admittedly inoffensive, but hopelessly vague, veneer of spirituality to the corporate environment. Narottam Bhindi and Patrick Duignan, for example, call for a "restoration of spirituality in leadership," by which they do not mean "a partisan religious view," but rather "that individuals and groups should experience a sense of deep and enduring meaning and significance from an appreciation of their interconnectedness and interdependency, and from their feelings of being connected to something greater than the self."[92] Southwest Airlines seems to have embraced this approach, priding itself on four "spiritual" values: "a strong emphasis on community," helping "employees feel that they are part of a cause," the "empowerment of all employees," and a cultural emphasis on "emotional and humor aspects."[93]

In many ways, workplace spirituality programs come across as a slightly jaded way to gain employee loyalty and avoid divisiveness. Douglas Hicks concludes, "[m]any accounts of spiritual leadership accept as unproblematic the view that it is possible to cull religions for their essential insights, while leaving behind the other parts of tradition and communal practices that might create disagreement or simply be inconvenient for modern, busy individuals."[94] Most management spirituality programs incorporate aspects of Eastern religion, humanistic ethics, and psychology, suggesting "that their programs are highly compatible with all religions, as well as secular viewpoints."[95] Like civil religion, a combination of religious and value-laden

---

[92] Narottam Bhindi and Patrick Duigan, *Leadership for a New Century: Authenticity, Intentionality, Spirituality and Sensibility*, 25 Educational Management & Administration 126 (1997).

[93] John F. Milliman et al., *Spirit and Community at Southwest Airlines: An Investigation of a Spiritual Values-Based Model*, 12 J. Organizational Change Management 3 (1999) (quoted in Hicks, *infra* note 94, at 58).

[94] Douglas A. Hicks, *Religion and the Workplace: Pluralism, Spirituality, Leadership*, 50 (2003).

[95] Laura Nash and Scotty McLennan, *Church on Sunday, Work on Monday: The Challenge of Fusing Christian Values with Business Life*, xxv (2001).

symbolism "is crafted in order not to offend anyone, but rather to appeal to all and to gain their loyalty to the company."[96]

Even if fears of divisiveness were overcome and employers created space for the authentic exercise and expression of conscience in the workplace, the efforts would not substitute for the parallel endeavor of constructing the corporation's institutional conscience. The corporation's moral identity is not simply the sum of its parts; the corporation needs discretion to shape its own identity. Under some circumstances, this will limit the conscience-driven conduct of individual employees, but that is the price of the corporation's mediating role.

Title VII, the federal statute governing employment discrimination, prohibits discrimination by adverse employment action (e.g., termination or demotion) or the creation of a hostile work environment. Employers are required to accommodate the religious beliefs of an employee unless such accommodation would cause an "undue hardship" for the employer. Courts have shown a tendency to interpret "undue hardship" in economic terms. In holding unlawful an employer's mandatory employee devotional, the Ninth Circuit went so far as to hold that an accommodation's impact on the spiritual aspects of the company is "irrelevant if it has no effect on [the company's] economic well-being."[97] This cramped view hinders the cultivation of a corporation's moral identity.

Courts do occasionally articulate noneconomic "undue burdens,"[98] and there may be room within case law to recognize undue burdens in terms of the corporate mission, but the area remains largely uncharted. Courts are split as to whether an employer's concern for its "public image" justifies limitations on an employee's religion-driven personal appearance,[99] although the limitations seem to be viewed by courts as "appeals to customer preference,"[100] which fall back into the realm of commercial concerns.

Other noneconomic burden cases are similarly ambiguous as to whether they would encompass the employer's moral claims. In *Peterson v. Hewlett-Packard*,[101] for example, the Ninth Circuit ruled that the employer did not need to accommodate an employee who responded to posters celebrating diversity in the workplace by prominently posting bible verses in his cubicle, including a passage from Leviticus referring

---

[96] Hicks, *supra* note 94, at 120; *see also* Michelle Conlin, *Religion in the Workplace: The Growing Presence of Spirituality in Corporate America*, Bus. Wk., Nov. 1, 1999, at 153 ("[T]he largest driver of this [spirituality] trend is the mounting evidence that spiritually minded programs in the workplace not only soothe workers' psyches, but also deliver improved productivity.").

[97] *EEOC v. Townley Eng'g & Mfg. Co.* 859 F.2d 610, 616 (9th Cir. 1988).

[98] *U.S. Airways, Inc. v. Barnett*, 527 U.S. 581 (2002) (holding that reassignment to another position, in violation of a company's seniority system, would pose undue burden on company).

[99] Cf. *Cloutier v. Costco Wholesale Corp.*, 390 F.3d 126 (1st Cir. 2004) (allowing exception to ban on facial jewelry would be undue hardship for employer), with *E.E.O.C. v. Red Robin Gourmet Burgers*, No. C04-1291JLR, 2005 WL 2090677 (W.D.Wash. Aug 29, 2005) (allowing employee to work with visible tattoos would not constitute undue burden).

[100] See, e.g., *Cloutier*, 390 F.3d at 136.

[101] 358 F.3d 599 (9th Cir. 2004).

to homosexual conduct as an abomination warranting death.[102] The employer's anti-harassment policy stated that "any comments or conduct relating to a person's race, gender, religion, disability, age, sexual orientation, or ethnic background that fail to respect the dignity and feeling [sic] of the individual are unacceptable."[103] After rejecting the employee's claim that the diversity campaign amounted to disparate treatment of him on account of his religious beliefs, the court ruled that accommodation would pose an undue burden for the employer by precluding its expression of tolerance for gays. Crucially, though, it was not simply the corporation's desire to define itself through this message, but rather the message's link to commercial success that drove the court's reasoning. Allowing the employee's religious beliefs to trump the diversity program would have hindered "efforts to attract and retain a qualified, diverse workforce, which the company reasonably views as vital to its commercial success."[104]

Even this approach, notwithstanding its ambiguity, is preferable to the proposed Workplace Religious Freedom Act (WFRA), which portrays the undue burden as pertaining only to economic impact.[105] Further, although the Supreme Court has interpreted Title VII to mean that an accommodation's impact on an employer's operations need only be *de minimis* to qualify as an "undue hardship,"[106] the WRFA would replace the *de minimis* standard with a requirement that the employer incur "significant difficulty or expense" in accommodating the employee's religious exercise. The factors prescribed by the WRFA for making this determination are framed narrowly in economic terms:

A) the identifiable cost of the accommodation, including the costs of loss of productivity and of retraining or hiring employees or transferring employees from one facility to another;

B) the overall financial resources and size of the employer involved, relative to the number of its employees; and

C) for an employer with multiple facilities, the geographic separateness or administrative or fiscal relationship of the facilities.[107]

Although the WRFA is lauded by religious liberty advocates and enjoys bipartisan support, imposing more stringent standards for accommodating the religious

---

[102] *Id.* at 602.

[103] *Id.*

[104] *Id.* at 607.

[105] Workplace Religious Freedom Act of 2007, H.R. 1431, 110th Congress (2007). The Senate version was identical to the House version, but it has subsequently been narrowed. *Cf.* Workplace Religious Freedom Act of 2005, S. 677, 109th Congress (2005), with Workplace Religious Freedom Act of 2008, S. 3628, 110th Congress (2008).

[106] *Trans World Airlines, Inc. v. Hardison*, 432 U.S. 63, 84 (1977) ("To require TWA to bear more than a de minimis cost in order to give Hardison Saturdays off is an undue hardship.").

[107] H.R. 1431.

exercise of individual employees contributes to an atomistic understanding of conscience. Individuals are empowered, as individuals, to abide by the dictates of their consciences, but the relational dimension of conscience is marginalized. The marketplace of ideas and convictions is replaced with an archipelago of individually held beliefs. As James Sonne observes, "to suspend religion from debate, discourse, or even difficulty, in the manner proposed by the [WRFA] is not authentic freedom, but an atrophic enabling that is harmful not only to legal and market systems, but also to the vitality of religion."[108]

The key question for our inquiry pertains not simply to the degree of harm that is sufficient – *de minimis* versus significant difficulty – but the type of harm. If an employee's workplace conduct compromises the company's deliberately crafted moral identity without a demonstrable economic impact, can accommodation constitute an undue burden? For example, suppose that Walgreen's stakes out a "pro-choice" position in the pharmacist wars, articulating its mission as offering all legal contraceptive products to anyone carrying a valid prescription, with no lectures or hassles from its pharmacists. Suppose that a pharmacist who works at one of its high-traffic pharmacies (where there are always at least two pharmacists on duty) believes, as a matter of conscience, that he must not knowingly facilitate premarital sex among teenagers. Accordingly, he decides to ask about the marital status of any teenager who requests contraceptives. If they are not married, he calls over the other pharmacist on duty to handle the prescription. Assuming that a second pharmacist is always on duty at that location, Walgreen's can accommodate the pharmacist's conscience without incurring extra costs.[109] But the corporate identity is compromised regardless of the economic burden. Having a pharmacist ask the customer whether she is married sends a message to the customer contrary to the moral claim intended by the company.

Respect for the consciences of individual employees precludes granting employers a blanket license to define their missions in whatever way maximizes their discretion in personnel decisions. The prudent degree of authority over employees correlates with the mediating role; just as the mediating role requires that constituents have notice of the moral claims they are supporting, if a company's moral claims are given precedence over an employee's contrary claims, those claims must be articulated as part of the institutional identity. This dimension of the corporate conscience would also be served by expanded disclosure practices.

Employees do not have an inviolable right to preemployment notice of the claims making up the corporate conscience – the institutional identity will evolve in light

---

[108] James A. Sonne, *The Perils of Universal Accommodation: The Workplace Religious Freedom Act of 2003 and the Affirmative Action of 147,096,000 Souls*, 79 Notre Dame L. Rev. 1023, 1032 (2004).

[109] In terms of "identifiable costs," it is possible that the pharmacist's question would drive some customers away, but it is also possible, depending on the prevailing norms of the surrounding community, that other customers would be drawn to support the moral claims implicit in either the pharmacist's question or in the pharmacy's accommodation of the pharmacist's question.

of changing business and moral environments – but the claims must originate apart from the employment dispute at issue. And certain moral claims must be deemed nonstarters in the undue burden analysis to the extent that they could justify the exclusion of whole categories of individuals from employment opportunities. Apart from the hiring practices of pervasively religious employers, cultivating the corporation's moral identity will entail fact-intensive inquiries into the compatibility of a particular employee's conduct with a particular moral claim. The corporate conscience is not a legitimate justification for categorical discrimination. In light of these caveats, this type of undue burden – noneconomic harm to the employer's deliberately cultivated moral identity – may be a narrow sliver of religious accommodation cases, but recognizing its legitimacy is key to ensuring the possibility of the corporation's mediating function.

Employee Conscience versus Employee Conscience

In the broad interstices where the employer's moral claims (or commercial interests) are not implicated by an employee's exercise of conscience, the corporation's internal environment should be a welcoming one. But the employer's openness to individual conscience does not resolve the other part of the dilemma: How do conflicting consciences coexist without transforming the workplace into another battleground of the culture wars?

Such conflicts cannot be avoided or glossed over, but we must accurately frame what is at stake. Protecting the exercise of conscience does not require a controversy-free workplace. An employee's conscience – understood as belief applied to conduct – is not violated through the involuntary exposure to debate, admonition, or even incivility on matters that touch on the employee's moral convictions. The rough and tumble dynamics of the public square may not belong in the workplace, but the benchmark of concern should be the level of discord that will interfere with the efficient operation of the business, not merely that which will give offense to any particular employee. Often these standards will overlap, but the "eggshell" employee cannot dictate the permissible exercise of conscience by her coworkers. In particular, the expression of moral or religious convictions should not be construed as harassment unless the expression directly targets a coworker in a way that interferes with job performance or would otherwise be deemed objectively unreasonable. Unlike racist and sexist speech, there is no compelling reason to disfavor categorically religious or moral speech in the workplace, whether engaged in by the employer or employee.

Resolving particular disputes will require stepping back to consider the competing conscience claims of individual employees in light of the corporation's own articulated claims. For example, an employee who spends every lunch hour in the company cafeteria trying to persuade her coworkers of the immorality of the American military's invasion of, and continued presence in, Iraq must be given space to express herself if our legal system takes conscience seriously. The objections of a coworker who disagrees should not alter the analysis because being exposed to alternative views does not interfere with the coworker's exercise of conscience. If the employee continues to harangue coworkers to the point of affecting a reasonable employee's ability to function effectively in the workplace, the employer needs to step in. At this point, coworkers are being forced to give up their ability to work as the price of maintaining their moral convictions. Unless and until that point is reached, the employee's exercise of conscience should be given latitude by the employer.

But suppose the employer is a contractor with a significant role in the Iraq reconstruction, and that the employer has issued statements supporting the military's efforts in Iraq in an effort to attract employees who would accept assignment there. In that case, the employee's persistent proselytizing may be problematic even absent a showing that a reasonable employee could not perform her work. If the company's ability to cultivate a distinct moral identity is compromised – for example, by hindering the hiring and retention of ideologically sympathetic employees, lowering morale, and fomenting dissent – the institutional conscience should take precedence over the individual employee's.

Transcending the Value-Free Workplace

The skeptic rightly wonders, why bother with any of this? An approach that complicates the already convoluted individual rights paradigm by introducing another level of moral actor – the institution – to the employment discrimination inquiry bears a heavy burden of proof. The premise that the very fabric of the corporate environment should be accessible to deeply held religious and moral claims is not met with enthusiasm in all circles.

The value of a conscience-friendly workplace does not turn on the value of any particular set of conscience-driven claims. Employees need as much space as possible to bring their core moral convictions, which often will spring from religious convictions, to bear on their workplace decision making. Bridging the personal-professional gap has three potential benefits. First, the integration can bring greater *coherence* to the lives of employees. Personal-professional segmentation exacts a heavy price on individuals forced to ignore their most deeply held convictions in performing their work. Second, by bringing moral convictions into the workplace, employees may be empowered to *transcend* the minimalist and visionless ethical regimes of most corporations. A morally proactive corporation can emerge, strengthening employee-employer bonds in the process. Third, living out deeply held moral convictions on the job makes meaningful ethical and moral *dialogue* possible. Such dialogue is a key path toward raising an employee's own ethical awareness, as well as a means by which to facilitate a richer conscience-driven conversation throughout the corporation. These benefits will not follow invariably whenever moral or religious convictions are brought into the workplace. Indeed, much can go off-track when an outspoken employee is insensitive to the diverse moral convictions held by her coworkers, using her own claims as a bludgeon, rather than as fertile ground for dialogue.

For any of these benefits to be realized, the corporation's internal environment cannot be a value-free zone; it should be replete with meaningful and motivating values, even if diverse, as long as they do not eviscerate the power of the corporation's articulated institutional values. What is at stake is not just the individual employee's well-being, but the corporation's well-being to the extent that its own moral compass lacks the substance that could be provided by the core convictions of its constituents. This is where the corporation's mediating function should be front and center. In other words, what if Ken Lay had been groomed for leadership within a corporate culture where his Christian devotion was viewed as an asset and not as irrelevant?

There are exceptions to Enron's profit-at-all-costs morality. Interstate Batteries' mission statement is "[t]o glorify God as we supply our customers worldwide with top quality, value-priced batteries, related electrical power-source products, and distribution services."[110] The fast food chain Chick-fil-A Inc., foregoes an obvious revenue stream by closing all of its stores on Sundays.[111] At ServiceMaster, a statue of Jesus washing his disciples' feet stands outside the company headquarters, and no one earns more than twelve times the amount earned by the lowest-paid employee.[112] After a fire burned down its mill, Malden Mills CEO Aaron Fuerstein cited his Jewish faith as the impetus for keeping his employees on the payroll and under the company's benefits coverage even though they had no work to do.[113]

These examples do not easily translate into a universalized sense of spirituality; they emanate from particular moral convictions held by particular individuals and embedded into the fabric of particular companies. Despite the claims of its advocates, the allure of "common morality" is illusory unless it maintains a connection with the motivational power of the truth claims revealed in the lived realities of the individuals who make up the corporation. To the extent that religious convictions undergird an institution-wide policy, a simple reference to divine revelation may not be as effective as a broader dialogue in which religiously rooted truth claims provide the foundation but are not the sole input.

Of course, regardless of the process through which they are enacted, corporate policies premised on moral truth claims will sometimes spark discord. Some of the

---

[110] Victor Godinez, *supra* note 88.

[111] See *Why We're Closed on Sundays*, http://www.chick-fil-a.com/#closedonsundays (accessed Sep. 6, 2009).

[112] See Marc Gunther, *supra* note 89.

[113] See Timothy L. Fort, *Religion in the Workplace: Mediating Religion's Good, Bad, and Ugly Naturally*, 12 Notre Dame J.L. Ethics & Pub. Pol'y 121, 155 (1998). Morally distinctive corporations are not always successful corporations, of course. Malden Mills eventually filed for bankruptcy. See *A Change at Malden Mills*, N.Y. Times, Mar. 10, 2003, at C8.

discord can be avoided if the employer is able to distinguish between two paths by which to cultivate the institutional conscience. One path focuses on the employee's external conduct in setting boundaries that define the company mission, limiting an employee's ability to send mission-defying messages to other market participants or fellow constituents. (Consider a Ben & Jerry's employee defying the company's activism on environmental issues by sporting a "Global Warming is a Myth" button at work.) The other path veers into the substance of the individual employee's beliefs, effectively seeking employee assent to the substantive truth claims embodied in the company mission. This path becomes more problematic in that the employee is not simply called to limit her exercise of conscience, but to shape its dictates, or at least pretend that its dictates are something that they are not, as the price of employment. (Consider Ben & Jerry's requiring employees to write letters to their legislators urging government action to reduce global warming.) For many religious organizations, the work is ministry, and it is no affront to the dignity of conscience to ensure that the ministers are aligned in belief. For-profit corporations seeking to embrace religious or moral values as part of their missions need not force an artificial unity of conscience among employees to do so. More importantly, economic participation in our pluralist democracy should not be conditioned on the dictates of one's conscience.

These two paths – visible defiance of corporate identity versus subjective assent to corporate identity – are not always easily distinguished, though. Consider the litigation battles that have erupted over mandatory religious services for employees.[114] Holding religious meetings in the workplace is perfectly consistent with honoring individual and institutional conscience; making the meetings mandatory elevates institutional conscience and veers uncomfortably close to regulating the interior disposition of employees. Kent Greenawalt tentatively concludes that such meetings amount to unlawful discrimination, drawing parallels to the more obviously unlawful practice of an employer making attendance at a particular church a condition of employment.[115] Admittedly, an employee could go through the motions of participating in a religious service without allowing it to affect her own beliefs; however, the whole point of the mandatory meetings is to shape the employees' consciences into shared religious convictions. Participating employees flout the objective when they silently disengage or dissent from the content of the service. A mandatory meeting to inform employees of the content of the employer's moral identity is not similarly objectionable. Unlike religious services, which are a communal expression of religious belief, informational meetings are not problematic as long as the employer does not presume authority over the content of the employee's most deeply held beliefs.

[114] See, e.g., *EEOC v. Townley Eng'g & Mfg. Co.* 859 F.2d 610 (9th Cir. 1988); *Young v. Southwestern Savings & Loan Ass'n,* 509 F.2d 140 (5th Cir. 1975).
[115] Kent Greenawalt, *Title VII and Religious Liberty,* 33 Loy. U. Chi. L.J. 1, 10 (2001).

CONSCIENCE AND CORPORATIONS

The reactive corporation, captive to the prevailing culture, cannot be a significant agent for change in society or a meaningful venue for the formation or expression of conscience among its constituents. Part of the problem is the corporation's failure to identify, much less conduct its operations by, defined moral principles or truth claims. Just as this amoral pragmatism hinders the flourishing of corporate identity, it also muddles individual efforts to construct a coherent or stable personal identity. Whether or not Ken Lay fell victim to pragmatism's profit-fueled rationalizations, it is difficult to contest Robert Bellah's observation that "[t]he idea that institutions are objective mechanisms that are essentially separate from the lives of the individuals who inhabit them is an ideology that exacts a high moral and political price."[116] Within a culture that conditions us to look past the moral dimension of everyday corporate life and the corporation's potential to be "a great moral driver of many persons,"[117] encouraging the identification and articulation of the broad contours of institutional conscience may lead to a greater awareness among employees of how the corporate environment impacts individual conscience and vice versa.

The viability of our own freedom of conscience is not easily disentangled from the viability of the venues in which we gather around shared moral convictions. In marginalizing the identity-forming capacity of the corporation, much of our legal discourse's individualist rhetoric fails to account for the real-world context of actual individuals. The dictates of conscience are constitutive of our individual identities, but the constitution proceeds through our relationships, including those we enter into within the marketplace. When it comes to facilitating the living out of conscience, the relevance of the local church and Wal-Mart are different in degree, not in kind.

The fact that legislatures, rather than an aggressive judiciary, have more often than not been responsible for the current push to cabin the moral autonomy of both for-profit and nonprofit corporations is no comfort. Whatever the political popularity of measures that homogenize the corporate moral landscape, such measures ignore the lessons of pluralism and the social nature of the person. We must acknowledge that the flourishing of individual conscience requires more than the reflexive expansion and enshrinement of individual rights. One essential step is to resist using the levers of collective power to close down the social spaces, including the corporate form of those spaces, in which shared conceptions of the good can be identified, articulated, and lived out. Our legal system already values diversity in corporate structures and methods of governance; it is time to value diversity in the moral claims embodied in corporate identity.

---

[116] Robert Bellah, *The Good Society*, 12 (1991).
[117] Morrell Heald, *The Social Responsibilities of Business*, 275 (2005) (quoting Frank W. Abrams' 1951 statement of managerial responsibilities in inculcating sense of stewardship for company among employees).

8

Schools

The overly individualized conception of conscience is unmistakable in education. On the provider side, teachers have long claimed academic freedom on a variety of grounds, but the conscience-driven dimension of such claims recently received a high-profile media jolt in Cupertino, California, where an elementary school teacher sued the school district for religious discrimination after his curricular choices were subjected to screening for inappropriate religious content by the principal. His case, although ultimately unsuccessful legally, garnered widespread sympathy as a welcome effort to infuse a secularized educational orthodoxy with a teacher's own religious sensibility.

On the consumer side, the conscience of a student dissenting from prevailing social norms has been a pressing jurisprudential concern since the Supreme Court in *West Virginia Bd. of Ed. v. Barnette* recognized a student's right not to pledge allegiance to the majority's sacred ideals.[1] The latest evidence of the dissenting conscience's prominence comes from Dover, Pennsylvania, where a federal court invalidated the local school board's clumsy effort to introduce Intelligent Design to the high school science curriculum. The implicit religious underpinnings of the board policy, coupled with compulsory attendance laws, sensitized the court to the plight of the captive student conscience.[2]

Deference to the individual consciences of both educational provider and consumer make sense under our traditional "common school" framework. Where students and their families are presented with a single option of publicly financed schooling, and where public school teachers' employment opportunities are fungible in terms of the moral content of the curriculum and pedagogical mission, the school is functionally equivalent to the state. As such, invoking the sanctity

---

[1] *West Virginia Bd. of Ed. v. Barnette*, 319 U.S. 624 (1943).
[2] See *Kitzmiller v. Dover Area Sch. Dist.*, 400 F. Supp. 2d 707, 712–6 (6th Cir. 2005) (applying endorsement test).

of conscience can bolster the individual's authority in what otherwise would be a pronounced power disparity in the state's favor. If teachers and students are understood to operate within a monolithic, unitary educational system, their claims to be empowered legally to act (or not act) on conscience in the face of conflicting normative claims by the system are not to be dismissed lightly.

But the common school framework may be unraveling. School choice is on the rise, giving students and teachers an important tool that may change the power dynamic in their relationship with any particular school: an exit option. Only a few school districts have embraced private school vouchers, but many districts offer an array of charter, magnet, and other schooling options, thereby creating paths by which like-minded teachers and students can affirmatively choose to invest themselves in one school instead of another based on distinct normative claims embodied in the schools' respective missions. As school choice bolsters the ability of a school to create its own identity, the ability to maintain and defend that identity presupposes a reduced authority for the individual consciences of the school's prospective constituents.

Under these circumstances, schools no longer function as fungible components of an educational monopoly backed by coercive state power. Schools instead begin to serve a mediating function, linking students and teachers together in common support of a mission that is not shared by every school. The viability of this mediating function has two implications for individual conscience. First, to the extent that a teacher's conduct is inconsistent with the school's deliberately chosen mission, the school has a stronger claim to control it. Second, to the extent that the implementation of a school's mission creates tension with a dissenting student's conscience, the student's exit option gives the school a stronger claim to maintain its mission. Conscience is not marginalized within a marketplace of schooling options, but its relevance and authority must be viewed from a different, more relational perspective. This chapter aims to begin tracing the contours of that perspective.

CONSCIENCE IN CUPERTINO

Stephen Williams emerged from relative anonymity as a fifth-grade elementary school teacher to provide a rallying cry for culture war veterans who have finally found conclusive evidence of the public school system's hostility toward Christians. The media widely reported that Williams had "been forced to stop distributing copies of the Declaration of Independence to his students because the document on which our freedom was founded happens to mention God."[3] In reality, the principal required Williams to submit his lesson plans and readings for approval only after parents complained that the pervasive incorporation of pro-Christian viewpoints into Williams' teaching amounted to religious indoctrination. The court cut

---

[3] Transcript, *Scarborough Country* (MSNBC television broadcast Nov. 29, 2004).

through the hyperbole surrounding the case and observed that there "is a difference between teaching about religion, which is acceptable, and teaching religion, which is not."[4] The eventual settlement reflected the weakness of the case.[5]

For our purposes, the case's significance lies in the considerable traction that Williams' conscience-driven cause had with members of the public concerned with the efficacy of religious convictions in the educational sphere. Much of the case's notoriety undoubtedly stemmed from majoritarian concerns over the "Godless" public school, but the proffered vehicle for remedying that void was the religious sensibilities of an individual teacher. According to Williams' own understanding of the dispute, "he merely wanted to give his 5th graders an accurate picture of the nation's heritage by enriching his lessons with documents containing references to God, the Bible and Jesus Christ."[6] By violating his constitutional rights, one columnist insisted, the school district was "engaging in educational malpractice."[7] After all, another observed, "we hire teachers who bring their own backgrounds and passions and beliefs to their teaching" because "[w]e don't want robots."[8]

Numerous organizations devoted to the cause of religious liberty embraced his case, including the Alliance Defense Fund, which ultimately brought suit against the school district. The claims, of course, presumed that Williams should have the authority to act on the dictates of conscience: a right to "academic freedom – his ability to speak and teach freely in accordance with the state educational standards,"[9] protection from government discrimination based on his viewpoint "that this nation has a Christian history,"[10] and termination of the school's practice excluding "Mr. Williams' religious expression."[11] Such language comports with longstanding calls to give teachers academic freedom to ensure that students can "explore and develop new ideas," and to provide a bulwark against education becoming "indoctrination."[12]

---

[4] *Williams v. Vidmar*, 367 F. Supp. 2d 1265, 1273 (N.D. Cal. 2005).

[5] Wyatt Buchanan, *Cupertino Teacher, District Agree on Religious Materials*, S.F. Chron., Aug. 12, 2005, at B4; Editorial, San Jose Mercury News, Aug. 17, 2005, at A1 ("Let's call the agreement what it was: a total victory by the district over conservative lawyers who drummed up a bogus claim of religious persecution.").

[6] Caroline Hendrie, *References to Religion in Teacher's Handouts Spur Calif. Legal Fight*, Educ. Week, Jan. 5, 2005, at 17.

[7] Nat Hentoff, *Sweet Land of Liberty*, Wash. Times, Dec. 20, 2004, at A21.

[8] Scott Herhold, *Give Teacher Benefit of Doubt Amid Uproar*, San Jose Mercury News, Dec. 9, 2004, at 1B.

[9] Verified Complaint for Declaratory and Injunctive Relief ¶ 107, *Williams v. Vidmar*, 367 F. Supp. 2d 1265 (N.D. Cal. 2005) (No. 5:04-CV-4946 JW PVT), available at http://fl1.findlaw.com/news.findlaw.com/hdocs/docs/religion/wmsvid112204cmp.pdf (accessed Sep. 6, 2009).

[10] *Id.* ¶ 106.

[11] *Id.* ¶ 118.

[12] David K. DeWolf, Stephen C. Meyer, Mark E. Deforrest, *Teaching the Origins Controversy: Science, or Religion, or Speech?* 2000 Utah L. Rev. 39, 105; see also Francis J. Beckwith, *A Liberty Not Fully Evolved?: The Case of Rodney LeVake and the Right of Public School Teachers to Criticize Darwinism*, 39 San Diego L. Rev. 1311, 1325 (2002) ("Bringing into the classroom relevant material

Supporters of Williams' cause lost sight of the fact that, if successful, his case would have been a significant setback for those who want to close the gap between the values and worldviews of families and the values and worldviews reflected in their children's educational environments. One key objective of conscience claims in public education is to increase the efficacy of parents' child-forming decisions, especially as those decisions relate to the maintenance of a family's faith tradition. Empowering teachers to speak their minds in defiance of school authorities threatens to do the opposite; that the substance of Williams' underlying faith commitments aligned with those of conservative Christians cannot obfuscate this fact.

The reaction of community parents to the Williams controversy reflects the tension between teachers' rights and parental authority.[13] If one facet of religious liberty is the freedom to transmit values across generations, and if parents' only power over a child's education lies in their choice of school, then equipping schools to create a more deliberate institutional identity is essential. Teacher autonomy precludes that identity, negating a more meaningful mediating role for schools in the process. For folks concerned with the hybrid right of parental autonomy and religious liberty,[14] then, the case for a robust vision of teachers' rights within the classroom should be a nonstarter.

CONSCIENCE IN DOVER

The problem posed by individual conscience on the consumer (i.e., student) side of the ledger is not nearly so stark. Indeed, as noted earlier in the book, one of our most widely cherished Supreme Court rulings is *Barnette*, which struck down, on free exercise grounds, a West Virginia law compelling students to salute the flag.[15] The question now is not whether a student's conscience merits such deference, but whether such deference can be at least partially facilitated by affording the student her choice of schools. If a student chooses to attend a school that has staked out an identity grounded in nonuniversal norms and ideals, should the student lose any portion of her constitutional right not to participate in the maintenance of those norms and ideals?

Many of these disputes arise under the Free Exercise and Establishment clauses of the First Amendment. Under the Supreme Court's test to determine whether a state action should be considered an unconstitutional "endorsement" of religion,

---

that supplements the curriculum (and does not violate any other legal duties), when public school teachers have adequately fulfilled all of their curricular obligations, is protected speech under the rubric of academic freedom.").

[13] Indeed, some parents formed an advocacy group, fearful that Williams' allegations and the ensuing media coverage would give the country the wrong impression of their community. Luis Zaragoza, *No Apology in Cupertino School Flap*, San Jose Mercury News, Jan. 30, 2005, at 1B.

[14] See *Wisconsin v. Yoder*, 406 U.S. 205 (1972).

[15] *West Virginia v. Barnette*, 319 U.S. 624 (1943).

school policy is viewed through the eyes of the reasonable student. The district court judge found such an endorsement when he invalidated the Intelligent Design "disclaimer" adopted by the Dover, Pennsylvania school board for inclusion in the evolution curriculum. The disclaimer read, in part, as follows:

> Because Darwin's Theory is a theory, it continues to be tested as new evidence is discovered. The Theory is not a fact. Gaps in the Theory exist for which there is no evidence. A theory is defined as a well-tested explanation that unifies a broad range of observations. Intelligent Design is an explanation of the origin of life that differs from Darwin's view. The reference book, *Of Pandas and People*, is available for students who might be interested in gaining an understanding of what Intelligent Design actually involves. With respect to any theory, students are encouraged to keep an open mind. The school leaves the discussion of the Origins of Life to individual students and their families.[16]

Defenders of the school board saw this as simply a safeguard against putting undue pressure on students' religious beliefs through the teaching of evolution. In this regard, the court's ruling confirmed for some that "we cannot trust government schools to teach our children without undermining our values and our worldview," and that the only viable way of ensuring "that our children are taught properly" is to "consider the form of education our Founding Fathers believed in and practiced – private and home schools."[17] For many others, though, the ruling was a sensible acknowledgment of the fact that inserting contested views on life's transcendent origins into the science curriculum creates problems for families whose worldviews do not acknowledge such transcendence. As the district court recognized,

> School sponsorship of a religious message is impermissible because it sends the ancillary message to members of the audience who are nonadherents "that they are outsiders, not full members of the political community, and an accompanying message to adherents that they are insiders, favored members of the political community."[18]

To the extent that school choice becomes a reality, that straightforward summation does not pack the same punch. It is by no means obvious that the message received by students and their families will remain the same when a system of fungible schools with monopoly power is replaced by a marketplace of schools offering distinct normative identities, especially if those identities are articulated and cultivated from below, by the association of like-minded families, teachers, and

---

[16] *Kitzmiller v. Dover Area Sch. Dist.*, 400 F. Supp. 2d 707, 708–9 (M.D. Pa. 2005).

[17] John Eidsmore, *An Intelligently Designed Ruling?* New American, Jan. 23, 2006, at 35.

[18] *Kitzmiller*, 400 F. Supp. 2d at 713 (quoting *Lynch v. Donnelly*, 465 U.S. 668, 688 (1984) [O'Connor, J., concurring]).

administrators, rather than imposed from above by a centralized government body. Certainly for explicitly religious activities or unmistakably sectarian environments, the Establishment clause is an insurmountable obstacle to the direct government funding that drives public school choice programs. In contexts in which the religious nature of the school's curriculum is less clear – such as Intelligent Design or abstinence-only sex education – the obstacle does not appear so absolute. On a closely related question, the free speech rights of students to contest the values that the school seeks to inculcate may also stand on shakier ground when students have viable exit options. At a minimum, the constitutional analysis may need to account for a diminished ability to rely on individual conscience as the rationale for constraining the mediating function of individual schools.

COMMON SCHOOL PARADIGMS

The elevation of individual conscience has been a sensible reaction to the paradigms of public schooling that have traditionally prevailed in the United States. The two most influential paradigms – the assimilationist model popularized by John Dewey in the early twentieth century and the individualist model emerging from the antiauthoritarian movement of the 1960s – adopt a critical stance toward the moral presumptions with which a student emerges from her family of origin. As Rick Garnett explains, this stance emanates from the stakes of the project:

> Education is the process of and vocation of shaping souls. Now more than ever, though, the shape our souls ought to take, and the ends toward which they ought to be directed, are contested matters. Education is, therefore, in many ways a contest that the liberal state, no less than any other, wants to win and is invariably tempted to "fix."[19]

Especially in matters of morality that are highly contested or closely linked to religious convictions, private schools are available to protect some students and their families from the state's pedagogical overreaching, but for the vast number of students for whom private schools are not a financially viable option, a limited right of conscience serves a much cruder, but equally crucial, bulwark function. A teacher's right of conscience – usually articulated in the language of academic freedom – facilitates students' critical reflection on the state's homogenizing impetus (under the assimilationist model) or makes possible the day-to-day realization of the marketplace of ideas.

---

[19] Richard W. Garnett, *The Story of Henry Adams's Soul: Education and the Expressive Association*, 85 Minn. L. Rev. 1841, 1882 (2001).

The Assimilationist Common School

When common schools were avowedly religious, the push to assimilate students into a shared moral identity was unmistakable.[20] The assimilationist project was secularized, but did not noticeably dissipate, under the influential work of John Dewey. The ambition of his vision was made evident by his famous aspiration that "[w]hat the best and wisest parent wants for his own child, that must the community want for all of its children."[21] It is not difficult to perceive a collectivist angle to this ambition, especially when read against Dewey's profound distrust of subcommunities that cling to tradition instead of embracing the promise of liberalism:

> The isolation and exclusiveness of a gang or clique brings its antisocial spirit into relief. But this same spirit is found wherever one group has interests 'of its own' which shut it out from full interaction with other groups, so that its prevailing purpose is the protection of what it has got, instead of reorganization and progress through wider relationships. That savage tribes regard aliens and enemies as synonymous is not accidental. It springs from the fact that they have identified their experience with rigid adherence to their past customs.[22]

Dewey invoked such groups as support for his skepticism that moral education could ever be accomplished by targeting students' character directly. After all, "direct instruction in morals has been effective only in social groups where it was a part of the authoritative control of the many by the few."[23] To attempt a similar feat in an enlightened democracy "is to rely upon sentimental magic."[24]

This is not to suggest that Dewey shunned the possibility of moral education, for he believed that "[a]ll education which develops power to share effectively in social life is moral" because "[i]t forms a character which not only does the particular deed socially necessary but one which is interested in that continuous readjustment which is essential to growth."[25] The "essential moral interest," then, is "[i]nterest in learning from all the contacts of life."[26] In other words, the moralizing force of education consists of its ability to foster a willingness to adapt among students as they encounter the worldviews and lived realities of others. The homogenizing implications are clear. As Diane Ravitch puts it, in Dewey's "conception of democracy . . . the particularities of neighborhood, region, religion, ethnicity, race, and other

---

[20] See, e.g., Noah Feldman, *Divided by God*, 69 (2005) ("The Catholic bid for a constitutional right to liberty of conscience foundered on the Protestant perception that an exemption from Bible reading would undermine the schools' project of teaching a shared republican, Christian morality.").

[21] Amy Gutmann, *Democratic Education*, 13 (1987) (quoting John Dewey, *The School in Society* [1900]).

[22] John Dewey, *Democracy and Education*, 99 (1916).

[23] *Id.* at 411.

[24] *Id.*

[25] *Id.* at 418.

[26] *Id.*

distinctive features of communal life are isolating factors, all of which may be expected to dissolve as individuals interact and share their concerns."[27]

In a significant sense, Dewey succeeded in replacing the homogenizing Protestant common school with the homogenizing secular common school. Joseph Viteritti observes that this "aggressive secularism would become a creed in itself."[28] Indeed, Dewey seemed to revel in that fact, insisting that by "bringing together those of different nationalities, languages, traditions and creeds, in assimilating them together upon a basis of what is common and public in endeavor and achievement," the schools "are performing an infinitely significant religious work."[29] He was, according to Viteritti, "incapable of comprehending the oppressive nature of his own self-righteous approach to education."[30]

Dewey helped shape our nation's understanding of public education, but he was not alone in espousing the assimilationist message. To take one prominent example, when Oregon passed a law in 1922 that required all children to attend public schools,[31] much of the credit went to a campaign in which supporters argued that public schools should "[m]ix those with prejudices in the public school melting pot for a few years while their minds are plastic, and finally bring out the finished product – a true American."[32]

The Individualist Common School

The presumption that schools should function primarily as socializing institutions held sway, to varying degrees, until the 1960s, when antiauthoritarianism triggered educational innovations grounded in critical thinking skills.[33] Schools began to be reimagined as venues in which students would not be indoctrinated into collectively shared moral norms, but would be exposed to a "values clarification" curriculum. The autonomy-stifling nature of Dewey's assimilationist program was recognized, but it was replaced with an individualist understanding of student well-being that not only marginalized parents, but affirmatively strived to achieve critical distance between them and their child.

---

[27] Diane Ravitch, "Education and Democracy," in *Making Good Citizens: Education and Civil Society*, 15, 21 (D. Ravitch and J. Viteritti, eds., 2001).

[28] Joseph Viteritti, *Choosing Equality: School Choice, the Constitution, and Civil Society*, 158 (1999).

[29] *Id.* at 159 (quoting John Dewey, *Religion in Our Schools*, 6 Hibbert J. 800, 806–7 (July 1908)).

[30] *Id.*

[31] The law was subsequently invalidated as an unconstitutional intrusion on parental autonomy by the Supreme Court. See *Pierce v. Society of Sisters*, 268 U.S. 510 (1925).

[32] Edward M. Gaffney, Jr., *Pierce and Parental Liberty as a Core Value in Educational Policy*, 78 U. Det. Mercy L. Rev. 491, 492 (2001) (quoting statement of the Imperial Council, A.A.O. Nobles Mystic Shrine).

[33] Bruce Hafen, *Developing Student Expression Through Institutional Authority: Public Schools as Mediating Structures*, 48 Ohio St. L.J. 663, 667 (1987).

The very rationale of common schools, under the individualist approach, stems from "the basic fact that children are independent persons-in-the-making with their own basic interests and their own lives to lead."[34] And the person-to-be-made should, at a minimum, honor the basic premises of liberalism, meaning that they "should be alert to the possibility that religious imperatives, or even inherited notions of what it means to be a good parent, spouse, or lover, might in fact run afoul of guarantees of equal freedom."[35] Those who resist should not stand in the way. Stephen Macedo, for example, perceives no reason "why public educational policy should be guided by the peculiarities of a small number of people whose needs for psychological closure place them in opposition to liberal democratic civic practices and virtues, including mutual respect amidst diversity and cooperation among group lines."[36]

The autonomy-driven approach comported nicely with rulings by the Supreme Court from the same era, most notably *Tinker v. Des Moines Independent School District*, in which the majority reasoned that:

> In our system, state-operated schools may not be enclaves of totalitarianism. School officials do not possess absolute authority over our students. Students in school as well as out of school are "persons" under our Constitution. They are possessed of fundamental rights which the State must respect, just as they themselves must respect their obligations to the State. In our system, students may not be regarded as closed-circuit recipients of only that which the State chooses to communicate. They may not be confined to the expression of those sentiments that are officially approved. In the absence of a specific showing of constitutionally valid reasons to regulate their speech, students are entitled to freedom of expression of their views.[37]

Note that the central place for individual autonomy – secured by collectively observed liberal norms – is a departure from Dewey's emphasis on the creation of socially amenable and infinitely adaptable American citizens. But the student's attainment of individual autonomy through schooling still places tremendous pressure on the student's continued identification with her family's worldview. John Goodland, for example, asserts that "[s]chools should liberate students from the ways of thinking imposed by religions and other traditions of thought."[38] In turning the individualist norm into a reality, Macedo observes that today's urban high schools "embody the variety and choice of the liberal community as a whole: They aim not to reinforce particularistic communal norms but to provide access to a world beyond the family and its closest affiliations."[39]

For some, this individualist model does not go nearly far enough. Martin Redish and Kevin Finnerty caution that, through public schooling, "the state is able to

---

[34] Stephen Macedo, *Diversity and Distrust: Civic Education in a Multicultural Democracy*, 233 (2000).

[35] *Id.* at 239.

[36] *Id.* at 252.

[37] *Tinker v. Des Moines Indep. Sch. Dist.*, 393 U.S. 503, 511 (1969), discussed *infra*.

[38] Viteritti, *supra* note 28, at 167 (quoting Goodland).

[39] Macedo, *supra* note 34, at 257.

engage in a dangerous form of political, social, or moral thought control that potentially interferes with a citizen's subsequent exercise of individual autonomy."[40] They propose an "anti-indoctrination" model of the First Amendment, urging "the judiciary to reasonably police the educational process in order to restrict values inculcation to that essential minimum degree required for the educational process to function."[41] School programs or messages regarding racial or gender equality, patriotism, or ethnic tolerance would be "presumptively unconstitutional because they are improper government attempts to inculcate socio-political values in a uniquely impressionable audience."[42] Under this approach, the autonomy of individual students is of such paramount importance that the school must abdicate completely any value-inculcative role.

One problem in facilitating critical moral reasoning by liberating students from direct value inculcation is that it disregards the inherently social nature of moral judgment, as explored in chapters 2 and 3. Because values are embedded in relationships, the notion that lessons can be imparted through the teacher–student relationship without accompanying moral messages is dubious.[43] More broadly, seeking to foster critical reflection by drawing out a child from her embeddedness within a particular culture, family, and faith tradition may compromise the realization of a more fulsome autonomy by imposing on her a critical stance toward life choices that she may authentically be inclined to make.[44] To the extent that the message purports to offer a smorgasbord of values from which to pick, schools may be encouraging "in children a false subjectivism or relativism, giving rise to the logical inference that no one set of values can be right."[45]

These grounds for skepticism toward values clarification have led some to question the relentless focus on the autonomy of individual students. Amy Gutmann, for example, asks "[w]hy must freedom be the sole end of education, given that most of us value things that conflict with freedom?," and so why should we "prevent teachers from cultivating moral character by biasing the choices of children toward good

---

[40] Martin H. Redish and Kevin Finnerty, *What Did You Learn in School Today? Free Speech, Values Inculcation, and the Democratic-Educational Paradox*, 88 Cornell L. Rev. 62, 67 (2002).

[41] *Id.* at 69.

[42] *Id.* at 70.

[43] See Susan H. Bitensky, *A Contemporary Proposal for Reconciling the Free Speech Clause with Curricular Values Inculcation in the Public Schools*, 70 Notre Dame L. Rev. 769, 778 (1995).

[44] Rosemary Salomone explains that the educational process:

> touches children deeply through specific visions of the good life. These visions typically reaffirm those valued by the larger secular culture, but they may also negate the vision fostered by the family. Education exerts a powerful indoctrinative force. The scope and direction of that force are largely a function of district policy, school practice, and teacher discretion. In effect, this process potentially can undermine children's autonomy by forcing them to choose a life contrary to that of their parents and community.

> Rosemary Salomone, "Common Education and the Democratic Ideal," *in Making Good Citizens, supra* note 27 at 223.

[45] Bitensky, *supra* note 43, at 778.

lives and, if necessary, by constraining the range of lives that children are capable of choosing when they mature?"[46] Gutmann's vision of moral teaching should not necessarily reassure families whose worldviews do not align with secularist norms, though, for she also sees education as functioning to "convert children away from the intensely held [religious] beliefs of their parents."[47]

Viewed against the assimilationist and individualist conceptions of public education, the case for conscience is formidable. By presuming to shape students from wildly divergent backgrounds into a common model of the right-thinking American citizen, the assimilationist approach invites the creation of a limited constitutional buffer around individual students who resist the more aggressive efforts to shape them. To a lesser extent, the assimilationist approach also justifies protecting teachers who are called to conform in their conduct and pedagogy to the prescribed model, both for their own liberty interests and for the instrumental value of that liberty to the extent that it provides students with critical perspectives on the state's indoctrination.

The individualist model's success in achieving critical distance between the student and the traditions from which she emerges provides a rationale for conscience claims not so much for any unified message it imparts, but for the alienating implications of the fact that so many messages are imparted without concern for the tension they create – both by their substance and by their sheer number – with the student's governing worldview or values. And the teacher's claim of conscience is instrumentally valuable, for without an empowered and independent voice for teachers, the marketplace approach's very premise could easily be compromised by the collectivizing reach of school authorities.[48]

Both the teachers' and students' claims to conscience under the assimilationist and individualist approaches to public education gain traction because of the lack of an exit option and because of the collective manner in which a school's moral identity is imposed within a monopolistic, centralized system of fungible schools. The concerns driving the case for conscience change markedly with the advent of school choice, although the common school still predominates in many areas of the country.

---

[46] Gutmann, *supra* note 21, at 37.
[47] *Id.* at 121.
[48] In a Supreme Court ruling invalidating New York's loyalty oath requirement for teachers, Justice Brennan wrote:

> Our nation is deeply committed to safeguarding academic freedom, which is of transcendent value to all of us and not merely to the teachers concerned. That freedom is therefore a special concern of the First Amendment, which does not tolerate laws that cast a pall of orthodoxy over the classroom.... The classroom is peculiarly the "marketplace of ideas." The Nation's future depends upon leaders trained through wide exposures to that robust exchange of ideas which discovers truth "out of a multitude of tongues, [rather] than through any kind of authoritative selection."

Keyishian v. Board of Regents, 385 U.S. 589, 603 (1967) (citation omitted).

THE COMMON SCHOOL AND CONSCIENCE

For most American students, there is not yet a viable market of schooling options, and thus individual conscience – rather than institutional conscience – remains an important bulwark against overreaching government indoctrination. Building the inculcation of contested moral values of any stripe into the public school mission engenders significant resistance as long as each school functions as a fungible component of the state's monopoly power,[49] and attempts to stake out uncontested norms have become more difficult in modern public schools as the varied constituents and accompanying moral claims erode any sense of common identity.[50]

Nevertheless, few are comforted by the specter of "value-free" public schools, as though we can remove any potentially contested moral claims from the curriculum without jeopardizing a significant part of what we expect from public education. Our schools do not just impart knowledge to our children; they provide nurturing and challenging environments in which children can grow in their capacity for moral and civic engagement. Schools teach literacy, but they also shape citizens. Given our ambitious charge to public education, the authority of individual conscience within a public school – particularly as it finds legal traction via the First Amendment – is unclear. In contrast to universities, which serve as sites for the *production* of free speech, Paul Horwitz notes that public schools serve as "sites for the production of the *facility* for free speech: They teach children so that they will have the capacity to be engaged and active citizens elsewhere and later in life."[51] As Rick Garnett puts it, how can the First Amendment, which is designed to "constrain the government from interfering in or directing a diverse and pluralistic society's conversations about the common good," apply in a context in which the state is charged with "producing not just certain facilities, but certain core values, loyalties, and commitments?"[52]

Student Speech in the Common School

Perhaps in light of this tension, free speech rights for students have been embraced tentatively by the Supreme Court. The high-water mark for such rights is *Tinker v. Des Moines Indep. Sch. Dist.*, a 1968 case in which the court held unconstitutional

---

[49] Mark Holmes, "Education and Pluralism in an Age of Pluralism," in *Making Good Citizens, supra* note 27, at 196 ("Can a state monopoly of schooling successfully inculcate values that are foreign to the larger society?").

[50] *Id.* at 205 ("A genuine citizenship is more likely to be found in a fundamentalist school, despite its intolerance, than in a comprehensive high school, with its tolerance of almost everything and parallel belief in almost nothing.").

[51] Posting of Paul Horwitz to PrawfsBlawg, Public Schools as First Amendment Institutions? http://prawfsblawg.blogs.com/prawfsblawg/2007/03/public_schools_.html (Mar. 21, 2007).

[52] Richard W. Garnett, *Can There Really Be Free Speech in Public Schools?* 12 Lewis & Clark L. Rev. 101, 114 (2008).

the school's decision to prohibit students from wearing black armbands to protest the Vietnam War. The court laid down the default rule for these disputes, holding that a public high school student has a constitutional right to "express his opinions, even on controversial subjects like the conflict in Vietnam, if he does so without 'materially and substantially interfer(ing) with the requirements of appropriate discipline in the operation of the school' and without colliding with the rights of others."[53] Subsequent exceptions to this rule were carved out in situations when the speech at issue was officially sanctioned by the school (as with the publication of a school newspaper),[54] or when the student speaks in a lewd or indecent manner.[55]

The limits of students' speech rights were underscored further by the Supreme Court in *Morse v. Frederick*, a case in which a high school principal suspended a student for refusing to take down a "Bong Hits for Jesus" banner outside the school while the Olympic torch relay passed by. The Ninth Circuit Court of Appeals had held that the principal's actions violated the student's right to free speech, because there was no demonstration that the speech created "a risk of substantial disruption."[56] Further, the Ninth Circuit ruled that the student's right was so clearly established as to deprive the principal of immunity for her actions.

The Supreme Court reversed, but framed its decision narrowly. The court was careful to note that the student's speech was not constitutionally proscribable simply because it was "offensive;"[57] rather, the principal's conduct was permissible because the banner "was reasonably viewed as promoting illegal drug use" in violation of "established school policy."[58] The three-justice dissent took the majority to task for upholding "a school's decision to punish [a student] for expressing a view with which it disagreed."[59] Indeed, the dissenters cautioned, "a full and frank discussion of the costs and benefits of the attempt to prohibit the use of marijuana is far wiser than suppression of speech because it is unpopular."[60]

The facts of *Morse* indicate that the student was acting less on the dictates of his deeply held moral convictions about marijuana (or Jesus), and more on the adolescent drive for attention and notoriety. Nevertheless, the majority's rationale is

---

[53] *Tinker v. Des Moines Indep. Sch. Dist.*, 393 U.S. 503, 513 (1968).

[54] *Hazelwood Sch. Dist. v. Kuhlmeier*, 484 U.S. 260, 272–73 (1988) ("[T]he standard articulated in *Tinker* for determining when a school may punish student expression need not also be the standard for determining when a school may refuse to lend its name and resources to the dissemination of student expression.").

[55] *Bethel Sch. Dist. No. 403 v. Fraser*, 478 U.S. 675, 683 (1986) ("The schools, as instruments of the state, may determine that the essential lessons of civil, mature conduct cannot be conveyed in a school that tolerates lewd, indecent, or offensive speech and conduct such as that indulged in by this confused boy.").

[56] 439 F.3d 1114, 1123 (9th Cir. 2006).

[57] 127 S. Ct. 2618, 2629 (2007).

[58] *Id.*

[59] *Id.* at 2644 (Stevens, J., dissenting)

[60] *Id.* at 2651.

puzzling in light of *Tinker*'s focus on the speech's tendency to disrupt substantially the educational environment. Without question, the state has authority to teach students about the dangers of drug abuse and the importance of following the law, but it is less clear why that authority includes the power to shut down dissenting students from publicly displaying their disagreement with those messages in a manner that does not disrupt the educational environment. When students (and their parents) lack an exit option, there must be substantial latitude given for dissent, even on matters held inviolate by society (such as drug abuse by adolescents).

Whatever constitutional right is the vehicle of choice in a given dispute, for our purposes it is important to recognize that compulsory attendance laws, coupled with the lack of an exit option for students who cannot afford private schools, means that the marketplace approach to conscience's flourishing that pervades much of this book holds different lessons here. Respect for the dissenting consciences of students – an essentially captive audience – and their parents demands that the common school act less like an institution possessing its own robust moral identity in a marketplace of other morally distinct institutions, and more like the facilitator of its own marketplace in which contrasting moral claims are given space to coexist. For those concerned with maintaining a robust liberty of conscience in public schools, *Morse* should give pause. The decision's practical impact is limited given its narrow framing – school officials can silence a student's advocacy of illegal drug use at a school-sanctioned event – but its departure from a focus on disruption is problematic.

The marketplace analogy is limited here. High school students might experience a marketplace of curricular offerings at a single school, but there is no meaningful range of moral viewpoints embodied in such curricular offerings. Younger students, of course, lack even a choice of curricular offerings. Nevertheless, the state's focus remains the same here as in its regulation of pharmacies or attorneys: ensuring access to the goods in question. When there is only one pharmacy serving an area, the state may appropriately require a full range of pharmaceuticals to be offered as a condition of licensing. When students lack any choice in the educational marketplace, the state must ensure that they can receive a full education at the school to which they are assigned. This means that the common school should impart the knowledge and values deemed essential by society to function and thrive as adults, but it also means that the state should resist placing (or tolerating) more obstacles to full participation in the common school than absolutely necessary. Such obstacles include bans on student speech, but they also may include the disruptive, or in extreme cases, demeaning speech of other students (which means that the *Tinker* approach may prudently facilitate participation). Less obviously, such obstacles also may include the common school's efforts to teach students to affirm contested moral claims, which may marginalize some students by creating tension within their other conscience-forming relationships, such as family and church. With a focus on participation, fact-intensive inquiries, not categorical line drawing, will be the norm for resolving conscience-related disputes in the common school.

First, when it comes to student speech, the prudent boundaries of a marketplace within the common school will differ significantly from the wider marketplace in which consenting adults allow moral claims to shape their own transactions for goods and services. (We must avoid what Fred Schauer refers to as the "institutionally oblivious First Amendment."[61]) Keeping in mind, however, the captive nature of the common school student body highlights the wisdom of extending constitutional protection to student speech, notwithstanding the temptation for courts to defer to an amorphous "educational mission" of the school. Judging by the briefs in the case, *Morse* could have been much more damaging to the cause of conscience in the common school. The United States, for example, intervened on behalf of the school principal and argued that public schools can prohibit student speech if it is "inconsistent with their basic educational mission in order to disassociate themselves from such speech and thereby reinforce the values . . . they seek to teach."[62] The National School Boards Association filed its own brief in the case, arguing that school officials may prohibit "pro-drug and other messages inimical to a school's core educational mission and ability to instill fundamental civic values and appropriate behavior."[63]

The problem is the state's difficulty in articulating an "educational mission" that is substantive enough to justify prohibitions on student speech even when speech has not disrupted the learning environment. If, as the briefs in *Morse* suggested, the school can shut down any speech that is inconsistent with the educational or civic "values" that school officials choose to impose, space for dissenting consciences could drastically shrink. *Tinker* allowed for prohibitions on disruptive speech, and mentioned in passing that speech could also be prohibited if it interfered with the rights of other students. Certainly a school can define its mission in more expansive terms than avoiding disruption and respecting each other's rights, but in a society that values liberty of conscience, the common school's mission "cannot be to instill religious or political conformity or to suppress speech with which it disagrees."[64] Beyond that (hopefully) noncontroversial point, the question for the common school is to what extent can its mission justify limits on the dissenting speech of the captive student audience?

One current batch of disputes involves in-school debates over the moral status of homosexuality. In *Harper v. Poway Unified Sch. Dist.*,[65] a high school student was ordered not to wear a shirt with the message "BE ASHAMED, OUR SCHOOL

---

[61] Frederick Schauer, *Towards an Institutional First Amendment*, 89 Minn. L. Rev. 1256, 1264 (2005).

[62] Solicitor General's Br. at 19 (available on Westlaw at 2007 WL 118978).

[63] Br. of Amici Curiae Nat'l Sch. Bd. Ass'n at 4 (available on Westlaw at 2007 WL 140999).

[64] Douglas Laycock, *High-Value Speech and the Basic Educational Mission of a Public School: Some Preliminary Thoughts*, 12 Lewis & Clark L. Rev. 111, 117 (2008).

[65] 445 F.3d 1166 (9th Cir. 2006).

HAS EMBRACED WHAT GOD HAS CONDEMNED" handwritten on front, and "HOMOSEXUALITY IS SHAMEFUL" handwritten on the back. The student wore the shirt in response to a "Day of Silence" event that had taken place at the school the day before in which some students and staff had worn duct tape over their mouths to symbolize the silencing effect of antigay discrimination and worn shirts commemorating the event.[66] The Ninth Circuit upheld the school's action, reasoning that under *Tinker*, the student's antigay shirt collided with other students' rights to be secure "from psychological attacks that cause young people to question their self-worth and their rightful place in society."[67] Obviously, courts would be very busy if high school students possess a cognizable right to be free of psychological attacks that cause them to question their self-worth, so the court limited its holding to "injurious speech that strikes at a core identifying characteristic of students on the basis of their membership in a minority group."[68]

As the Seventh Circuit pointed out under the similar facts of *Nuxoll v. Indian Prairie School District*, though, "people do not have a legal right to prevent criticism of their beliefs or for that matter their way of life."[69] In that case, a student responded to the Day of Silence protest by wearing a shirt that read "be happy, not gay." A school official crossed out the "not gay" phrase pursuant to a school policy forbidding "derogatory comments that refer to race, ethnicity, religion, gender, sexual orientation, or disability."[70] The Seventh Circuit ruled that this action violated the student's freedom of speech because the facts were not of the sort that would "reasonably lead school officials to forecast substantial disruption" to the school's operation.[71] There was no problem with the school's rule prohibiting those categories of derogatory comments because the rule seeks to "maintain a civilized school environment conducive to learning, and it does so in an even-handed way."[72] But the phrase "be happy, not gay," in the court's view, was only "tepidly negative," and it is "highly speculative" whether a t-shirt with the phrase would "poison the educational atmosphere."[73]

Whether or not the Seventh Circuit was correct in its characterization of the disputed phrase as "tepidly negative," rather than derogatory, the court's focus on disruption to the educational atmosphere, rather than an expansive understanding of other students' "rights," is more conducive to the cause of conscience in the common school. Apart from the degree necessary to ensure access to education, the state should not forbid students from expressing their own moral claims. Unlike

[66] *Id.* at 1171 n. 3.
[67] *Id.* at 1178.
[68] *Id.* at 1182 n. 27.
[69] *Nuxoll v. Indian Prairie Sch. Dist. #204*, 523 F.2d 668, 672 (7th Cir. 2008).
[70] *Id.* at 670.
[71] *Id.* at 673.
[72] *Id.* at 674.
[73] *Id.* at 676.

the pharmacy context, the question of access here does not refer to an arms-length exchange for a particular good or service. Instead, the state must protect students' access to full participation in the educational opportunities afforded by the school. If student speech can reasonably be foreseen to disrupt another student's ability to participate, the state can and should step in. The inquiry is inescapably nuanced and fact intensive; it is less susceptible to the all-or-nothing trump of a rights-based approach, as used by the Ninth Circuit. Judicially declaring that gay or lesbian students have a right not to be exposed to any speech from fellow students that criticizes homosexuality shuts down the marketplace of moral claims on a matter that has not been subject to a longstanding social conversation, much less the establishment of significant consensus. If the criticism rises to the level that could reasonably be foreseen to disrupt the educational environment – and referring to homosexuality as "shameful" might well rise to that level – school officials prudently step in. In other words, the Ninth Circuit may have reached the proper result, but for the wrong reason.

A captive student audience needs substantial space to express their own perspectives on contested moral issues. The space is not absolute, though, because the public school – even the public school with no exit option – is a place where everyone should feel like a member of the community, even if they do not feel like a member of the community of which every other member approves. Schools need not replicate the rough-and-tumble marketplace of moral claims that (hopefully) flourishes outside their walls, and elementary school officials are justifiably more cautious than high school officials in allowing potentially inflammatory speech. In general, though, the cause of conscience compels the state to recognize a student's right to free speech, bounded by the need to maintain access for all students by avoiding substantial disruption to the educational environment.

Constitutional litigation will not always be the most effective tool by which to further the cause of conscience in public schools. As a matter of course, the day-to-day regulation of student speech is better handled by local school officials than by judges. The need to recognize a constitutional dimension to the boundaries of that regulation is what makes the Seventh Circuit's holding so valuable. We should hope that judgments as to what constitutes materially disruptive student speech can be handled without recourse to a decidedly distant and nonexpert judiciary, but setting forth the proper constitutional standard will help ensure that the local decisions begin from conscience-friendly premises.

Opting Out Within the Common School

Framing students' arguments in terms of constitutional rights is distinctly less helpful when the state, instead of prohibiting certain types of student speech, seeks to teach certain contested values to all students. In cases challenging the school's inculcation of values or exposure of students to offensive views, the path by which conscience may best be defended proceeds through policymakers, not through constitutional interpretation.

Admittedly, it is tempting to reach for the Constitution when school officials abuse their authority. It is easy to appreciate that an empowered school does not invariably bring about a heightened mediating function. In those cases in which school autonomy is unhinged from parental choice, the outcome can be jolting. This was evident recently when parents brought suit against a California school district after their first-, third-, and fifth-grade children were given a research survey in class that, unbeknownst to the parents, inquired about sexual topics such as the frequency of "thinking about having sex" and "thinking about touching other people's private parts."[74] The Ninth Circuit ruled that the district's failure to disclose the survey's contents to the parents before obtaining their consent was not actionable under the Constitution because the parental right to control the upbringing of children – as recognized in the landmark cases of *Pierce v. Society of Sisters*[75] and *Meyer v. Nebraska*[76] – "does not extend beyond the threshold of the school door."[77] In other words, "once parents make the choice as to which school their children will attend, their fundamental right to control the education of their children is, at least, substantially diminished."[78] The problem is that for parents without the financial means to choose a nonpublic school, the right to control their children's education is illusory, and the school's potential mediating power appears, to dissenting families, more akin to heavy-handed indoctrination.

The impracticality of framing parents' legitimate objections as constitutional rights becomes evident in *Parker v. Hurley*, a case in which parents claimed that the school district violated their right to direct the religious upbringing of their children by failing to give parents an opportunity to exempt their children from exposure to books portraying same-sex relationships in a positive light. The parents acknowledged the district's "legitimate secular interest in seeking to eradicate bias against same-gender couples and to ensure the safety of all public school students,"[79] but insisted that the Constitution requires the accommodation "of their own religious beliefs and

---

[74] *Fields v. Palmdale School Dist.*, 427 F.3d 1197, 1201 n. 3 (9th Cir. 2005).

[75] In *Pierce*, the Court held that the state could not require parents to send their children to public schools because "[t]he fundamental theory of liberty upon which all governments in this Union repose excludes any general power of the state to standardize its children by forcing them to accept instruction from public teachers only." 268 U.S. 510, 535 (1925).

[76] In *Meyer*, the court struck down a state law banning the teaching of foreign languages to students before they graduated from eighth grade, reasoning that there was insufficient justification for state interference "with the opportunities of pupils to acquire knowledge, and with the power of parents to control the education of their own." 262 U.S. 390, 401 (1923). These cases are discussed further in the next chapter.

[77] *Fields v. Palmdale School Dist.*, 427 F.3d at 1206.

[78] *Id.*

[79] 514 F.3d 87, 102 (1st Cir. 2008).

of the diversity represented by their contrary views."[80] The First Circuit rejected their claims, ruling that the parents did not allege facts suggesting a constitutional violation, although they could seek change to their school's practices through the political system. The court noted, "the mere fact that a child is exposed on occasion in public school to a concept offensive to a parent's religious belief does not inhibit the parent from instructing the child differently."[81] Even though the book at issue was chosen precisely "to influence the listening children toward tolerance of gay marriage," the students were not asked to affirm gay marriage and requiring students to read a particular book "is generally not coercive of free exercise rights."[82]

The *Parker* court found support for its holding in an earlier ruling by the Sixth Circuit in a factually similar case. In *Mozert v. Hawkins County Board of Education*, parents objected to a prescribed set of textbooks as an infringement on their free exercise rights. The range of objections illustrates the problem with recognizing a constitutional right to shield one's child from exposure to objectionable school lessons.

> [One parent] stated that the offending materials fell into seventeen categories [ranging] from such familiar concerns of fundamentalist Christians as evolution and "secular humanism" to less familiar themes such as "futuristic supernaturalism," pacifism, magic and false views of death. [She] identified passages from stories and poems used in the Holt series that fell into each category. Illustrative is her first category, futuristic supernaturalism, which she defined as teaching "Man As God." Passages that she found offensive described Leonardo da Vinci as the human with a creative mind that "came closest to the divine touch." Similarly, she felt that a passage entitled "Seeing Beneath the Surface" related to an occult theme, by describing the use of imagination as a vehicle for seeing things not discernible through our physical eyes. She interpreted a poem, "Look at Anything," as presenting the idea that by using imagination a child can become part of anything and thus understand it better. Mrs. Frost testified that it is an "occult practice" for children to use imagination beyond the limitation of scriptural authority. She testified that the story that alerted her to the problem with the reading series fell into the category of futuristic supernaturalism. Entitled "A Visit to Mars," the story portrays thought transfer and telepathy in such a way that "it could be considered a scientific concept," according to this witness.[83]

No doubt cognizant of how difficult it would be to carve out exemptions for such an expansive range of objections, the court emphasized the importance of drawing distinctions "between those governmental actions that actually interfere with the exercise of religion, and those that merely require or result in exposure to attitudes

---

[80] *Id.*
[81] *Id.* at 105.
[82] *Id.* at 106.
[83] 827 F.2d 1058, 1062 (6th Cir. 1987).

and outlooks at odds with perspectives prompted by religion."[84] There is no constitutional violation absent any "compulsion to affirm or deny a religious belief or to
engage or refrain from engaging in a practice forbidden or required in the exercise
of a plaintiff's religion."[85]

The approaches taken by the *Mozert* and *Parker* courts help bring the common
school marketplace into relief. It cannot be a free exercise or substantive due process
violation for a school to teach children civil toleration of other religious and moral
perspectives, even if those perspectives conflict with the religious or moral beliefs of
the child and her parents. (It could, however, be a constitutional violation to teach
children to reject the truth claims of their own religious tradition.[86]) A constitutional
right to shield one's child from exposure to such perspectives would unduly hinder
the state's ability to provide an education and ensure full participation in the school
community through which the education is provided. Determining when "opt outs"
should be made available to children and their families does not lend itself to bright-
line categorization; it is a nuanced judgment based on the depth and breadth of
the moral controversy to which the teaching pertains, as well as the pervasiveness of
the teaching across the curriculum and corresponding difficulty of providing an opt
out. It is a determination best made by school officials, within parameters set by the
political process.

Providing parents with a constitutional trump card distorts the common school
marketplace by making it much more difficult for the state to expose students to
any common set of potentially contested values or truth claims. By contrast, maintaining a constitutional bulwark against the state's prohibition of student speech
does not similarly distort the common school marketplace. Instead, it facilitates a
well-functioning marketplace by ensuring students' ability to contest controversial
views to which they are exposed. Requiring the state to establish that a particular
instance of student speech threatened significant disruption to the learning environment before shutting it down maximizes a student's participation in the marketplace
without threatening other students' ability to participate. The factual application of
that standard will require a nuanced judgment, but a categorical standard is appropriate. When it comes to parents' right to shield their children from any viewpoints
with which the parents disagree, placing a similar categorical burden on the state is
impractical and inimical to the common school's prudent operation.

This is not to suggest that allowing parents to shield their children from exposure
to views that offend their own religious or moral convictions is always imprudent, just
that there should not be a constitutional right to avoid such exposure. Especially for
young children – when the stability of parental moral authority may be more essential

---

[84] *Id.* at 1068.

[85] *Id.* at 1069.

[86] See, e.g., *id.* at 1080 (Boggs, J., concurring) ("[T]he state may teach that all religions have the same
civil and political rights, and must be dealt with civilly in civil society.... It may not teach as truth
that the religions of others are just as correct as religions as plaintiffs' own.").

compared with teenage years – opportunities for opting out of certain classroom activities support the relational dimension of conscience. Reliance on the availability of opt outs should not, however, be used to justify moral overreaching by the state in the operation of common schools; a degree of humility is needed across the board as the school engages children on morally contested issues. Conscience's relational dimension does not just require a functioning marketplace of moral actors and their claims; it also reminds us that we are not self-created or self-sufficient beings, particularly when it comes to our moral identities. Even though John Dewey's ideas do not dominate educational theory as they once did, the temptation remains to view students as free-standing lumps of clay, ready to be molded into whatever sort of moral agent the surrounding society deems prudent.

One elementary school curriculum that has been adopted by a few districts to increase sensitivity toward students from nontraditional families reflects the problem. The curriculum includes positive portrayals of families headed by single parents and by same-sex couples, in addition to traditional families. This appropriately supports the school's legitimate objective of teaching mutual tolerance and respect among students – facilitating the full participation of all students in the common school marketplace. However, the same curriculum suggests a classroom exercise designed to replace students' "stereotypes" about nontraditional family arrangements with "facts." Students are asked to fill in the blank: "I used to believe [x], but now I know [y]."[87]

To the extent that schools take a more aggressive stance in pushing students to embrace affirmatively certain conclusions about nontraditional family arrangements and reject their previous beliefs about family, there is a twofold risk. First, if the school directly criticizes traditional teachings about family, the student (especially young students) are led to question not only the validity of that particular teaching, but the credibility of the authority figures responsible for that teaching. Second, by portraying other views as illegitimate in comparison to the "truth" espoused by this curriculum, students are led to view the school as the source of moral truth. Admittedly, these risks will always be present to some degree when the school enters the debate over contested moral issues, but a stance of moral humility (not moral agnosticism or apathy) can lessen the risk. The relational dimension of conscience cautions the state against fostering skeptical attitudes among children toward their nonstate sources of moral formation, and although concern for the common good warrants the full inclusion of all students within the life of the common school, it does not warrant short-circuiting the "bottom-up" nature of moral suasion and engagement by elevating the state as the primary teacher of contested moral values. The family's role in the cultivation of conscience and the common good will be explored more fully in the next chapter.

---

[87] Katherine Kersten, *The Real Agenda Behind Schools' Anti-bullying Curriculum*, Mpls. Star-Trib., May 11, 2008 (discussing "Welcoming Schools" curriculum created by Human Rights Campaign and adopted on a trial basis by Minneapolis public schools).

PUBLIC CHARTER SCHOOLS AND CONSCIENCE

Although voucher programs encompassing private schools have generated most of the publicity in the school choice debate, the rise of choice within the public school system warrants attention as well. Public school choice is much more widespread than voucher programs encompassing private schools, which have thus far been limited largely to districts in Florida, Cleveland, Washington D.C., and Milwaukee. Public school choice also presents more challenging and nuanced conscience implications than voucher programs do because the latter entail spending decisions by parents who have been given government funds, while the former entail direct spending decisions by the government. An expansive understanding of school autonomy will at some point bump into the First Amendment; the question is whether school choice alters the relevant boundaries, even in the public school sphere.

The Charter School Movement

Charter schools are at the center of these developments because they so fundamentally change the prevailing conceptions of public schools while remaining unmistakably public institutions. Approved by a school board for a fixed period of time and funded by a combination of public and private sources, charter schools fall "between the ultimate independence of private schools and the bureaucratic constraints of traditional public schools."[88] Nearly 3,000 new schools have been launched since states began enacting charter legislation in the early 1990s.[89] In states with strong charter laws,[90] "school-level personnel [have] wide discretion over their budgetary and personnel decisions and [are released] from all regulations except those that deal with civil rights, health, and safety."[91] As a result, individual schools are empowered to determine "dress codes, teaching materials, and the overall theme of the curriculum."[92] Across the nation, charter schools are proposed by community members along myriad lines of distinctiveness in their pedagogy, environments, and service objectives, including emphases of themes like leadership, particular fields like technology, music, or dance, or specific cultural traditions or underserved minority populations.[93]

Those willing to put forth the considerable effort necessary to create and maintain a charter school are generally motivated to do so by the insufficiency of current public school offerings within their district. They indicate a desire "to achieve more

---

[88] John F. Witte, *The Market Approach to Education*, 17 (2000).

[89] See Charter Schools History http://www.uscharterschools.org/pub/uscs_docs/o/history.htm (accessed Sep. 6, 2009).

[90] These include Arizona, Michigan, Massachusetts, and Washington, D.C.

[91] Viteritti, *supra* note 28, at 65.

[92] *Id.*

[93] *Id.*

managerial autonomy" to "realize an alternative educational vision or to serve a special target population of students whose needs were not adequately being met in existing schools."[94] Although nothing precludes a given charter school from organizing itself around the assimilation or marketplace approaches,[95] they do not all limit themselves to those two models. The result is an array of educational offerings that replaces "the rigid, and frankly anachronistic, concept of the common school" with "the more flexible and accommodating notion of common education."[96] Rosemary Salomone offers a helpful comparison:

> The one seeks to homogenize students by imparting a fixed set of values through a system of neighborhood schools funded partially by the state and controlled by local government. This 'one size fits all' approach historically has shown little if any regard for differences in family values or divergent perspectives on educational practice. The other aims to impart a common core of political principles, virtues, and understandings while recognizing differences at the broad margins. The focus on common education supports contemporary initiatives that allow families greater choice, and therefore voice, in the education of their children.[97]

In this regard, schools have the potential to be important relationally, because their connection to both the individual and the state equips them to fulfill a mediating role, serving as bridges between families and the surrounding, impersonal society. Public schools already serve a limited mediating function whenever the state or federal governments defer to the judgment of local communities in the schools' operation,[98] especially as that judgment pertains to the values properly embodied in the educational environment.[99] But the efforts to cultivate individualist or assimilationist norms within the common school have drastically reduced the efficacy of particular parents' values in the educational experience.

By contrast, when there are varieties of schools from which to choose representing different normative ideals, schools can bring a greater sense of identity, meaning, and shared purpose to students and their families. Witness the dramatic impact of the Harvey Milk School in New York City, a high school devoted to providing a safe haven for gay, lesbian, bisexual, and transgender youth. The school, which

---

[94] *Id.* at 72–3.
[95] "A court faced with twin teacher-speech cases arising out of two such dissimilar hypothetical schools should employ a legal rubric allowing consideration of the unique school goals and school designs." Kevin G. Welner, *Locking Up the Marketplace of Ideas and Locking Out School Reform: Courts' Imprudent Treatment of Controversial Teaching in America's Public Schools,* 50 UCLA L. Rev. 959, 1019 (2003).
[96] Salomone, *supra* note 44, at 226–7.
[97] *Id.*
[98] *See* Bruce Hafen, *Developing Student Expression Through Institutional Authority: Public Schools as Mediating Structures,* 48 Ohio St. L.J. 663 (1987).
[99] See, e.g., *Bethel Sch. Dist. No. 403 v. Fraser,* 478 U.S. 675, 683 (1986) ("The determination of what manner of speech in the classroom or in school assembly is inappropriate properly rests with the school board.")

requires the consent of parents before students can enroll, is permeated by normative messages that are far from universally accepted – many conservatives object to its legitimization of homosexuality and many progressives object to its "self-exile" of gay students from the straight community.[100] The mediating power, though, is unmistakable: The high school serves as a thick community centered on a common ideal that is hotly disputed by the surrounding society, providing students with a shared sense of identity, purpose, and meaning.[101] If a student enrolled or a teacher sought employment at Harvey Milk with knowledge of its unique mission, they would be hard pressed to earn a sympathetic audience for a claim that the school's environment and curriculum unfairly impinged on their deeply held convictions that homosexuality is immoral. The claim to conscience, from a common-sense perspective, would be a nonstarter.

Even those who defend a fairly aggressive state role in transmitting liberal values through the schools have begun to appreciate the appeal of decentralized authority in that process. Amy Gutmann rejects the value-free presumptions of the marketplace approach,[102] but she also rejects the collectivizing premise of Dewey's value-laden approach, conceding that "[a] democratic society must not be constrained to legislate what the wisest parents want for their child," as long as the society does not "legislate policies that render democracy repressive or discriminatory."[103] And Stephen Macedo embraces some differentiation, at least in process and form, advocating for schools as "moral communities":

> The public high school could be more like the Catholic school by being organized on a scale capable of sustaining a sense of community among students and teachers. The schools must also have enough autonomy so that they can be self-governing and develop a shared ethos. An element of parental choice is important so that children want to be there. Individual schools should have the ability to hire and fire teachers to ensure that a shared sense of mission and purpose can be sustained – that is, to ensure that the teachers want to be there as much as the students do."[104]

Although some might quibble with the substance or the nonnegotiable status of the values prudently transmitted according to these theorists, it is significant that the

---

[100] See John Colapinto, *The Harvey Milk School Has No Right to Exist: Discuss*, New York Mag. Feb. 7, 2005.

[101] *Id.* (describing school's "aging out" policy requiring students to leave the school by the age of 21 years because they are so resistant to departure).

[102] Gutmann supports the "nonneutral education of states and families" because "the good of children includes not just freedom of choice, but also identification with and participation in the good of their family and the politics of their society. . . . To focus exclusively on the value of freedom, or even on the value of moral freedom, neglects the value that parents and citizens may legitimately place on partially prejudicing the choices of children by their familial and political heritages." Gutmann, *supra* note 21, at 43.

[103] *Id.* at 15.

[104] Macedo, *supra* note 34, at 264.

broader trend appears to be toward reconceiving schools as "voluntary associations that participants have joined as a matter of their own free will."[105]

So while Stephen Williams' supporters sympathetically portray him as the noble individual standing alone against monolithic state power, the spread of school choice may require us to shift our perspective. If there are a range of distinct schools embodying a variety of deliberately crafted normative ideals, teachers' rights cases may be more accurately portrayed as pitting a voluntarily constructed subcommunity founded on a distinct identity against a designated agent of that subcommunity who threatens its continued viability. If the teacher's exercise of conscience threatens the identity staked out by the school, school autonomy must trump. There is no obvious legal impediment to such an approach once we leave behind the intraschool marketplace model,[106] especially where knowledge of the basis for a particular restraint on conscience can be imputed to the teacher before any dispute arises by virtue of the school's ongoing articulation of its mission.[107]

Charter Schools and the First Amendment

It is fairly easy to see how school choice could reduce the persuasive power of a dissenting student's claim of conscience. In light of *Tinker's* focus on student speech's capacity to disrupt the educational environment, a student's right to free speech may be a function, at least in part, of the particular school she attends. Perhaps the "be happy, not gay" shirt is more disruptive – as measured by likelihood and degree of disruption – at the Harvey Milk School, where students and teachers have deliberately chosen an environment that supports and affirms homosexuality. It is not difficult to imagine a heightened capacity for disruption from student speech inimical to the missions of charter schools devoted to environmental stewardship or Middle Eastern cultures.[108] It is not helpful to frame the differences categorically – the

---

[105] Viteritti, *supra* note 28, at 217.

[106] Stephen R. Goldstein, *The Asserted Constitutional Right of Public School Teachers to Determine What They Teach*, 124 U. Pa. L. Rev. 1293, 1356 (1976) ("The freedom of expression justification for teacher control is premised on an analytical model of education which views schools as a market place of ideas. There is no historical or precedential basis, however, for concluding that the market place of ideas model is constitutionally compelled over the traditional value inculcation model. Thus, in the final analysis, teachers' constitutional rights, in and out of the classroom, do not extend beyond the first amendment rights of all citizens."); see also Ralph D. Mawdsley, *School Board Control Over Education and a Teacher's Right to Privacy*, 23 St. Louis U. Pub. L. Rev. 609, 624–5 (2004) ("Efforts under a variety of legal theories to change or to personalize school curriculum have generally been rejected.").

[107] See Vikram Amar and Alan Brownstein, *Academic Freedom*, 9 Green Bag 2d 17, 24 (2005) (suggesting that "public school restrictions on teacher speech should emphasize substantial before-the-fact control, while curtailing the availability of after-the-fact sanction").

[108] See, e.g., Andrea Elliott, *Critics Cost Muslim Educator Her Dream School*, N.Y. Times, Apr. 28, 2008, at A1 (reporting on controversy surrounding Khalil Gibran International Academy in New York City, a public charter school founded to foster understanding between American and Arab cultures, but also accused of harboring an "Islamist agenda").

First Amendment should never be interpreted to allow blanket prohibitions on any student speech that dissents from the majority view, even when there is a vibrant marketplace of other majority views from which to choose. It is more helpful to view the differences as a question of degree: If there is a line between constitutionally protected dissent and unprotected disruption, there is no reason to believe that the line never shifts depending on the environment in question.

It is less clear whether an expanded array of charter schools expands a particular school's discretion to implement policies or practices that would otherwise run afoul of the Establishment clause. This chapter does not purport to reach conclusive answers on this question, but it will offer preliminary reflections on why we may need to rethink the role of conscience in our understanding of the Establishment clause as applied to public school districts where meaningful parental choice is available.

One reason is the rationale underlying the Supreme Court's ruling in *Simmons-Harris v. Zelman* that state voucher funds directed by parents to religious schools do not violate the Establishment clause.[109] *Zelman* makes more difficult any sharp demarcation between publicly and privately funded schools when it comes to religion. The court suggested that the availability of magnet schools and privately run community schools, in addition to the traditional public schools, made religious schools' inclusion in the voucher program less problematic.[110] *Zelman*'s relevance is limited, however, by the fact that parents under the Cleveland plan were provided with government funds and they, in turn, directed the funds to the school of their choice.[111] The constitutional inquiry is different when a government agency approves a proposal for a new school and then funds its start-up directly. It bears further exploration whether the *Zelman* court's approval of state funding of expressly religious educational programs pursuant to the decisions of private individuals may suggest that even charter schools could merit a different Establishment clause analysis than the traditional public school system.

Three facts in combination could warrant broader discretion for the school: first, if the disputed element of the charter school is not sectarian or even expressly religious, but represents a moral claim that may be driven in significant part by a religious worldview (such as abstinence-only sex education[112]); second, if the element has been introduced by the self-selected constituents of the school, rather than imposed

---

[109] See *Simmons-Harris v. Zelman*, 122 S. Ct. 2460 (2002).

[110] *Id.* at 2469.

[111] *Id.* at 2468 ("[W]e have repeatedly recognized that no reasonable observer would think a neutral program of private choice, where state aid reaches religious schools solely as a result of the numerous independent decisions of private individuals, carries with it the *imprimatur* of government endorsement.").

[112] See Frank Ravitch, *Some Thoughts on Religion, Abstinence Only, and Sex Education in the Public Schools*, 26 Child. Legal Rts. J. 48 (2006) (arguing that abstinence-only sex education programs may be unconstitutional because they are religiously motivated).

top-down on all schools in the district;[113] and third, if the state action involved – granting a charter to the school, which triggers the funding – was based on unquestionably legitimate educational objectives, not on the disputed element, which may be but one of many components of the school's stated mission. The two pre-*Zelman* cases in which charter school practices were alleged to violate the Establishment clause do not seem to have triggered different treatment by the courts than a traditional public school,[114] but the rationale of *Zelman*, along with the proper set of facts and understanding of conscience, may shift the analysis, if not the outcome.

Even apart from *Zelman*, the rationale of the endorsement test espoused by Justice O'Connor may not be as confining in a choice regime as when it is enforced against schools functioning as fungible components of the state's monopoly power. The test holds that the Establishment clause prohibits the government from either endorsing or disapproving religion and endorsement is understood as sending "a message to nonadherents that they are outsiders, not full members of the political community, and an accompanying message to adherents that they are insiders, members of the political community."[115] Courts must evaluate the nature of the relationship between the government and any religious organizations involved, as well as the content of the message embodied in the policy or practice at issue. Determining whether the government acted neutrally toward religion will turn on "the judicial interpretation of social facts."[116]

As a matter of logic, the exit option made available by school choice makes it less reasonable for a student to view herself as a political outsider simply because a particular school embraces a moral claim with which she disagrees. By way of obvious example, the existence of the Harvey Milk School hardly justifies a conclusion that gay, lesbian, bisexual, and transgender youth are "insiders," while those who disagree with the school's premise are "not full members of the political community." What is not clear is whether the exit option changes the endorsement dynamic on religious matters. Certainly if a charter school was proposed with a mission of spreading the gospel of Jesus Christ, the government's decision to grant the charter would send a strong message of endorsing religion, regardless of how many viable alternative schools students could choose. Suppose that the proposal stated only that the school would shape students holistically: physically, mentally, emotionally, and

---

[113] Rich Schragger advocates for "a jurisprudence that shows both some increased respect for local choices and some increased suspicion of centralized ones, whether those choices appear to favor or disfavor religion in any particular case." Richard Schragger, *The Role of the Local in the Doctrine and Discourse of Religious Liberty*, 117 Harv. L. Rev. 1810, 1817 (2004). The "fragmented authority" reflected in school choice "ensures that no one political authority has a monopoly on religion-regulating and -benefiting powers, thereby diffusing both the state's power over religion and religion's power over the state." *Id.* at 1873–4.

[114] See Robert J. Martin, *Charting the Court Challenges to Charter Schools*, 109 Penn St. L. Rev. 43, 97–9 (2004) (discussing *Daugherty v. Vanguard Charter Sch. Acad.*, 116 F. Supp. 2d 897, 903 (W.D. Mich. 2000) and *Porta v. Klagholz*, 19 F. Supp. 2d 290, 293 (D.N.J. 1998)).

[115] *Lynch v. Donnelly*, 465 U.S. at 687–9 (O'Connor, J., concurring).

[116] *Id.* at 693–4.

spiritually, and that each student was to be treated as "a significant creature entrusted with the weighty role of steward of Earth."[117] And although not communicating any overtly religious messages through the curriculum, assume that the school decides to set aside time in each day for student reflection, meditation or prayer,[118] create an externship program that included opportunities to work with a variety of religious or secular organizations, institute abstinence-only sex education based on the school's perception of adolescents' lack of emotional readiness for sexual activity, and offer a class in which the existential implications of Darwinian evolution are explored.

If such measures were introduced as a legislative package to be imposed on all schools within a jurisdiction, would that pose a more formidable Establishment clause problem than when a single charter school adopts them? Two reasons suggest an answer in the affirmative: First, the state's role as overseer of the educational marketplace, rather than as arbiter of collectivized educational norms, makes the appearance of government endorsement more attenuated; and second, the student's exit option and perception of the broader marketplace makes the subjective impact of a potential government endorsement less problematic. This is, of course, no guarantee that the Supreme Court's Establishment clause jurisprudence will carve out a special place for charter schools; it simply reflects a rationale for the court to do so.

PRIVATE SCHOOL VOUCHERS AND CONSCIENCE

Much of the debate surrounding the school choice movement has focused on the inclusion of private schools in voucher programs, particularly in the wake of the Supreme Court's ruling in *Zelman*.[119] Clearly, if students are financially empowered to choose among a variety of secular and religious schools, the compulsion to protect their individual consciences from the moral or religious content embodied in the curriculum or environment at any particular school dissipates significantly. A student whose faith tradition rejects Darwinian evolution, for example, has a much less compelling conscience claim when she can choose to attend a religious school that introduces Intelligent Design theory in science class than if her only option is a public school where evolution is the only theory presented.

Zelman and Conscience

This basic point does not require much extrapolation, but it is important to see how the Supreme Court's resolution of the vouchers issue in *Zelman* bears on the

---

[117] This particular phrase comes from the mission statement of Tarek Ibn Ziyad Academy, a charter school in Minnesota focusing on the Arabic language and the cultural traditions of the Middle East, East Africa, North Africa, and South Asia. (http://www.tizacademy.com/Our_School.html) (accessed Feb. 27, 2009).

[118] See *Wallace v. Jaffree*, 472 U.S. 38 (1985) (striking down Alabama law that added words "or voluntary prayer" to statute authorizing student moment of silence).

[119] See *Simmons-Harris v. Zelman*, 122 S. Ct. 2460 (2002).

relational dimension of conscience. Put simply, the majority's approach ensures that the religiously motivated school choices of students and their parents are not unduly penalized in an otherwise well-functioning marketplace. The common good's bottom-up orientation presumes that families' educational priorities and values will actually be reflected in their children's education, and *Zelman* represents a key step in that direction.

The Court held five-four that Cleveland's school voucher program did not violate the Establishment clause, thereby reversing the Sixth Circuit Court of Appeals, which had invalidated the program in light of the fact that eighty-six percent of the participating schools (46 of 56) were religious and ninety-six percent of students using vouchers enrolled in religious schools.[120] In the Sixth Circuit's view, the statistical predominance of religious schools precluded students from having a "meaningful" choice between religious and secular schools, and thus the program impermissibly advanced religion. The Sixth Circuit relied in part on its belief that nonreligious schools were dissuaded from participating because the program placed caps on the amount of tuition chargeable to voucher students – thereby forcing the school to bear any per-student costs in excess of the caps – but that religious schools were not similarly dissuaded because the sponsoring church could pick up the tab for any tuition shortfall.

The Supreme Court disagreed, finding that: 1) nonreligious private schools, like their religious counterparts, received substantial third-party contributions supporting their operation; 2) all ten secular private schools operating within the school district at the time of the program's implementation had chosen to participate, and continue to do so; and 3) although no religious schools have yet been created in response to the financial incentives offered by the voucher program, several nonreligious schools have been created.[121] Because these facts showed that the structure of the program did not favor the participation of religious over nonreligious schools and given the lack of evidence that "any voucher-eligible student was turned away from a nonreligious private school in the voucher program,"[122] the fact that most participating private schools were religious, or that most participating students chose religious schools, is constitutionally irrelevant.

If every student in the Cleveland voucher program who wanted to attend a private secular school was able to do so, the Sixth Circuit and the four-justice Supreme Court dissent are hard-pressed to assert that the students lacked a meaningful choice between religious and nonreligious educational alternatives. It would be another matter, of course, if the lack of choice derived from a significant disparity in academic quality between the participating nonreligious schools and participating religious schools. This was not a factor in *Zelman*, however. Rather, the judges finding

---

[120] 234 F.3d 945 (6th Cir. 2000).
[121] 122 S. Ct. at 2470 n. 4.
[122] 122 S. Ct. at 2477 (O'Connor, J., concurring).

an Establishment clause violation seem to have inferred an advancement of religion simply because, in their view, too many religious schools and not enough nonreligious schools elected to accept voucher students, and too many students chose to use their vouchers to attend those religious schools.

This mindset unnecessarily hinders the ability of religious associations to pursue their chosen purposes to the extent that such pursuit hinges on their ability to compete with the operators of public schools (i.e., the government) and nonreligious private schools (i.e., mainly nonprofit and for-profit corporations, along with some nonreligious civic associations). In effect, this approach places a heavier burden on religious associations relative to their nonreligious competitors: For religious schools to participate in a facially unobjectionable voucher program, they would have to hope that a sufficient number of nonreligious schools choose to participate, and that a sufficient number of students choose to use vouchers to attend the nonreligious schools; obviously, the participation of nonreligious schools in a voucher program does not similarly turn on the participation rates of their religious counterparts. Provided that public resources are made available without either explicit or implicit regard to religion and that individual beneficiaries (i.e., the voucher recipients) are able to choose from at least one legitimate nonreligious entity, the nonreligious versus religious composition of entities that have chosen to utilize public resources is immaterial. Meaningful choice is not precluded simply because there are more opportunities to choose religious schools; such a notion is attractive only to a court looking for ways to preclude the utilization of public resources by religious entities. Such predispositions are unnecessary from a constitutional standpoint and distinctly unhelpful to the efforts of religious organizations to maintain conscience-forming educational venues.

Vouchers and Public Norms

This is not to suggest that any religious or secular group holding itself out as a school has unfettered discretion to tap into public funds. As in the Charitable Choice context, the provider must be able to fulfill the objectives for which the government funds are made available. Certainly, a school must be able to educate students effectively to be eligible to receive vouchers. Because public funds are involved, the government should have reasonable discretion to inject its own view of effectiveness into those requirements. Although it is patently unreasonable to conclude that all religious schools are incapable of educating students effectively, it is not so unreasonable to conclude that effective education in our day precludes the categorical exclusion of students from a school based, for example, on their religious beliefs. In this regard, the government may require voucher schools to adopt a more inclusive admission policy than the school would choose absent such funding. The fact that the relational dimension of conscience demands freedom for groups to pursue their own identities does not give them a blanket license to maintain the same degree of freedom when they accept government funds in pursuit of their chosen purpose. In other words, the combination of *Dale* (giving the Boy Scouts a right to discriminate against gays) and *Zelman* (permitting religious schools' access to public funds) does not create the specter of students using voucher money to attend exclusionary private schools. Whether or not such schools have the right to exist, they do not have the right to government funds. A healthy marketplace of moral norms and ideals presumes a meaningful role for the state, especially when it comes to taxpayer-facilitated access to a foundational good like education.

The "strings" accompanying the funds may, as in the Charitable Choice context, warrant hesitation before a religious school rushes headlong to participate in a voucher program. The need for caution is reflected, perhaps unintentionally, in an observation by Martha Minow, who suggests that urban Catholic schools have embraced public values – which to her means dropping specific religious instruction and focusing instead on tolerance and civic virtue – without jeopardizing their missions.[123] Regardless of whether one supports or opposes the mission of Catholic schools, it seems far-fetched to suggest that the omission of religious instruction does not jeopardize their mission.

The regulations accompanying vouchers should be prudently tailored toward ensuring nondiscriminatory access to publicly funded education and toward achieving the widely shared cognitive objectives of education, not on mandating the inculcation of certain contested values, such as individual autonomy. James Dwyer, a leading children's rights scholar, welcomes the rise of school choice, as he sees government funding as the perfect vehicle to justify more intensive regulation of private schools, which can ensure that children are not precluded from meaningful self-development simply by the accident of their birth into a family that rejects the educational promises of modern liberalism. Dwyer urges states implementing voucher programs to attach to the vouchers "whatever regulatory strings are needed to ensure that children in all private schools receive a good secular education," and if this means that "some parents cannot use their children's schooling to proclaim the 'good news,' because in the state's judgment the parents' news is not so good, then so be it."[124] This translates into proposals to regulate the content of private school curricula, stamping out even subtle forms of discriminatory and biased content that could result, for example, in "diminished self-esteem, inhibited cognitive development, passivity, reduced aspirations, and lower achievement on the part of female students."[125] Similar concerns underlie calls to regulate home schooling more closely.[126]

[123] Martha Minow, *Partners, Not Rivals: Redrawing the Lines Between Public and Private, Non-profit and Profit, and Secular and Religious*, 80 B.U. L. Rev. 1061, 1092–3 (2000).

[124] James G. Dwyer, *School Vouchers: Inviting the Public Into the Religious Square*, 42 Wm. & Mary L. Rev. 992, 1005 (2001).

[125] James G. Dwyer, *Religious Schools v. Children's Rights*, 10 (1998).

[126] See, e.g., Kimberly Yuracko, *Education Off the Grid: Constitutional Constraints on Homeschooling*, 96 Cal. L. Rev. 123, 183 (2008) (arguing that state constitutions should be interpreted to "limit the

Emily Buss starts from the same premises as Dwyer, but arrives at a different regulatory target: the makeup of student populations at both private and public schools. Buss insists, "a state interest in fostering the capacity for independent thought in its children could justify policies encouraging and even, perhaps, compelling some amount of exposure to ideologically unlike peers," especially among older adolescents.[127] When a family chooses a school based on a student population that reflects the family's values or worldview, the state may be justified in stepping in to avoid the resulting compromise of the child's autonomy, at least as that autonomy is understood by Buss. She argues that peer relationships that reinforce the child's existing value structure are actually doing a disservice to the child.

> While these relationships with like peers still offer the child an opportunity to 'try on' an identity by acting independently of parents and reflecting on that identity through peer interactions, this opportunity for exploration will be more narrowly circumscribed. The child's choice of friendships may offer some range in personality types, but not in value structures or long-term ambitions. The child's conversations with friends may allow her to understand her own value structure better, but they will be less likely to push her to question her own choices because they will not offer her alternative values and plans to compare with her own.[128]

In these terms, the child's best interests require separation from the child's family-formed identity, and that separation is important enough to justify state intervention into the family's effort to protect and maintain the identity, regardless of whether or not the child objects to such efforts.

Many proposed private school regulations have already emerged from this conception of the child, and several have already been adopted in districts implementing school voucher programs. Some suggested regulations seem relatively innocuous, but by no means unobjectionable, such as mandating certain curricular requirements, requiring teachers to be state-certified, ensuring that religious instruction or services are optional for voucher students, and prohibiting the use of religious criteria in the admission of students. Others are more problematic, most notably the state power to censor the transmission of illiberal religious teachings. Whatever our view of a particular regulation's reasonableness, the content is not as significant as the underlying notion that the state is equipped to define and pursue collectively the child's autonomy-centered interests, even if it negates the efficacy of parents' child-forming, conscience-shaped decisions. The dangers of that approach will be explored more fully in the next chapter.

extent to which parents may teach their children idiosyncratic and illiberal beliefs and values without labeling or framing them as such. In other words, the minimum may require that if parents want to teach against the enlightenment they have to label what they are doing as such.").
[127] Emily Buss, *The Adolescent's Stake in the Allocation of Educational Control Between Parent and State*, 67 U. Chi. L. Rev. 1233, 1234 (2000).
[128] *Id.* at 1274.

CONSCIENCE AND SCHOOLS

This analysis is not meant to suggest that our gradually expanding embrace of school choice diminishes the relevance of individual conscience to such an extent that schools are free to espouse any normative vision that is sustainable in the marketplace. An educational provider should still be expected to fulfill the objectives for which public education exists in a liberal democracy in the first place. The fact that a school's mediating role demands freedom to pursue its own identity does not mean that the mediating role merits a degree of freedom that would effectively trump every other government interest. But there is considerable space within the broad constraints of liberalism for schools to pursue divergent moral values. When there is meaningful school choice, the broad constraints should be defined and articulated primarily by the state through its oversight function, not through the constitutionally empowered resistance of individual teachers and students. Teacher autonomy, and to a lesser extent student autonomy, are inconsistent with the level of school autonomy that is necessary to cultivate a system of public education that is accountable to its constituents and does not shirk from the task of value inculcation.

Among schools that embody legitimate educational visions, the school's autonomy, even under the most robust framework of parental choice, is not unlimited. A reduced focus on individual conscience does not justify institutional power that runs roughshod over nonconforming students and teachers. Individual conscience must give way only when the substance of the constituent's conscience-driven claim directly threatens the realization or maintenance of the institutional identity previously staked out by the school. School choice brings a skeptical eye toward individual conscience not because it seeks to replace dissent with an all-powerful government indoctrination zone. Rather, school choice seeks to maximize the efficacy of parents' child-forming decisions in a way that takes values, and value pluralism, seriously. Under a one-size-fits-all approach to public education, an individualized right of conscience provides a voice to individuals who do not fit.

In the currently unfolding era, however, in which public education does not presume that one size will suffice, it becomes more difficult to defend the individualized right of conscience, and the relational dimension of conscience comes into relief. If institutional diversity becomes a reality in publicly funded education, then we can begin to view a particular school less as a monolithic arm of the state, and more as an affirmatively chosen communal venue for the formation of conscience. In the meantime, in light of students' lack of an exit option, the state must be careful not to use its monopoly power to marginalize nonstate sources of moral authority over children's lives. This requires a degree of self-restraint in pushing students to affirm contested moral claims, as well as the maintenance of sufficient space in which essentially captive students (and parents) may express their own dissenting claims of conscience.

9

Families

To take stock fully of conscience's relational dimension and its implications for the law, we must explore what that dimension means for our treatment of the most important relational venue in the lives of most people – the family. This exploration is by no means straightforward or obvious, for the marketplace model that has shaped this book's recommendations in other areas is of limited applicability when it comes to the family. Put simply, how should we view conscience's relational dimension in a venue where we have traditionally functioned more as members than as choosers? To the extent that the law empowers individual family members to function more as choosers, what are the implications for conscience?

One possible implication is an expanded state role to protect those deemed incapable of choosing the moral commitments imposed on them by those exercising authority within the family. Consider the recent well-publicized government raid of the Yearning for Zion ranch associated with the Fundamentalist Church of Jesus Christ of Latter Day Saints in Texas. Acting on an anonymous telephone call reporting that a 16 year-old girl named Sarah was being physically and sexually abused at the ranch, the state removed 463 children from their parents despite failing to locate "Sarah." A state agency would not typically enter and remove all children from their families in a population the size of a small town absent some particularized and substantiated allegations of serious abuse. It is no stretch to conclude that the aggressiveness shown by the state of Texas may have been motivated, in significant part, by the fact that the abuse allegations were raised against a community that practices polygamy and pushes its daughters to marry at a younger age than the age considered prudent by the broader society.

Although the Texas Supreme Court ultimately ordered the children to be reunited with their parents pending further investigation,[1] the case, while notable for its massive scope, is not an anomaly – criminal prosecutions for polygamy continue

---

[1] In re *Texas Dep't of Family and Protective Servs.*, 255 S.W.3d 613 (Tex. 2008).

to this day. More broadly, the state does not take a hands-off approach to family matters. The law sets forth bright-line, if shifting, boundaries governing the nature of, and eligibility to participate in, the institution of marriage. The state also has long taken an active role in defining child-rearing obligations and in favoring certain categories of adults' intimate relationships over others. Given the state's regulation-heavy approach to the make-up and function of family, the bottom-up model of moral suasion central to the rest of this book's recommendations appears to be largely inoperative in this context.

A top-down approach to family, however, should give pause when we consider the centrality of family to the moral lives of its members. If ever the cause of conscience demanded autonomy for a particular relational venue, the family appears as the most obvious candidate. In this context, we are not talking about arms-length bargains for contraceptives; we are talking about comprehensive relationships of dependency that, to a significant extent, can establish, not just shape, a person's moral worldview. It is one thing for the state to require a photographer to shoot an event that she finds morally objectionable; it is quite another for the state to impair a parent's ability to pass on her beliefs to her child or to hinder her ability to enter or exit certain adult consensual relationships of her choice.

At the same time, the comprehensiveness and intimacy of family relationships gives rise to a level of vulnerability not often found in other social settings. In particular, the lack of an exit option for many family members – children and, to a lesser extent, an economically dependent spouse – makes the marketplace model a nonstarter. Children do not get to choose their families, and they generally cannot escape parental authority until they become adults. A spouse, usually the wife, may forego developing her own earning capacity and financial independence to raise children or maintain the home. For these and other reasons, family relationships entail vulnerability, and the state has an obvious interest in protecting the interests of individuals who cannot protect themselves. This interest may, under certain circumstances, justify state intervention into the affairs of the family.

But the intervention must be limited, and the relational dimension of conscience can help inform our ongoing efforts to articulate those limitations. Stated broadly, the state should take family relationships as constitutive elements of a person's moral identity, not as obstacles to its development. Consciences are formed in families, and the process of formation is itself among conscience's most vital expressions. Elevating the cultivation of individual autonomy as an objective of family law discounts the myriad moral traditions in which individual autonomy is not the ultimate good. Honoring family members' moral identities does not always require the state to push for members' achievement of individual autonomy. That said, the state's need to recognize the centrality of family relationships to individual identity does not mean that the state must remain neutral on the question of which types of relationships are most conducive to the healthy development of individuals within the family structure.

FROM STATUS TO CONTRACT

At first glance, an observer might conclude that family law is well tailored to protecting conscience within the family under a marketplace approach given the law's longstanding and broad move from status to contract. In past eras, family members' rights and responsibilities were defined, in large part, by their status: wife, husband, parent, and child. Increasingly, the law's inquiry turns on individuals' agreement (express or implied) to take on certain obligations. A contractual approach presumes that individuals should have the freedom to define their own intimate relationships.

We have replaced the traditional view of family as an institution defined by public norms with a vision of the family as more of a sphere of private ordering in which participants can set the terms of the endeavor. No-fault divorce, for example, has made marriage an at-will relationship, rather than a lifelong commitment. The law's enforcement of prenuptial agreements allows the terms of separation to be set by the spouses, not by society. The rise of cohabitation, the advent of easy contraception, and the availability of abortion have effectively made sexual intimacy, marriage, and parenting separately chosen life experiences, rather than a package deal. Even the considerable commitments imposed on parents are not triggered exclusively by simple biological parentage, but by affirmative acts toward establishing a caregiving relationship. With the expanding relevance of choice in matters of family, one might see promise for the law's protection of conscience in matters of family. If we define ourselves and our moral identities in significant part through our relationships, surely the law's elevation of chosen relationships over status-defined relationships bodes well for conscience.

Such optimism, however, misreads the connection between relationships and identity. When everything is a matter of choice, the chooser can be made to feel isolated, as though her relationships are not really part of her, but something external that she decides (or not) to add. By opening up our family relationships to choice, the law (and culture more broadly) can engender the expectation that we are constantly choosing. For example, critics contend that at-will divorce sends the message to spouses that their marriage is subject to an ongoing cost-benefit analysis. When an individual spouse's perception of the costs exceeds the perceived benefits, the law provides an easy exit option. The effect can be profoundly distancing. As Milton Regan puts it, the contractual approach's vision of intimacy is premised on "the model of the acontextual self – a belief in the existence of an authentic self who stands apart from any social relationship in which he or she is involved."[2] Being a husband, under this view, "is a role that I play, not part of who I am in any fundamental way," and thus "I am truly myself insofar as I am free to choose which role to play, not insofar as I carry out the prescriptions of any one of them."[3] Reframing the family as

---

[2] Milton C. Regan, *Family Law and the Pursuit of Intimacy*, 2 (1993).
[3] *Id.*

a freely chosen interaction of rights-bearing individuals may give short shrift to the relational dimension of conscience, compromising the identity-shaping capacity of families in the process.

Status to Contract: Adult Intimacy

There is a trend toward viewing as illegitimate, or at least as dangerously moralistic, the state's interest in regulating relationships between consenting adults unless there is a clear nexus between the regulation and the caregiving function of families.[4] Some feminist legal scholars maintain, in fact, that the state privileges marriage as a "crucial component of contemporary patriarchal ideology" because "it ensures that men are perceived as central to the family."[5] Whatever the grounds from which the critique is offered, there is a growing set of voices contending that the law should be decidedly neutral toward adults' relationship choices. One of the best known voices within this set belongs to Martha Fineman, who advocates for "equality" of "sexual relational affiliations," meaning that we should "destroy the marital model altogether and collapse all sexual relationships into the same category – private – not sanctioned, privileged, or preferred by law."[6] In her ideal world, "the interactions of female and male sexual affiliates would be governed by the same rules that regulate other interactions in our society – specifically those of contract and property, as well as tort and criminal law."[7] Relational transactions between and among women and men would proceed unfettered by "legalities that they did not voluntarily choose."[8]

The law is still a long way from reflecting Fineman's approach, but without question the state has become more restrained in its regulation of adults' intimate relationships. This movement has been compelled in part by the Supreme Court's interpretation of the right to privacy. In 1965, the court first articulated a right to privacy in striking down a state prohibition on the use of contraception by married couples. The court's reasoning, though, was far from individualistic, grounded in a finding of "marital privacy." Ruling that the law unconstitutionally intruded on the "intimate relations of husband and wife," the court observed:

> Marriage is a coming together for better or for worse, hopefully enduring, and intimate to the degree of being sacred. It is an association that promotes a way of life, not causes; a harmony in living, not political faiths; a bilateral loyalty, not commercial or social projects. Yet it is an association for as noble a purpose as any involved in our prior decisions.[9]

---

[4] See, e.g., Robin West, *Marriage, Sexuality, and Gender*, 208 (2007).
[5] Martha Fineman, *The Neutered Mother, the Sexual Family, and Other Twentieth Century Tragedies*, 146 (1995).
[6] *Id.* at 5.
[7] *Id.* at 229.
[8] *Id.*
[9] *Griswold v. Connecticut*, 381 U.S. 479, 486 (1965).

Despite its focus on the marital relationship, *Griswold* served as the foundation for the individual right to privacy we know today. In 1972, the court extended *Griswold's* ruling to cover unmarried individuals, discounting the notion of "marital privacy," by asserting that "the marital couple is not an independent entity with a mind and heart of its own, but an association of two individuals each with a separate intellectual and emotional makeup." As such, "[i]f the right of privacy means anything, it is the right of the individual, married or single, to be free from unwarranted governmental intrusion into matters so fundamentally affecting a person as the decision whether to bear or beget a child."[10] The following year, in *Roe v. Wade*, the court extended that rationale to encompass a woman's decision to abort her fetus.[11]

Twenty years after *Roe*, the court pushed the right to sexual privacy beyond the reproductive realm. In *Lawrence v. Texas*, the court struck down a state prohibition on same-sex sodomy, ruling that "the State cannot demean [petitioners'] existence or control their destiny by making their private sexual conduct a crime."[12] In the eyes of appellate courts charged with interpreting the decision,[13] *Lawrence* established a constitutional right to sexual autonomy. There is a growing consensus that laws authorizing state intrusion on matters as intimate and personal as contraceptive use or sodomy are, in the words of Justice Clarence Thomas, "uncommonly silly."[14] Perhaps the costs of waiting for that consensus to result in the laws' repeal are high enough to justify courts' enshrinement of constitutional bulwarks against such intrusion. There is a cost, though, to the extent that a rights-driven approach to intimate relationships makes it more difficult to discern, articulate, and pursue a vision of the family as an entity that is greater than the sum of its rights-bearing parts.

An even more significant aspect of the movement from state-defined status to participant-defined contract has been legislatively driven. The enactment of no-fault divorce and the validation of prenuptial agreements, to cite two prominent examples, reflect a more neutral stance by the state toward the duration and scope of the marital commitment. The Uniform Premarital Agreement provides that such agreements are enforceable unless: 1) a party did not enter into the agreement voluntarily; 2) the agreement was substantively unconscionable at the time of execution, and the party did not receive, and did not waive, fair and reasonable disclosure of the other party's assets at the time of execution; or 3) the agreement waives spousal support and would cause the spouse to require public assistance.[15] Some courts have gone so far as to hold that premarital agreements should be treated as any other commercial

---

[10] *Eisenstadt v. Baird*, 405 U.S. 438, 453 (1972).

[11] *Roe v. Wade*, 410 U.S. 113 (1973).

[12] *Lawrence v. Texas*, 539 U.S. 558 (2003).

[13] *Cook v. Gates*, 528 F.3d 42, 53 (1st Cir. 2008); *Witt v. Dep't of the Air Force*, 527 F.3d 806, 819 (9th Cir. 2008).

[14] *Lawrence v. Texas*, 539 U.S. at 605 (Thomas, J., dissenting) (quoting *Griswold v. Connecticut*, 381 U.S. 479, 527 (Stewart, J. dissenting)).

[15] Uniform Premarital Agreement Act § 6.

contract,[16] although the pendulum may be swinging back toward a more nuanced approach.[17]

The changes in divorce law have justifiably garnered much more attention. Traditionally, spouses desiring a divorce were required to engage in an adversarial proceeding in which the divorcing spouse was to establish that the other spouse violated a marital obligation, usually adultery, cruelty, or abandonment. This system was completely transformed over the 1960s and early 1970s. By the middle of the 1970s, "no fault" divorce reigned supreme, requiring only that one spouse allege that the marriage had broken down. One consequence of this transformation was that the wife's bargaining position became much weaker than her husband's. As June Carbone and Margaret Brinig explain:

> The effect, probably unintended, of precluding consideration of fault was to change marriage from a lifetime commitment whose obligations were enforced, albeit selectively, through a form of specific performance, to a contract terminable at will. Either party could end the marriage; the other has no ability to prevent termination. Most of the states to address the matter have ruled that the reasons why the marriage ended are irrelevant. The husband's promise of life-long support became meaningless; the new standard emphasized the parties' self-sufficiency. Upon divorce, the property was divided, and dependent spouses were given transitional awards intended to encourage their financial independence. Protection of the standard of living enjoyed during the marriage, though discussed in the case law, disappeared from practice. The result... was a divorce system that left men financially better off and women worse off than they had been when they were married.[18]

Apart from its tendency to recast spouses as self-interested combatants in a zero-sum financial battle, the no-fault regime also shapes our perception of marriage, which has an impact on the reality of marriage. Marriage as an at-will contract plays a different role in the relational aspirations of its participants (and those who choose not to participate) than does marriage as a lifelong covenant.

These observations are not intended to imply that developments in the right to privacy, the validation of prenuptial agreements, or the rise of no-fault divorce are invariably unhealthy for the cause of conscience. The right to privacy has proved a powerful weapon against the overbearing state, which itself is a formidable threat to conscience. Prenuptial agreements allow spouses – especially older spouses or those entering second marriages – to protect prior financial commitments and obligations against the default rules of property distribution. Providing an exit option from marriage for unhappy spouses is hardly inimical to the morally engaged life. These examples are intended to underscore a simpler claim: Our laws increasingly

---

[16] *Simeone v. Simeone*, 581 A.2d 162 (Pa. 1990).

[17] See *American Law Institute, Principles of the Law of Family Dissolution*, chapter 7 (2002) (embracing contractual freedom, but within limitations shaped by public policy).

[18] June Carbone and Margaret F. Brinig, *Rethinking Marriage: Feminist Ideology, Economic Change, and Divorce Reform*, 65 Tulane L. Rev. 953, 979 (1991).

approach adult relationships by presuming that the starting point should be the participant as an individual, rather than the relationship as an entity. The costs are not certain, but they are real: The relational dimension of conscience suffers if expansive readings of the individual right to privacy handcuff state efforts to promote certain relationships as possessing a quality and depth more conducive to individual flourishing and the common good, or if state deference to spouses' freedom to contract precludes the law from embedding into certain relationships substantive commitments that transcend individual self-interest, or if the state dismisses as moralizing paternalism any effort to buttress the marital commitment's durability by making the exit option a bit less easy and immediate. Before unpacking the reasons why this is so, we must flesh out the other category of family relationships: the parent and child.

Status to Contract: Parent and Child

It is easy to see how the law in areas such as divorce and reproductive rights has, for good and for ill, contributed to a more individualist understanding of relationships between consenting adults. In the area of parent-child relationships, though, the law has maintained a robust set of caretaking obligations given the obvious dependency and vulnerability of children. Even in this area, there is an expanding individualist, rights-based rhetoric coming from legal academics who appear inclined to utilize the law to groom children for their own autonomous moral identities, as already noted in our discussion of education.[19] The (often unstated) operative premise is that children need to achieve critical distance from the moral traditions and commitments embedded in their family life in order to construct their own moral identities. Such a vision is antithetical to conscience's relational dimension.

Mainstream scholars are not pushing for the blanket extension of legal autonomy to children, but many seek to guard against parental actions that are seen to hinder the child's full exercise of autonomy in the future. An uncritical inculcation of religious beliefs by parents over the course of childhood is a leading concern underlying calls for limiting parental authority. Childhood is understood primarily as either an obstacle to, or instrument of, autonomy, and "family" as an entity is dismissed as "a legal fiction that may have an ancient pedigree but [that] has hidden a multitude of wrongs."[20]

One key dimension of this advocacy portrays the constitutional right to privacy as applying only to individuals, not families. For example, leading family law scholar Barbara Bennett Woodhouse argues that state intervention into the family unit should not be blocked legally because the family's dominant member is thereby given license "to engage in clearly (although not grossly) wrongful conduct while

---

[19] See chapter 8.
[20] Barbara Bennett Woodhouse, *The Dark Side of Family Privacy*, 67 Geo. Wash. L. Rev. 1247, 1251–2 (1999).

the dependent members are compelled to suffer it."[21] The notion of privacy as a "right to caretaker autonomy," according to Woodhouse, "runs counter to the principle of public responsibility and public accountability."[22] State intervention into the parent-child relationship should be rendered unnecessary by making sure that families follow "a clear set of social and legal expectations so that adults will be educated in their 'responsibility' and will be deterred from misusing their powers over children."[23]

As such, limitations on a child's autonomy must be justified rationally, not by tradition or biology. Gareth Matthews explains that the children's rights movement arises from a vision of "authorities in our society as rational authorities, people who, even if they first came to occupy their positions of authority by biological accident, can be appropriately called upon to justify their exercise of authority, and justify it in the presence of their children, as soon as those children are capable of making reasonable judgments about their own interests."[24] Even among scholars who defend some semblance of parental autonomy, rationality is central. Emily Buss, for example, defends limited parental autonomy because "we can expect the heavily invested parent to do a better job than the state would do, and under most circumstances, we will have no way of knowing when this will not be so," but cautions that the focus should remain on the "relative competence" of parents and the state.[25] The state's "special competence" on this score includes its ability to shape children "to become citizens capable of meeting the demands of a successfully functioning society," to "identify behavior that the majority of citizens considers harmful to children, no matter what the circumstances," and to "impose some negative limits on the parents' exercise of developmental control."[26]

When parental authority turns on the parents' rationally accessible, context-specific competence, the authority exists, in a real sense, as a state license. Woodhouse makes the state's predominance explicit, asserting that "power over children is conferred by the community, with children's interests and their emerging capacities the foremost consideration," and that parental rights of "[s]tewardship must be earned through actual care giving, and lost if not exercised with responsibility."[27] Her approach "would place children, not adults, firmly at the center and take as its central values not adult individualism, possession, and autonomy, as embodied in parental rights, nor even the dyadic intimacy of parent/child relationships," but instead "would value most highly concrete service to the needs of the next generation,

[21] *Id.* at 1255.
[22] *Id.* at 1260.
[23] *Id.* at 1256.
[24] Gareth B. Matthews, *The Philosophy of Childhood*, 80 (1994).
[25] Emily Buss, *Allocating Developmental Control Among Parent, Child and the State*, 2004 Univ. of Chi. Leg. Forum 27, 32 (2004).
[26] *Id.* at 32–3.
[27] Barbara Bennett Woodhouse, *Hatching the Egg: A Child-Centered Perspective on Parents' Rights*, 14 Cardozo L. Rev. 1747, 1814–5 (1993).

in public and private spheres, and encourage . . . collective community responsibility for the well-being of children."[28] If parental authority is grounded in rights, rather than "demonstrated responsibility," it "constitute[s] a form of bondage."[29]

To the extent that this skepticism toward parental rights goes beyond redressing instances of parents inflicting serious and readily discernible harm on their children, the family's capacity to function as a venue for conscience may be threatened. By "serious and readily discernible," I do not purport to supply a comprehensive or uncontested definition of the harms in which the state legitimately takes an interest. Rather, for purposes of the present discussion, I mean primarily to exclude from the field of state interest those parenting outcomes that are cognizable as "harm" only to the extent that we presume that all children must be equipped to adopt an operative moral worldview as a matter of affirmative, conscious choice. Elevating the facilitation of a child's moral autonomy as an objective to which all parents are accountable precludes commitments for which individual moral autonomy is not an ultimate good. It is no answer to say that the child is free to choose her parents' tradition from a position of autonomy, for the process by which the child achieves autonomy likely entails the inculcation of critical, distancing attitudes by the child toward that tradition.

Further, there is an inescapably top-down element to this purportedly child-centered vision. When parental or family autonomy exist only to the extent that they support the child's individual autonomy, the state has already inserted itself into family life because some degree of intrusion is necessary to judge the acceptability of the relationship between a specific exercise of parental authority and the child's prospects for autonomy. Because autonomy is not a self-defining concept, the law's pursuit of autonomy as an ultimate objective of its treatment of children requires the state to supply autonomy's content with normative claims that will invariably be contested by a significant portion of the families affected.

Another strand of this expanding debate is spatial: Laura Rosenbury, for example, concedes the prudence of recognizing parental authority within the home, but contends that the state should play a role in regulating the myriad spaces between home and school, such as the Boy Scouts, sports leagues, and other civic or religious activities. More striking than the proposed objects of the state's attention is the impetus for that attention. The objective appears to be the achievement of critical distance between the child and her family's moral identity. Rosenbury laments the fact that pluralism only exists between families. She explains:

> Our society is pluralistic because many types of families are permitted to exist largely free from state indoctrination. In contrast, pluralism rarely exists within families. Children are generally exposed to just one belief system within the family, or at most two. Therefore, although children may not be standardized by the state, they

---

[28] *Id.*
[29] *Id.* at 1816.

often are standardized within their own families. Pluralism may exist on a broad, societal level, but children rarely experience pluralism on a micro level, within their own families.[30]

We should be hesitant to "cede childrearing between home and school to the control of parents and their surrogates," she contends, because we stand to lose "[i]mportant opportunities to expose children to the diversity of the broader society."[31]

In Rosenbury's analysis, the childrearing-as-autonomy-promotion norm comes into relief. We do not encounter the family as a given moral community, but as an accidental moral community, created by the happenstance of birth. The law's aim is to minimize the legacy of that accident on the child's long-term moral identity by exposing the child to diverse moral influences. In contrast to the bottom-up orientation of the common good, here parents are constrained in their ability to join together in pursuit of shared norms that are contested by the broader society. Because the formation of children is at issue, the state is empowered to step in. Our respect for conscience, under this view, requires state intervention to ensure that the child's conscience is not unduly shaped by her unquestioning embrace of her family's worldview. Conscience is still respected, but only as an outgrowth of a morally autonomous individual.

Abstract discussions of authority allocations between parents and the state become clearer upon reading the United Nations (UN) Convention on the Rights of the Child, a treaty that has been ratified by every nation except Somalia and the United States. Adopted by the UN General Assembly in 1989, the Convention is a sweeping attempt to encapsulate children's well-being in a rights-based framework consisting of 53 separate articles. Most are relatively uncontroversial to anyone who embraces even a modicum of legal protection for children, including measures designed to protect family integrity, such as Article 11, which requires signatory states to "take measures to combat the illicit transfer and non-return of children abroad." In other provisions, though, the Convention enshrines a more robust vision of human rights than has been seen in international law, even as applied to adults. For example:

- Article 13 grants the child freedom of expression, which includes the "freedom to seek, receive and impart information and ideas of all kinds, regardless of frontiers, either orally, in writing or in print, in the form of art, or through any other media of the child's choice."
- Article 14 grants the child freedom of thought, conscience, and religion, and instructs that parents' rights to direct the child in the exercise of these rights should be respected "in a manner consistent with the evolving capacities of the child."

---

[30] Laura Rosenbury, *Between Home and School*, 155 U. Pa. L. Rev. 833, 893 (2007).
[31] *Id.* at 894–5.

- Article 16 gives the child "the right to the protection of the law against" interference with the child's privacy.
- Article 17 requires states to "ensure that the child has access to information and material from a diversity of national and international sources, especially those aimed at the promotion of his or her social, spiritual and moral well-being and physical and mental health."

Through provisions such as these, the Convention's supporters explain, the Convention portrays the child as more than a "being in need of services": the child is "an individual with the right to have an opinion, to be a participant in decisions affecting his or her life, and to be respected for his or her human dignity."[32] With this vision, the Convention "moves beyond protection rights to choice rights for children."[33]

This move is key to understanding the autonomy-driven conception of the child. "Protection rights" – including rights to property, to physical care and security, and to procedural due process – were the focus of the children's rights movement for much of the twentieth century because such rights do not depend on a minimum level of decision-making capacity. Choice rights, though, "grant individuals the authority to make affirmative and legally binding decisions, such as voting, marrying, making contracts, exercising religious preferences, or choosing whether and how to be educated." Traditionally, denying these rights to children was not seen as discriminating against them, but as protecting them, for "[t]o confer the full range of choice rights on a child is also to confer the burdens and responsibilities of adult legal status."[34]

The organizing premise of all these provisions is found in the Convention's Article 3, which provides that, "[i]n all actions concerning children, whether undertaken by public or private social welfare institutions, courts of law, administrative authorities or legislative bodies, the best interests of the child shall be a primary consideration." The "best interests" standard thus is to be imposed globally through a framework of choice rights on both private and public actors in their dealings with children. In conjunction with the panoply of corresponding substantive rights, the elevation of the best interests standard as a universal, state-enforced (and as a consequence, state-defined) norm begins to bring into relief the extent to which the law's protection of the child's well-being is disconnected from the parents' understanding of the child's well-being. Further, even when parents are not acting as impediments to the child's best interests, they are owed respect, under the Convention, only to the extent that their efforts to "direct the child" are consistent with the child's "evolving

[32] Cynthia Price Cohen and Susan Kilbourne, *Jurisprudence of the Committee on the Rights of the Child: A Guide for Research and Analysis*, 19 Mich. J. Int'l Law 637–8 (1998).

[33] Bruce C. Hafen and Jonathan O. Hafen, *Abandoning Children to Their Autonomy: The United Nations Convention on the Rights of the Child*, 37 Harv. Int'l L.J. 450 (1996).

[34] *Id.* at 461.

capacities." The presumption is that when the state deems the child old enough to act for herself in a given context, the parent begins to recede from the picture, even if there is no apparent conflict between the parents' wishes and the state's understanding of the child's best interests. According to the UN's own description, the Convention "promotes a 'new concept of separate rights for children with the Government accepting responsibility [for] protecting the child from the power of parents.'"[35] The pursuit of autonomy has led to a legal posture toward children that increasingly stands for "the right to be left alone, even within the family structure."[36]

The Convention's challenge to parental authority stands in some tension with a longstanding triumvirate of American Supreme Court cases. In *Meyer v. Nebraska*,[37] the court invalidated a state law banning the teaching of foreign languages to students before they graduated from eighth grade, reasoning that there was insufficient justification for state interference "with the opportunities of pupils to acquire knowledge, and with the power of parents to control the education of their own."[38] In *Pierce v. Society of Sisters*,[39] the court ruled that the state could not require parents to send their children to public schools because "[t]he fundamental theory of liberty upon which all governments in this Union repose excludes any general power of the state to standardize its children by forcing them to accept instruction from public teachers only."[40] Finally, in *Wisconsin v. Yoder*,[41] the court rejected on religious liberty grounds the state's efforts to compel high school education for Amish children, recognizing that a "State's interest in universal education" must be balanced against the reality that "the values of parental direction of the religious upbringing and education of their children in their early and formative years have a high place in our society."[42]

Taken together, these cases establish the right of parents to direct the education of their children. For purposes of this chapter, the more salient point is that the three decisions are premised on the recognition that the parent-child relationship is not a creation of the law and that the parental caregiving authority on which the relationship rests does not represent a delegation of state authority. Echoing Kuyper's sphere sovereignty, the Supreme Court deferred to a prelegal sovereignty within the family that stems from the natural fact of caregiving relationships and the moral formation that is central to that care.

As made clear in the previous chapter, these cases do not completely foreclose state regulation of a child's education, even if the education is pursued in private

---

[35] *Id.* at 450.
[36] *Id.* at 452.
[37] 262 U.S. 390 (1923).
[38] *Id.* at 401.
[39] 268 U.S. 510 (1925).
[40] *Id.* at 535.
[41] 406 U.S. 205 (1972).
[42] *Id.* at 213–4.

schools, and the skeptics of parental authority concentrate their advocacy efforts on creating more space for such regulation based on both the state's interest in producing an educated citizenry and on the child's interest in acquiring an education sufficient to allow her full exercise of autonomy. For example, given the rare cultural separation achieved by the Amish community, *Yoder* does not pose a problem for the broad enforcement of state compulsory attendance laws, nor is there a constitutional impediment to states requiring that private schools teach certain core subjects in order to satisfy those laws.

Notwithstanding this regulatory window, criticism of the triumvirate abounds, even on issues outside the education arena. *Meyer* and *Pierce*, for example, are accused by Barbara Woodhouse of being animated by "a conservative attachment to the patriarchal family, to a class-stratified society, and to a parent's private property rights in his children and their labor," reflecting a "narrow, tradition-bound vision of the child as essentially private property."[43] *Meyer* in particular is seen as having "announced a dangerous form of liberty, the right to control another human being."[44] The legal recognition of parental authority in such cases generally underscores the "bias towards adults' possessive individualism," which "objectifies children and places physical control and possession of the children, rather than demonstrated service or shared concern for their well-being, at the center of controversy."[45]

The UN Convention, the push to regulate private schools (discussed in chapter 8), and the theories underlying recent children's rights advocacy reflect a distinct conception of a child's best interests. For our purposes, the relevant characteristics are threefold: first, the optimal childhood will support a child's attainment of individual moral autonomy at the earliest practicable age and to the fullest possible extent; second, the child's autonomy requires cognitive separation from the cultural or religious traditions in which the child has been raised; and third, the child's best interests are a universalized construct, grounded in self-reflection and independence from whatever particular social milieu has shaped the preautonomous child.

To be sure, greater public accountability for parents' treatment of their children has secured important advances in children's well-being. Adequate food, clothing, and shelter are nonnegotiable elements of any meaningful definition of a child's best interests. Many instances of emotional abuse, neglect, and absence of meaningful access to education should trouble any fully formed conscience. But a categorical expansion of the very concept of childhood best interests should be troubling, especially as the expansion proceeds to define the concept without reference to – or, more glaringly, in opposition to – a family's moral or religious tradition.

---

[43] Barbara Bennett Woodhouse, *"Who Owns the Child?": Meyer and Pierce and the Child as Property*, 33 Wm. & Mary L. Rev. 995, 997 (1992).
[44] *Id.* at 1001.
[45] Woodhouse, *Hatching the Egg, supra* note 27, at 1811.

THE FAMILY AS MORAL COMMUNITY

In tracing the history of conscience in chapter 2, we established that conscience can only be understood fully when it is considered in light of the human person's social nature. Rooted in external sources of moral belief, conscience calls the individual into relationship with others. Nowhere is this dynamic more profound than in the family. When the law posits spouses as parties to an at-will economic venture or presumes that the child must achieve critical distance from the worldview in which she is raised, the family as moral community is compromised. To be sure, the moral community is not erased, but its nature is altered in the eyes of participants and the broader society. The move from status to contract portrays the "authentic" self as a chooser over being a member. Membership in the moral community, absent the individual's exercise of deliberate choice, becomes a problem for the law to overcome, not a natural outgrowth of the person's identity.

The status-defined family is not costless, of course, especially as status has tradition-ally been a vehicle for legally sanctioned power disparities, both between husband and wife and parent and child. Status does have a significant upside, as explored in the work of Milton Regan. He explains, "[s]tatus expresses the social aspects of the self that are the precondition for its exercise of autonomy and its participation in inti-mate relationships," and thus the family "can be seen as a form of discourse about the relational self – a self that acknowledges the constitutive character of certain contexts in which we participate."[46] The relational self is to be distinguished from the detached self, "who is free to take or leave alternatives as she wishes." By contrast, the relational self "is defined in part by her relationships with others," which "places constraints on her, because certain courses of action now seem foreclosed in light of their consequences for those with whom she is enmeshed."[47] Given the potential for harm in the disruption of relationships that are constitutive of our identities, an emphasis on status can actually promote intimacy because it better protects family members "from the disruption that changes in sentiment can bring."[48]

Marriage

When it comes to marriage, Regan draws a helpful distinction between external and internal stances toward marriage. The former "represents an individual's capacity to reflect critically upon, rather than simply identify with, her commitments and attachments," which "enables a person to keep in focus the extent to which any given commitment serves her interests as a distinct individual."[49] The external stance, by facilitating reflection on traditional gender roles, was a key development in women

---

[46] Regan, *supra* note 2, at 104.
[47] *Id.* at 113.
[48] *Id.* at 89.
[49] Milton C. Regan, *Alone Together: Law and the Meanings of Marriage*, 5 (1999).

seeking more empowerment within marriage. But adopting an external stance alone does not do justice to the good of marriage. An internal stance allows marriage to function "as a universe of shared meaning that serves as the taken-for-granted background for individual conduct."[50] A perpetually critical, or even evaluative, stance toward the claims of marriage can be profoundly distancing. Accepting the claims of marriage, not as a conscious cost-benefit analysis, but as a constitutive element of one's moral identity, "makes possible the experience of lives lived in intimate concert, rather than mere parallel association."[51]

The internal point of view comports with research suggesting that individuals are not simply pursuing their own intangible self-interest through their relationships. Even in the absence of rewards, a person's prosocial behavior may stem from the fact that she has adopted "a more expansive and less individualized sense of self," acting "on the basis of norms that deemphasize attention to individual costs and benefits."[52] The self, as constituted by her attachments to others, is encumbered, but in a way that may actually facilitate autonomy. As Michael Sandel puts it, "some relative fixity of character appears essential to prevent the lapse into arbitrariness which the deontological self is unable to avoid."[53] The normative background provided by marriage is not, and should not be, immune from criticism, but we must recognize the cost when we allow the episodic need for criticism to become a categorical need for the marriage relationship to justify itself in terms of participants' self-interest. The law does not explicitly adopt such a view, of course, but the messages emanating from the no-fault divorce and prenuptial agreement regimes take us farther down that path.

Children's Rights

As outlined previously, more autonomy-focused strains within the children's rights movement may not be consistent with the relational dimension of conscience. The answer, though, does not necessarily lie in the expansion and buttressing of parental rights. Realistically, parental rights today often appear as the only shield against state encroachment, but the language of rights, whether the child's or the parent's, tends to further elevate notions of autonomy and marginalize the centrality of the relationship.

In general, the presence of children deepens and strengthens the family as a moral community. Margaret Brinig and others have found that the divorce rate falls when the family includes children born during the marriage.[54] Along with obvious reasons such as a sense of responsibility, altruism, and joy in creation, perhaps children also

---

[50] *Id.*
[51] *Id.*
[52] *Id.* at 73.
[53] Regan, *supra* note 2, at 115 (quoting Michael Sandel, *Liberalism and the Limits of Justice*, 180 [1982]).
[54] Margaret F. Brinig, *Troxel and the Limits of Community*, 32 Rutgers L.J. 733, 760 (2001).

inculcate the values of unconditional love, generosity, and selflessness.[55] Because of
the devotion to their children that most parents naturally experience, it is difficult
to contest reasonably the wisdom of the law's deference to parents as caretakers.
It is also difficult, however, to maintain reasonably that the deference should be
absolute, as parents' natural devotion is not without exception. The difficulty is
respecting the unsurpassed caregiving competence and motivation of parents as a
class without sacrificing the interests of children who comprise the exceptions to the
rule of nature.

One key is to keep the law's focus on the parent and child in relationship, rather
than on the child's needs or parent's rights standing alone. In this regard, Elizabeth
and Robert Scott have proposed viewing the parent's responsibilities to the child in
the context of a fiduciary relationship.[56] The law should encounter the parent-child
relationship as a given, and its rare interventions should be geared toward supporting
that relationship. As the Scotts recognize, "[p]arents are not fungible child rearers,"
because "[t]he link between parent and child has substantial and intrinsic value to
the child; the substitution of another parent and/or termination of the relationship
is accomplished only at considerable cost to the child."[57]

State intervention into the parent-child relationship comes at significant cost to
the parent as well. Just as parents are not fungible, neither are the myriad ways in
which parents exercise responsibility for the child. As Katherine Bartlett explains,
responsible action "expresses a particular set of internalized limits and constraints
that define the person," and this expression "provides to the individual a sense of his
or her own particularity that is essential to the subjective freedom required for moral
decision-making."[58] The law accordingly must "contribute to the creation of high
expectations for parents, while leaving sufficient leeway so that parents are free to
become responsible in the true sense."[59] The law honors both children and parents
by honoring the relationships in which they are most likely to thrive.

The challenge is resisting the urge to step in whenever the state believes that a
child is more likely to thrive if parental authority and influence are circumscribed.
Particularly when parents are part of a tradition that does not embrace modern
liberal values such as equality and individual autonomy, the temptation to intervene
is enormous. Absent serious and readily discernible harm to the child, the temptation
should be resisted.

Contrary to the implied premises of some of the recent children's rights rhetoric,
worldviews are shared normative backgrounds, not mix-and-match items to be
selected off the shelf from a range of choices. From the parent's perspective, a
worldview is intrinsically valuable because it is true, and it is instrumentally valuable

[55] *Id.* at 761.
[56] Elizabeth S. Scott and Robert E. Scott, *Parents as Fiduciaries*, 81 Va. L. Rev. 2401 (1995).
[57] *Id.* at 2414–5.
[58] Katherine Bartlett, *Re-expressing Parenthood*, 98 Yale L.J. 293, 301 (1988).
[59] *Id.*

because, by being true, it comports with the reality that the child will experience in life. Both the intrinsic and instrumental values are threatened if the purported legitimacy of the child's moral identity is conditioned on a deliberate and informed choice to adopt that worldview as her own. The critical distance on which the deliberate and informed choice rests can itself make the perceived value of the worldview more elusive. If the worldview provides the touchstone against which personal virtues and priorities are measured, approaching the very question of worldview as a smorgasbord also calls into question the cultivation of personal virtues and priorities. Subverting the idea that responsible child rearing occurs *within* a normative worldview also challenges the very integrity and coherence of child rearing as moral formation.

WHEN AND HOW SHOULD THE STATE INTERVENE?

So how can the state respect the family as the foundational venue for conscience without sacrificing the well-being of its members? As noted, the state cannot simply function as the facilitator of a marketplace of families because there is no marketplace of families. There is no exit option for children, dependent spouses can exit only with great difficulty, and any dissolution of a family unit comes at a cost of an entirely different sort than the transaction costs incurred in commercial settings. As such, even a minimalist vision of the state's role suggests that the state must ensure that parents' monopoly over child rearing does not lead to physical abuse or neglect, that the power disparity present in many marriages does not lead to economic abandonment, and that the costs of family break-up are accounted for in the incentives and disincentives provided by family law. At the same time, conscience's relational dimension – and the bottom-up orientation of the common good that it contemplates – underscores the importance of maintaining space in which families can live out, transmit, and shape their own moral identities in a manner that is not reducible to the same processes as practiced by members individually. The state must be supportive of family members' relationships without abandoning members to those relationships. This balance is not susceptible to bright-line rules, but a few examples might help flesh out its implications.

Physical Abuse/Medical Neglect

The intact family usually lacks the need for arbitral intervention by the state, but the pressing needs of individual members may justify a state role. Even within staunchly libertarian camps, few would advocate for a return to the laissez-faire days of the nineteenth century, when the nation's first prosecution for child abuse could only be brought under a creative interpretation of animal cruelty laws. Physical abuse and neglect are obvious cases for state intervention. Harm sufficient to justify intervention should be articulable and readily recognizable as actual harm – as Emily Buss puts it, "the suffering of serious and demonstrable detriment," not just "falling short of some developmental ideal."[60] Laws against physical abuse of children do not impose a contested idea of flourishing; they are aimed at ensuring a nonnegotiable minimum requirement for the child's ability to function in any moral community.

In the same vein, the state does not violate the cause of conscience by requiring medical treatment of a child's life-threatening or debilitating medical condition over the parent's religious objection. Law enforcement officials in Minnesota, to take one widely publicized example, did not overreach when they sought the arrest of a woman who fled the state with her 13 year-old son after she refused continued chemotherapy treatments for his advanced, but still treatable, cancer.[61] The parental monopoly does and should enjoy considerable sway over the child's moral formation, but that monopoly cannot be empowered to extend to the child's very existence. For the same reason, state-mandated vaccines can be consistent with our respect for conscience, particularly when there is no reasonable dispute about their medical necessity or concern about significant side-effects. When the link between a morally objectionable vaccine and harm to the child is more attenuated – especially when the likelihood of the link is itself based on a morally objectionable premise – the balance shifts.

For example, several states have decided to require eleven- and twelve-year-old girls to receive the human papilloma virus vaccine, which prevents a sexually trans-mitted disease that can lead to cervical cancer. In this case, the cost to conscience incurred by the imposition of a medical treatment that presumes that the adolescent girl will engage in unprotected sex may warrant state restraint.[62] To the extent that the family as moral community embodies a moral opposition to extramarital sex, a state-mandated message that the family's shared belief is, in effect, unworldly or unrealistic is more than an inconsequential intrusion. At the same time, the teenage girl may reject her family's worldview, and the health fallout could be considerable. Although this is a close call, the state should not operate on the presumption that a child will reject the tenets of her family's worldview. The most prudent path in this case might be to encourage the vaccine, but allow for a parental opt-out.

The State's Arbitral Role in Divorce and Custody

One relevant context alluded to earlier is the no-fault divorce regime. When the family breaks up, an arbitral role for the state is often unavoidable, especially when parents cannot reach agreement on property distribution or custody rights. Con-ditioning eligibility for divorce on a showing of fault is undoubtedly a political

[60] Emily Buss, *Allocating Developmental Control Among Parent, Child and the State*, 2004 U. Chi. Legal F. 27, 33–4 (2004).

[61] Maura Lerner and Jenna Ross, *Daniel Obeys Court, Shows Up At Hospital Appointment*, Mpls. Star Tribune, May 28, 2009, at 1B.

[62] See Susan Levine, *Parents Question HPV Vaccine: Push to Mandate Shots Rapidly Creates Backlash*, Wash. Post, Mar. 4, 2007, at C1.

nonstarter (and may simply resurrect earlier practices of collusion and perjury in "proving" fault), especially considering the low rates of participation so far in the few states that have offered the option of "covenant" marriage in which the availability of no-fault divorce is drastically curtailed. However, the relationship-affirming power of fault findings arises not only at the stage of eligibility for divorce, but also at the stage of financial determinations upon divorce. In most states, fault is irrelevant to such questions unless it is linked to the dissipation of marital assets, for example. This irrelevance, according to Milton Regan, "sends the message that those who abuse the marital relationship ought to share its fruits equally with those whom they have abused."[63] The misconduct does not occur in a vacuum, and its impact cannot be isolated to a particular asset; marital misconduct "occurs within a context of inter-dependence in which cause and effect can't be easily isolated,"[64] and it constitutes harm to the family as an entity. The law could more accurately reflect that relational truth.

Custody disputes between divorcing parents are one of the most difficult categories to resolve, particularly when the substance of the dispute implicates one or both of the parents' deeply held beliefs. Again, when the family remains intact, there is no cause for state intervention, even when the family's practices confound liberal sensibilities. But, in a custody dispute, the state's deference to the family as moral community solves little; one parent's exercise of authority is perceived by the other parent as infringing on her own authority. A famous example of this conundrum occurred in *Quiner v. Quiner*, a case in which the father sought custody based in significant part on the mother's membership in a fundamentalist sect that taught that nonmembers of the sect were unclean and must be avoided. The mother, as a consequence, would not allow the child to play with children outside school who were not members of the sect, forbade civic participation, and sought to avoid having the child interact with his father. The trial court awarded custody to the father, ruling that the child's best interests "include the opportunities for intellectual, character, and personality growth, and the development of those social graces and amenities without which one cannot live comfortably or successfully in a complex, integrated society."[65] The court also noted its concern that the child's relationship with his father would be destroyed if he was "taught to believe that his father is an evil sinner to be shunned."[66]

The appellate court reversed, employing reasoning that appears well-suited to the bottom-up flourishing of conscience. The court explained,

> The fact that judged by the common norm, it may be logically concluded that custody in the father is for the child's best interests, does not warrant us in taking

---

[63] Regan, *supra* note 2, at 141.
[64] *Id.*
[65] *Quiner v. Quiner*, 59 Cal. Rptr. 503, 527 (Cal. App. 1967).
[66] *Id.* at 526.

custody away from the mother when such an order must be bottomed on our opinion that the mother's religious beliefs and teachings, in their effect on the child, are and continue to be contrary to the child's best interests.[67]

To justify the trial court's ruling, in the appellate court's view, there needed to have been evidence sufficient to "sustain a finding that there is actual impairment of physical, emotional and mental well-being contrary to the best interests of the child."[68]

The question is, how should a court treat parental child-rearing decisions that arise as claims of conscience? One option is for a court engaged in the best interests analysis to disregard any aspect of a parent's plans that arise out of claims of conscience (which in most custody cases are religious claims). As Kent Greenawalt rightly observes, this approach would give effective immunity to all parental conduct colorably attributable to religion.[69] Systematically removing religiously motivated parental decisions from the analysis might skew the analysis in favor of deeply religious parents and ignores the fact that some such decisions are unmistakably contrary to any reasonable conception of the child's best interests.

Another option is for the court to assess parental plans "with 'blinders' about their religious source – for example, assessing her proposals not to have her son watch television or read outside material detached from their religious motivations."[70] Leading family law scholar Carl Schneider appears to favor this approach, urging courts to "consider all the behavior and attitudes that might affect a parent's qualities as a guardian, without looking into the religious or ideological basis for them."[71] This approach, however, might provide an unrealistic picture of how Mrs. Quiner's plans – or their negation by the state – would affect the son, for a given deprivation is likely to appear senseless, incoherent, and alienating when removed from its communal context and rationale.

An intermediate approach makes the most sense, one which, as stated by Greenawalt, "would not treat Mrs. Quiner's religiously based choices just like any other unusual plans but would take them into account if their negative effects were likely to be significant."[72] This is a nuanced, fact-driven inquiry, but its lack of conceptual clarity reflects a prudent concession to the complications posed by competing parent-child relationships. In analyzing the facts, it is essential that the court take an expansive view of the connection between the parent's claim of conscience and the child's well-being.

[67] *Id.* at 518.
[68] *Id.* at 516.
[69] Kent Greenawalt, *Child Custody, Religious Practices, and Conscience*, 76 U. Colo. L. Rev. 965, 972 (2005).
[70] *Id.*
[71] Carl E. Schneider, *Religion and Child Custody*, 25 U. Mich. J. L. Ref. 879, 885 (1992).
[72] Greenawalt, *supra* note 69, at 972.

That is to say, although a secular court cannot put itself squarely into whatever worldview is at issue in the custody dispute, it can endeavor to take a comprehensive account of the harms and benefits that are likely to flow from a childhood within the parameters set out by that worldview. For example, in the *Quiner* case, the trial court needed to account not only for the relationships that would be forbidden to the child, but also for the depth and strength of the relationships that would be afforded by such a robust sense of community. In this regard, a parent who seeks to isolate her child from the outside world, but who does so based on her own idiosyncratic convictions of conscience rather than as part of a vibrant and nurturing community, should face a tougher task in court.[73] Conscience matters, but so do relationships, and when a court is faced with deciding which parent is better suited to raise the child, conscience exercised in a relational context deserves, for the well-being of the child, more deference.

A more solid ground for the *Quiner* court to grant custody to the father was the mother's stated intention to discourage the child's relationship with his father by portraying the father as an unclean outsider to be avoided. The relational dimension of conscience demands that courts take family relationships as a given, even in a custody dispute. The court is not distributing caretaking obligations and privileges among a set of rights-bearing individuals; the court is making necessary practical adjustments to the day-to-day arrangements that govern existing relationships. When one parent uses her relationship to threaten the viability of the other relationship, a court should consider such conduct in its analysis.[74] When the family is no longer a single moral community, state intervention may be unavoidable, but it should still be done with humility and restraint. Divorce does not justify state efforts to reconstruct the family as a moral community in the state's own image, nor to ignore the family's community status altogether by treating claimants as freestanding individuals in conflict. Absent readily discernible, serious harm to the child, relationships in the postdivorce family should be given the chance to embody the same coherent, formative moral experience as those in the predivorce family.

Biology versus the Family as Community

Understanding family as a given set of relationships, rather than as a group of rights-bearing individuals, also has implications for courts' handling of disputes between biology-based parental claimants and relationship-based parental claimants. In most states, men who are not married to the mother must do more than show paternity to gain parental rights; they must show some effort to establish a relationship with the child. This is as it should be. It can become more complicated in some cases, such as

---

[73] *Id.* at 977.
[74] Eugene Volokh, *Parent-Child Speech and Child Custody Speech Restrictions*, 81 N.Y.U. L. Rev. 631, 645 (2006) (asserting that parents in split families have First Amendment rights to speak freely to their children "except when the speech undermines the child's relationship with the other parent").

when the mother obstructs the father's efforts to establish a parent-child relationship or, as in one famous case, the biological father has established a relationship, but his claim threatens an existing family unit. In *Michael H. v. Gerald*, the Supreme Court rejected a biological father's claim of a constitutionally protected liberty interest in maintaining a relationship with his child. Carole and Gerald were married, but Carole had an adulterous affair with Michael, resulting in the birth of a child. Gerald was listed as the father on the birth certificate, but, for several years, Carole and the child lived with different men, including Michael. Carole and Gerald ultimately reconciled, had two more children, and the entire family lived together at the time of suit. California law established a presumption that the child of a wife living with her husband is the child of the marriage unless the husband or the wife challenges the presumption within two years of the birth. Because neither the husband nor the wife was willing to challenge the presumption, Michael had no way to establish his parental status under state law.[75]

Justice Scalia, writing for the plurality, observed that the Michael's claim was not the only liberty interest at stake, for "to provide protection to an adulterous natural father is to deny protection to a marital father, and vice versa."[76] Ultimately, the plurality held, "[i]t is a question of legislative policy and not constitutional law whether California will allow the presumed parenthood of a couple desiring to retain a child conceived within and born into their marriage to be rebutted."[77] This ruling, although widely ridiculed as being out of step with changing social norms of marriage and procreation, wisely resisted the urge to inject a framework of individual constitutional rights even more deeply into the family as community. Approaching parental disputes as a rights-driven scramble for the child by individual adults marginalizes the centrality of the family as community. This is not to say that rights are not relevant, just that rights are best embedded within the functioning family, not simply left to operate as freestanding weapons attached to biology. As Emily Buss puts it, "we should conceive of identity rights as a form of familial right, the right of the family to control its child-rearing structure free from state interference." Parental rights can be invoked as individual rights, but "the assignment of that right derives from family status."[78] Allowing the states to work through these conflicts was a prudent measure by the court. California, by deferring to existing family relationships, provided a workable model for a difficult situation.

Third Parties versus the Family as Community

Existing parent-child relationships also warrant deference against the claims of third parties, even when the family unit has dissolved. This principle was implicated in

---

[75] *Michael H. v. Gerald D.*, 491 U.S. 110 (1989).
[76] *Id.* at 130.
[77] *Id.* at 129–30.
[78] Emily Buss, *"Parental" Rights*, 88 Va. L. Rev. 635, 651–2 (2002).

Troxel v. Granville, a case in which the Supreme Court invalidated the application
of a state statute permitting any person to petition at any time for the right to visit a
child and authorizing courts to grant such rights when visitation "may serve the best
interests of the child." Justice O'Connor, writing for the plurality, observed that the
state court, in granting grandparents' visitation request over the parent's objection,
violated the traditional presumption that a parent will act in her child's best interests.
Accordingly, the state court failed to protect the parent's fundamental right to make
decisions concerning the rearing of her child. As Margaret Brinig explains, "with
families, outside involvement benefits everyone up to a point, the point at which the
third-party claims a legal right to be involved," and then at that point, "the balance
tips, and the greater the right to intrude claimed, the more devastating it is to the
family."[79]

    Troxel is an instance when the language of rights is a necessary measure to protect
family autonomy. On occasion, rights are the only means by which courts can
defend parents' natural authority to raise their children against well-intentioned
encroachment by the state. In this context, recognizing the right does not splinter
the family into individual rights bearers; it maintains the family's viability as a
meaningfully autonomous entity. And while a meaningful conception of "family"
can extend beyond the parents and children, embedding that conception in law is
problematic. Grandparents may have natural moral claims to a relationship with
their grandchildren, but once the dispute concerning that relationship reaches the
courtroom, it is no longer an intrafamily dispute; it is state power brought to bear
against parents' assessment of their children's best interests. As discussed previously,
parental rights cannot be absolute shields against state intervention, but absent
readily discernible and serious harm, they can and should function to protect the
parent-defined boundaries of the family community.

THE STATE'S CHANNELING FUNCTION

Because the family as a meaningful moral community presupposes a significant
degree of family autonomy, the state should intervene in family relationships rarely
and with the minimum possible disruption. This is not the limit of the state role,
however. Perhaps counterintuitively, the state's limited role within the family warrants the state taking an interest in the choices individuals make about the family
relationships they form (or do not form). Because there is no marketplace of families
from which children can choose and because the state cannot (and should not) take
on the role of child rearing for every family deemed deficient, for the most part
children either will get the caregiving they need within their family or they will not
get it at all. The state can promote family structures in which children are more
likely to get what they need. This "channeling" function by the state encourages

[79] Margaret F. Brinig, *Troxel and the Limits of Community*, 32 Rutgers L.J. 733, 735 (2001).

and facilitates the type of relationships that are most conducive to the sort of human flourishing that is consistent with our social natures and the common good.

Beyond Paternalism

To modern sensibilities, this rationale reeks of paternalism. One emerging strand in family law advocacy is for the state to get out of the channeling business entirely, especially as it pertains to consensual relationships between adults. Martha Fineman, for example, calls for the abolition of marriage as a legal category so that "[a]dult, voluntary sexual interactions would be of no concern to the state since there would no longer be a state-preferred model of family intimacy to protect and support," and "all such sexual relationships would be permitted – nothing prohibited, nothing privileged."[80] Elizabeth Emens insists that the "the existence of some number of people choosing to live polyamorous lives" should prompt us to rethink "the ways that our norms and laws urge upon us one model rather than pressing us to make informed, affirmative choices about what might best suit our needs and desires."[81] Others, such as Nancy Polikoff, "value equally all family forms and therefore want just social policies that facilitate maximum economic well-being and emotional flourishing for all, not only for those who marry."[82]

Consider the widely publicized 2006 statement, *Beyond Same-Sex Marriage*, from a variety of activists and scholars calling for the lesbian, gay, bisexual, and transgender community to stop focusing on same-sex marriage as a stand-alone issue. The problem, the statement asserts, is that the current debate obfuscates the need for marriage itself to be dislodged from its privileged position, to allow for the full possibility of caregiving arrangements to be valued equally:

> Our vision is the creation of communities in which we are encouraged to explore the widest range of non-exploitive, non-abusive possibilities in love, gender, desire and sex – and in the creation of new forms of constructed families without fear that this searching will potentially forfeit for us our right to be honored and valued within our communities and in the wider world. Many of us, too, across all identities, yearn for an end to repressive attempts to control our personal lives. [83]

Arrangements explicitly embraced by the statement include grandparents raising children, blended families, single-parent families, "households with more than one conjugal partner," and "queer couples who decide to jointly create and raise a child with another queer person or couple, in two households."[84] Mainstream media have

---

[80] Martha Fineman, *The Neutered Mother, the Sexual Family, and Other Twentieth Century Tragedies*, 229 (1995).

[81] Elizabeth F. Emens, "Just Monogamy?" in *Just Marriage*, 75, 79 (2004).

[82] Nancy D. Polikoff, *Ending Marriage as We Know It*, 32 Hofstra L. Rev. 201, 228 (2003).

[83] *Beyond Same-Sex Marriage: A New Strategic for All Our Families and Relationships* (2006) (available at www.beyondmarriage.org) (accessed Sep. 6, 2009).

[84] *Id.*

begun to take note of the movement to grant marriage-like legal recognition to nonconjugal relationships of the participants' choosing.[85]

These calls for state neutrality appeal, at one level, to the common good's bottom-up orientation. If conscience is formed and lived out in relationship, the state's privileging of certain relationships over others seems to challenge the very thesis of this book. As noted, however, a hands-off role by the state presumes a functioning market – for example, if only one pharmacy serves a rural area, requiring the pharmacy to offer the morning-after pill as a condition of licensing may be in order. There is no functioning market of families to the extent that vulnerable and dependent family members lack a viable (or, in some cases, any) exit option. Channeling may be appropriate.

Such channeling should support a vision of relationships that calls individuals to commit themselves to a self-transcendent good. Marriage is the leading example. As Milton Regan puts it, marriage "provides a distinct social form that expresses intimate commitment as an impersonal good, whose value transcends the mere fact that it is personally chosen."[86] It is not that marriage needs state support because it defies human nature; such commitments channel natural human functions such as sexual desire, affection, procreation, and child rearing into one institution. Don Browning explains that this integration, to remain stable, warrants "powerful social, legal, cultural, and religious reinforcements" in addition to the natural human inclinations.[87] The integration of these goods makes up the core family unit. Seen in this light, the family as moral community is not some arbitrary state creation; the state simply encourages and stabilizes the integration through a range of policy supports. The primary form of support, though, is not legal, but social. Family law reinforces institutions "which have significant social support and which, optimally, come to seem so natural that people use them almost unreflectively."[88]

The Need for Critical Discourse

But what if law simply reflects social norms that themselves embody injustice and the marginalization of dissenting voices of conscience? Unless the law shows a capacity to foster a critical discourse regarding prevailing social norms, the threat to conscience is real. The channeling function can only be defended in a society that values conscience if it is tailored to securing demonstrably better outcomes for family

---

[85] Rebecca Tuhus-Dubrow, *I Now Pronounce You . . . Friend and Friend*, Jun. 8, 2008, Boston Globe.

[86] Milton C. Regan, Jr., *Law, Marriage, and Intimate Commitment*, 9 Va. J. Soc. Pol'y & L. 116, 123–4 (2001).

[87] Don S. Browning, *Equality and the Family: A Fundamental, Practical Theology of Children, Mothers and Fathers*, 342 (2007).

[88] Carl E. Schneider, *The Channeling Function in Family Law*, 20 Hofstra L. Rev. 495, 504 (1992) (quoting Peter L. Berger and Thomas Luckmann, *The Social Construction of Reality: A Treatise in the Sociology of Knowledge*, 52 (1966)).

members who lack real marketplace choices. This does not mean that the law's channeling focus must be limited to encouraging committed parent-child relationships
standing alone; committed adult relationships are relevant to the caretaking that
occurs within the family. Linda McClain, for example, criticizes Martha Fineman's
proposal to abolish legal marriage and focus on caretaking-dependent relationships.
McClain points out that the proposal removes, and treats primarily as a matter of
private contract, "another valuable dimension of families: the intimate, committed
bonds between adults and the role that such relationships play in fostering goods
as well as interdependencies."[89] Adult relationships have obvious implications for
the well-being of children. A multitude of studies confirm that "the rise of unwed
parenting is not benign" for children,[90] and the relationships of cohabiting couples
are significantly less durable than those of married couples.[91] Don Browning contends that, without being moralistic, we need to recognize that intact, two-parent
families "have, on the whole, more emotional and material resources" for child
rearing,[92] and that "family pluralism has too often meant exempting men from their
responsibilities in raising children, leaving women to do the job."[93] One reason why
marriage is so important, and why the state has a legitimate interest in supporting it,
is its capacity "to channel males into recognizing their offspring as part of their own
being and hence lead them to invest in the care of their child as a continuation of
their existence."[94]

Opponents of same-sex marriage often contend that the state, in changing the
longstanding definition of marriage, is abdicating its channeling responsibility. One
interesting dynamic of the legal debate over same-sex marriage, however, is the
judiciary's use of certain social norms associated with marriage – caregiving, stability, commitment – to reflect critically on the law's embodiment of other social
norms associated with marriage – that is, limiting the institution of marriage to
heterosexual couples.[95] Judges upholding and overturning bans on same-sex marriage have embraced social narratives about marriage's function and purpose. They
take different views of marriage's malleability, but they are decidedly not neutral
about consensual adult relationships. Milton Regan, an advocate of same-sex marriage, nevertheless opposes the legal strategy of insisting that the state must defer to
the private ordering of intimate relationships. Instead, same-sex marriage advocates

---

[89] Linda C. McClain: *The Place of Families: Fostering Capacity, Equality and Responsibility*, 193 (2006).
[90] Margaret F. Brinig, *From Contract to Covenant: Beyond the Law and Economics of the Family*, 59
      (2000).
[91] See Regan, *supra* note 2, at 123.
[92] Statistics show that "the children of white single-parent families are two-and-a-half times more likely
      to be living in poverty [than] are the children in black two-parent families." Browning, *supra* note 87,
      at 69 (quoting William Galston).
[93] *Id.* at 57.
[94] Don S. Browning, *Linda McClain's The Place of Families and Contemporary Family Law: A Critique
      from Critical Familism*, 56 Emory L.J. 1383, 1395–6 (2007).
[95] Linda C. McClain, *Love, Marriage, and the Baby Carriage: Revisiting the Channelling Function of
      Family Law*, 28 Cardozo L. Rev. 2133, 2179 (2007).

should invite "an imaginative reconstruction of the traditional values promoted by marriage that supports legal recognition of same-sex relationships."[96] In the debate over changing social and legal norms, the focus should remain "on the importance of the family as an arena of relational responsibility," rather than "on individual privacy."[97]

The Limits of Channeling

The channeling function should not be misinterpreted as a justification for empowering the state to function as moral arbiter when it comes to adults' consensual relationships. Just as the state can signal its disagreement with racially discriminatory organizations without shutting them down, the state's support for certain types of relationship need not preclude tolerance for relationships that are not as conducive to the well-being of dependents. In other words, the state can encourage without foreclosing. Adults form intimate relationships that flout social and legal norms, and, just as state-privileged relationships do, these relationships produce instances of vulnerability and dependence. The state should approach these relationships as constitutive elements of their participants' identities, not as expressions of social deviance to be willed out of existence by state fiat (or disregard).

When possible, the state should support participants within a relationship specifically without creating incentives for the formation of such relationships categorically. When a type of relationship is less conducive to the stable commitments on which caregiving, especially child rearing, relies, legal support should flow more from contractual liberty than from any sort of privileged relational status. For example, courts have been wise to allow unmarried cohabitants to bring contractual and reliance-based claims against each other upon dissolution of the relationship.[98] Excluding nonmarital relationships from the enjoyment of general equitable principles would, as Milton Regan recognizes, "undermine the cultivation of relational identity by reinforcing the idea that by refusing to marry one can escape the responsibilities that flow from an intimate relationship."[99] Relationship-based claims to benefits from the state or third parties warrant different treatment than claims against one's partner. In the latter case, "the issue is not how the parties should act toward each other, but what kind of recognition the relationship should receive from those outside it."[100] The categories of relationships that the state encourages may change, of course, depending on our understanding of the connections between family structure and function.

The line between the state's categorical encouragement of certain relationships and the state's support of particular existing relationships will not always be clear.

[96] Regan, supra note 2, at 120.
[97] *Id.* at 122.
[98] See, e.g., *Marvin v. Marvin*, 557 P.2d 106 (Cal. 1976).
[99] Regan, *supra* note 2, at 124.
[100] *Id.* at 127.

Take the hotly contested matter of adoption by same-sex couples. Proponents of banning such adoptions warn that children's best interests should not be sacrificed in the service of equality for same-sex couples, and that society should not so quickly abandon the belief that children need a father and a mother for their optimal development. This argument wisely recognizes the community's interest in the well-being of children, particularly when the state is charged with placing children with adoptive parents. In these cases, the state is not being asked to interfere in an existing parent-child relationship; the state is creating the parent-child relationship. As such, identifying the criteria by which prospective adoptive parents will be approved is a prudent exercise of state power. Given the current state of knowledge, however, a categorical prohibition of adoption by same-sex couples may be pushing the law's channeling function too far, for two reasons.

First, in many cases, a legal prohibition on gay adoption amounts to a refusal to recognize parent-child relationships that already exist. Second-parent adoptions by the partner of a child's biological (and legal) parent are increasingly common. Their prohibition would not end the functional caregiving relationship between the parent's partner and the child, but it would foreclose the stabilizing and protective role that the law can play within the relationship.

Second, in cases in which there is no existing parent-child relationship, there is still a significant relational cost to a categorical prohibition. Bans on same-sex marriage, by comparison, may marginalize or stigmatize committed same-sex relationships between adults, but they do not preclude the existence of the relationships themselves. The law's power over adoption can function to preclude the very existence of parent-child relationships. Unless there is sound empirical evidence establishing that same-sex couples are less effective parents than heterosexual couples, or that not having both a mother and a father will have a negative impact on a child's psychological well-being, a legal ban on gay adoption stands in tension with the bottom-up orientation of conscience's relational dimension because it presumptively defines same-sex relationships as inherently unsuited to parental caregiving. The common good demands that the law not abandon its channeling function, but the cause of conscience demands that the function be exercised with restraint.

CONSCIENCE AND FAMILIES

One of the fathers from the Yearning for Zion ranch tried to convince reporters of the merits of the particularly insular moral community to which he had committed his children. He asked, "What honorable father and parent would not give their all to preserve their children from a traumatic, hostile to them, even abhorrent society?"[101] When those commitments entail, as they allegedly did at this ranch, the arranged "marriages" of multiple underage girls to a single older man, the father is

---

[101] David von Drehle, *The Sins of the Fathers*, May 5, 2008, Time, at 32.

hard-pressed to persuade many of his fellow citizens. But to what extent should that failure to persuade result in the loss of his and his wives' children? And why should we value the father's ideas of the good life over the daughter's ability to function as a member of modern society? This is the crux of the conscience problem when we leave the marketplace and enter the family.

The relational dimension of conscience holds different lessons here than virtually anywhere else. Their substantive differences, though, do not lessen their practical importance. Three lessons stand out:

First, the centrality of family to a person's moral identity suggests that the law should approach family relationships as a given part of the background against which the law operates, not as vehicles for the calculated defense and maximization of individual self-interest. The law's focus should be primarily on supporting the relationship, not on facilitating the exercise of individual autonomy within the relationship. If marriage is a commitment to a relational entity that is bigger than one's self, the spouse should not assume legal authority to break that commitment and return to his premarriage identity with the identical bundle of obligations and assets. The enforcement of prenuptial agreements should be limited to reflect the notion that some relational commitments are nonnegotiable. When it comes to the parent-child relationship, removal of the child and termination of parental rights are steps of last resort; every intermediate step of education, support, and supervision must be exhausted beforehand. Rhetoric matters here: The law should not endeavor to balance the individual interests of parents and child; the focus must be on ensuring the child's well-being within the family as community.

Second, state termination of the parent-child relationship should be limited to serious and readily discernible harm. Coercing sexual activity by girls who have not reached the minimum age that our society considers necessary for consent qualifies as such. Being part of a community that seeks to maintain a unique though widely despised way of life, shuns engagement with the outside world, and produces women who are presumed to exhibit "a limited cultural mentality" does not so qualify.[102] This is not to suggest that such upbringings are ideal to the realization of what most Americans would consider a life well-lived; it is, rather, to suggest that the state, if charged with the responsibility for ensuring the realization of lives well-lived, threatens more harm than good.

Finally, the state need not sit on the sidelines as a neutral bystander to the panoply of intimate adult relationships that appear and thrive or wither on the landscape. Because those relationships create situations of human vulnerability – chiefly among the children they produce – the state has a vital interest in supporting those that are demonstrably and favorably related to the well-being of dependents. If the state can show that polygamy is less conducive to the well-being of wives and children, the state can and should refuse to sanction polygamous marriage. But in a society

---

[102] See Mary Zeiss Stange, *What Does Texas Church Raid Say About Us?* May 12, 2008, USA Today, at 11A (reporting that a "tip sheet" given to state employees dealing with the case warned that mothers from the ranch may exhibit a limited cultural mentality).

that values conscience in its full relational dimension, a lack of state support should never be mistaken for a lack of state tolerance. The residents of the Yearning for Zion ranch may justifiably lose out on the array of benefits that flow through the institution of civil marriage, but – absent proof of physical or sexual abuse – they should not lose their children.

The stakes of family law are incredibly high. Children's physical care, emotional development, and moral formation proceed primarily through intimate relationships that are not of their own choosing, and a significant determinant of women's well-being has been marital relationships that were traditionally marked by pronounced (and legally supported) power disparities not easily escaped. In protecting vulnerable family members, though, the law must be careful to recognize – and remind society – that the family is not a set of disposable resources for individual fulfillment.[103] The family is a relational community that is bigger than the sum of its parts. In some ways, family is a remarkable embodiment of conscience's relational dimension, connecting us in self-transcendent and identify-forming ways even when those connections are not products of our own conscious choices.

---

[103] Robert Bellah, et al., *The Good Society*, 48 (1991).

10

The Legal Profession

In tracing the implications of conscience's relational dimension for law, this book has thus far focused on law's substance. But the law's substance is relevant only in so far as it applies to the real-world experiences of citizens, and the paths of application are not automated. Human gatekeepers – lawyers and judges – are at the heart of the rule of law. If we aim to figure out how law can best facilitate conscience's flourishing, we need to figure out how conscience should (or should not) shape the professional roles of those who provide access to the law. If our society's commitment to conscience demands that the law maintain space for marketplace participants to integrate moral claims with their provision of goods and services – as I have argued in the previous chapters – do different rules apply when the good or service in question is the law itself?

From much of the legal profession, the traditional answer has been an emphatic "yes!" The predominant view of the lawyer is as a common carrier, charged with maximizing the client's interests within the bounds of the law. The lawyer's own claims of conscience are a threat to the client's autonomy if introduced into the representation. Far from being a venue for conscience's flourishing, the attorney-client relationship tends to be portrayed as a technical venture in which the client's stated objectives are translated by the lawyer into legal strategy. The relationship between a lawyer and the law is akin to that between a photocopier and a technician; we need the technician to make it work, but it is not the technician's "concern whether the content of what is about to be copied is morally good or bad."[1]

Consider the infamous "torture memos." Even from an American public conditioned not to expect many signs of integrity from the legal profession, news that attorneys from the Department of Justice's Office of Legal Counsel (OLC) provided an aggressive legal analysis facilitating the torture of suspected terrorists unleashed a

---

[1] Stephen Pepper, *The Lawyer's Amoral Ethical Role: A Defense, A Problem, and Some Possibilities*, 1986 Am. B. Found. Res. J. 613, 624 (1986).

torrent of condemnation and hand wringing. Following closely on the heels of the photographs depicting abuse at Iraq's Abu Ghraib prison, a steady stream of leaked OLC memoranda painted a picture of government lawyers engaged in jurisprudential gymnastics in an effort to validate the sort of practices that had sparked worldwide revulsion. The White House eventually released many of the memoranda in hopes of minimizing the political fallout, but the attention to the conduct of the attorneys involved only intensified. Americans may have grown accustomed to tales of attorney dishonesty, self-aggrandizement, and incivility, but twisting the common-sense definition of torture and constructing blanket claims of immunity from international and domestic torture prohibitions struck many as beyond the pale.

The critics spanned the political spectrum, reflecting a remarkable degree of consensual outrage. The Senate was moved to reaffirm by acclamation that the United States "shall not engage in torture or cruel, inhuman or degrading treatment."[2] One journalist, having read the OLC's legal analysis of torture, compared it with "the advice of a mob lawyer to a mafia don on how to skirt the law and stay out of prison."[3] Other descriptions attached to the memoranda in question included "patently outrageous and un-American,"[4] a "shocking cover for cruel, inhuman and degrading treatment,"[5] and a "legal incantation to cover whatever misdeeds the leaders want to commit."[6] Even the White House disavowed the work of its own lawyers as the scandal intensified, labeling the more controversial of the memoranda "overbroad and irrelevant."[7]

Some lawyers, however, met the news with a dramatically different take. Charles Fried, for example, defended the OLC's work, asserting, "[t]here's nothing wrong with exploring any topic to find out what the legal requirements are."[8] A former deputy attorney general, George Terwilliger, expressed skepticism that "legal opinions have ever caused anyone any injury."[9] Eric Posner and Adrien Vermeule characterized the analysis as "standard lawyerly fare, routine stuff."[10] Other lawyers who did criticize the memoranda concerned themselves with the deficiencies of the legal analysis[11] or the more stringent ethical obligations presumably faced by

[2] Pauline Jelinek, *Senate Reaffirms U.S. Opposition to Torture*, Hous. Chron., Jun. 17, 2004, at 3.
[3] Anthony Lewis, *Making Torture Legal*, NY Rev. of Books, July 15, 2004.
[4] Stuart Taylor Jr., *How Bush's Overreaching Hurts the War Against Terrorism*, Nat'l J., July 3, 2004.
[5] Lincoln Caplan, *Lawyers' Standards in Free Fall*, L.A. Times, July 20, 2004, at B13.
[6] Ann Woolner, *Law Twisted to Justify Presidential Tolerance of Torture*, L.A. Bus. J., Jun. 21, 2004.
[7] Stephen Henderson et al, *Memos on Detainees Released*, Phila. Inquirer, Jun. 23, 2004, at A1.
[8] Adam Liptak, *Legal Scholars Criticize Memos on Torture*, N.Y. Times, Jun. 25, 2004, at A14.
[9] Vanessa Blum, *Culture of Yes: Signing Off On a Strategy*, Legal Times, Jun. 14, 2004, at 1.
[10] Eric Posner and Adrien Vermeule, *A 'Torture' Memo and Its Tortuous Critics*, Wall St. J., July 6, 2004, at A22.
[11] See, e.g., R. Jeffrey Smith, *Slim Legal Grounds for Torture Memos: Most Scholars Reject Broad View of Executive's Power*, Wash. Post, July 4, 2004, at A12; Adam Liptak, *Legal Scholars Criticize Memos on Torture*, N.Y. Times, Jun. 25, 2004, at A14; Kathleen Clark and Julie Mertus, *Torturing the Law: The Justice Department's Legal Contortions on Interrogation*, Wash. Post, Jun. 20, 2004, at B3.

government lawyers.[12] Even among critics, there was less of the moral condemnation that marked responses from outside the bar.[13]

This divergence is not attributable simply to a guild-like protectionist mentality or circling of the professional wagons, but rather reflects the fact that, for the most part, the legal profession lacks discernible moral resources with which to condemn the OLC attorneys, notwithstanding their perceived facilitation of torture. The dominant view of legal practice is founded on a purported demarcation between the legality and morality of a proposed course of conduct, with lawyers providing information on the former, but leaving the latter untouched, to be resolved only at the client's discretion. Those defending the OLC attorneys are quick to point out that they "were not asked for political or moral advice; they were asked about legal limits on interrogation," and accordingly "provided reasonable legal advice and no more."[14] It is immaterial, under this view, that the legal advice may have contributed to an environment in which repeated and blatant instances of prisoner abuse occurred.

This legality-morality demarcation complicates the role of conscience in the provision of legal services. In contrast to fields such as education, where moral claims are unavoidably on the table, the professional norms that have shaped a lawyer's understanding of her role suggest that moral claims can be separated from the advice for which she is paid. As such, figuring out what the relational dimension of conscience means for an attorney's provision of legal services requires us to figure out whether and how an attorney's conscience is, in the first place, even relevant to her provision of legal services. What role do moral claims play in the lawyer's work?

THE MORAL DIMENSION OF LEGAL ADVICE

John Yoo, a principal drafter of some of the more controversial OLC memoranda, defended his work as simply "an abstract analysis of the meaning of a treaty and a statute," and portrayed his critics as "confusing the difference between law and moral choice."[15] Yoo accurately reflects the modern attorney's understanding of her role, and therein lies the crux of the problem. To face Abu Ghraib and other manifestations of the amoral lawyering paradigm, we must talk freely about morality; specifically, we must allow – indeed, encourage – lawyers to talk about morality, even if they can only do so through claims that are grounded in their own consciences

---

[12] *See* Stephen Gillers, *Tortured Reasoning*, Am. Law., July 1, 2004; Vanessa Blum, *Culture of Yes: Signing Off On a Strategy*, Legal Times, Jun. 14, 2004, at 1.

[13] There are exceptions to this characterization, although it bears noting that perhaps the most pointed moral criticism of the memoranda from within the legal academy has come from legal ethics scholar David Luban, who is trained as a philosopher, not as a lawyer. See, e.g., David Luban, *Legal Ethics and Human Dignity*, 163 (2007) ("Torture is among the most fundamental affronts to human dignity, and hardly anything lawyers might do assaults human dignity more drastically than providing legal cover for torture and degradation.").

[14] Posner and Vermeule, *supra* note 10, at A22.

[15] Edward Alden, *US Interrogation Debate*, Fin. Times, Jun. 10, 2004, at 7.

and are not binding on – or perhaps even accessible to – the political community as a whole.

There is a rich moral dimension to legal advice, consisting not only of lawyers' own moral claims, but also their perception of their clients' moral claims and their understanding of the profession's moral claims. In light of the countervailing professional norms, the relational dimension of conscience operates more subtly within the attorney-client dialogue than in the pro-life pharmacy or environmentally conscious charter school. Nevertheless, its impact is unmistakable.

Lawyers' Personal Moral Claims

From the nineteenth-century exhortations of legal ethics pioneer David Hoffman[16] to the current pop culture provocations of Al Pacino,[17] the story of the legal profession has been told through the religious imagery of the priesthood.[18] Although this analogy carries a bit of rhetorical flourish, it reflects the widespread perception of the unifying, central role that the law plays in modern American society. Past eras may have looked to religion as the common framework under which everyday existence proceeds, but the law has long since usurped it. So although priests, as administrators providing access to that unifying framework in their role as mediators between God and man, were essential figures in the collective life of society, today their place has been taken by lawyers, who provide access to our common framework of legal rights and privileges.

There is another, more subtle perception underlying the priesthood analogy. The consistent emphasis on the thoroughly secular nature of the lawyer-as-priest carries certain implications for the identity of the modern American lawyer. That is, the imagery of the priesthood not only connotes something about the centrality of the law, but also about the fungibility of lawyers. In the Judeo-Christian tradition, the priest is the primary means by which the faithful access the rites and sacraments of the religious community. This access is not to be a function of a particular priest's

---

[16] David Hoffman, *Resolutions in Regard to Professional Deportment*, Resolution 15 (1836) (referring to lawyers as "ministers at a holy altar"), quoted in Thomas Shaffer, *On Being a Christian and a Lawyer*, 61 (1981).

[17] Playing the role of Satan in the guise of a managing partner at a big New York law firm in the movie "Devil's Advocate," Pacino bragged to an underling that lawyers are "the new priesthood, baby." Rebecca Porter, *Lawyers on the Big Screen*, 38 Trial 54, 56 (Mar. 2002).

[18] See, e.g., Harold J. Berman, *Faith and Order: The Reconciliation of Law and Religion*, 351 (1993) ("In the Western political tradition, and especially in that of the United States, the legal profession constitutes a secular priesthood."); David T. Johnson, *American Law in Japanese Perspective*, 28 Law & Soc. Inquiry 771, 790 (2003) (noting analogy that "law is our national religion; lawyers constitute our priesthood; the courtroom is our cathedral, where contemporary passion plays are enacted"); Kay L. Levine, *Negotiating the Boundaries of Crime and Culture: A Sociolegal Perspective on Cultural Defense Strategies*, 28 Law & Soc. Inquiry 39, 40 (2003) (same); Lawrence J. Fox, *Accountants, the Hawks of the Professional World*, 84 Minn. L. Rev. 1097 (2000) (concluding that lawyers "indeed . . . are a priesthood").

personality, feelings toward the community member, or misgivings about the rite at issue. Although a priest's performance of his duties is affected by his own individual gifts or shortcomings, the access is to remain untrammeled and unadulterated by the priest's personal opinions or foibles. The priest is not to detract or distract from the experience of the divine, but should simply facilitate the experience within the bounds established by his community's faith tradition.

Similarly, the lawyer as priest is a gatekeeper, an agent who provides access to the law – access unfettered by the lawyer's personal affiliations, motivations, or world-views. The lawyer, in providing such access, is constrained by the law, but not by any perceived need to reconcile her own conscience or personal values with the client or the client's cause. As the Model Code of Professional Responsibility provides, clients are "entitled to . . . seek any lawful objective through legally permissible means."[19] The lawyer as priest is an "amoral technician,"[20] aiming not to inject her own vision of the good into the representation, but simply to pursue the client's vision of the good through the maximization of the client's legal rights. Whether or not the OLC attorneys find the torture of suspected terrorists to be abhorrent is irrelevant, as reflected in the Model Rules of Professional Conduct's admonition that representation of a client does not constitute an endorsement of the client's morality,[21] and in the Rules' suggestion that an attorney should defer to her client's views on whether potential harm to third parties warrants rethinking the means or ends of the representation.[22] Stephen Pepper's view nicely captures the paradigm's essence: "For access to the law to be filtered unequally through the disparate moral views of each individual's lawyer does not appear to be justifiable."[23]

Resistance to this amoral lawyering paradigm is evidenced in part by the tension between the compulsions of conscience and the compulsions of the profession. The tension is unmistakable when a state ethics board, in requiring a devout Christian lawyer to represent a minor seeking an abortion without parental consent, reasons that religious beliefs are not a legitimate basis for declining a court appointment.[24] It is also unmistakable when a lawyer who opposes capital punishment is faced with a death row client who wishes to forego all court challenges to the imposition of his

---

[19] Model Code of Prof'l Resp. EC 7–1 (1969).
[20] Richard Wasserstrom, *Lawyers as Professionals: Some Moral Issues*, 5 Human Rights 1, 5–6 (1975).
[21] Model Rules of Prof'l Conduct R. 1.2(b) (2009) ("A lawyer's representation of a client, including representation by appointment, does not constitute an endorsement of the client's political, economic, social or moral views or activities.").
[22] *Id.* cmt. 2 (explaining that "lawyers usually defer to the client regarding such questions as . . . concern for third persons who might be adversely affected").
[23] Stephen Pepper, *The Lawyer's Amoral Ethical Role: A Defense, A Problem, and Some Possibilities*, 1986 Am. B. Found. Res. J. 613 (1986).
[24] See Bd. of Prof'l Responsibility of the Sup. Ct. of Tenn., Formal Op. 96-F-140 (1996) (requiring Catholic lawyer to proceed with a court appointment in such a case despite his religiously grounded objection); see also Teresa Stanton Collett, *Professional Versus Moral Duty: Accepting Appointments in Unjust Civil Cases*, 32 Wake Forest L. Rev. 635 (1997) (discussing case).

sentence,[25] when a Muslim litigator is expected to make an opposing witness look like a liar on the stand, even if she believes that the witness is testifying truthfully,[26] or when a lawyer whose conscience compels her to stand up for the oppressed is told by her client to initiate eviction proceedings against low-income tenants who lack alternative shelter.[27] On a broader stage, the tension is unmistakable when the leader of the Catholic Church seems to suggest publicly that Catholic divorce lawyers can remain Catholic or can remain divorce lawyers, but they cannot persist in both identities.[28]

Beyond the sense of personal incoherence it spawns, the resistance to bringing lawyers' own moral convictions into the attorney-client dialogue is especially problematic given that such convictions are often part of that dialogue, whether acknowledged by the attorney or not. Whenever an attorney makes sense of her client's stated intentions, she utilizes an interpretive judgment that is shaped by the attorney's own moral experience, and this same experience, in turn, helps form whatever response the attorney offers to the client. When the response is pitched in exclusively legal terms – as was the OLC's torture analysis – the moral component is not erased, but rather is forced into the background, where it is not susceptible to exploration by the client. As such, the lawyer's interpretive morality is neither challenged nor endorsed by the client; it simply holds sway over the course of representation, albeit implicitly. While the amorality of legal advice is a fiction, it is not a harmless fiction because it facilitates the tendency of clients to equate legality with permissibility.

Especially in cases in which the law is indeterminate, an attorney's conscience will often shape the advice she gives, and clients will be better off if the attorney's moral perspective is articulated openly and deliberately instead of being left to operate beneath the surface of the attorney-client dialogue. Consider the most infamous of the "torture memoranda," an August 2002 memo written by John Yoo setting forth the OLC's "views regarding the standards of conduct under the Convention Against Torture and Other Cruel, Inhuman and Degrading Treatment or Punishment." The Convention's implementing statute provides that pain or suffering must be

---

[25] See Richard W. Garnett, *Sectarian Reflections on Lawyers' Ethics and Death-Row Volunteers*, 77 Notre Dame L. Rev. 795 (2002).

[26] *See* Azizah Y. Al-Hibri, *Faith and the Attorney-Client Relationship: A Muslim Perspective*, 66 Fordham L. Rev. 1131, 1136 (1998) (highlighting Muslim lawyer's difficulty functioning in "a legal system where the lawyer's loyalty is viewed as belonging to the client," especially in light of Qur'anic injunctions "to be just" and "not to suppress testimony because it may harm one's own interest").

[27] For a broader discussion of this example, see Robert K. Vischer, *Faith, Pluralism and the Practice of Law*, 49 Cath. Law. 1 (2004).

[28] Pope John Paul II cautioned that Catholic lawyers "must always decline the use of their profession for an end that is counter to justice, like divorce." David O'Reilly, *Pope's Words Unsettle Catholic Lawyers*, Phil. Inquirer, Feb. 3, 2002, at B05. Some observers contend that the Pope did not intend to foreclose a role for Catholic lawyers in situations of inevitable family breakdown, but rather that Catholic lawyers should not use their professional tools as instruments for further breakdown or exacerbation of conflict. Thanks to Amy Uelmen for raising this point.

"severe" to constitute torture, but does not define the term.[29] Based on the dictionary definition, Yoo concludes that, "the adjective 'severe' conveys that the pain or suffering must be of such a high level of intensity that the pain is difficult for the subject to endure."[30] Certainly this understanding makes sense, for the subject's difficulty enduring the pain inflicted is the whole point of torture – coercing the subject to provide information because he is unable to endure the pain.

The linking of torture with the ability to endure, however, potentially encompasses any interrogation technique premised on physical pain, and Yoo does not allow this conception to stand. Invoking the legal principle that courts construe statutory terms "to contain that permissible meaning which fits most logically and comfortably into the body of both previously and subsequently enacted law,"[31] Yoo looks to the use of the term "severe pain" in statutes "defining an emergency medical condition for the purposes of providing health benefits."[32] The language he looks to – and on which the memorandum's ultimate narrow conception of torture is based – defines an emergency condition as one

> manifesting itself by acute symptoms of sufficient severity (including *severe pain*) such that a prudent lay person, who possesses an average knowledge of health and medicine, could reasonably expect the absence of immediate medical attention to result in – placing the health of the individual . . . (i) in serious jeopardy, (ii) serious impairment to bodily functions, or (iii) serious dysfunction of any bodily organ or part.[33]

The statute does not purport to define "severe pain;" the statute provides that severe pain is one type of symptom that *might* lead a person to believe that her health was in serious jeopardy, her bodily functions would be seriously impaired, or an organ would suffer serious dysfunction. Other symptoms, the language implies, might also lead a person to such a belief. Nevertheless, Yoo decides to *equate* severe pain with the three conditions, extracting from the quoted language the conclusion that "severe pain," as used in the entirely unrelated torture statute, must rise to "the level that would ordinarily be associated with a sufficiently serious physical condition or injury such as death, organ failure, or serious impairment of bodily functions – in order to constitute torture."[34] Plainly, this conclusion was not driven exclusively by the settled meaning of governing legal directives.

[29] Memorandum from Jay S. Bybee, Assistant Attorney General, to White House Counsel Alberto Gonzales, Aug. 1, 2002, at 5 (available at http://www.washingtonpost.com/wp-srv/politics/documents/cheney/torture_memo_aug2002.pdf) (accessed Feb. 12, 2009). See also Michael Hirsch, et al., *A Tortured Debate*, Newsweek, Jun. 21, 2004 (reporting that John Yoo drafted the Bybee memorandum).
[30] *Id.*
[31] *Id.* (quoting *West Va. Univ. Hosps., Inc. v. Casey*, 499 U.S. 83, 100 (1991)).
[32] *Id.*
[33] *Id.* at 6 (quoting 18 U.S.C. § 1395w-22(d)(3)(B)).
[34] *Id.*

Having opened up a broad range of interrogation approaches designed to inflict physical pain, Yoo turns to mental pain and suffering. He concludes that for "purely mental pain or suffering to amount to torture under Section 2340, it must result in significant psychological harm of significant duration, e.g., lasting for months or even years."[35] This follows, in Yoo's estimation, from the statute's requirement that for "severe mental pain or suffering" to qualify as torture, it must be "prolonged mental harm."[36] The phrase "prolonged mental harm" is not defined, nor does it appear elsewhere in the U.S. Code, in relevant medical literature, or in international human rights reports.[37] The dictionary definition of "prolong" – to "lengthen in time" or to "extend the duration of, to draw out" – gives little temporal insight,[38] so Yoo strikes out on his own.

Without any supporting citation, Yoo opines that "the mental strain experienced by an individual during a lengthy and intense interrogation – such as one that state or local police might conduct upon a criminal suspect – would not" qualify as prolonged harm.[39] By contrast, "the development of a mental disorder such as posttraumatic stress disorder, which can last months or even years, or even chronic depression, which also can last for a considerable period of time if untreated, *might* satisfy the prolonged harm requirement."[40] He cites medical literature on posttraumatic stress disorder, as well as two sources noting that torture victims frequently suffer from posttraumatic stress disorder, but no sources suggesting that prolonged harm must last months or years, not days. Nevertheless, Yoo provides the White House with the conclusion that the deliberate infliction of mental pain or suffering will not qualify as torture unless it results in "long-term mental harm,"[41] understood as "significant psychological harm of significant duration, e.g., lasting for months or even years."[42] The temporal aspect of this conclusion is entirely of Yoo's creation.

In the memorandum's concluding section, Yoo offers a partial glimpse into the moral convictions that may have driven his analysis of these indeterminate legal directives. Put simply, he appears to view the prospect of harm inflicted by torture through the lens of utilitarian morality. On the assumption that the torture statute could apply constitutionally to the interrogation of suspected al Qaeda members, Yoo explores the availability of the necessity defense, noting that it "can justify the intentional killing of one person to save two others."[43] In, perhaps, the most morally laden statement of the memorandum, he asserts: "Clearly, any harm that might

---

[35] *Id.*
[36] *Id.* (quoting 18 U.S.C. § 2340(2)).
[37] *Id.*
[38] *Id.* at 7 (quoting Webster's Third International Dictionary).
[39] *Id.*
[40] *Id.* (emphasis added).
[41] *Id.* at 13.
[42] *Id.* at 1.
[43] *Id.* at 40.

occur during an interrogation would pale to *insignificance* compared to the harm avoided by preventing such an attack, which could take hundreds or thousands of lives."[44] Exploring the legal defense of necessity and its potential applicability to a situation is one thing; labeling as insignificant any possible harm that might be inflicted on an individual to extract information that would avert a terrorist attack is quite another. As we have seen, the memorandum is replete with normative assertions founded in unarticulated beliefs that have very little to do with law; this statement is the closest we have to an articulation of those beliefs, albeit framed as the straightforward application of black-letter legal standards.

If Yoo had acted on the opportunity for moral engagement with his client, the Bush administration would have been led to view the issue, at least in passing, through moral terms, not just through the narrowing, obfuscating lens of purportedly strict legal analysis. Further, perhaps Yoo would have been led to couch his advice with less legal certainty and bright-line pronouncements once he took stock of the role played by his own underlying moral convictions. As it stood, Yoo's moral understanding of the war against terrorism appears to have shaped his analysis without ever being acknowledged and engaged as such. Instead, the language of law drove the inquiry, as evidenced by Alberto Gonzales' testimony at the Senate hearing weighing his nomination to become Attorney General. On the subject of the torture memorandum, Gonzales remarked that he did not "have a disagreement with the conclusions reached" in the memorandum at the time it was written because it is ultimately "the responsibility of the [OLC] to tell us what the law means."[45]

The unspoken and unexamined moral impetus of Yoo's torture analysis is not some anomaly, out of step with other lawyers' ability to maintain a sharp morality-legality demarcation in the advice they give. In cases in which the law bears any significant degree of indeterminacy as applied to a given set of facts, the attorney's interpretive judgment will often emerge from the attorney's own deeply held moral claims. Most lawyers are not advising the White House about torture, but their consciences may implicitly shape the advice they give in a variety of routine scenarios, ranging from determining whether a home seller must return the down payment to a purchaser who lost his job and thus cannot proceed with the transaction, to advising a company whether to close a plant in a small town that is economically dependent on the company for jobs, to the drafting of a will for a client who is estranged from her children, to plea bargain negotiations, to custody disputes, to interpreting a litigation opponent's requests for sensitive documents.

Lawyers' discomfort with discussing moral considerations may tempt them to maintain the efficacy of their moral convictions by conforming the legal advice to those convictions. Even in cases in which the law is clear, the inaccessibility of

[44] *Id.* at 41 (emphasis added).
[45] *See* Eric Lichtblau, *Gonzales Speaks Against Torture During Hearing*, N.Y. Times, Jan. 7, 2005, at A1.

legal knowledge to nonlawyers – that is, the ease with which lawyers can cloud the legal-moral distinction without detection by their clients – makes morally engaged lawyering a potential threat to client autonomy. One way to counter that threat is to encourage lawyers to bring the moral dimension into the open, unpacking relevant moral considerations for the client's own decision making.

Imagine that Yoo had raised explicitly in the memorandum his own conscience-shaped presumptions toward the prospect of sacrificing suspected terrorists' lives or bodily integrity in exchange for a reduced possibility of another deadly attack on the United States. Imagine that he then embarked on a series of questions – ideally face-to-face, but on paper as a fallback – pressing White House and CIA officials on whether they shared his moral presumptions, and to what degree they did so. Whether consisting of fact-specific hypotheticals or posited abstract formulations of moral permissibility, Yoo would frame the inquiry so as to remain open to a range of responses and communicated ideals. Through the questions and their stated premises, Yoo would have brought the moral presumptions on which his "legal" recommendations were based to the surface, all the while maintaining appropriate respect for the client-directed nature of his services.

Legal advice, at its heart, requires the attorney to connect ends and means; this cannot be done in a vacuum, but is shaped inexorably by the decision maker's own past experiences. An attorney asked to explore potential measures by which the government may permissibly seek to gain information from suspected terrorists will necessarily fall back on her own experience. Crucially, the attorney's past experience is not readily segregated based on legal versus moral relevance. Even if the attorney, for example, concludes that the text of an applicable statute does not, on its face, foreclose the government's physical abuse of an individual during interrogation, the text of that statute will not be the only source of meaning that speaks to the attorney's exploration of the issue. If she has spent time reading about Nazi Germany, or representing victims of spousal abuse, or suffering through the agonies of a family member in the throes of a painful illness, her experiences will bear powerful witness to her project. They undoubtedly will have less impact on her recommendations than the text of the statute, but that is only because the attorney has trained herself to filter such experiences out of her analysis – or at least trained herself to believe that such experiences can be filtered out.

Seen in this light, the debate over whether an attorney should bring her personal moral convictions into the attorney-client relationship is moot: Such morality inexorably plays a role as a component of the identity-shaping tradition in which every attorney finds herself. Put simply, in the process of knowing, the "knower's own being is involved."[46] The attorney's choice is whether to allow the client to grasp the impact that the attorney's "own being" has had on the representation.

---

[46] Hans-George Gadamer, *Truth and Method*, 447 (1975).

Lawyers' Reflective Moral Claims

What if Yoo's utilitarian analysis emanated not so much from his own conscience, but from his own moral claims about the primacy of his client's moral claims? That is, what if the torture memo reflects his perception of what the Bush administration's moral convictions were? If so, the need for explicit moral engagement remains stark. If, for example, Yoo presumed that the administration embraced a utilitarian approach to the interrogation of suspected terrorists, making this presumption explicit would have strengthened the quality of the attorney-client dialogue in three potential ways. First, by explaining his perception of the administration's moral perspective, Yoo would have given the administration an opportunity to rectify any errors in that perception. Second, the disclosure could have cued the administration that Yoo's legal reasoning was a function, in part, of the administration's utilitarian moral premise, rather than a straightforward explication of settled law. Third, by setting forth his moral perception, Yoo would have forced the administration to face the content of the moral claims embodied in its policies.

An attorney's *reflective* moral perspective – that is, decision making derived from what she perceives to be her client's moral perspective – embodies a judgment as to what the client's moral claims actually are, and a tacit concession, if the perception is not articulated for the client's benefit, that those claims are not amenable to engagement through moral dialogue. Especially in cases in which the governing legal directives are ambiguous or otherwise indeterminate, attorneys become tools for facilitating morally problematic conduct, even in contexts in which the client may not have deliberately embraced the moral claims embodied therein or where the client would have benefited from being pressed on the wisdom of those claims.

One prime example of this is the demise of Enron. Lawyers from Vinson & Elkins were so enmeshed in Enron's management culture that their legal advice became tailored to supporting the maximization of share price, to the exclusion of other considerations more in keeping with the company's long-term interests. The moral content of this legal strategy remained beneath the surface – there is no indication that Enron's managers were made to face the moral implications of the lawyers' manipulation of governing law. Whether or not the managers would have embraced or disavowed the moral dimension of the legal strategy, they should have been brought to such a point of decision through a meaningful moral dialogue with their attorneys.

Enron used off-balance sheet partnerships to enter into transactions deemed too risky for ordinary commercial entities.[47] Because these partnerships were not consolidated with Enron's other activities on its financial statements, Enron's losses and debts were kept hidden from public disclosure.[48] This system began to unravel

---

[47] Deborah L. Rhode and Paul D. Paton, *Lawyers, Ethics, and Enron*, 8 Stan. J. L. Bus. & Fin. 9, 13 (2002).

[48] *Id.*

throughout 2001, as the partnerships experienced credit problems and could not make payments to Enron.[49] In November 2001, Enron announced that it had failed to account properly for its transactions with certain partnerships, requiring the company to revise its financial statements for the years 1997 through 2001.[50] Enron also disclosed that certain employees had profited from these transactions and that these profits had not been previously disclosed.[51] The company's stock price plummeted, and on December 2, 2001, Enron became the largest bankruptcy filing (at that time) in American history.[52]

Theories abound as to the root causes of the Enron debacle. Every colorable explanation, however, implicates Enron's lawyers as having failed to provide a needed check on the self-aggrandizing transgressions of Enron's management. There is little doubt that "Enron sought and received professional advice that reassured Enron's management that its strategies legally could be realized."[53] Lawyers wrote opinions certifying loan transactions as "true sales,"[54] provided nonsensical justifications for the CFO who wished to avoid disclosure of his compensation,[55] complied with the CEO's request that they not explore the accountants' treatment of transactions before certifying the transactions' validity,[56] and "repeatedly facilitated Enron's strategy of structuring dubious transactions so that nobody could understand them, by using language to describe them in proxy and financial statements that, although literally and technically correct, was in practice completely opaque."[57] At bottom, lawyers were "the but-for cause" of Enron's demise because the transactions at issue "could not have closed in their original form" without their participation.[58]

This uncritical adoption of the managers' perspective precluded Enron's lawyers from exercising a vital function of the legal profession: articulating limits grounded in public norms beyond which the client's pursuit of self-interest will not be permitted.[59] Especially in contexts in which public norms are ambiguous or malleable, this articulation can be compromised because it becomes easier for the lawyer to lose her grounding in the public norms and gravitate toward the client's self-defined norms. This elevation of client norms to the status of dispositive norms likely resulted from a combination of factors. First, it may have been difficult for the lawyers at Enron's primary outside law firm, Vinson & Elkins, to distinguish between

[49] *Id.* at 16.
[50] David A. Westbrook, *Corporation Law After Enron: The Possibility of a Capitalist Reimagination*, 92 Geo. L.J. 61, 64 (2003).
[51] *Id.*
[52] *Id.*
[53] *Id.* at 98.
[54] Robert W. Gordon, *A New Role for Lawyers? The Corporate Counselor After Enron*, 35 Conn. L. Rev. 1186 (2003).
[55] *Id.* at 1187.
[56] *Id.*
[57] *Id.* at 1186.
[58] W. Bradley Wendel, *Professionalism as Interpretation*, 99 Nw. L. Rev. 1167, 1167 (2005).
[59] Westbrook, *supra* note 50, at 120.

client and colleague: At the time of the collapse, Enron's general counsel and deputy general counsel were former Vinson & Elkins partners, and another twenty lawyers from the firm had jumped to Enron since 1991.[60] In a real sense, when the outside lawyers sat down to talk to Enron, they saw themselves staring back. Second, Enron's lawyers may have been lulled into complacency by the seeming unified and uncontroversial interests of the corporate constituents. When managers, directors, and shareholders alike appeared devoted to the same conception of self-interest (the maximization of share price), it became far too tempting to employ the indeterminacy of the governing public norms as a tool by which to facilitate the unbounded pursuit of that self-interest. Third, under the prevailing investor euphoria of the 1990s, naysayers – whether stock analysts, accountants, or lawyers – were largely ignored. Consequently, the competitive environment among professionals served to intensify the allure of acquiescence to the client's perspective of unchecked optimism, leading Vinson & Elkins lawyers to occupy a position characterized by critics as the Enron CFO's "own personal vassals."[61]

Make no mistake, Enron's demise is a tale steeped in moral claims. The transactions on which Enron's skyrocketing share price was built were made possible only by the distinct acts and omissions of the company's managers, directors, accountants, and lawyers. The creation and treatment of these transactions constituted an unmistakable moral perspective, which holds that profit trumps principle, that public perception of profit is a matter for advocacy and manipulation, that the corporation's only duty to its shareholders is the maximization of share price, and that the corporation owes no duties to the public at large whatsoever. This perspective is helpfully illustrated by a former Enron employee's infamous explanation of the company's approach to the governing rules:

> Say you have a dog, but you need to create a duck on the financial statements. Fortunately, there are specific accounting rules for what constitutes a duck: yellow feet, white covering, orange beak. So you take the dog and paint its feet yellow and its fur white and you paste an orange plastic beak on its nose, and then you say to our accountants, "This is a duck! Don't you agree that it's a duck?" And the accountants say, "Yes, according to the rules, this is a duck." Everybody knows that it's a dog, not a duck, but that doesn't matter, because you've met the rule for calling it a duck.[62]

This is not to suggest that there is some fixed, objectively ascertainable set of moral claims for lawyers to substitute in place of those that called a dog a duck, and

[60] Rhode and Paton, *supra* note 47, at 25.
[61] *See* Gordon, *supra* note 54, at 1187; Rhode and Paton, *supra* note 47, at 26 ("Increased competition from within and outside the bar has led to increased pressure on firms to favor responsiveness to client demands over broader societal concerns.").
[62] Bethany McLean and Peter Elkind, *The Smartest Guys in the Room: The Amazing Rise and Scandalous Fall of Enron*, 142–3 (2003) (quoting unidentified former Enron employee), *quoted in* Wendel, *supra* note 58, at 1171.

that held sway over Enron's demise. Ameliorative moral claims are fluid, plural, and best discovered through dialogue, not unilateral imposition. The failure of Enron's lawyers is not that they failed to interject the "correct" moral perspective, but that they acted on their perception of the client's moral perspective without engaging in the moral dialogue necessary to confirm that perception, much less challenge it. In acting on their perception of the client's norms, Enron's lawyers were deeply immersed in a moral endeavor, implicating not only the client's moral claims, but also their own. Facilitating the transformation of an actual dog into a fictional duck is not a value-free exercise; pretending otherwise is a delusion made possible by the amoral lawyering paradigm. The exercise implicates the moral perspective of the client who wishes the facilitation as well as that of the lawyers who accomplish it. The exercise begs for its moral components to be brought to the surface.

Lawyers' Professional Moral Claims

In many cases, legal advice is shaped by a set of moral claims that originate with neither the attorney nor the client. An attorney's *professional* moral perspective entails decision making derived from moral claims embedded in the legal profession's adversarial tradition. The lawyer generally is not speaking as an independent, rational agent, but as a product of a professional ideology that has pushed her to emphasize qualities such as secrecy, defensiveness, and rights maximization, and to minimize qualities such as compassion, vulnerability, and risk taking.

A telling example of the professional moral perspective's impact is the Catholic Church's legal response to the priest sex abuse scandal. Reliance on lawyers contributed to the church's utter failure to exercise its duties of pastoral care toward the victims, opting instead for secrecy, discovery stonewalling, hardball litigation tactics, and prohibitions on apologies or other conciliatory acts that could be construed as admissions. Instead of building a legal strategy around the particular functions and responsibilities of the client, too often the church's lawyers build a legal strategy around the presumptions of the legal profession. Integrating the profession's adversarial mindset with the church's defense should only have been undertaken after a full and frank conversation regarding the implications of that integration. Bringing the profession's moral perspective to bear on the client's case or cause presupposes a moral dialogue.

Since early 2002, the Catholic Church in the United States has been enveloped by the revelations of priests' sexual abuse of minors. The fallout was magnified by the disclosure of evidence that church leaders facilitated the abuse by relocating accused perpetrators and shrouding the incidents in secrecy. These personal and institutional failures are familiar to anyone exposed to the blanket media coverage afforded the scandal. For present purposes, however, the needed insight can be gained not by rehashing the many omissions of the bishops, but the omissions of the bishops' lawyers.

The United States Conference of Catholic Bishops commissioned a review board composed of lay Catholics to evaluate the "causes and context" of the clergy abuse crisis.[63] In cataloguing the failures of the church's response to abuse allegations, one entire section of the report was devoted to "Reliance on Attorneys."[64] In short, the review board faulted the bishops for adopting the presumptions and prejudices of their legal counsel in their effort to minimize the impact of the allegations. The report provides a clear example of attorneys bringing the moral perspective of their professional tradition to bear on the representation without allowing the client to engage, much less challenge, that moral perspective on its terms.

The review board's attorney-related criticisms are readily classifiable into three broad groups. First, several of the criticisms are indicative of an overly aggressive legal posture toward the victims. These include assertions that the church's lawyers raised "inappropriate defenses that could be construed as blaming the victim, such as assumption of risk or contributory negligence," and disclaimed "responsibility for . . . priests by claiming that they were 'independent contractors.'"[65] In other cases, lawyers for the church forced plaintiffs who wished to remain anonymous to reveal their identities publicly in bringing litigation;[66] sought to depose the therapist the church had hired to help abuse victims, notwithstanding the therapist's insistence that she was hired with the understanding that her communications with the victims would remain confidential;[67] demanded that a victim present himself without an attorney for questioning by church officials if he wished to have his request that a priest be defrocked considered (a demand quickly disavowed by church officials themselves);[68] and filed countersuits accusing victims' parents of negligence for entrusting their children to priests.[69]

A second set of criticisms suggests defensive tactics that directly precluded the church's exercise of pastoral care of the victims. According to the review board, many of the church's attorneys "counseled Church leaders not to meet with, or apologize to, victims even when the allegations had been substantiated on grounds that apologies could be used against the Church in court."[70] In the words of one bishop:

> We made terrible mistakes. Because the attorneys said over and over "Don't talk to the victims, don't go near them," and here they were victims. I heard victims say

---

[63] The National Review Board for the Protection of Children and Young People, *A Report on the Crisis in the Catholic Church in the United States* 1 (Feb. 27, 2004) (available at http://www.usccb.org/nrb/nrbstudy/nrbreport.pdf) (accessed Feb. 12, 2009) ["Review Board"].

[64] *Id.* at 119.

[65] *Id.* at 120.

[66] Michael Paulson and Michael Rezendes, *Openness of Bishops Still at Issue*, Boston Globe, Jun. 17, 2003, at A1.

[67] Ralph Ranalli, *Clergy Abuse Settlement Seen Unlikely*, Boston Globe, May 19, 2003, at A1.

[68] *Id.*

[69] Michael Powell and Lois Romano, *Roman Catholic Church Shifts Legal Strategy*, Wash. Post, May 13, 2002, at A1.

[70] Review Board, *supra* note 63, at 121.

"We would not have taken it to [plaintiffs' attorneys] had someone just come to us and said 'I'm sorry.'" But we listened to the attorneys.[71]

Finally, certain criticisms focus on the systemic impact resulting from the lawyers' adoption of a fractured, secrecy-driven approach to the allegations. When cases settled, lawyers frequently recommended that the victims sign confidentiality agreements as a prerequisite to settlement. In the review board's estimation, these agreements stifled victims' "ability to discuss their experience openly and thwarted awareness by the laity of the problem."[72] The climate of secrecy was also maintained through a range of hard-hitting discovery tactics.[73] Even when the church released records of complaints against certain priests, the church steadfastly resisted releasing information regarding the church's handling of the complaints,[74] drawing judicial accusations of "sandbagging" plaintiffs' lawyers in seeking to delay key depositions on the subject.[75] A Connecticut judge accused church lawyers of inappropriately blocking the release of court documents, adding that the court would "not be a party to a cover up."[76]

Were the church's lawyers acting out of loyalty to their client or out of loyalty to the profession's adversarial ideals? The lawyers were understandably concerned about their client's financial well-being, particularly in light of the aggressive arguments by plaintiffs' lawyers to lift the statutes of limitations, for example. Compare the values and priorities of the church's litigators with those of the church's canon lawyers – the lawyers charged with interpreting and enforcing the church's own legal code. The objectives of canon law are starkly different from those of the civil law, but it is nevertheless telling that canon lawyers are indeed held to "abstract moral standards" as they endeavor to serve the church. The Canon Law Society's Code of Professional Responsibility, for example, reminds canonists that they are "to foster and to promote justice and love in the public life of the Church."[77] Far from ignoring the church's pastoral role, canonists are called to "cooperate in the pastoral care of persons involved in canonical cases," and to "make known to pastoral counselors and to concerned parties the pastoral options available under the law in a given case, and [to] encourage those involved to seek the counseling they need."[78] If canon lawyers are called to integrate love and justice with their professional service

[71] *Id.*

[72] *Id.* at 120.

[73] *Id.*

[74] Michael Rezendes and Walter V. Robinson, *Church Tries to Block Public Access to Files*, Bost. Globe, Nov. 23, 2002, at A1.

[75] Kathleen Burge, *Judge Rebukes Law's Lawyer for Bid to Delay Deposition*, Bost. Globe, Jan. 22, 2003, at A10.

[76] Powell and Romano, *supra* note 69, at A1.

[77] Canon Law Society of America, Code of Prof'l Resp. prologue.

[78] *Id.* I(B)(4).

to the church, what makes the church's civil lawyers so confident that the church eschews such values when they have entered the secular legal sphere?

As the Catholic Church's lawyers imported "Rambo-style" tactics into their litigation strategy, they were also importing an alternative set of moral claims regarding the dignity of the victim, the relationship of trust with parishioners, and the preeminence of concerns over financial liability. The lawyers certainly did not erase the moral perspective, they just substituted the profession's for their client's. The Church's institutional tendency toward clericalism and secrecy already made a pastoral response to the crisis more difficult than it needed to be. The overlay of the lawyers' professional values exacerbated the problem, given the widespread recognition that, in the words of one victim, "Folks, this is the Catholic Church," and so "[p]eople expect a higher moral standard"[79] than the one embodied in the adversarial mindset. Whether or not the bishops who hired the lawyers would have embraced the profession's adversarial mindset, they should have been engaged by their attorneys in an ongoing dialogue that explored the mindset not just as a set of legal tactics, but as the moral perspective that it is.

LAWYERS AS MARKET ACTORS

If moral claims are discernible in the legal advice an attorney provides, is the attorney morally accountable for her decision to take on a case or for the myriad decisions she makes in the course of working on the case? If John Yoo, or Vinson & Elkins, or the Catholic Church's trial lawyers should have raised moral considerations with their clients, does that mean that the attorneys should have engaged in their own moral evaluation of the causes and clients to which they committed themselves? In other words, even if we are comfortable with an attorney bringing up moral claims with their clients, we may not be comfortable if the attorney – based on those moral claims – declines a given representation or declines to undertake a certain course of conduct within the representation. Further, we may not be comfortable if third parties express moral approval or condemnation of an attorney's decision to undertake a particular representation or otherwise legal course of conduct.

Consider a recent flap in Boston, where the law firm Ropes & Gray represented Catholic Charities as it searched for a way around a new state requirement that adoption agencies not discriminate against same-sex couples in placing children.[80] The Harvard Law School's student chapter of Lambda protested the firm's decision to work on that case, threatening to picket future on-campus interviewing by the firm, and the threats appear to have had their desired effect, as the firm announced that it would no longer work on the case.[81] Regardless of one's view of the moral claims

---

[79] Review Board, *supra* note 63, at 123.
[80] Patricia Wen, *Catholic Charities Stuns State, Ends Adoptions*, Boston Globe, Mar. 11, 2006.
[81] See Sacha Pfeiffer, *Harvard Law Group Hits Ropes & Gray*, Boston Globe, Mar. 15, 2006.

raised in Lambda's protest, I submit that the students' recognition of the moral dimension of a firm's decision to represent a given client or cause is commendable. For our purposes, it is essential to recognize that the moral dimension of lawyering amounts to more than the uncritical provision of access to the law: The conduct of the representation, and the acceptance of the representation itself, must be included in the moral evaluation of the lawyer's role. The claims of conscience – those of the lawyer and of others – are not irrelevant to any such evaluation. To see why this is the case, we need to understand the lawyer's role as a market actor.

Prophet versus Judge

Obviously, we do not approve of an actor's stance toward the legal system simply because he has invoked conscience to justify his stance; our evaluation of the stance depends, in significant part, on the role the actor plays. This can be readily illustrated by our reactions to the following statements:

- Actor 1, in reference to his public disobedience of a law he perceived to be unjust, said that "I have been ordered to do something I cannot do, and that is violate my conscience."[82]
- Actor 2, in defending his own violation of a law, claims that it is appropriate to defy a law that "conscience tells him is unjust."[83]

Should we react differently to these essentially identical invocations of conscience as justifications for violating the law? Whether or not we should, we do: actor 1 is Roy Moore, former Chief Justice of the Alabama Supreme Court, explaining his refusal to obey a federal court order that he remove an enormous Ten Commandments monument from the courthouse rotunda.[84] Actor 2 is Martin Luther King Jr., as he sat in a Birmingham jail, arrested for marching without a permit.

It is safe to say that even among those who believe that the Ten Commandments should not have been banished from the courthouse, Roy Moore's understanding of conscience is problematic. At the same time, very few, regardless of political leanings, will condemn Martin Luther King Jr. for his version of the same claim. One basis for this discrepancy lies in role. Specifically, we resist the conflation of the role of the judge with that of the prophet: Those who are called to apply the laws of a nation

---

[82] Jeffrey Gettleman, *Thou Shall Not, Colleagues Tell Alabama Judge*, N.Y. Times, Aug. 22, 2003, at A1 (quoting Chief Justice Roy Moore of the Alabama Supreme Court at a rally).

[83] Martin Luther King Jr., *Letter from a Birmingham Jail* (Apr. 16, 1963), available at http://www.stanford.edu/group/King/frequentdocs/birmingham.pdf (accessed Feb. 27, 2009).

[84] Chief Justice Moore testified that he placed the monument in the Supreme Court rotunda "to acknowledge God's law and God's sovereignty." *Glassroth v. Moore*, 335 F.3d 1282, 1287 (11th Cir. 2003). He rejected a request to permit a monument displaying a historically significant speech in the same space on the grounds that "[t]he placement of a speech of any man alongside the revealed law of God would tend in consequence to diminish the very purpose of the Ten Commandments monument." *Id.* at 1284.

evenhandedly, and uniformly, are evaluated on a substantively different moral scale than those who are called to engage critically the nation on the content of those laws.

There is not a universal resistance to that conflation, though. The late Yale law professor Robert Cover skewered judges during the Vietnam War for not publicly engaging "in creative judicial obstruction of the war effort."[85] Although there is a huge gulf between Roy Moore and Robert Cover on the political spectrum, they both seem to conceive of the judge's function as calling for the full integration of moral truth with official role.

Justice Scalia's thought runs in the opposite direction, as he has long railed against what he calls the "judge moralist."[86] In his famous discussions of the death penalty, he argues that if a judge is morally opposed to the death penalty, his only option is to resign from the bench.[87] At least on this issue,[88] he sees no space for judges who hold moral convictions that diverge from the positive law machinery they are obliged to operate. He stands with Moore and Cover in recognizing that a judge may not ignore his conscience, but he sees resignation, not subversion, as the acceptable outcome.

The positions espoused by Moore, Cover, and Scalia fail to account adequately for professional role. Suggesting that conscience automatically compels the judge to subvert the law, or conversely, to resign from his role, misses the bigger picture. A comparison of judges to lawyers brings greater clarity, underscoring the need to account for the context in which the legal professional works. In a modern pluralist democracy, the marketplace is a key dimension of that context. Lawyers can act as modern-day prophets, speaking truth to power,[89] because their moral claims do not threaten the legal access of citizens who dissent from those claims. Judges, by contrast, are constrained by their exercise of monopoly power.

Lawyer versus Judge

Judges should be discouraged from bringing in extralegal, conscience-driven norms to their work, and lawyers may be encouraged to bring in extralegal norms to their work, because lawyers are market actors and judges are not. If a lawyer decides to

---

[85] Robert Cover, *Book Review*, 68 Colum. L. Rev. 1003, 1005 (1968) (reviewing R. Hildreth, *Atrocious Judges: Lives of Judges Infamous as Tools of Tyrants and Instruments of Oppression* (1856)).

[86] The Associated Press, *Scalia Critical of What He Calls the 'Judge-Moralist,'* Boston Globe, Mar. 15, 2006.

[87] "[W]hile my views on the morality of the death penalty have nothing to do with how I vote as a judge, they have a lot to do with whether I can or should be a judge at all. My vote, when joined with at least four others, is, in most cases, the last step that permits an execution to proceed. I could not take part in that process if I believed what was being done to be immoral." Antonin Scalia, *God's Justice and Ours*, First Things (May 2002).

[88] *Cf. id.* ("[A] judge, I think, bears no moral guilt for the laws society has failed to enact. Thus, my difficulty with *Roe v. Wade* is a legal rather than a moral one.").

[89] For a vision of the lawyer as prophet, see Thomas L. Shaffer, *Lawyers as Prophets*, 15 St. Thomas L. Rev. 469 (2003).

integrate her own moral convictions into her legal practice, and her integration leads her to tell the client, for example, that the lawyer will not attempt to impeach a witness if she is certain that the witness is telling the truth, the client's moral agency has not been denied. The client can embrace that approach or decline to proceed with the representation and choose another lawyer. The American Bar Association's Model Rules are clear that "[a] client has a right to discharge a lawyer at any time, with or without cause."[90]

The theoretical ability to choose another lawyer may not always mean much in practice, of course. If a litigant can reject her court-appointed lawyer only by paying for one herself, market dynamics are illusory. Even in the corporate sphere, the market had less vitality in earlier times given the tendency of large companies to attach themselves to a single law firm for decades and to give all their legal business to that firm, ensuring that switching representation would incur a huge cost in terms of the firm's accumulated knowledge of and familiarity with the client.

The power dynamics have changed, though. Ronald Gilson identifies the rise of the in-house legal counsel as having largely eliminated "the information asymmetry between client and lawyer, so that no relationship specific assets are created and no lock-in effect results."[91] The consequence is "a dramatic reduction in the switching costs facing clients and an elimination of lawyers' market power."[92] Companies shop around among a variety of firms for each significant matter, staging beauty contests at which firms parade through a conference room and do their best to sell themselves to the client. Much of the decision-making power now resides with in-house legal departments. At least for corporate clients who are able to pay, they have a variety of options when it comes to their legal representation.

Anyone who doubts the power of market forces in the legal profession need look no farther than the savings and loan scandal of the 1980s. One of the central figures, Charles Keating, expected his lawyers to push the envelope farther than they were comfortable doing, and they resisted. His response was to fire the firm and hire Kaye Scholer. The rest is well documented in any legal ethics casebook, as Kaye Scholer ended up paying $41 million to the government stemming from the firm's various ethical transgressions committed in deference to the market forces that kept its relationship with Keating so precarious.[93] A similar dynamic is evidenced in the Enron debacle. As David Wilkins observes, "[i]n a competitive market filled with sophisticated repeat players, outside firms have little incentive to fail to seek their client's objectives,"[94] even as those objectives push the bounds of the law.

[90] Model Rules of Prof'l Conduct R. 1.16 cmt. 4 (2009).
[91] Ronald Gilson, *The Devolution of the Legal Profession: A Demand Side Perspective*, 49 Md. L. Rev. 869, 902–3 (1990).
[92] *Id.*
[93] William H. Simon, *The Kaye Scholer Affair: The Lawyer's Duty of Candor and the Bar's Temptations of Evasion and Apology*, 23 Law & Social Inquiry 243 (1998).
[94] David B. Wilkins, *Do Clients Have Ethical Obligations to Lawyers? Some Lessons From the Diversity Wars*, 11 Geo. J. Legal Ethics 855, 884 (1998).

Litigants do not have remotely similar discretion in choosing their judge as clients have in choosing their lawyers. They may be able to seek recusal in cases in which the judge's impartiality might reasonably be questioned, but that is a far cry from a deliberate ability to align one's understanding of a proper judicial function with a judge who actually embodies that understanding. Witness the minor media storm in Chicago several years ago when two lawyers filed five identical suits within fourteen minutes on behalf of their client, hoping to land one of them with a preferred judge.[95] The lawyers and their firm were fined, and the state ethics committee opened an investigation.

There is no marketplace of judges, and more than that, there is no marketplace of judicial authority. Judges are the gatekeepers for the legitimate exercise of the state's coercive power on behalf of citizens. If individuals have a dispute that they cannot work out through private ordering, they need the authority that judges provide.

Conscience versus the Rule of Law

The absence of a market makes a provider's exercise of conscience much more problematic. It is not simply a begrudging concession to the rule of law that justifies a judge's self-restraint of conscience; there is an affirmative case to be made for why judges should embrace a certain degree of disconnection between their personal convictions and professional decision making. It flows from a vision of the rule of law as a constitutive element of the common good. The relationship between the morally restrained judge and the common good is discernible from three vantage points.

First, subsidiarity, as explained in chapter 4, holds that the lowest body that can address a problem effectively in society should be empowered to do so. In keeping with subsidiarity, individual judges cannot be assigned to settle legal disputes by invoking their own consciences because such an individualized approach effectively disempowers citizens by negating the law-making efficacy of their democratic participation. Citizens would not enjoy full access to the law, but an access limited by the substance of the judge's convictions. Because the judge acts with the power of the state, the judge's personal moral convictions would serve as a top-down short-circuiting of the bottom-up process of democratic law making. If, for example, a judge were to ignore the settled principles of contract law to preclude enforcement of an agreement that facilitated a company's production of pornography, the company and its members no longer have the space to order their affairs that is contemplated by law, but simply the space contemplated by the judge's own moral convictions. The moral good of reducing pornography may be furthered, but by a path that precludes a meaningful role for citizens in the resolution of the issue. This problem is most pronounced in cases that turn on statutory law; for common

[95] See Randall Samborn, *Chicago Judge Sanctions Firm*, Nat'l L.J., April 18, 1994, at A4.

law cases, the cost is felt in the loss of the law's predictability and stability, necessary ingredients for localized empowerment. The judge's conscience-driven embrace of extralegal norms hampers the ability of associations and individuals to pursue and protect their own interests via unfettered access to the law.

By contrast, when a lawyer stakes out a position based on an extralegal norm with which the client disagrees, the client has an exit option, assuming that the norms are brought to the surface and made known to the client. If lawyers introduce their own extralegal moral norms into the representation without the client's knowledge, they are functioning more like judges, narrowing a client's access without allowing the client to seek other avenues. A lawyer who advises her client that a contract is unenforceable without revealing that the conclusion is grounded in her opposition to pornography, rather than the settled law, becomes a moral arbiter, rather than a partner in moral discourse. When a client has adequate information and viable market options, a lawyer is hard-pressed to justify the facilitation of immoral ends by invoking subsidiarity's impetus of localized empowerment.

Second, the contours of an individual's professional role cannot be defined without reference to the relationships in which it is embedded. When judges put their own conscience-driven claims to the side to adjudicate cases based on the settled law, they are serving the litigants appearing before them. This service is not a one-way act of charity, but a recognition of the mutual self-restraint between citizens on which the rule of law is founded. Judges as private citizens enjoy the liberty of action made possible by the rule of law, a rule for which a degree of self-restraint by all citizens is necessary. With lawyers, their integration of extralegal norms with their practice, if done openly, does not threaten a prospective client's liberty of action. The self-restraint needed by lawyers is simply to resist the temptation to subvert the client's autonomy through the covert introduction of extralegal norms.

Third, as a trigger for the invocation of the state's coercive force, the judicial voice must speak with deference toward the dimension of the common good that is not defined by the collective will. This is why it is so important that judges recognize and invoke the rights needed to protect the human person from overbearing state incursions on individual and associational autonomy. By the same token, the judge must not close down the space needed for individual self-direction by substituting her own extralegal norms for the collective will. Judicial self-restraint helps ensure that the common good is not defined and imposed from above as either a uniform, fixed norm or as an idiosyncratic product of the judge's own conscience, but is instead realized from the bottom up, constituted by the decisions and day-to-day actions of individuals and the communities to which they belong.

When lawyers within a functioning marketplace introduce extralegal norms into the advice they give clients or as the basis for declining a representation, they do not close down the divergent paths by which the common good is realized. In fact, lawyers who bring conscience to bear on their professional identities can help expand and enrich the common good by challenging the presumptions of the governing legal paradigm, whether by critically engaging the substance of the positive law or the objectives that the client wishes to pursue through the positive law. In keeping with the common good, the judge must facilitate the exercise of autonomy by nonstate actors; the lawyer, by contrast, can and should help shape the exercise of autonomy itself.

LAWYERS IN RELATIONSHIP

Not only does a lawyer's conscience have a role to play in her work, but its relational dimension will loom large because the lawyer's moral claims will be articulated, and perhaps even formed, in dialogue with the client's claims. Further, even outside the attorney-client relationship, there is an expanding array of venues for the development of relationships conducive to the formation, articulation, and living out of professionally relevant moral claims. Such venues run against the tradition of the profession, which has been shaped by powerful individualist imagery. Fortunately for the relational dimension of conscience, that tradition may be changing.

Client Autonomy and the Lawyer's Conscience

Moral dialogue between the attorney and client aims not simply at the protection of interests external to the client, but at the well-being of the client herself. Tom Shaffer, for example, traces the scope of our devotion to individual autonomy, observing that, "[i]n moral discourse, as in political and legal discourse, we don't talk about good people, we talk about rights," and we assume "that what citizens want for one another, or lawyers for their clients, is not goodness but isolation and independence."[96] Joseph Raz reminds us that our devotion to individual autonomy is functional – "to enable people to have a good life" – and that "[p]roviding, preserving or protecting bad options does not enable one to enjoy valuable autonomy."[97] David Luban strikes a similar chord, stating that "[a]utonomy is a precondition for things of great value, but it has no value of its own."[98]

Approaching the client's stated objectives as fully formed or fixed precludes the lawyer from having any substantive role in the client's definition or pursuit of the good.[99] A dialogical relationship allows lawyers "to help their clients decide what it is they really want, to help them make up their minds as to what their ends should be, a function that differs importantly from the instrumental servicing of

---

[96] Thomas L. Shaffer, *Ethics After Babel*, 19 Cap. U. L. Rev. 989, 997–8 (1990).

[97] Joseph Raz, *The Morality of Freedom*, 412 (1986).

[98] David Luban, *Partisanship, Betrayal and Autonomy in the Lawyer-Client Relationship: A Reply to Stephen Ellman*, 90 Colum. L. Rev. 1004, 1037–38 (1990).

[99] David B. Wilkins, "Everyday Practice is the Troubling Case: Confronting Context in Legal Ethics," in *Everyday Practices and Trouble Cases*, 68, 70–2 (Sarat et al., eds., 1998).

preestablished goals."[100] Such morally active legal practice presumes that "the lawyer who disagrees with the morality or justice of a client's ends does not simply terminate the relationship, but tries to influence the client for the better."[101] Requiring a lawyer to ignore her conception of truth in formulating or pursuing her client's objectives is to ask her to deny her own moral agency, to have her act as a mere tool of technique without moral standing, and to treat her client as an object of servitude incapable of moral reflection.

Although unfettered client autonomy is undoubtedly a bad idea, few would dispute the understanding that a lawyer should aim to serve the client's interests, not her own, in a given matter. Absolute truth or not, a lawyer cannot be empowered to hijack the representation to further her own conception of the good, perhaps even in a way that goes undetected by the client. This compels a clear limitation on the role of a lawyer's conscience in her work: The client-directed quality of legal representation must be honored. Role differentiation is not to be replaced by the trump of the lawyer's morality, but by moral dialogue in which both the lawyer and client treat each other as agents capable of meaningful moral thought and reflection. Lawyers must be vigilant against overreaching or subtle coercion when it comes to any contact with the client, and morality-driven conversations are no exception.

This vigilance is not just defensive, but requires a proactive mindset on the part of the lawyer, for we will have to rely on the lawyer to initiate conversations regarding the paths by which the lawyer's identity may have an impact on the representation. One fear common to those troubled by the morally engaged lawyer is the prospect of unknowing clients being swept along in service of the lawyer's overarching moral commitments. For example, if a lawyer makes a point of never lying in a negotiation on behalf of her client, the client may never be aware of the fact that the Model Rules permit certain misrepresentations in negotiation[102] or of the strategic advantage that could have accrued to the client's cause if such misrepresentations were made. The attorney must bring up this limitation in consultation with the client – the earlier the better – even though such a conversation will be awkward at best and may result in a loss of business.

This does not necessarily mean that lawyers should emblazon their moral commitments or religious affiliations on their letterhead, for such overt self-categorization will not tell prospective clients much about the likely relationship between the lawyer's identity and the course of the representation, and it may have the unintended and unwelcome consequence of functioning as a signal that individuals who do not share the lawyer's identity should look elsewhere for counsel. A lawyer is obligated to keep the client apprised to the extent that the lawyer recognizes the bearing her own moral convictions will have on the decisions presented by the

---

[100] Anthony Kronman, *The Lost Lawyer*, 27.
[101] David Luban, *Lawyers and Justice: An Ethical Study*, 160 (1989).
[102] See Model Rules of Prof'l Conduct R. 4.1 cmt. 2 (2009).

matter. Often, the identity-representation interplay will be obvious at the initial lawyer-client conversation as the lawyer learns of the client's objectives, such as a lawyer asked by a minor to help her procure court permission for an abortion. At other times, the lawyer's own identity will remain relatively immaterial pending unforeseen developments over the course of the representation, such as a discovery dispute in which the client expects the lawyer to engage in "hardball" tactics. Whatever the timing, a lawyer bold enough to bring her personal values into her provision of legal services must also be bold enough to ensure that her client is aware of those values and approves of their entry into the representation.

The focus is not so much on whether the lawyer's deeply held beliefs are ultimately reflected in the outcome of the representation, but whether the values emanating from those beliefs, once implicated by the representation, were offered for consideration. Of course, often a fully informed client will take issue either with the lawyer's values, or, as is more likely, with the specific way in which the values are brought to bear on the pursuit of the client's lawful objectives. When there is an irreconcilable conflict between the lawyer's conscience and the client's wishes, the lawyer must give way, either by acceding to the client's wishes or by stepping aside in favor of another lawyer.

The Religious Lawyering Movement

The attorney-client relationship is not the only venue for the intersubjective exploration of an attorney's moral claims. Other venues run against the presumptions of the profession even more starkly. In the few instances in which the Model Code does acknowledge a moral side to lawyers, the acknowledgment is steeped in the language of individualism. For example, the preamble to the Code explains that "each lawyer must find within *his own* conscience the touchstone against which to test the extent to which his actions should rise above the minimum standards."[103] Morals, to the extent they are acknowledged at all, are viewed as strictly a "private affair."[104] Today one of the most frequent injunctions is for each lawyer "to be charted by one's own 'moral compass.'"[105]

This tendency to individualize legal ethics implicitly marginalizes a lawyer's communal identities and allegiances. In the traditional view, a lawyer is presented with an ethical dilemma, and, within the framework of the profession's universal norms, determines the proper course of conduct as a free, rational choice. What the traditional view fails to notice, however, is that, as Tom Shaffer observes, "[w]e are

[103] Model Code of Prof'l Responsibility Preamble (1969). Similarly, the 1908 Canons of Professional Ethics directed a lawyer to 'obey his own conscience.'
[104] Thomas Shaffer, *On Being a Christian and a Lawyer*, 20 (1981).
[105] Bruce A. Green, *The Role of Personal Values in Professional Decisionmaking*, 11 Geo. J. Legal Ethics 19, 20 (1997). Green is skeptical about the wisdom of introducing a lawyer's personal values into the representation.

primarily members, not choosers," and that "we belong because of our choices, but that we make the choices we do because we are connected to the people we are connected to."[106] Any account of legal ethics, in this regard, must "take into account the evidence and commonsense primacy of organic groups, to see if we can build plausible common-good arguments there and from there."[107]

Any attempt by the legal profession, as an overarching entity, to claim the mantle of community faces an uphill struggle with reality. One of the modern architects of our ethical regime, Geoffrey Hazard, observes that the profession's "governing norms no longer represent the shared understandings of a substantially cohesive group."[108] Instead, the governing norms "are simply rules of public law regulating a widely pursued technical vocation."[109] David Wilkins notes, "[t]he traditional image of a homogenous profession united by a common normative culture is increasingly out of touch with the realities of contemporary law practice,"[110] and Ted Schneyer sees a profession that "has become vastly more differentiated than it was when the ABA [American Bar Association] adopted its first ethics code in 1908."[111]

Clinging to the image of the profession as an overarching community of fungible technicians whose personal values are peripheral to the services they provide deprives many lawyers of the meaningful community that they crave. Especially for religious lawyers, the paradigm's marginalization of meaningful professional communities is personally and professionally detrimental. An expanding array of groups such as the Christian Legal Society, the National Association of Muslim Lawyers, the International Association of Jewish Lawyers and Jurists, and the St. Thomas More Society dot the professional landscape. The extent to which these groups actually serve as venues for moral reflection and formation – rather than for run-of-the-mill professional networking – varies widely, but their potential is obvious.[112]

These groups can bring coherence to religious lawyers by facilitating the integration of faith and practice. They can also promote the type of conversations that should be foundational to a meaningful sense of professionalism, but that elude the technical, regulatory approach that dominates today's conversations about professional "ethics." Further, religious lawyering groups can ameliorate some of the dangers that critics fear will accompany the introduction of a lawyer's religious or moral convictions into her representation of a client. Communities of religious lawyers can bring individual convictions into the open, subjecting them to review

---

[106] Shaffer, *supra* note 104, at 20–1.

[107] *Id.* at 113–4.

[108] Geoffrey C. Hazard, *The Future of Legal Ethics*, 100 Yale L.J. 1239, 1278–9 (1991).

[109] *Id.*

[110] Wilkins, *supra* note 99, at 1542.

[111] Ted Schneyer, *Professionalism as Bar Politics: The Making of the Model Rules of Professional Conduct*, 14 Law & Social Inquiry 677, 734 (1989).

[112] See generally Robert K. Vischer, *Heretics in the Temple of Law: The Promise and Peril of the Religious Lawyering Movement*, 19 J. Law & Relig. 427 (2003–04).

by fellow believers, and requiring the individual to express and examine her own views, thereby separating motivations of faith from personal predilections that may have found a convenient, but untested, faith cover.

By placing individual convictions within a communal framework, the intracommunity dialogue not only helps the lawyer strengthen and sort her convictions, but it also protects the client by increasing the likelihood that the convictions will be knowable by the client. By facilitating the distillation of lawyers' religious convictions into professional norms, the community engages in a sort of translation that makes the convictions more accessible to the client. Further, to the extent that the norms are implemented on a community-wide basis – either as obligations of conduct or aspirations of character – the vague leanings of an individual lawyer's conscience are fleshed out and made explicit, enhancing the likelihood that the norms will be communicated in some fashion to the client.

The Cause Lawyering Movement

The religious lawyering movement, to a significant extent, can be understood as another incarnation of "cause lawyering," a broader phenomenon, which has a longstanding and well-entrenched foothold within the profession. Cause lawyering generally is associated with legal efforts to "achieve greater social justice – both for particular individuals (drawing on individualistic 'helping' orientations) and for disadvantaged groups."[113] Cause lawyers are, in David Luban's words, "morally activist lawyers," which means that they "hold themselves morally accountable for the means they employ and the ends they pursue on behalf of clients."[114]

Like religious lawyering, cause lawyering presumes that the dictates of a lawyer's conscience will – and should – play a role in her professional life. For example, the priesthood paradigm embodies a "bleached out professionalism,"[115] under which a lawyer's own identity, including her racial identity, is deemed wholly irrelevant to her practice of law. David Wilkins, among others, challenges at least this aspect of the paradigm, contending that "black lawyers have moral obligations to the black community that these women and men are entitled to consider when deciding how to act in particular cases, and more generally, in determining what it means to live a morally acceptable life in the law."[116] Gay and lesbian attorneys are similarly seen as subject to certain overarching commitments by virtue of their membership in that community, as William Rubenstein urges "the gay bar" to "attend

[113] Carrie Menkel-Meadow, "The Causes of Cause Lawyering," in *Cause Lawyering*, 31, 37 (A. Sarat and S. Scheingold, eds., 1998).
[114] Luban, *supra* note 101, at 1005.
[115] Sanford Levinson, *Identifying the Jewish Lawyer: Reflections on the Construction of Professional Identity*, 14 Cardozo L. Rev. 1577, 1577 (1993).
[116] Wilkins, *supra* note 99, at 1506.

more self-consciously than it has to date to the concept of intra-community 'responsibilities.'"[117] Rubenstein suggests that the label "gay attorney" is more than descriptive. Under his vision, it is a "placeholder for . . . a set of responsibilities that result from her embrace (however tenuous) of, or her occupying (and/or taking advantage of the benefits) of, this identity position."[118]

Certainly a prime justification for elevating a lawyer's consciousness of her racial and sexual identities is the role such identity plays in overcoming the historical discrimination and marginalization of these groups within the profession and the legal system more generally. But the emergence of identity-conscious lawyering among disadvantaged communities reflects something broader than the pursuit of a favored societal objective. Wilkins and Rubenstein are not simply urging all lawyers to show special concern for the standing of racial and sexual minorities within the legal system. Rather, they are urging members of those communities to show such concern based on the fact of their membership. That is, it matters not simply that a particular end-result is realized, but that lawyers with an identity-driven affinity for that end-result are intimately involved in its realization. Whether or not the end-result has been endorsed by the entire profession is irrelevant; it is enough that it matters to the individual lawyer and the community to which she belongs.

So cause lawyering, even understood expressly in social justice terms, cannot be explained away as a simple derivation of the priesthood paradigm. It is not that some segments of the profession emphasize certain collectively determined conceptions of the good over others, as if the secular priesthood as a whole delegated certain social reform functions to a subset of perfectly fungible gatekeepers. The ends to be sought are inextricably intertwined with the lawyer's identity, and the justification for the endeavor consists not simply in the endeavor's ultimate success, but in the paths of personal reflection, realization, and sacrifice by which the endeavor is under-taken. Cause lawyering shows not simply that a lawyer's moral identity matters as a descriptive fact, but that it should matter as a normative proposition. This identity is informed, in significant ways, by her membership in a given community, particularly when that membership is itself shaped by her conscience-driven commitments.

THE JUDGE'S CONSCIENCE

Focusing on the legal system provides a suitable opportunity to explore whether, and the extent to which, conscience can be professionally relevant outside a functioning marketplace. As already discussed, the marketplace for legal services does not extend to the judicial bench. Does conscience play any legitimate role whatsoever in the provision of access to the law by those who are not market actors? Imagining judges as

---

[117] William B. Rubenstein, *In Communities Begin Responsibilities: Obligations at the Gay Bar*, 48 Hastings L.J. 1101, 1102 (1997).
[118] *Id.* at 1118.

some sort of robotic, amoral interpreters of the law runs counter to our association of the judicial temperament with decidedly human virtues such as creativity, empathy, and integrity. What place, if any, does a judge's own moral claims have in the performance of her official duties?

Our discomfort with the integration of a judge's conscience with her decision making is readily discerned. Consider the "judicial conscience," a concept that occurs sporadically in case law, though it is rarely defined explicitly. Its invocation can function as praise or an indictment of the judge, depending on the epistemological basis of the judicial act in question. When referring to a judge's good-faith application of enacted law to the facts, the judicial conscience represents the heart of the judicial function, but when it refers to the judge's introduction of her own extralegal moral claims, the concept is more problematic.

As an example of the first context, courts speak of "evidence sufficient to satisfy the judicial conscience" that the applicable legal standard has been satisfied.[119] In this sense, the judicial conscience refers to the judge's reasonable certainty, rather than to any substantive moral claim. If conscience is, as was traditionally held, the application of the moral law to a particular set of circumstances, then the judicial conscience poses little controversy. One reason conscience has become so problematic in the broader society is the breakdown in consensus about the moral law's content; the judicial conscience, subject to the positive law, faces no comparable epistemological obstacle. To the extent that we know the law, we know the object of the judicial conscience.

When "judicial conscience" is invoked to refer to the judge's own moral convictions, it is more often than not done to criticize the introduction of the judge's idiosyncratic views into the rule of law. As far back as 1888, a Pennsylvania appellate court noted that lower courts had based their contrasting decisions on their "judicial conscience," meaning "personal conscience in the breast of the judge."[120] The court was quick to note, however, that the conscience of the judge is not to be understood in the strictly personal sense because the judge must "with a clear conscience administer the law as they find it, irrespective of their private views of its propriety," and that "if the law is wrong, it is with the people to alter it."[121] Greg Sisk reflects the traditional conception that "a well-formed judicial conscience draws upon the rule of law, adheres to neutral principles and impartial procedures, and embraces humility lest a decree improperly override democratic governance."[122]

The most strident contests over the possibility of injecting moral content into the judicial conscience have occurred in Supreme Court jurisprudence. In 1952, the Supreme Court ruled that police had violated a suspect's due process rights by having

[119] *Grady v. Wallace*, 272 So.2d 21, 24 (Ala. 1961).
[120] In re *Lackawanna County Licenses*, 5 Pa. C.C. 462, at *3 (1888).
[121] *Id.* at *3.
[122] Gregory C. Sisk, *The Willful Judging of Harry Blackmun*, 70 Mo. L. Rev. 1049, 1050 (2005).

his stomach pumped to recover illegal morphine pills. Justice Frankfurter, writing for the majority, based the ruling on the fact that the conduct "shocked the conscience."[123] Hinging a constitutional violation on conduct's capacity to shock the judicial conscience was widely criticized as subjective and unprincipled, akin to transforming due process liberties into "the policy preferences of the Members of this Court."[124]

The more accepted approach to identifying a substantive due process violation is to examine whether the interests at stake are "those fundamental rights and liberties which are objectively deeply rooted in this Nation's history and tradition, and implicit in the concept of ordered liberty such that neither liberty nor justice would exist if they were sacrificed."[125] Even this "objective" analysis of history and tradition frequently stands accused of serving as a vehicle for the judge's own views, particularly in light of the tendency of our traditions to "evolve." For example, when the court recently held the execution of minors to be unconstitutional under the Eighth Amendment based on "evolving standards of decency," Justice Scalia insisted that the majority had neglected to "identify a moral consensus of the American people," and had instead presumed, as a group of unelected lawyers, "to be the authoritative conscience of the Nation."[126]

Eric Muller reflects the widely accepted nature of judicial conscience when he calls for a "constitutional conscience" standard for determining substantive due process violations based on morally outrageous executive actions in the criminal setting. The relevant question is not whether the judge finds the executive's conduct "viscerally shocking," but whether it shocks a "constitutional conscience," one that is "formed by reference to the historical foundation and fundamental commitments of the Constitution itself."[127] Although Muller admits that there will be "healthy differences of opinion about the content of constitutional conscience just as there are healthy differences about the scope of history and tradition in substantive due process cases and in search-and-seizure law," these are differences that can be approached through "a reasoned discourse – something that is impossible when the conscience by which judges measure executive action is, to borrow Justice Scalia's sarcastic words, their 'still, soft voice within.'"[128]

The notion that "reasoned discourse" is impossible whenever individual conscience enters the scene stands in some tension with the picture of conscience that has been painted in this book. Suffice it to say that a judge's individual conscience is not a particularly welcome guest in our legal system given its perceived threat to equal access to, and equal justice under, the law. The judicial conscience becomes

[123] *Rochin v. California*, 342 U.S. 165 (1952).
[124] *Id.*
[125] *Washington v. Glucksberg*, 521 U.S. 702, 720–1 (1997) (internal quotation marks omitted).
[126] *Roper v. Simmons*, 543 U.S. 551, 616 (2005) (Scalia, J., dissenting).
[127] Eric L. Muller, *Constitutional Conscience*, 83 B.U. L. Rev. 1017, 1021 (2003).
[128] *Id.* at 1068 (quoting County of Sacramento v. Lewis, 523 U.S. 833, 865 (1998)).

more problematic the more it becomes associated with the judge's own views rather than the dictates of the law. Even a noted progressive legal scholar such as Pam Karlan warns, "a conception of judicial independence that insists that each judge be free to follow her own conception of what the law demands threatens a constellation of interests that may ultimately be more important than a judge's autonomy."[129] Witness the extent to which the Senate confirmation hearings of Supreme Court Justice Sonia Sotomayor fixed on a past speech in which she expressed her hope "that a wise Latina woman with the richness of her experiences would more often than not reach a better conclusion than a white male who hasn't lived that life."[130] It is arguable whether she would have secured the confirmation without repeatedly clarifying that her judicial philosophy "is simple: fidelity to the law."[131] The judicial-conscience-as-law rests easily within our legal system only to the extent that its content is defined and accessible, qualities thought to be lacking from personal conscience.

For a judge, extralegal moral norms should be kept at the margins when evaluating the performance of her professional role. This is not to pretend that a judge can function as an amoral robot, stepping out of her own morally laden identity whenever she picks up the gavel. But by looking beyond her own moral convictions (which is a starkly different proposition than pretending her moral convictions do not exist), she can acknowledge the moral significance of judging without subverting the rule of law. Often the judge's moral convictions will spark no tension with the legal framework, either because of substantive consistency between the two or because the law defers to – indeed, welcomes – the judge's exercise of discretion. When the judge's convictions encounter resistance from the law, however, the value of the restrained judicial conscience comes into relief. Contrary to Justice Scalia's assertion that the judge who opposes capital punishment should resign, a morally dissenting judge still contributes to the rule of law and, more broadly, to the common good. Three essential functions stand out.

First, judicial decision making can have a meaningful pedagogical impact, especially when the judge who upholds a settled rule of law nevertheless dissents from the moral implications of the rule. In other words, what does the judge say in her opinion about the legal rule she upholds? This dynamic can be seen in federal District Court Judge Richard Casey's ruling in which he struck down a partial-birth abortion ban in light of binding Supreme Court precedent,[132] but nevertheless stated in the opinion that the practice is "gruesome, brutal, barbaric and uncivilized."[133] Other judges have called attention to the injustice of sentencing disparities for crimes involving crack versus powder cocaine, but have, nevertheless, imposed sentence as instructed by the guidelines. Although judges should not utilize their public pedestals in a

---

[129] Pamela S. Karlan, *Judicial Independence*, 95 Geo. L.J. 1041, 1056 (2007).
[130] Sonia Sotomayor, *A Latina Judge's Voice*, 13 Berkeley La Raza L.J. 87, 92 (2002).
[131] Peter Baker and Neil Lewis, *Sotomayor Vows "Fidelity to the Law"*, N.Y. Times, Jul. 13, 2009, at A1.
[132] *Stenberg v. Carhart*, 530 U.S. 914 (2000).
[133] *Nat'l Abortion Fed. v. Ashcroft*, 330 F. Supp. 2d 436, 479 (2004).

way that inspires hostility toward the rule of law, there is nothing inherent in their professional role that disqualifies them from drawing the public's attention to the law's moral dimension.

Second, judges serve the structural good of maintaining access to the law even when they facilitate particular problematic ends in a particular case. A judge's moral qualms about a particular provision of law may actually deepen and enrich the quality of justice afforded under that provision. Of course, participating in the enforcement of morally objectionable laws is not without cost, particularly in terms of the legitimacy lent by the participation, and that must be considered in the calculus. The calculus cannot simply consist of whatever moral weight is given to the specific problematic law to be enforced; there is a broader, systemic value to the morally dissenting judge's continued presence that must be factored into the equation.

Third, in cases in which the exercise of prudence suggests that the structural good is outweighed by the particular harm to be facilitated by a law's enforcement, the judge's ability to recuse herself preserves the good they do in other cases in which the law's indeterminacy may allow a judge's rightly formed conception of justice to have a positive impact on the law's development. "The judge's sense of right and wrong," after all, "shapes, to some extent, the direction in which the law evolves,"[134] and "resignation deprives the bench of some of those who may be most inclined to try to encourage positive changes in controlling law."[135]

These three functions will resolve many questions over a judge's culpability in the enforcement of immoral laws, but they will not resolve all of them. One thorny question that arises in light of this analysis concerns the moral responsibility and professional obligations of the judge in Nazi Germany. David Luban captures the "central jurisprudential question" of the Nazi judge as being, "In what way, to what extent, does the rule of law . . . immunize jurists from the still small voice of conscience?"[136] German historian Ingo Muller notes that, thanks to legal positivism, "no professional group emerged from the Nazi era with so good a conscience as that of the jurists."[137] Given my insistence that a judge should facilitate morally problematic ends in a particular case in light of the overarching moral good occasioned by the continued rule of law, should the Nazi judge have enforced the legal rules of Hitler's democratically elected regime?

The case of the Nazi judge serves as a tragic reflection of the fact that the governing legal order is not always coextensive with the rule of law, especially when entire

---

[134] Avery Cardinal Dulles, *Catholic Social Teaching and American Legal Practice*, 30 Fordham Urb. L.J. 277, 288 (2002).

[135] Hon. Jack B. Weinstein, *Every Day is a Good Day for a Judge to Lay Down His Professional Life for Justice*, 32 Fordham Urb. L.J. 131, 140 (2004).

[136] David Luban, *A Report on the Legality of Evil: The Case of the Nazi Judges*, 61 Brook. L. Rev. 1139, 1140 (1995) (symposium panel comments).

[137] Ingo Muller, *Hitler's Justice: The Courts of the Third Reich*, 219 (D. Schneider, trans., 1991).

classes of persons are categorically excluded from the law's protection. Favoring circumscribed discretion for a judge to bring her conscience to bear on the law's substance should not be construed as requiring unquestioned judicial support of the existing legal order. Revolution cannot be excluded as the prudent path of last resort, and the covert subversion of the legal order by judges could be contemplated within that revolution. At some point, a society reaches a tipping point where the judges should aim to avoid or minimize the harm caused by a morally bankrupt legal system, and they can do so most effectively as judges, not simply in their personal capacities. The precise tipping point may be difficult to discern – much less define in the abstract – and it will not be enough to point to isolated injustices as a defense for judges who elevate their own extralegal moral norms above the settled law. Further, the greater space for conscience enjoyed by lawyers, as market actors, remains instructive: If judges, as judges, are justified in subverting the legal order, lawyers should have also joined the revolution long before.

CONSCIENCE AND THE LEGAL PROFESSION

The relationships through which conscience thrives include those relationships that provide access to the law because legal questions are often inescapably moral questions as well. The relational dimension of conscience, however, takes on a different gloss within the legal profession. With some exceptions, the attorney-client relationship will tend not to be a venue in which the participants gather around a shared commitment to a particular moral claim. It is a fiduciary relationship in which the lawyer is obliged to protect the client's interests. But those interests are not easily disentangled from moral claims, and the lawyer should not pretend that they are.

That said, the interests at stake and the potential power disparities within those relationships warrant caution in carving out space for the lawyer's moral agency. The client-centered nature of legal services must not be subverted, but we should not presume that the lawyer encroaches on client autonomy by raising moral considerations implicated by the representation. If the lawyer approaches such conversations with deference to the client's ultimate authority over the direction of the representation, moral dialogue can actually enhance client autonomy.

Further, as long as a viable market for legal services exists, the lawyer's adherence to her own conscience-informed professional boundaries does not threaten the rule of law. For many lawyers, such adherence is essential to the coherence and integrity of their own moral identity. As the late civil rights lawyer William Kunstler observed, "Everyone has a right to a lawyer, that's true. But they don't have a right to me."[138] Kunstler's quip embodies our commitment to conscience, not only in the legal profession, but in any field in which consumers have a choice among providers.

[138] *Sonya Live* (CNN television broadcast, Nov. 5, 1993).

Once the regulatory ambition expands beyond the securing of access to a morally contested good or service, the specter of the provider as amoral technician looms. A vibrant marketplace secures providers' ability to exercise their moral agency in choosing the ends to which they commit themselves and the means by which they pursue those ends and allows consumers to bring their own moral commitments to bear on their day-to-day decision making. Using access as the benchmark can help check intrusive, albeit well-intentioned, state ambitions, thereby allowing our liberty of conscience to account for the fact that our moral convictions gain real-world traction primarily through our relationships.

Conclusion

Let us return briefly to the case that began this book's inquiry – the husband-and-wife photography agency that refused on moral grounds to shoot a same-sex commitment ceremony.[1] It is safe to say that state-coerced photography in violation of conscience elicits nowhere near the amount of public sympathy as state-coerced military combat in violation of conscience does. If Daniel Seeger is the poster boy for the sanctity of conscience, the Huguenins appear, to many, to be misguided zealots who should seek another line of work or, at best, unfortunate but unavoidable casualties in the noble struggle for human equality. As one noted civil rights scholar remarked, "if you run a wedding photography service, even if you don't like the fact that those two gays are getting married, you'd better have someone on your staff who will take those pictures."[2]

As this book has tried to show, these responses derive from a superficial conception of conscience, one that lacks the depth and breadth of conscience's relational dimension. Suggesting that the Huguenins can honor their consciences by keeping their moral beliefs out of the marketplace ignores the external orientation of conscience, discernible from its earliest invocations as moral belief *applied* to conduct. Respecting conscience as an internalized set of beliefs does not authentically respect conscience.

Similarly short sighted is the idea that the Huguenins can avoid the problem by hiring an employee who is willing to shoot events that their own moral convictions do not permit them to shoot. This approach solves nothing unless we conceive of conscience in individualist terms, as though its claims apply to my own conduct and no further. In reality, conscience refers (literally) to shared moral belief, and

---

[1] See pages 2–5.
[2] *Gay Rights Law Faces Legal, Religious Challenges*, NPR Talk of the Nation (Jun. 16, 2008) (comments of Chai Feldblum).

while not every claim of conscience will actually be shared, such claims are, by their nature, susceptible to sharing. As such, the Huguenins' resistance to offering, through creative hiring, a "full service" photography agency is not an imperialist expansion of conscience's interior domain; it is a natural outgrowth of conscience's relational dimension. Institutions do not possess a conscience in some ontological sense, but they do embody distinct moral identities that are shaped by their con- stituents' consciences. When we preclude the cultivation and maintenance of such institutional identities, it is not just moral pluralism that suffers; it is the cause of conscience itself.

If we care about conscience, we have to care about the Huguenins – in particular, about the state's punishment of their refusal to photograph an event they find immoral. Indeed, we have to care enough to have a conversation about how to handle these cases that does not resort to simplistic platitudes about equality (from one side) or freedom (from the other). That is not an easy conversation to have, for two reasons. First, at least from today's vantage point, it seems easier to have rooted for conscience in traditional cases, which tended to involve the courageous individual standing up to the oppressive and impersonal state. In the current wave of conflicts, not only is the cause of conscience often represented by individuals or organizations committed to moral claims that appear outdated and regressive, but, in addition, the claims are brought to bear against sympathy-inspiring individuals who seek equal treatment after longstanding marginalization by society. In our rights- soaked legal culture, it is easy to choose sides against the state; less so against those battling discrimination.

We must remember, though, that sympathetic individuals like Vanessa Willock, who simply wanted her commitment ceremony to be photographed, are functional stand-ins for the state. It is one thing to rush to Willock's cause by targeting the hearts, minds, and wallets of our fellow citizens through advocacy, protests, and boycotts; it is quite another to bring state power down on the heads of those who have aggrieved her. In the short term, the state can vindicate the majority's conviction that gays and lesbians should enjoy the same treatment as heterosexuals in their attempt to secure goods and services in the marketplace. In the long term, as the state enacts legal short-cuts to social equality, the bottom-up vision of the common good recedes further from view, and a decidedly more statist understanding becomes more firmly entrenched. Even if we applaud a particular moral claim imposed by the state on dissenting consciences, each instance paves the way for an increasingly top-down approach to the common good. This not only jeopardizes the moral autonomy of those who flout prevailing wisdom, it also further atomizes the citizenry by decreasing the practical relevance of our ongoing moral conversations. If the state imposes the good, the state is the primary audience for conversations regarding the good. One- time political contests to determine which vision of the good will prevail in law and which will be vanquished are no substitute for the day-to-day contests over which visions of the good will find support and sustenance among the citizenry, which visions will wither for lack of moral persuasiveness, and which can flourish alongside each other. Sometimes claims of conscience must be denied, but they should not be denied without counting the cost. Giving any particular public norm – equality, in this case – a categorical trump over conscience precludes such an accounting because it ignores context.

Conversations regarding conscience disputes like the Huguenins' also become more difficult because there is no sure-fire remedy available via resort to bright-line constitutional principles. In other words, once we decide that we do care, it is not obvious what the law is supposed to do. In a case such as *Barnette*, it is obvious that a state-compelled pledge of allegiance violates our commitment to conscience, and fortunately, the Free Speech clause stands ready to vindicate that commitment. Freedom of speech includes protection against the compelled expression of ideas that violate one's moral convictions. (The Huguenins' attorney, in fact, focused on the free speech aspect of their claim.) This is an imperfect proxy for conscience because although the freedom to express one's conscience is essential, it is only one aspect of conscience's viability. Photographers are engaged in expression through their work, but it is difficult to see how taxi drivers are. Still, when Muslims in Minneapolis are compelled – by the threat of losing their licenses – to transport passengers carrying alcohol, the cost to conscience is no less significant than that experienced by the Huguenins.[3]

The Free Exercise clause is another possibility, but in light of the Supreme Court's ruling in *Smith* that neutral laws of general applicability do not create free exercise problems,[4] it is far from evident how nondiscrimination laws can be overcome by free exercise principles. Many states have enacted Religious Freedom Restoration Acts that aim to restore the pre-*Smith* weighing of state and individual interests in religious liberty cases. This restoration furthers the cause of conscience, though New Mexico's did not help Elane Photography.[5] More broadly, as outlined in this book, freedom of conscience is not coextensive with freedom of religion.

Other even less perfect proxies for conscience can be invoked in certain contexts: Substantive due process, though wildly underspecified, maintains some degree of moral autonomy regarding relationships, particularly intimate relationships. The right of association is key to the extent that it goes beyond expression and protects venues for the formation and implementation of conscience's claims, although its application to commercial entities is dubious and its power to resist state interests is uncertain, even in the wake of *Dale*.[6]

---

3 Curt Brown, *Cabbies Ordered to Pick Up All Riders*, Mpls. Star-Trib, Apr. 17, 2007, at A1.

4 See *Employment Div. v. Smith*, 494 U.S. 872 (1990).

5 The New Mexico Human Rights Commission refused to consider the RFRA claim, reasoning that such claims only are cognizable in judicial proceedings, not administrative proceedings.

6 See *Dale v. Boy Scouts*, 530 U.S. 640 (2000).

Put simply, conscience's vitality depends on more than the identification and application of particular constitutional rights. Much of the responsibility for conscience falls on political actors. Statutes such as California's Unruh Civil Rights Act are perfectly constitutional (on their face, at least), but they are not conducive to conscience. The Act provides that:

> All persons within the jurisdiction of this state are free and equal, and no matter what their sex, race, color, religion, ancestry, national origin, disability, medical condition, marital status, or sexual orientation are entitled to the full and equal accommodations, advantages, facilities, privileges, or services in all business establishments of every kind whatsoever.[7]

In a society that values conscience, this is a bad law because it is not premised on securing individuals' access to essential goods and services. Instead, it is premised on the expressive value of nondiscrimination as a universal norm in the marketplace. That is a legitimate value for the state to express, to be sure, but the state should limit itself to expressing such a contested value as a marketplace actor, not as the marketplace gatekeeper. The state can (and should) express the value of nondiscrimination by refusing to enter into contracts with discriminatory vendors, or by trumpeting the importance of nondiscrimination through public awareness campaigns. Apart from the areas of employment and housing,[8] the state should not impose nondiscrimination as the nonnegotiable precondition for marketplace participation.

Bright-line rules, such as the Unruh Act, are relatively simple to administer, but the cost to conscience is high. The state has a legitimate interest in ensuring access, and thus the inquiry into appropriate state action must be empirical, that is, if there are ten wedding photographers in Albuquerque willing to shoot a same-sex commitment ceremony, the justification for state action looks much different than if the Huguenins are the only photographers in town. Administering an empirical regime may be messier, but it is not impossible. In fields in which state licenses are required, an access-centered framework may warrant legislative grants of authority to state agencies to condition licenses on the provision of morally contested goods and services that are not otherwise available in the area. In nonlicensed fields, the legislature could allow a "market access" defense to discrimination law, with the accused bearing the burden of proving the availability of comparable goods or services in a reasonably defined area.

An access-centered framework does not invariably translate into victories for conscience. If there is no viable marketplace for an essential good or service, state intervention is appropriate. Consider the recent lawsuit filed by Guadalupe Benitez against a fertility clinic near San Diego and two of its physicians for refusing to provide intrauterine fertilization because she was unmarried (according to the doctors)

---

[7] Calif. Civil Code § 51.
[8] These are discussed further in chapter 1.

or because she was a lesbian (according to Benitez).[9] Ideally, the resolution of this conflict would not hinge on elevating freedom or equality over the other, but on whether Benitez could obtain those services elsewhere without incurring substantial hardship. (In that particular case, although there are many reproductive specialists in San Diego who would have provided their services to Benitez, she alleges that the defendant clinic was the only provider covered under her employer's health insurance policy.[10])

In the case of the Muslim taxi drivers, the access inquiry looks a bit different. The fact that many taxi drivers licensed to serve the Minneapolis airport do not object to transporting alcohol is not dispositive because the relevant marketplace – the taxis available at the time a passenger emerges from the terminal – is a function of happenstance and often may not reflect the overall ratio of nondiscriminatory drivers. The limited marketplace encountered by a given passenger, combined with the significant percentage of drivers in Minneapolis who object to transporting alcohol, may warrant the airport commission's refusal to accommodate drivers' consciences under these circumstances. Nuanced, access-centered resolutions like these are not contemplated by sweeping edicts like the Unruh Act, and they cannot be created by the courts absent some grounding in positive law.

Conscience entails much more than the authority to exclude, however. It broadly concerns the ability to stake out, and live according to, a set of moral claims, even (especially) when such claims are disputed by much of society. Respect for conscience also entails respect for the relationships through which consciences are formed. Admittedly, this is the point at which even some civil libertarians will object to my prescription, arguing that our commitment to permit the exercise of already-formed illiberal consciences does not justify supporting the formation of illiberal consciences. Our discomfort with the prospect of the state shutting down the expression of racist views, for example, does not mean that we should be similarly uncomfortable with the state shutting down the inculcation of racist values in our children.

Viewed from the perspective of the moral marketplace, however, the state's respect for the exercise of conscience is inexorably linked with the state's respect for the formation of conscience. State intrusions into the marketplace should be limited and marked with humility because we should not be confident in the state's ability to weed out good from bad formative venues and moral claims. Expanded state authority over the formation of conscience also affects the marketplace for the expression and living out of conscience's claims. The alternative to maintaining space for formation is the specter of state-approved formation, which shuts down the life-blood of the moral marketplace and substitutes a top-down social order for the

[9] See North Coast Women's Care Medical Group, Inc. v. San Diego Cty. Sup. Ct., 189 P.3d 959 (Cal. 2008).
[10] *See* Plaintiff's Opening Br. at 4 (available at http://data.lambdalegal.org/pdf/legal/benitez/benitez-opening-brief.pdf) (accessed Sep. 6, 2009).

bottom-up social order that part I of the book establishes as essential for conscience's (and the common good's) flourishing.

As described in chapter 8, the state may justifiably inject its own moral claims into public education, but even there the state should proceed with caution. In other venues of formation, the state should resist the temptation to intrude, even when it comes to a claim as fundamental as racial equality. This is not because those venues are incapable of causing social harm, but because the autonomy of those venues, and their independence from the state, are vital to a conscience-honoring social order. The two most obvious venues within this category are churches and families. Within both of these venues, it is important that members do not perceive their projects as operating within the state's purview or permission; the depth of the personal investment called for and the object of the calling transcend the governing political will. They belong to separate spheres. The state's interference thus should be limited to protecting vulnerable members from readily discernible, serious harm (e.g., physical or sexual abuse of a child; financial fraud by church officials), not from moral claims that the political community rejects (e.g., Fred Phelps' homophobic church should remain free to operate, as should a patriarchal family that teaches its daughters to submit to their future husbands).

This restraint by the state is not in blind service to some abstract theory of society, but stems from the conviction that human beings are most likely to flourish in a society where their moral convictions can be brought to bear on their lived realities. Circumscribing formative relationships based on the content of the moral claims that they transmit is not a costless endeavor, for building life narratives of integrity and coherence presumes a degree of accountability to sources other than the state. The common good arises from the myriad sources of accountability that drive moral agents to translate the convictions on which their life narratives are built into action. As society becomes more and more sanguine about making the state a party to these formative relationships, a targeted set of disfavored moral claims will not be the only casualty; we will also threaten the social dynamic by which conscience's motivational power is realized.

Whether we are talking about the formation, expression, or living out of our citizenry's wildly divergent sets of moral claims, it is too early to tell how much space for conscience's relational dimension will be forthcoming under the law. In corporate law, is there room to include distinct moral claims within the protection of the business judgment rule? In health care, will licensing agencies tolerate the rise of morally distinct pharmacies? In education, will the expanding array of schooling options feature anything resembling a marketplace of institutional moral identities? Can and should charities maintain allegiance to their foundational moral commitments without defying the public expectations that attach to public funds? In other areas, it remains to be seen whether professional identity is malleable enough to incorporate the moral claims that traditionally have operated beneath the surface, as in the attorney-client relationship. Perhaps the most crucial test of our commitment to conscience is whether we will resist the temptation to mold our foundational moral relationships in the state's image, or will we eventually replicate public individual autonomy norms within the family? In all of these areas, the debates are underway, but the outcomes are far from clear.

Emphasizing these emerging areas of concern should not be read as minimizing or undermining the importance of the individual-versus-state paradigm that has long governed our legal understanding of conscience. The paradigm has served us well – and continues to serve us well – to the extent that it has cast as a "fixed star in our constitutional constellation," as Justice Jackson wrote for the court in *Barnette*, the principle "that no official, high or petty, can prescribe what shall be orthodox in politics, nationalism, religion, or other matters of opinion or force citizens to confess by word or act their faith therein."[11] Until now, this understanding has been presumed to fulfill our nation's duty to preserve "freedom of conscience to the full."[12] With due respect to Justice Jackson and his colleagues, this conception of the freedom of conscience must be expanded. If we intend to maintain a robust commitment to conscience, the individual-versus-state paradigm provides only a baseline for a conversation that may be just getting started. Conscience, and the self-transcending paths by which it forms the common good, bear a legitimacy founded on human nature and the inescapable intersubjectivity of moral claims. This legitimacy warrants the state's deference, but should not require its approval.

[11] *West Virginia Bd. of Ed. v. Barnette*, 319 U.S. 624, 642 (1943).
[12] *Id.* at 646 (Murphy, J., concurring).

Index

Canon Law Society, 284
Carbone, June, 244
Carpenter, Dale, 130
Carter, Stephen, 103, 132
Casey, Richard, 299
Catholic Charities: adoption services, 7, 125,
    149–50, 285; and contraceptives, 7, 151
cause lawyering, 295–96
Charitable Choice, 140, 235–36
Charo, Alta, 166
charter schools, 227–33. *See also* schools
children: abuse of, 239, 282–85; autonomy,
    246–47; custody of, 256–60; exit options, 207,
    216, 219, 232, 255; formation, 209, 237, 248, 258;
    rights of, 248–51
Christian Legal Society, 131–32, 294
Cicero, 49
Civil Rights Act of 1964, 26–29
civil rights movement, 26–30
Clark, Sherman, 31
Clinton administration, 140
cognitivism, 79
cohabitation, 241
coherentist conception of rationality, 64
Cole, David, 175–76
communitarians, 102, 186–90
community conscience, 30–32
conscience: 'lived out' dimension, 132;
    accommodation of, 16–47, 198–201, 206–11; and
    authority, 17–23, 74–78; and reason, 21, 53, 62;
    and rule of law, 289–91; and self-transcendence,
    74, 76, 82; and will, 38, 50–52, 55, 72, 82; as a
    black box, 20–23, 48, 59, 61; as individual
    liberty, 34–36, 155–56; as judicial authority,
    50–51; as legislative authority, 50–51; as
    motivation, 68, 99–101, 103, 179, 202–3; as
    self-revelation, 48; internal and external
    aspects, 50–51, 59; outward orientation, 11, 23;
    relational dimension, 3, 6, 23, 59, 76–77, 154;
    religious roots, 18, 57, 76–77; secularized, 25,
    45, 76; social nature, 58, 71; subjective
    dimensions, 51, 53
conscientia, 3, 52–54
conscientious objector status, 1, 16–18
contraceptives, 6–7, 151, 156–57, 159–62, 164,
    166–67, 170–74, 242
contractarians, 186–90
*Convention Against Torture and Other Cruel,
    Inhuman and Degrading Treatment or
    Punishment*, 274–76
corporate social responsibility movement, 181,
    183–86, 189–90
corporations: and employee dissent, 10;
    communitarian conception of, 186–90;

conscience, 197–201; contractarian conception
    of, 186–90; directors, 192–94; duty to
    shareholders, 181–84, 186–90; moral identity, 10,
    167, 179–80, 185, 194–201; religious view of, 186;
    undue burdens, 198–201
covenant marriage, 257
Cover, Robert, 287
criminal law, 31
cultural cognition, 9, 115
Cuomo, Mario, 109

Dale, James, 7
Damascene, John, 52
Darwall, Stephen, 89–91
death penalty, 20
Declaration of Independence, 207–9
Dessables, Mary Jane, 143–44
Dewey, John, 211–14, 229
Dickens, Bernard, 163, 170
Diet of Worms, 56
divorce, 241, 243–44, 256–59
Domini, Amy, 189
Dooyeweerd, Herman, 109
Duignan, Patrick, 197
Duncan-Jones, Austin, 60
Durkheim, Emile, 74, 78, 110–12
Dworkin, Ronald, 165–66
Dwyer, James, 236

Easterbrook, Frank, 190
Eberle, Ed, 34
education. *See also* schools: curriculum, 10;
    equal access, 28; racial discrimination, 32–33;
    school choice, 10, 207, 209–10, 216–17, 223,
    227–38
Eighth Amendment, 298
Elane Photography, 2–5, 303–5
Elhauge, Einer, 182–83
Elshtain, Jean Bethke, 105, 109
embryonic stem cells, 159, 161
Emens, Elizabeth, 262
emotivism, 79
employees: health care benefits, 7, 151; moral
    values of, 6–7; work-related misconduct,
    37–38
employment discrimination, 27–28, 157–59,
    198–200
Employment Division v. Smith, 37, 305
end-of-life decisions, 36
Enlightenment, 58–63, 112
Enron, 195–96, 203, 279–82, 288
Establishment clause. *See* First Amendment
exit options: dependent spouses, 255; from
    attorney-client relationships, 11, 288, 290; from